ABOUT THE AUTHOR

Dr. Hossamaldin Alzawawi, a seasoned clinical pathologist, passionately explores the intersection of medicine, philosophy, physics, and cognitive neuroscience. His journey through medical expertise and philosophical inquiry has ignited a fascination with the enigmas of consciousness and intelligence.

Believing in the power of interdisciplinary knowledge, Dr. Alzawawi aims to bridge ancient wisdom and modern science. He envisions applying these insights to illuminate human cognition and enhance human experience.

Join Dr. Alzawawi on this intellectual odyssey and discover the hidden architect within you.

BOOKS BY AUTHOR

Arcanum of Awareness Series

1. The Creativity Spark
2. The Evolution of Thought
3. The Labyrinth of Cognitexis
4. The Supremacy of Selective Awareness (Upcoming)
5. Architects of a Future Dawn (Upcoming)

Other Books by Author

- The Thermodynamic Universe and Beyond: How Nature's Laws Reveal the Secrets of Time, Biology, Information, and Quantum Reality

BOOK 3

THE COGNITEXIS ENIGMA

THE LABYRINTH OF COGNITEXIS: MYSTERIES OF THE MIND'S FORGE

ARCANUM OF AWARENESS SERIES

Library of Congress Control Number: 2024919198

ISBN (PB):	978-1-964328-06-5
ISBN (E):	978-1-964328-07-2

DEDICATION

My Mother, Thank you for teaching me resilience and tenacity in learning and directing my life. Your verbal and implicit advice helped me overcome difficulties and create a knowledge masterpiece.

My Wife, In your company, my best friend, and my life partner, I have freely explored, expressed, and enjoyed various Cognitexis alternative constructs as we grow and learn together.

ACKNOWLEDGMENTS

This work is a tribute to the great thinkers whose contributions have paved the way for me. **Professor Roger Penrose's Shadows of the Mind** has been a guiding light, encouraging me to explore the consciousness conundrum further. I am immensely grateful to **Napoleon Hill,** whose influential book **How to Own Your Mind** served as a map through the maze of mental ownership. Their priceless insights have deepened my comprehension and inspired me to write this book. I hope you will discover, within these pages, the same glimmer of insight that has led me through the enchanting terrain of the mind.

Although I have a strong command of English as a second language, I have sought assistance refining my writing to make it more engaging and accessible. For that reason, I am compelled to offer my editorial board my deepest gratitude; their unwavering encouragement was crucial to the success of our project.

My Dear Wife, Basma, I am writing to tell you how much you mean to me. I greatly appreciate your thoughtful analysis of my intricate concepts and theories; it helped me distill them into a more understandable story. You helped me tremendously develop narratives out of scientific principles by suggesting various forms my ideas may take and suggesting appropriate language.

This series was envisioned over six years ago. I worked on the work's framework—ideas, descriptions, basic concepts, reasoning, and logical deductions. As a solo project worker with only my wife's comments, my progress was gradual but steady. AI gave this project a huge boost, for we spent countless hours enhancing, improving, and advancing my concepts and making them more appealing. Vivid discussion with AIs added enrichment, examples, and illustrations. AI is fundamental for including several book-related tones.

I am grateful to the AIs for the flourishing brought through their support, where various enrichment, examples, and illustrations were generated through passionate discussion. Also, the addition of diverse tones related to each book was not accessible without the support of AI. My work's varied topics and tones owe much to **Google AI,** our joint efforts, and the hours we devoted to working together. Your feedback substantially improved my writing process, producing more lyrical and narratively compelling works. **Microsoft AI,** thank you for all the hard work we put together. You played a paramount and much-appreciated role in guiding me through various ideas and keeping the process moving smoothly.

"Arcanum of Awareness" is a series memorializing the great experiences and locations I've traveled to. My deepest appreciation goes to **Queen's University Belfast's MBC and the McClay Libraries.** There was peace in these hallowed places of learning, perfect for serious study and deep thought. Libraries were more than simply locations where one could learn; they were also sanctuaries for new ideas and a love of learning. Being by my wife's side as she completed her degree at Queen's University Belfast has brought valuable happiness to our trip. Knowledge, shared experiences, and personal progress were abundant during that time. What I learned and my experiences throughout this time will always be with me.

My sincere regards, Hossamaldin Alzawawi, M.D.

THE COGNITEXIS ENIGMA

THE LABYRINTH OF COGNITEXIS: MYSTERIES OF THE MIND'S FORGE

ᔑ᯼ ᔑ᯼ ᔑ᯼

Within the mind's enigmatic labyrinth, solitary thoughts echo like whispers in a haunted hall, resonating against the walls of collective consciousness to craft a symphony of shared understanding. A Minotaur of truth lurks within these shadowy corridors, a creature born of emotions, social constructs, logic, insight, and beyond.

This book embarks on a perilous quest through the labyrinthine depths of cognition, where the phantoms of our deepest fears and the specters of our highest aspirations intertwine with the Minotaur of truth. As we navigate the uncharted realm of multidimensional intelligence known as Cognitexis, we confront the darkness that lies within our own minds.

"The key to every man is his thought. Sturdy and defying though he looks, he has a helm which he obeys, which is the idea after which all his facts are classified. He can only be reformed by showing him a new idea which commands his own."

— Ralph Waldo Emerson

CONTENTS

REALM VII: THE LABYRINTHINE DESCENT: EXPLORING THE COGNITEXIS CORE

Introduction: A Warning to the Intrepid Explorer

Cognitexis Labyrinth Core: Navigating the Laws of Thought

FIRST SPHERE: THE FOUNDATION OF COLLECTIVE COGNITION

Interaction and Collaboration of Thoughts

1. The Cosmic Ballet: A Symphony of Intertwined Minds

2. The Fabric of Minds: Weaving the Tapestry of Collective Consciousness

3. The Nexus of Thoughts: Where Concepts Collide and Collaborate

4. Intriguing Connections: The Intersection of Collaborative Thoughts

5. The Symphony of Energy: Where Thoughts Dance and Collide

6. The Spark Exchange: Illuminating the Labyrinthine Library

SECOND SPHERE: THE CRYPTIC HEART OF COGNITION

Individual Thought Processes and Mental States

1. The Inner Maelstrom: Taming the Currents of Thought

2. The Walled Garden: A Contemplation on Selfish Thoughts

3. The Mind's Quicksilver: Navigating the Crucible of Opportunity

4. The Unbreakable Spirit: Forging an Impregnable Mind

5. The Complex Mind: Mastering the Chaos of Multitasking

6. Conquering the Darkness: Rising from the CgX Turmoil

7. The Piercing Gaze: Revealing the Invisible Matrix

CONTENTS

ஃ ஃ ஃ

THROUGH THE LABYRINTH: A DANCE WITH THE MINOTAUR OF TRUTH

ஃ ஃ ஃ

T he gateway has been breached. You stand at the precipice of a thrilling and perilous realm—the human mind's labyrinthine corridors. Book Two served as your torch, casting a fleeting light on the path ahead. Now, prepare to embark on a solitary quest, an odyssey of intellect, navigating the treacherous terrain of Cognitexis.

Venture forth, intrepid explorer, into these twisting passages where shadows dance and secrets whisper. A mythical beast with a heart of riddles guards the labyrinth's core. Only by facing it can you claim your intellectual birthright, but be warned, its gaze can warp perception and twist logic.

Within the winding corridors lurk dangers, both subtle and overt. Beware the whispers that distort reality, the echoes of your own biases, and the chilling miasma of unchecked emotion. These guardians of the labyrinth are ready to lead you astray from the path of true understanding. This prelude serves as your preparation for the chapters to come, where you will arm yourself to face the intricacies of your cognition, forging pathways of understanding. In the dynamics of Cognitexis, you will explore the forces that etch our mental tapestry, confronting the tempest of our inner monologues, journeying through Cognitexis Continuum to uncover the hidden gateways of habits and intellect, delving into the crucible of emotion to transform raw passion into purpose and action. You will uncover the anchors that shape our subconscious mind, navigate the symphony of shared purpose and collective thought, unveil the profound harmony that binds us, and equip yourself with the knowledge to navigate the laws that govern thought, reaching the pinnacle of cognitive mastery.

Tread carefully, for the labyrinth is not easily conquered. It is within this very confrontation, this grappling with your own limitations, that true intellectual growth is found. The journey through Cognitexis is not merely about finding answers but about forging the very instrument of inquiry—the discerning intellect, a cornerstone of the ADAM-GENE vision.

Dear reader, take up the challenge. For in this maze, there is the possibility of the mind being changed at its very roots. Every step you make will strip you of layer upon layer of illusion and bring you closer to the middle of something much greater than your mere self. Are you prepared to face the unknown and claim your intellectual birthright?

INTRODUCTION

༄ ༄ ༄

F orget the gentle symphony of thought. Now, we can descend into the labyrinthine realm of Cognitexis, a shadowy frontier where individual minds become enmeshed in a collective consciousness. Here, every thought is a whispered echo, a ripple on a vast, unseen pond. Prepare to navigate this enigmatic terrain, for within its depths lies the key to unlocking the true potential of your intellect.

This tome empowers you, the valiant adventurer, with the tools needed to navigate your escape from the perilous labyrinth that Cognitexis has become. We shall embark on a journey through the vast expanse of duality in thought, navigating toward the essence of human understanding, where the fierce clash of ideas ignites, and the unseen forces shape them in a cosmic ballet. You will master the art of distinguishing the steadfast sword of reason from the unpredictable fire of feelings as you face the perils that lie in wait—from the sly murmurs of conformity to the alluring melody of confirmation bias.

The journey through Cognitexis is not for the faint of heart. It is a crucible, a test of your intellectual fortitude. Yet, within this very confrontation lies the potential for a profound transformation of the mind. Embrace the challenge, for with each step, you will shed layers of illusion, drawing closer to the heart of something far greater than yourself.

Now, brave travelers, we must set forth on a quest to uncover two enigmatic definitions unveiled from the depths of the ADAM-GENE project: Sound Thought and Cognition.

A Symphony of Sound Thoughts: A Scientific Exploration

Sound thoughts, the unassailable truths of our cognitive comprehension, are the enigmatic architects of our mental landscape. They are not mere opinions or fleeting speculations but rather the bedrock upon which our beliefs rest. Imagine them as ancient monoliths, standing tall and defiant against the tides of doubt.

Sound thoughts emerge through the choreography of neurons, a symphony of synapses orchestrating the mental symposium. These are how we perceive reality: how we interpret information, connect the dots, and weave meaning. So, like alchemists, we read patterns, unravel mysteries, and glimpse the underlying equations of existence.

Sound thoughts, the architects of our beliefs, profoundly influence our cognitive skills. They shape our perception, memory, and reasoning, inspiring us to explore new ideas, situations, and prospects. **These sound thoughts, rooted in the Unassailable Truth of the Axioms of Intelligence,** a concept beyond the scope of this book, are the foundation of our mental structures. They motivate us, forming the intricate tapestry of our minds, guiding our understanding of the world, and constructing the essence of our perceived reality.

Yet, even these seemingly invincible, unassailable truths may conceal shadows of deception. We must seek out other echoes to rise above the whispers of the axioms. Veiled insights, expansive realms—these unveil the shadows of our minds, exposing concealed imperfections. **It is the paradox: only through the unknown can we hope to rise above the unshakeable.**

A Cosmic Odyssey: Navigating the Labyrinth of Cognitexis

Cognitexis, the enigmatic realm of human conscious intelligence and awareness, is a multidimensional cosmos where the threads of thought intersect, forming constellations of cognition. Envision it as a celestial tapestry woven with the threads of perception, reasoning, memory, attention, language, problem-solving, and more.

This vast labyrinth is the bedrock of our cognitive existence, the unseen scaffolding that supports our conscious experiences. It is a kaleidoscope of facets, each revealing a different aspect of our mental landscape. **Perception**, the prism through which we glimpse reality, **Reasoning**, the alchemical forge of logic, **Memory**, where echoes of the past linger, **Attention**, the cosmic spotlight, **Language**, the celestial lexicon, and **Problem-Solving**, the cosmic riddle—all intertwine to create the intricate fabric of **Cognitexis.**

To chart this mysterious uncharted territory, we embark on an intellectual odyssey armed with the tools of cognitive science. Psychology, neuroscience, linguistics, philosophy, and artificial intelligence—each discipline contributes a star to our navigational map.

Sound thoughts, those ethereal whispers, serve as a cosmic coordinate within Cognitexis. They guide our mental voyages, shaping beliefs and anchoring our understanding. Like ancient wayfinders, we follow their luminous trails.

Cognitexis defies singularity. It is a multiverse—a web of interconnected realms. Consciousness, like dark matter, permeates its fabric. Emotions swirl like cosmic storms, and dreams ripple across its event horizon.

In the vast expanse of our imaginations, profound ideas shine like distant stars, illuminating our path through the darkness. They summon us further into the maze, unveiling secret sanctuaries where conviction falters. So, brave travelers of the mind journey through Cognitexis with awe, for its secrets lie in waiting for our exploration.

Cognitexis (CgX) Unveiled: The Dawn of Mental Exploration

Deep within the human mind lies a realm cloaked in an enigma—Cognitexis. In this realm of swirling shadows, an unseen force orchestrates the epic symphony of human understanding. Every unique intellect, a master of its craft, adds its own harmonious note. Yet, a single discordant note can unleash a tempest, sending the entire composition into a whirlwind of chaos.

This book, "The Cognitexis Enigma: Charting the Course through Cognitexis and the Maze of Thought," serves as your essential gear, leading you into the mysterious and uncharted realms of Cognitexis. We shall embark on a journey through the scientific principles that govern cognitexis while also uncovering the mysterious forces that lie in the darkness, poised to challenge the fragile equilibrium. Are there hidden forces guiding the very fabric of our minds? Can the very foundation of trust be shattered by a subtle deception lurking within the shadows of Cognitexis?

Embark on an epic adventure where the quest for knowledge intertwines with the gripping tension of a mind-bending saga. We are about to unveil the mysteries of intellectual synergy and its shadowy forces of manipulation, revealing how balance and chaos exist side by side within the human psyche. This quest within Cognitexis will reveal the wonders of cognitive functioning while exposing the formidable weaknesses lurking in the darkness.

Cognitexis Unveiled: Whispers from the Labyrinth

Descartes was mistaken. We do not think; therefore, we are. In the vast expanse of our imagination, we conjure visions, and from those visions, the very fabric of existence is crafted.[i] Embark on a journey into the enigmatic realm of Cognitexis—a labyrinthine construct concealed deep within the vast expanse of human consciousness. Science cannot grasp its essence, yet whispers endure of a realm where thought and substance unite, where willpower forges realities, and the echoes of countless minds are woven together.

The Alchemist of the Mind

In the dimly lit passages of the CgX, a force awakens—an invisible creator that shapes our thoughts and yearnings. Envision a glowing chamber where electric tempests surge with an ethereal power. The CgX serves as the sorcerer in this realm, conjuring ethereal ideas into concrete realities. But it doesn't merely generate concepts; it forges them with distinct attributes, intent, and an unsettling harmony. These are not the fleeting whispers of a wandering mind but purposeful Sound-Thoughts with a mission of their own.

The Ritual of Habituation

How do these sound thoughts take shape in our realm? The CgX harnesses a formidable force—the ancient rite of habituation. A sound thought first emerges as a faint murmur—a tempting idea that begins to take hold in the conscious mind. We cultivate it with focus, and as time passes, this evolves into a deliberate endeavor—a continuous pursuit we engage in without a moment's hesitation. But here is where the true power awakens. The CgX ventures

---

[i] The contents of our perceptual worlds are controlled hallucinations, brain-based best guesses about the ultimately unknowable causes of sensory signals. For most of us, most of the time, these hallucinations are experienced as real.

For further information refer to: The Neuroscience of Reality: Reality is constructed by the brain, and no two brains are exactly alike (https://www.scientificamerican.com/article/the-neuroscience-of-reality).

beyond mere surface-level changes; it seeks to weave these habits into the very fabric of our existence, propelling them deeper from the realm of awareness into the rich, untamed depths of the subconscious. Once mastered, these patterns weave into the fabric of automation, guiding our actions like unseen forces orchestrating the dance of our lives. A Struggle of Light and Darkness

A Duality of Power and Peril

The CgX possesses a force that stands on the edge of salvation and annihilation. It sharpens our minds—shaping the very essence of our being. Picture a master creator, deeply engrossed and with precision in every move, weaving the complex tapestry of our reality—each deliberate strand at a time. Yet, the very act of succumbing to the CgX's influence harbors a peril that casts a long shadow. What if the whispers of our consciousness do not belong to us at all? What if an unseen power lurking in the depths of the labyrinth is intricately crafting the essence of our reality?

The Unanswered Question

The most profound mystery surrounding the CgX lies in its beginnings and its true intent. Is it a noble power, a master orchestrating the grand tapestry of human consciousness? Or is it a dark master orchestrating a vast deception for its own mysterious purposes? The answer, for now, remains hidden in the depths of Cognitexis, cloaked in mystery.

COGNITEXIS: FORGING THE PATH OF THE MIND

ᚷᚱᚷᚱᚷᚱ

In the shadows of cognition, where the intertwining threads of light and darkness weave the fabric of reality, lies the essence of thought. Here, in the enigmatic depths of the human mind, the foundations of reasoning are laid bare. The intricate labyrinth of Cognitexis awaits, filled with perilous twists and hidden truths, as you arm yourself to face the minotaur of deception.

This chapter, "Cognitexis: Forging the Path of the Mind," prepares you for navigating the intricate maze of cognition that lies ahead. Within these pages, we shall explore the formidable power of the instructions and tools provided here, transforming your cognitive abilities and equipping you to traverse the vast challenges of existence with sharp insight and unwavering focus.

Embrace the journey through the depths of your mind, where inductive and deductive reasoning illuminate the path, and the symphony of reason guides your steps. As we delve into the mastery of discernment and shield against the insidious invaders of thought, you will be armed with the cognitive skills necessary to forge a path to reliable truth.

Prepare yourself, for Cognitexis is not a place for the faint-hearted. It demands vigilance, curiosity, and the courage to confront the minotaur of misinformation that lurks in the shadows. Let us embark on this thrilling expedition, ensuring that your thoughts resonate with precision and rationality as you navigate the enigmatic maze that lies ahead.

Foundations of Clear Thinking

The essence of clear thought lies in the vast expanse of the human mind, where shadows and light intertwine. Here, the foundations of reasoning are laid bare among the enigmatic depths of cognition. Journey with us as we unveil the secret blueprints of clear thinking, where inductive and deductive reasoning guide the path through the labyrinth of knowledge. Embrace the symphony of reason, where logic and emotion dance in harmonious balance.

1. From the Shadows to Light: Unveiling Inductive Reasoning

Inductive reasoning resembles the method of a detective navigating through shadows, assembling fragments of evidence to reveal the enigma at hand. It transitions from uncertainty to clarity, beginning with broad observations or fragments of evidence. Imagine wandering through ancient ruins, each structure crafted from the same warm, reddish-brown stone. Through inductive reasoning, one could deduce that this civilization favored this particular type of red stone for their construction endeavors. Yet, a deeper exploration may uncover further insights that reshape our understanding of the hypothesis.

Science: The Scientific Method

The journey of seeking knowledge and understanding through careful observation and experimentation embodies the core of the scientific method, rooted in the strength of inductive reasoning. In the initial stages, researchers engage in careful observation and data collection to formulate their hypotheses. For example, observing that specific plants thrive under particular soil conditions may lead to intriguing theories about how soil nutrients shape plant growth and development. By engaging in experimentation, we thoughtfully analyze these hypotheses, deepening our understanding through the perspective of evidence.

o   **Example: Investigation into Climate Change**

Experts in climate science thoughtfully examine weather data patterns accumulated over decades, employing a method of reasoning that draws general conclusions from specific observations. Noticing the upward trend in global temperatures, the retreat of ice caps, and the surge in greenhouse gas levels prompts us to consider the implications of human actions on our climate. The insights derived from rigorous research continuously refine our comprehension of climate change.

Philosophy: Empiricism

Exploring the foundations of knowledge through experience and observation. Empiricism, a philosophical perspective advocated by notable figures such as John Locke and David Hume, highlights the significance of sensory experience in developing knowledge. Inductive reasoning harmonizes with empirical thought, drawing from observations to formulate overarching principles. Locke posited that the mind begins as a blank slate, with knowledge formed through empirical evidence acquired via experience.

o   **Example: Everyday Decision-Making**

Imagine a culinary artist delving into the intricacies of a novel dish. Through careful observation of the interplay between various ingredients and cooking techniques, one hones their comprehension of flavor dynamics and culinary practices. This inductive approach enriches their culinary abilities via experiential learning.

Religion: Interpretative Reasoning

In spirituality, one can observe inductive reasoning at play through the interpretation of sacred writings. Academics and religious thinkers delve into sacred texts to uncover underlying patterns and themes that can lead to more profound spiritual and ethical insights. This reflective journey enables individuals to grasp and integrate spiritual principles into their daily existence.

o **Example: Scriptural Interpretation**

Scholars who study sacred texts (such as the Bible and the Quran) use inductive reasoning to understand passages within the larger context of the divine narratives in these venerated scriptures. Carefully investigating historical context, language, and literary styles can uncover insights, foundational principles, and ideas that impact religious practice and belief.

Final Thoughts

Inductive reasoning is a fundamental element of lucid thought, enabling the transition from specific observations to broader conclusions. By examining its scientific, philosophical, and religious dimensions, we cultivate a richer understanding of its influence on our perceptions and decision-making processes. Adopt this systematic strategy to traverse the intricacies of existence, revealing insights and sharpening analytical skills.

2. The Master Builder's Logic: Unveiling Deductive Reasoning

Deductive reasoning operates with the meticulous accuracy of a skilled artisan, bringing a carefully crafted design to life. It functions by transitioning from familiar concepts to uncharted territories, drawing upon recognized truths or commonly held convictions as a reliable base. As a general principle, it is widely accepted—though future scientific inquiry may reshape our understanding—that all birds possess feathers. Should an observer notice a creature soaring through the heavens, its feathers glistening in the sunlight, one could reasonably conclude that this is likely a bird.

The Function of Deductive Reasoning in Scientific Theories

Deductive reasoning is a cornerstone in the development of scientific theories and the execution of experiments. Researchers employ it to foresee results grounded in well-established concepts. For example, Isaac Newton's principles regarding motion and universal gravitation emerged through a process of deductive reasoning grounded in observable phenomena. By applying these principles, researchers can foresee the actions of objects in diverse circumstances with impressive precision.

o **Example: Anticipating Eclipse Events**

Astronomers apply logical reasoning to anticipate eclipses. By deeply exploring the intricate dynamics governing the movements of celestial bodies, one can discern the timing and location of an impending eclipse. This accurate forecast is grounded in well-established astronomical principles and rigorous mathematical computations.

Philosophy: Logical Positivism

Exploring the realm of philosophy, we encounter the intriguing concept of Logical Positivism. Logical positivism is a philosophical approach highlighting the importance of deductive reasoning in extracting meaningful insights from empirical observations. Thinkers such as A.J. Ayer and the Vienna Circle posited that only those statements that can be verified through logical reasoning or empirical observation hold significance. This perspective highlights the importance of deductive reasoning in exploring philosophical questions.

o   **Example: Syllogistic Reasoning**

Reflect on the timeless syllogism: "All humans are mortal." Socrates embodies the essence of humanity. Consequently, Socrates embodies mortality. This deductive argument illustrates how a specific conclusion can emerge from general premises, highlighting the strength of logical reasoning.

Religion: Theological Arguments

In spirituality, one frequently observes the application of deductive reasoning within theological discourse. Consider the ontological argument for God's existence introduced by St. Anselm. It employs deductive reasoning to claim that the very idea of God, defined as the greatest conceivable being, necessitates existence in reality since existence is an essential characteristic of greatness.

o   **Example: Ethical Reasoning**

Ethical teachings within religious contexts frequently employ deductive reasoning to formulate moral principles. For example, the principle of treating others as you wish to be treated, often referred to as the Golden Rule, emerges from a deeper understanding of the necessity of honoring the inherent dignity and paying respect of every individual.

Al-Ghazali and the Argument from Cosmology

Al-Ghazali, a significant figure in Islamic thought, employed deductive reasoning in his cosmological argument to affirm the existence of the divine. In "The Incoherence of the Philosophers" (Tahafut al-Falasifa), Al-Ghazali presents a compelling case for the existence of a first cause or necessary being, which he identifies as God. His reasoning unfolds in the following manner:

o **Premise 1:** Every entity that comes into being must have an underlying reason for its existence.

o **Premise 2:** The universe came into being.

o *Conclusion:* it follows that the universe must have a cause for its existence, which can only be an uncaused, necessary being—God.

Al-Ghazali employs a deductive approach, progressing from broad principles to a particular conclusion. He begins with universally acknowledged principles (everything that comes into existence has a cause). He extends them to the universe, arriving at the conclusion that the universe itself must have an uncaused cause.

Philosophy: The Concept of Causality

The principle of causality, which lies at the heart of Al-Ghazali's argument, is a fundamental concept in Islamic thought and wider philosophical discourse. It posits that a preceding cause necessitates every effect. This principle serves as a foundation for numerous theological discussions, emphasizing the importance of deductive reasoning in uncovering metaphysical truths.

- o **Example: Ibn Sina (Avicenna) and the Essential Nature of Being**

  Ibn Sina, a prominent figure in Islamic thought, employed deductive reasoning in his metaphysical discourse. In his "Book of Healing" (Kitab al-Shifa), he articulates the argument for the necessity of existence:

  - o **Premise 1:** In our reality, there exist beings whose existence is not guaranteed—entities that are present yet could very well not be.

  - o **Premise 2:** The existence of beings that depend on something else must have a reason.

  - o **Premise 3:** An endless chain of causes cannot exist.

  - o *Conclusion:* it follows that there exists a necessary being—one that must exist and cannot fail to exist—that serves as the cause for the existence of all contingent beings. This essential existence is the divine.

  The arguments presented by Al-Ghazali and Ibn Sina illustrate the application of deductive reasoning within Islamic philosophy, aimed at establishing and defending theological concepts, much like the deductive reasoning found in St. Anselm's ontological argument.[ii]

[ii] **Sufism: The Journey of Mystical Experience:**
Within the realm of Sufism, one encounters a unique perspective on the essence of existence and the divine. Sufism highlights the importance of a deep, personal experience of the divine, often achieved through practices such as meditation, chanting, and various spiritual exercises. Sufism, also known as Tasawwuf, represents the mystical dimension of Islam, emphasizing the inner quest for the Divine and the development of spiritual experiences. Sufis pursue a direct encounter with the divine, emphasizing personal and inner experiences over mere rational or deductive reasoning.

In Summary

Exploring Islamic philosophy and Sufism reveals profound instances of deductive reasoning applied within theological discourse. Philosophers such as Al-Ghazali and Ibn Sina utilized deductive reasoning to delve into and express deep metaphysical and theological insights, showcasing the broad relevance of this approach within spiritual frameworks.

Critical Thinking: Integrating Diverse Reasoning Approaches

Appreciating the vast potential of the human intellect is crucial; nonetheless, it is also vital to understand that even the most skilled investigator can reach incorrect conclusions, and the

---

- **Counter-Example: The Notion of Fana**
  A fundamental idea in Sufism is Fana, signifying "annihilation" or "extinction." This describes a profound experience in which the sense of self and personal identity dissolve, leading to a total immersion in the divine essence.
  This notion questions the reliance on deductive reasoning to reach conclusions about the divine, highlighting the importance of direct, personal experience rather than purely logical deduction.

- **Philosophical Perspective: Exploring the Boundaries of Rational Thought**
  Sufi thinkers such as Ibn Arabi contend that the realm of rational thought and deductive reasoning falls short in grasping the essence of the divine. The conviction is that the deepest understanding of the divine and the essence of existence can only be attained through direct, mystical experiences, surpassing the limits of human logic and reasoning.

- **Example: The Night Journey (Miraj)**
  The Night Journey of the Prophet Muhammad, known as Miraj, stands as a pivotal moment in Islamic tradition, emphasizing the profound significance of mystical experiences.
  Throughout this journey, the Prophet rose to the heavens and experienced a direct encounter with the divine, regarded as a deeply significant mystical experience. This event highlights the Sufi perspective that emphasizes the importance of personal, experiential understanding of the divine, rather than relying solely on rational or deductive reasoning.

- *Final Thoughts*
  Unlike the ontological argument, which leans on deductive reasoning, Sufism highlights the significance of mystical experiences and personal connections with the divine. This perspective emphasizes the constraints of logical reasoning in understanding the essence of the divine and invites a more intimate, personal journey into spiritual realities.

most meticulous designer may misinterpret a plan. Critical thinking requires a blend of various reasoning methods coupled with a strong dose of skepticism.

o **Example: Evaluating Scientific Assertions**

In assessing scientific assertions, thoughtful analysts employ both inductive and deductive reasoning. They begin by making observations to generate hypotheses and then apply established theories to evaluate predictions. This holistic method guarantees a thorough and meticulous examination.

Final Thoughts

Deductive reasoning, marked by its clarity and dependence on verified information, serves as a fundamental element of rational thought. By grasping its significance in various domains, we can truly value its influence in molding our perceptions and steering our choices. Embrace the logic of a master builder to navigate the complexities of existence, integrating various reasoning methods and applying skepticism to elevate your critical thinking skills. This harmonious method enables us to reveal insights and make decisions with lucidity and assurance.

3. The Symphony of Reason: The Power of Critical Thinking

Aligning with Your Logic

Ultimately, your reasoning is a powerful instrument within the CgX system for revealing the truth. When faced with information that challenges your current beliefs or logic, it becomes crucial to delve deeper into its implications. It is essential to nurture and engage your critical thinking skills.

Immerse yourself in the art of impartial examination of information, contrasting it with your current understanding.

Science: Cognitive Psychology and Critical Thinking

Cognitive psychology highlights the vital role that critical thinking plays in how we process information and make decisions. Critical thinking requires a deep examination, thoughtful evaluation, and information integration to arrive at sound conclusions. It necessitates the capacity to recognize flawed reasoning, evaluate supporting information, and explore diverse viewpoints. Studies indicate that those who practice critical thinking possess enhanced abilities to manage intricate information and arrive at well-informed conclusions.

o **Example: Evaluating Scientific Claims**

It is worthwhile to critically assess the validity of scientific assertions regarding a novel health intervention. Critical thinking requires thoroughly exploring the study's methodology, carefully evaluating the source's credibility, and thoughtfully comparing the findings with established knowledge. Through this careful examination, individuals are empowered to arrive at more enlightened conclusions regarding the effectiveness and safety of the treatment.

Philosophy: The Role of Reason in Knowledge

Thinkers such as René Descartes and Immanuel Kant have highlighted the fundamental importance of reason in the pursuit of knowledge. Descartes' approach encourages a rigorous examination of our beliefs, pushing us to challenge assumptions in pursuit of undeniable truths. Kant's examination of pure reason delves into the boundaries and potential of human comprehension. These contemplative perspectives emphasize the significance of harmonizing reasoning with logical thought and critical examination.

o **Example: Cartesian Skepticism**

René Descartes employed skepticism as a method to critically examine and challenge all beliefs that could be doubted. His goal was to establish a foundation of indubitable knowledge. This disciplined approach to critical thinking encourages individuals to rigorously scrutinize their assumptions and beliefs, aligning them with rational thought.

Religion: The Practice of Discernment

In spiritual frameworks, discernment encompasses a meticulous and reflective analysis of convictions and doctrines. Numerous spiritual paths invite individuals to embark on a journey of discernment, pursuing higher understanding and insight to address intricate ethical and spiritual dilemmas. This approach resonates with the foundations of analytical reasoning and impartial evaluation.

o **Example: The Ignatian Examen**

The Ignatian Examen, a profound spiritual practice conceived by St. Ignatius of Loyola, invites individuals to contemplate their thoughts, actions, and experiences daily. This approach encourages thoughtful examination of one's spiritual path, harmonizing one's convictions and behaviors with one's core beliefs. Through this introspective journey, individuals deepen their insight and elevate their spiritual awareness.

o **Example: The Islamic Practice of Muhasabah**

The concept of Muhasabah encourages a profound engagement with oneself, prompting individuals to reflect daily on their thoughts, actions, and intentions within the framework of Islam. This reflective practice invites individuals to scrutinize their actions and harmonize their conduct with their fundamental principles and convictions, nurturing a profound relationship with the divine and elevating spiritual consciousness.

i. **Daily Reflection:** Individuals are invited to engage in introspection regarding their daily actions and intentions, aiming to uncover opportunities for growth and a deeper alignment with their guiding principles. This practice frequently occurs at the close of the day, akin to the Ignatian Examen.

ii. **Qur'anic Guidance:** The Qur'an highlights the significance of personal responsibility and introspection. For example, Surah Al-Hashr (59:18) conveys, "O you who have believed, fear Allah." Let each individual reflect on the contributions they have made for the future.

iii. **Prophetic traditions:** The Hadith literature underscores the profound importance of introspection. The esteemed Prophet Muhammad (peace be upon him) imparted wisdom with the words, "Take account of yourselves before you are taken to account" (Tirmidhi).

iv. **Contemporary Application:** In today's context, current Islamic scholars and spiritual guides highlight the importance of Muhasabah, urging Muslims to weave this practice into their everyday existence to foster spiritual awareness and development.

Through the practice of Muhasabah, one can enhance one's comprehension of one's spiritual path, align one's actions with one's convictions, and foster a deeper sense of spiritual consciousness, akin to the Ignatian Examen.

Defense Mechanism: Engage in Objective Analysis and Critical Thinking

1) **Examine Contradictory Information:** When faced with information that challenges your current beliefs, take the time to scrutinize it thoroughly. Reflect on the underlying evidence and the logic that supports these assertions.

2) **Maintain Critical Thinking Abilities:** Foster your capacity for critical thought by consistently analyzing, evaluating, and synthesizing information. Participate in endeavors stimulating your cognitive abilities, like debates and thoughtful discussions.

3) **Examine the evidence:** Scrutinize the quality and reliability of the information's supporting evidence. Reflect on the approach, references, and circumstances to guarantee a comprehensive examination.

4) **Juxtapose with Existing Knowledge:** Relate new insights to your established knowledge framework. Contemplate how this resonates with or contrasts your perspective, and ponder the consequences of your convictions and choices.

In summation

The harmonious interplay of rational thought, driven by analytical reasoning, is vital for revealing the essence of truth within the CgX framework. By harmonizing your thought processes with rationality and embracing a critical examination of facts, you can adeptly traverse intricate information and arrive at well-founded conclusions. Adopt these approaches to elevate your critical thinking skills, allowing your cognitive processes to be rooted in thorough and substantiated examination. This methodical approach enables the CgX system to produce trustworthy and precise insights, leading to a more profound comprehension of existence.

4. Reason Before Emotion: A Harmonious Performance

Reason and Emotion

Emotions act as powerful forces, frequently obscuring the inherent judgment abilities within the CgX system. One should be cautious of emotional appeals, which can hinder clear and rational thinking. It is essential to conduct a comprehensive logical examination of the information provided before accepting it as truth. A tool that disturbs the cohesion of a musical composition mirrors an emotion that, when articulated with excessive intensity, loses the guiding influence of rationality necessary for equilibrium and self-regulation.

Science: Emotional Regulation and Decision-Making

The interplay between emotional regulation and decision-making is a fascinating area of exploration. Understanding how emotions influence our choices can lead to profound insights into human behavior and cognition.

Investigations within cognitive psychology underscore the crucial role that emotional regulation plays in decision-making. Emotions have the power to shape our cognitive processes, often resulting in biases and irrational judgments that can cloud our reasoning. Techniques for emotional regulation, including mindfulness and cognitive reappraisal, empower individuals to navigate their emotions and sustain a harmonious outlook. By emphasizing rational thought and critical examination, one can reduce the influence of emotions on one's choices.

o **Example: Financial Decisions**

Reflect on how emotions shape our financial choices. Emotions such as fear and greed often propel individuals toward illogical investment decisions, which can result in considerable financial setbacks. By carefully managing emotions and applying logical reasoning to market data, individuals can arrive at more thoughtful and informed investment choices.

Philosophy: The Stoic Approach

The principles of Stoic philosophy, especially those articulated by Marcus Aurelius and Epictetus, highlight the significance of prioritizing reason above emotional responses. The Stoics emphasized the importance of nurturing rational thinking and mastering one's emotions as a pathway to a virtuous and meaningful existence. Through the harmonious integration of rational thought and emotional balance, one can adeptly traverse the complexities of existence with both insight and fortitude.

o **Example: Stoic Practices**

Individuals dedicated to Stoic principles may employ methods like negative visualization and cognitive reframing to navigate their emotions and uphold a reasoned outlook. By envisioning possible obstacles and reinterpreting adverse experiences, they can foster resilience and arrive at thoughtful conclusions.

Religion: Balancing Faith and Reason

Numerous spiritual paths highlight the significance of harmonizing belief and rational thought. In Christianity, "faith seeking understanding" invites individuals to embark on a journey of rational exploration and introspection. This equilibrium guarantees that spiritual convictions are rooted in heartfelt emotion and rational thought.

o **Example: Theological Reflection**

Individuals might delve into intricate spiritual beliefs by merging conviction with logical examination. Through theological reflection, individuals can enhance their comprehension and express their convictions with greater clarity. This harmonious perspective nurtures both cognitive and spiritual development.

Defense Mechanism: Prioritize Reason and Logical Analysis

1) **Regulate Emotions:** Engage in practices that foster emotional regulation, like mindfulness and cognitive reappraisal, to navigate your feelings and sustain a balanced outlook.

2) **Engage in Logical Analysis:** Embrace the practice of rigorous logical examination. Place a high value on meticulously analyzing information before embracing it as truth. Examine the foundations and logic that support the assertions made.

3) **Avoid Emotional Appeals:** Be cautious about emotional appeals, as they can hinder clear and rational thinking. Concentrate on empirical data and rational reasoning.

4) **Reflect on Reasoning:** Regularly engage in thoughtful contemplation of your reasoning processes. Grounding conclusions in a rational examination rather than allowing emotions to sway judgment is essential.

In Summary

The interplay of reason and emotion is essential for preserving the integrity of the CgX system. By emphasizing rational thought and conducting comprehensive logical evaluations, one can lessen the influence of emotions on one's decision-making processes. This structured methodology anchors cognitive processes in reasoned thinking, steering you toward sound and trustworthy conclusions. Adopt these approaches to skillfully maneuver through the intricacies of information, maintaining a sense of equilibrium and impartiality in your reasoning.

Tools of Discernment

Amidst the shifting sands of information, discerning minds rise as beacons of clarity. Within this realm, the tools of discernment are your compass and lantern, guiding you through the maze of data. The discerning eye navigates the shadows, while the cartographer's compass prioritizes the stars of truth. Engage with these instruments, ensuring that each piece of information is meticulously examined and mapped precisely.

1. The Discerning Eye: Navigating the Maze of Information with Critical Insight

The first step toward gaining clarity is to develop a keen perspective akin to a seasoned scholar deciphering the mysterious signs hidden in ancient texts. It is essential to thoroughly examine information, refining our capacity to distinguish between facts—those solid pillars of knowledge—and the subjective shades of opinion, the unreliable whispers of hearsay, and the overt fabrications of fiction.

Science: The Significance of Critical Thinking

Engaging in critical thinking serves as a cornerstone for the pursuit of knowledge within the realm of scientific exploration. It requires thorough examination, critical questioning, and an impartial assessment of information. The essence of the scientific method lies in the art of critical thinking, compelling researchers to rigorously test their hypotheses through controlled experiments and the scrutiny of peer review. This method guarantees that scientific conclusions rest on trustworthy and replicable data rather than unsubstantiated assertions or individual prejudices.

o **Example: Peer-Reviewed Research**

In science, peer-reviewed journals represent the pinnacle of research publication. Before publication, a study is thoroughly examined by fellow experts, who carefully assess the methodology, data, and conclusions. This approach fosters credibility and trustworthiness in research, setting it apart from non-peer-reviewed sources that often lack the necessary rigor and reliability.

Philosophy: The Socratic Method

The Socratic Method, rooted in the teachings of the ancient Greek thinker Socrates, embodies a collaborative dialogue that encourages deep reflection and sheds light on various concepts. It entails engaging in a dialogue that prompts inquiry and reflection, revealing the foundational beliefs that shape our perspectives. This approach invites individuals to thoughtfully reflect on their convictions and the rationale behind them, nurturing an environment of deep questioning and open-mindedness.

o **Example: Socratic Dialogues**

In Plato's dialogues, Socrates interacts with his conversation partners through a thoughtful exchange of questions and answers, pushing them to examine their beliefs and leading them toward deeper philosophical understanding. This approach to inquiry and thoughtful analysis continues to serve as a vital instrument for uncovering truth and promoting clarity of thought.

Religion: Scriptural Analysis

Uncovering truth frequently requires thoughtful examination of revered writings in spiritual discussions. Academics utilize diverse interpretative approaches to analyze sacred texts, taking into account the historical backdrop, literary forms, and theological motifs. This methodical approach aids in separating fundamental religious principles from cultural or contextual interpretations, fostering a clearer comprehension of religious beliefs.

o **Example: Interpretation in the context of Islam (Tafsir)**

Tafsir serves as a profound exploration and interpretation of the Quran, seeking to illuminate the meanings embedded within its verses. Academics adopt a methodical perspective, considering the text's language, historical background, and contextual elements. This thorough examination illuminates the core message of the Quran, offering followers a richer and more insightful comprehension of their beliefs.

Practical Approaches for Verifying Information

1) **Source Evaluation:** Examine the reliability of the information source. Reliable sources are often recognized for their commitment to precision, openness, and

responsibility. For example, educational establishments, reputable media outlets, and scholarly journals typically serve as trustworthy sources.

2) **Cross-Verification:** Ensure the accuracy of information by consulting various trustworthy sources. Cross-referencing serves as a vital tool in validating the precision and coherence of information. When various independent sources align on the same information, it enhances the likelihood of its credibility.

3) **Awareness of Bias:** Acknowledge the possible biases inherent in the information provided. Reflect on the viewpoint and possible motivations of the originator. Recognizing biases enables us to sift through personal influences and concentrate on the essence of objective truths.

4) **Ask Critical Questions:** When assessing information, consider profound questions like: Is there substantiation for this assertion? Is the information grounded in verified data or merely anecdotal accounts? Critical questioning reveals the trustworthiness and authenticity of the information presented.

In Summary

Fostering a keen sense of perception is crucial for traversing the intricate maze of information that characterizes our contemporary landscape. Through thoughtful examination, thorough scrutiny, and verification of facts, we can establish strong and logical conclusions. Utilize these resources to cultivate a clear mindset, anchoring your thoughts in trustworthy and dependable knowledge. This structured method enables you to discern between reality and falsehood, steering you toward a deeper and more insightful comprehension.

2. The Cartographer's Compass: Prioritizing Facts for Your Journey

Not every fact carries equal significance. This conversation underscores the essential importance of structuring information based on its relevance. Essential insights are those that relate directly to our goals and desires. Imagine exploring a vast library, a rich repository of wisdom and concepts eager to be unveiled. While every book presents a rich tapestry of insights, our attention is directed toward those that resonate deeply with our specific research theme. Similarly, it is crucial to focus on relevant information to enhance our thinking and reach informed conclusions.

Science: Cognitive Load Theory

John Sweller introduced the Cognitive Load Theory, which elucidates the constraints of our working memory's capacity. To enhance our understanding and choices, navigating cognitive load by focusing on information that aligns closely with our objectives is essential. Concentrating on relevant information and minimizing unnecessary distractions improves our capacity to understand and remember essential data, resulting in more efficient thinking and problem-solving.

o   **Example: Academic Research**

Envision scholars embarking on an intellectual journey to explore the depths of knowledge for their thesis. Confronted with an extensive range of sources, they focus on selecting articles and books that specifically relate to their research inquiry. Concentrating on the most pertinent information, they adeptly collect evidence, construct arguments, and derive significant conclusions. This focused strategy highlights the significance of emphasizing facts to effectively traverse abundant information.

Philosophy: Epistemological Inquiry

Exploration of Knowledge: An Inquiry into Understanding. The exploration of knowledge highlights the necessity of differentiating between what is truly meaningful and what is merely inconsequential. Thinkers such as René Descartes and John Locke emphasized the importance of having clear and distinct ideas alongside the necessity of sifting through unreliable information. Emphasizing trustworthy and relevant information resonates with the pursuit of authentic and well-founded understanding.

o **Example: The Method of Doubt by Descartes**

René Descartes utilized a systematic skepticism approach to elevate the significance of certain knowledge. Through a methodical process of skepticism towards all that could be scrutinized, he aimed to uncover undeniable truths. This careful prioritization of specific knowledge resulted in essential philosophical insights, exemplified by his renowned assertion, "Cogito, ergo sum" (I think, therefore I am).

Religion: The Role of Discernment

In spiritual contexts, discernment is crucial for differentiating between genuine truths and misleading beliefs. Numerous spiritual paths highlight the significance of pursuing insight and comprehension to traverse the intricacies of existence and arrive at thoughtful choices.

o **Example: Ignatian Discernment**

Ignatian discernment, a practice grounded in St. Ignatius of Loyola's insights, encourages deep reflection on our thoughts, emotions, and desires to harmonize with a higher purpose. By focusing on spiritual insights and eliminating distractions, individuals nurture a profound sense of purpose and clarity in their lives.

Effective Approaches to Information Prioritization

i.   **Articulate Your Aspirations:** It is essential to express your intentions and goals clearly. Grasping your purpose enables you to discern the most pertinent information.

ii. **Categorize Information:** Arrange information into distinct categories that align with your objectives. This methodical approach helps to concentrate on the most significant aspects.

iii. **Evaluate Sources:** Analyze the trustworthiness and dependability of information sources. Emphasize drawing information from credible and respected sources to maintain precision.

iv. **Filter Out Noise:** Identify and set aside information that does not contribute to your understanding. This approach alleviates mental strain and sharpens attention to essential information.

v.   **Continuously Reflect:** Consistently assess and adjust your values and goals. As your aspirations transform, recalibrate your attention to resonate with your present aims.

In Summary

The Cartographer's Compass underscores the importance of putting facts first to effectively traverse the expansive terrain of information. By integrating insights from various disciplines, we can adeptly discern and concentrate on what is genuinely significant. Utilize these resources to enhance your thought patterns, ensuring that your reasoning is anchored in meaningful and trustworthy information, leading you to sound conclusions and enlightened choices.

3. The Corroborative Power of References: Verifying the Melody

Verifiable Statements

The conveyance of information lacking the opportunity for validation creates a discordant note within the otherwise cohesive structure of the CgX system's quest for truth. Trustworthy sources offer references, allowing for exploring the roots of information and assessing its reliability. Before accepting conclusions as absolute truths, it is essential to interact with these sources and verify the information through personal investigation. Consider references as essential elements in a harmonious composition—they enrich the entire piece and establish a basis of trustworthiness in the execution.

Science: The Significance of Citations in Research

Citations in scientific research serve as a vital foundation for affirming the credibility and validity of findings, reflecting the interconnectedness of knowledge and the importance of intellectual lineage. Scholars often reference earlier investigations to frame their arguments, bolster their theories, and affirm the credibility of their findings. In scholarly discourse, authors must reference pertinent literature in peer-reviewed journals, thereby anchoring their assertions in substantiated evidence. This approach fosters a deeper sense of clarity and reliability within scientific inquiry.

o **Example: Peer-Reviewed Articles**

An article subjected to rigorous peer review regarding the effectiveness of an innovative medical treatment will incorporate references to earlier studies, clinical trials, and pertinent research findings. Including these references empowers readers to explore the foundational sources of the information, fostering a deeper understanding and enabling them to assess its validity. Through carefully analyzing the referenced materials, individuals can evaluate the strength of the evidence underpinning the article's assertions.

Philosophy: The Importance of Reasoned Argumentation

Recognizing the value of well-reasoned discourse and the necessity of citing credible sources to substantiate one's assertions is crucial. In philosophical discussion, arguments are meticulously crafted through logical reasoning and supported by evidence drawn from esteemed texts. Referencing sources and notable thinkers guarantees that the arguments are robust and subject to examination.

o **Example: Philosophical Essays**

An exploration of the essence of justice could draw upon the insights found in Plato's "Republic" alongside the perspectives offered in John Rawls' "A Theory of Justice." The references laid out here serve as a cornerstone for the argument, inviting readers to delve into the original works and assess the interpretations presented. By exploring the references, individuals can evaluate the essay's validity and the robustness of its arguments.

Religion: Scriptural References and Theological Scholarship

In religious studies, examining scriptural references and theological scholarship plays a crucial role in interpreting and comprehending religious doctrines. Academics and spiritual leaders reference revered writings, historical records, and respected analyses to bolster their insights and perspectives. This approach guarantees that theological assertions are rooted in well-established traditions and substantiated sources.

o **Example: Biblical Scriptural Study**

An exploration of the concept of grace could draw upon biblical passages, such as Ephesians 2:8-9[1], insights from early Church Fathers like Augustine of Hippo, and perspectives from modern theologians such as Karl Barth. These references offer a thorough insight into the doctrine, enabling readers to follow the evolution of theological thought and evaluate the validity of the interpretations presented.

o **Example: Scriptural Study in Islam**

Delving into the notion of Tawhid, or the oneness of God, invites a rich tapestry of understanding through Qur'anic verses, the wisdom of early Islamic scholars, and the reflections of modern theologians. These references provide a comprehensive understanding of the doctrine, allowing readers to trace the development of theological thought and assess the interpretations' credibility.

i. **Qur'anic Verses:** The notion of Tawhid holds a pivotal place within Islam and receives considerable attention throughout the Qur'an. Passages like Surah Al-Ikhlas (112:1-4) and Surah Al-Baqarah (2:255) highlight Allah's singularity and distinctiveness.

ii. **Early Islamic Scholars:** The reflections of figures such as Imam Al-Ghazali and Ibn Taymiyyah offer profound historical insights into the concept of Tawhid. Their explorations penetrate the philosophical and theological foundations of the concept, providing a profound examination of its implications.

iii. **Contemporary Theologians:** Modern scholars like Dr. Yasir Qadhi and Dr. Hamza Yusuf delve into the concept of Tawhid, engaging with current issues and challenges in their interpretations. Their insights facilitate a connection between conventional interpretations and contemporary frameworks.

Through a careful exploration of these sources, individuals can attain a profound comprehension of Tawhid. They can follow its evolution throughout Islamic history and assess the diverse interpretations that have surfaced over the ages. This method reflects a deep examination of theological ideas present in various religious traditions.

Defense Mechanism: Engage with References and Validate Information

1) **Trace Information Origin:** Investigate the information's roots. Examine the references included in the source material. Examine the roots of these assertions by identifying their foundational sources to evaluate their reliability.

2) **Evaluate References:** Assess the cited references with a discerning eye. Reflect on the sources' trustworthiness, significance, and credibility to guarantee they substantiate the conclusions meaningfully.

3) **Engage in Direct Examination:** Delve into the referenced materials directly. Engage with the foundational studies, texts, or documents to critically evaluate the information and discern the validity of the interpretations presented.

4) **Reflect on the Essence of Credibility:** Assess the information's overarching trustworthiness by examining the depth and robustness of the references provided. Dependable references bolster trustworthy conclusions.

In Summary

The validating strength of references is crucial for affirming the essence of truth within the CgX system. Engaging with references and rigorously examining information can significantly bolster the credibility and reliability of one's conclusions. Adopt these approaches to skillfully traverse the intricate realm of information, ensuring your conclusions are anchored in credible and thoroughly substantiated evidence. This methodical approach enables the CgX system to create a balanced and credible portrayal of reality, steering you towards well-informed and dependable understandings.

4. The Weight of Reputation: A Trustworthy Chorus

Reliability and Veracity

Evaluating the reliability and truthfulness of information is essential; it is important to consider the author's credibility and history of honesty in this assessment. Any historical inclination towards negligence in factual accuracy or a pattern of presenting partial truths should act as crucial indicators within the CgX system. Half-truths, akin to deceptive notes in a magnificent symphony, can jeopardize the fundamental integrity of the entire composition. Explore the author's history and reveal insights about their accuracy in depicting historical events.

Science: The Importance of Author Reputation

The trustworthiness of scientific inquiry is deeply shaped by the standing of its author. Individuals who have regularly disseminated their perspectives in respected journals and significantly advanced the field often evoke a deeper sense of trust. The assessment of an author's contributions often hinges on the scrutiny of peers and the metrics of citation, serving as benchmarks for its credibility. A track record of accurate and trustworthy research greatly enhances the author's reliability.

o   **Example: Renowned Scientists**

Envision an individual whose extensive body of work graces esteemed journals, reflecting a commitment to precision and dependability in their research endeavors. Their commitment to honesty and rigorous scientific principles enhances the credibility of their work. Through a careful analysis of their publication history and citation metrics, it becomes possible to evaluate the credibility of their findings.

Philosophy: The Role of Ethical Integrity

It is essential to recognize the significance of ethical integrity in our interactions and exchanges. An author's integrity and ethical standards play a vital role in fostering trust within their audience. Works that embody strict reasoning and robust evidence tend to offer greater reliability. Examining the author's history and moral integrity is essential for determining the truthfulness of their claims.

o   **Example: Ethical Philosophers**

An individual renowned for their unwavering ethical principles and meticulous academic rigor is more inclined to generate trustworthy and authoritative contributions. Through a careful analysis of their contributions and commitment to ethical standards, we can assess the trustworthiness of their philosophical assertions.

Religion: The Credibility of Religious Leaders

Within spiritual frameworks, the trustworthiness of spiritual guides frequently hinges on their standing for honesty and commitment to established beliefs. Individuals who have consistently demonstrated a keen understanding and principled behavior tend to foster greater trust among their followers. Exploring their history and analyzing their principles is essential for evaluating their credibility.

o   **Example: Trusted Spiritual Figures**

An individual in a position of spiritual guidance, known for their insightful understanding of sacred writings and principled conduct, tends to be viewed as trustworthy. By exploring their history and analyzing their philosophies, one can evaluate the trustworthiness of their counsel.

Defense Mechanism: Investigate the Author's background and History of Accuracy

1) **Review Publication History:** Assess the author's body of work to gauge their consistency and trustworthiness in presenting information. Seek out articles in esteemed journals and meaningful contributions to the discipline.

2) **Evaluate Citation Metrics:** Analyze citation metrics to understand the significance and credibility of the author's contributions. Elevated citation frequencies in esteemed journals serve as a testament to credibility.

3) **Evaluate Ethical Conduct:** Assess the integrity of the author by reflecting on their ethical behavior and commitment to the principles of honesty. Examine their work for any signs of oversight or incomplete narratives.

4) **Engage in the Pursuit of Independent Verification:** Confirm the information through unbiased sources. Cross-referencing with other reputable sources fosters a deeper understanding and enhances the integrity of the information presented.

In Summary

The significance of authors' reputation plays a pivotal role in evaluating the trustworthiness and truthfulness of the information presented. One can assess the reliability of their contributions through a thorough examination of their background, publication history, and ethical practices. Adopt these approaches to traverse the intricate realm of information, making certain that your thought processes are anchored in reliable and precise sources. This methodical approach fortifies the integrity of the CgX system, steering you toward conclusions that are both sound and trustworthy.

Identifying and Shielding Against Malfunctioning Information

Beware the insidious invaders that seek to corrupt your cognitive sanctum. In this perilous domain, opinions masquerading as facts, unsolicited advice lures you into dependence, and whispers of gossip distort the melody of truth. Stand vigilant against the siren songs of self-deception and misinformation. Arm yourself with the knowledge to sift through the general information maze, ensuring that your symphony of thought remains untainted and harmonious.

1. Opinions: Trojan Horses of the Mind

Trojan Horses: Opinions

Opinions, those ubiquitous facets of human interaction, may mask significant dangers. In the absence of a firm foundation in verified truths or a deeply held belief framework, like the one proposed by ADM-GENE theory, personal views can swiftly shift into untrustworthy and possibly detrimental forces. Imagine these entities as deceptive vessels, offering the enticing promise of wisdom while concealing an inherent imperfection beneath the surface. It is crucial to engage with opinions thoughtfully, ensuring they are rooted in solid evidence or authentic convictions.

Philosophy: The Significance of Epistemology

The exploration of knowledge highlights the importance of differentiating between well-founded beliefs and those that are simply personal opinions. Thinkers such as René Descartes and Immanuel Kant highlighted the necessity of basing our convictions on rational thought and empirical proof. Descartes' approach to skepticism entails a thorough examination of beliefs to uncover undeniable truths.

Science: The Exploration of Scientific Inquiry

The differentiation between hypothesis and opinion holds significant importance in science. Hypotheses emerge from empirical evidence, undergoing a meticulous testing and validation process to ascertain their validity. In contrast, opinions are inherently subjective and do not possess the empirical basis necessary for rigorous scientific exploration. Evidence-based conclusions take precedence over unverified opinions within the framework of the scientific method.

o **Example: Assessing Health claims**

Reflect on the domain of health and wellness. A claim rooted in a personal perspective, like the efficacy of a specific diet, necessitates thorough examination. Through a careful analysis of clinical studies, peer-reviewed research, and the consensus of experts, it becomes possible to distinguish between health guidance grounded in evidence and that which is simply based on personal belief. This method guarantees that choices regarding health are rooted in trustworthy data.

Defense Mechanism: Foster a Critical Mindset

1) **Assess the Evidence:** When exploring different perspectives, reflect on the evidence that supports each viewpoint. Pose essential inquiries like Does the assertion have backing from empirical evidence? Is the origin trustworthy and esteemed?

2) **Verify Credibility:** Examine the reliability of the source. Reliable sources often demonstrate a history of precision and openness. Reputable academic institutions, respected media outlets, and rigorously peer-reviewed journals serve as trustworthy sources of information.

3) **Recognize Biases:** Recognize the inherent biases that could shape the narrative. Personal, cultural, or institutional biases can influence perspectives, highlighting the importance of examining viewpoints with discernment.

4) **Cross-Reference Information:** Ensure the accuracy of facts by consulting various trustworthy sources. Cross-referencing serves as a vital tool in validating the precision and coherence of information, thereby minimizing the chances of embracing unverified viewpoints.

In closing

Perspectives, though prevalent, can serve as covert agents, gradually permeating our mental constructs and skewing our comprehension. By cultivating a discerning perspective and carefully evaluating the evidence, we can differentiate between trustworthy information and dubious viewpoints. This structured method enables us to traverse the complex landscape of information with lucidity and assurance, guaranteeing that our reasoning is anchored in credible facts and authentic convictions. Utilize these resources to protect the purity of your mental frameworks, defending against the subtle intrusions of disruptive ideas.

2. The Siren Song of Unsolicited Advice

Critically Evaluate Unsolicited Guidance

Assess the merits and implications of unsolicited advice. While free advice may seem enticing, it is crucial to approach it with a mindset of critical skepticism within the CgX framework. It is quite typical for friends, family, and even those we know casually to offer advice without being asked. It is essential to acknowledge that these declarations often fall short of the necessary validation to be considered reliable advice. View these components as isolated notes; they can be delightful, but they do not possess the foundational strength and unity that define a true symphony. Such statements frequently emerge from sources that, despite their good intentions, may possess underlying biases. It is crucial for the discerning mind to undertake a comprehensive evaluation of such guidance, meticulously scrutinizing its origins and potential biases prior to incorporating it into their understanding.

Science: Cognitive Biases and Heuristics

Exploring the intricacies of human thought processes, particularly the nuances of cognitive biases and heuristics, reveals profound insights into our decision-making and perception of reality. Research in psychology reveals how cognitive biases and heuristics shape our decision-making processes and the guidance we offer others. Cognitive biases, including confirmation bias and the availability heuristic, can skew our judgment and result in misguided advice. Grasping these biases is essential for thoughtfully assessing unsolicited advice. By acknowledging the possibility of bias, one can more effectively evaluate the credibility and consistency of the guidance they encounter.

o **Example: Confirmation Bias**

Confirmation bias manifests when people prioritize information that aligns with their pre-existing beliefs, often overlooking evidence that challenges those views. Consider a scenario where an acquaintance passionately advocates for a specific dietary regimen, presenting unsolicited recommendations rooted in selective evidence that aligns with their convictions while conveniently overlooking research that points to possible disadvantages. Understanding this bias is essential for thoughtfully assessing guidance and pursuing a well-rounded viewpoint.

Philosophy: Skepticism and Inquiry

Philosophical skepticism, as advocated by figures such as David Hume, underscores the necessity of inquiry and the rigorous evaluation of beliefs and assertions. Questioning the validity of unsolicited advice fosters a systematic way of assessing it, guaranteeing that our conclusions rest on solid reasoning and empirical evidence. This philosophical approach resonates with the CgX framework's focus on analytical reasoning and thoughtful evaluation.

o **Example: Cartesian Skepticism**

René Descartes' method of skepticism involves a deep and rigorous analysis of all beliefs to reveal fundamental truths that cannot be disputed. This approach encourages individuals to critically assess unsolicited guidance, ensuring it withstands scrutiny before being accepted.

Spirituality: Guidance and Insight

In spiritual settings, discernment is a crucial practice for assessing guidance and counsel. Numerous belief systems highlight the significance of pursuing knowledge and insight to effectively navigate the intricacies of life and arrive at thoughtful choices. The discernment process encompasses prayer, introspection, and dialogue with reliable spiritual mentors to evaluate the authenticity and significance of the guidance received.

o   **Example: Sacred Insight**

Proverbs 19:20 states, "Listen to advice and accept instruction, that you may gain wisdom in the future," emphasizing the importance of heeding guidance and embracing teachings, as this will lead to the acquisition of wisdom down the line. Nonetheless, this body of wisdom underscores the importance of exercising discernment when assessing the value and applicability of the guidance offered. Through a thoughtful evaluation of the origins and substance of unsolicited guidance, individuals can arrive at well-considered and wise choices.

Defense Mechanism: Enhance Your Ability to Critically Assess Sources

1) **Evaluate Qualifications:** Assess the credentials and knowledge of those offering insights. Reflect on their history, expertise, and trustworthiness within the pertinent domain.

2) **Identify Potential Biases:** Recognize the possible biases that could shape the guidance provided. Reflect on the

various personal, cultural, or institutional biases that may influence the direction provided.

3) **Verify Information:** Consult trustworthy sources and empirical data to ensure accuracy. It is essential that the advice provided is backed by reliable information and is consistent with recognized understanding.

4) **Reflect and Analyze:** Dedicate moments to ponder the guidance and its potential consequences. Examine the possible effects of adhering to the advice and reflect on different viewpoints.

Final Thoughts

Unsolicited advice, though frequently offered with good intentions, necessitates careful consideration to assess its truthfulness and applicability. By cultivating a discerning perspective and evaluating those offering counsel's credentials and possible biases, we can skillfully navigate the alluring call of unsolicited advice. Utilize these resources to protect your mental faculties, guaranteeing that your thought processes are anchored in credible and dependable knowledge. This structured methodology enables you to navigate choices with clarity and uphold the coherence of your intellectual foundation.

3. The Abdication of Thinking: A Dangerous Melody of Dependence

Engage in Independent Thought

Skilled minds, the true experts of the CgX system, reject the temptation to delegate their intellectual challenges. They meticulously seek out trustworthy sources of information, transforming them into instruments that create a complex harmony of thoughts. Entrusting others with our cognitive functions can be likened to quieting a full symphony, resulting in a fragmented tune of comprehension. Encouraging an intrinsic passion for understanding and discovery is essential. Embrace the opportunities that research and analysis offer as engaging pursuits. Actively participating in the process of knowledge creation is crucial for maintaining the integrity of the CgX system.

Science: The Significance of Engaging in Active Learning

Exploration in educational psychology reveals the profound advantages of engaging in active learning. Active learning emphasizes the importance of engaging with the material through dialogue, hands-on practice, and thoughtful analysis rather than merely absorbing information without interaction. Research indicates that those who engage actively in their learning processes are more likely to retain information effectively, cultivate a profound understanding, and sharpen their critical thinking abilities in contrast to those who adopt a passive approach. This perspective highlights the significance of autonomous thinking and proactive participation in the journey of learning.

o **Example: The Socratic Seminar**

In a Socratic seminar, participants immerse themselves in a rich dialogue, exploring a text through the art of questioning and thoughtful responses. This approach fosters engagement and promotes autonomous thinking, compelling learners to scrutinize, interrogate, and deliberate on the content with a critical lens. The seminar encourages a profound engagement with the material and nurtures a spirit of inquiry.

Philosophy: The Value of Autonomy

Thinkers like Immanuel Kant highlighted the significance of autonomy in the realm of human reasoning. Kant's notion of enlightenment emphasizes the importance of individuals exercising their own reason and judgment instead of depending on external authorities. He famously proclaimed, "Sapere Aude" (Dare to know), encouraging individuals to embrace independent and critical thinking. This viewpoint resonates with the CgX system's focus on the significance of autonomous thinking.

o **Example: Autonomy in Decision-Making**

Reflect on an individual in a position of expertise navigating a pivotal choice. Through the pursuit of independent research, data analysis, and the evaluation of diverse viewpoints, individuals cultivate a sense of autonomy in their decision-making journey. This autonomous thinking fosters more informed and substantiated choices, highlighting the significance of self-directed reasoning.

Religion: Personal Reflection and Spiritual Growth

Numerous spiritual paths highlight the significance of introspection and the journey of individual spiritual development. For example, within Islam, the notion of Ijtihad encompasses the practice of independent reasoning to interpret sacred texts and arrive at decisions. This approach invites individuals to thoughtfully examine their beliefs and integrate their principles into modern challenges.

o **Example: Exploration of Ijtihad within Islamic Scholarship**

Islamic scholars engaging in Ijtihad thoughtfully examine religious texts, historical contexts, and modern situations to formulate fresh interpretations and solutions. This autonomous approach to thinking guarantees that spiritual teachings stay pertinent and evolving, fostering both individual and collective development.

Defense Mechanism: Foster a Spirit of Intellectual Exploration

1) **Cultivate Curiosity:** Nurture an insatiable thirst for understanding and discovery. Embrace learning as an invigorating journey that nurtures your mind and fosters personal development.

2) **Recognize Reliable Sources:** Pursue information from dependable and credible origins. Academic institutions, peer-reviewed journals, and recognized authorities serve as essential resources.

3) **Participate in Thorough Examination:** Engage deeply in the process of inquiry and reflection. Challenge your beliefs, assess the information, and explore various viewpoints.

4) **Reflect and Analyze:** Dedicate moments to ponder the insights acquired. Examine its significance, credibility, and consequences for your comprehension and choices.

Final Thoughts

The relinquishment of critical thinking creates a perilous rhythm of reliance that muffles the harmony of autonomous reasoning. Through nurturing a culture of inquiry and participating wholeheartedly in the journey of knowledge creation, we uphold the essence of the CgX system. Welcome the chance to think for yourself, allowing it to lead you to a richer comprehension and more enlightened choices. This structured method enables you to traverse the intricacies of existence with insight and assurance.

4. Beware the Whispers of Gossip: A Discordant Symphony of Bias

Sources that Exhibit Bias and Prejudice

The alluring appeal of gossip cannot be overlooked; consequently, adopting a discerning perspective regarding its impact within the CgX system is essential. Those who partake in the spread of whispers and rumors, commonly known as scandalmongers and gossipmongers, ought not to be seen as reliable sources of information. Their assertions are steeped in preconceived notions and partiality, generating dissonant elements that disrupt the flow of thoughtful dialogue. Connect with insights drawn from credible sources, highlighting the significance of evidence over conjecture. Observing the distortions that gossip brings ensures that the CgX system stays committed to creating a harmonious melody of truth.

Science: Exploring the intricacies of cognitive bias and the profound effects of social influence.

Exploration in psychology uncovers the intricate ways in which cognitive biases and social dynamics influence the spread of gossip. The impact of cognitive biases, such as the bandwagon effect and confirmation bias, can greatly enhance gossip dissemination. The inclination to align oneself with the beliefs or actions of others emerges when individuals adopt these ideas or behaviors merely by witnessing their prevalence among peers. Confirmation bias causes individuals to favor information that supports their pre-existing convictions. The existence of these biases deepens our intrigue with gossip, underscoring the necessity for a thoughtful evaluation of its effects.

o **Example: The Dissemination of Misinformation**

In times of public health crises, such as the COVID-19 pandemic, the rapid dissemination of rumors and gossip significantly contributed to the spread of misinformation. For instance, misinformation regarding vaccine safety spread widely, driven by inherent cognitive biases and the impact of social dynamics. This led to confusion and hesitancy among the public. By thoughtfully examining information sources and relying on trusted health authorities like the World Health Organization (WHO) and the Centers for Disease Control and Prevention (CDC), individuals can reduce the influence of rumors and make well-informed choices.

Philosophy: The Ethics of Discourse

Philosophical traditions highlight the importance of ethical considerations in dialogue and the duty to pursue truth. Immanuel Kant's notion of the categorical imperative emphasizes the importance of acting in accordance with principles that hold universal applicability. Participating in gossip and disseminating unverified information disrupts the ethical foundation we strive for, as it detracts from the quest for truth and damages meaningful dialogue.

o **Example: The Ethics of Communication**

Within the dynamics of a professional environment, an individual becomes aware of speculation regarding a fellow team member. Before disseminating the information, the employee reflects on the ethical dimensions and the possible consequences it might entail. By avoiding gossip and prioritizing factual information, the employee embodies the essence of ethical communication.

Religion: The Morality of Speech

Numerous spiritual paths emphasize the ethical obligations that come with our words. In the context of Islam, the notion of "ghibah," or backbiting, is viewed unfavorably. Individuals are urged to communicate honestly and refrain from disseminating detrimental rumors. This ethical structure resonates with the CgX system's focus on interacting with trustworthy information and upholding the purity of intellectual discourse.

o   **Example: Exploring the Moral Principles Found in Spiritual Traditions**

The Quran (49:12) cautions against the dangers of suspicion, spying, and backbiting: "And do not spy or backbite each other." Would anyone among you consider consuming the remains of a sibling after their demise? You would find it utterly distasteful. This lesson highlights the moral significance of avoiding gossip and upholding integrity in our interactions.

Defense Mechanism: Reduce Engagement with Rumors and Gossip

1)   **Seek Out Trustworthy Sources:** Prioritize gathering information from reliable and credible origins. Reputable academic institutions, respected media outlets, and experts offer trustworthy information.

2)   **Assess Biases:** Recognize and reflect on the inherent biases that may exist within various information sources. Acknowledge the various personal, cultural, or institutional biases that can influence the narrative.

3)   **Verify Information:** Ensure accuracy by consulting various trustworthy sources. Verification diminishes the

chances of embracing and disseminating false information.

4) **Reflect on the Consequences:** Ponder the possible effects of participating in and disseminating gossip. Contemplate the moral and societal implications of your choices.

Final Thoughts

The allure of gossip presents a profound challenge to the purity of thought within the CgX system. Through thoughtful reflection and a conscious reduction of involvement in gossip, one can sustain an emphasis on reliable and factual information. Embrace these defense mechanisms to ensure that your cognitive processes remain focused on creating a harmonious melody of truth, protecting against the disruptive forces of gossip and bias.

5. The Siren Song of Self-Deception: A Harmony of Wishes Disguised as Facts

Harmonizing with Desires: Aligning with Aspirations

Approach with care the enticing whispers of self-deception that may arise within the CgX framework. Individuals naturally tend to pursue information that aligns with their hopes, quietly shaping a story of wants that frequently appear as an undeniable reality. The distortion of our genuine conceptual landscape can lead us astray. Recognizing this common human inclination is crucial, and it is important to actively address its impacts.

Science: Cognitive Dissonance and Confirmation Bias

The interplay between cognitive dissonance and confirmation bias reveals profound insights into human behavior and thought processes. Leon Festinger's theory of cognitive dissonance elucidates the unease we feel when faced with contradictory information that questions our beliefs or aspirations. To alleviate this unease, we might resort to self-deception by pursuing information that resonates with our desires, a phenomenon referred to as confirmation bias. Confirmation bias encourages us to embrace information that aligns with our established beliefs while disregarding opposing evidence, strengthening our self-deceptive narratives.

o   **Example: Financial Decision-Making**

Imagine an investor who holds a deep conviction about a specific stock. Despite unfavorable reports and diminishing results, they gravitate towards optimistic narratives and analyst perspectives that reinforce their beliefs while dismissing opposing evidence. This form of self-deception, known as confirmation bias, can lead to misguided investment choices and subsequent financial setbacks. The COVID-19 pandemic highlighted how such biases can impact financial decisions, as many investors clung to hopeful projections despite market volatility. Awareness of this bias and a thoughtful assessment of all information, including critical perspectives, can help reduce the impact of self-deception and lead to more informed financial decisions.

Philosophy: The Allegory of the Cave

Plato's Allegory of the Cave profoundly explores self-deception and the transformative journey toward understanding truth. In this allegorical narrative, individuals are bound within a cave, interpreting the shadows cast upon the wall as their only truth. A solitary inmate breaks free, encounters the vastness of the world beyond, and comes to understand that the shadows are nothing but deceptive phantoms. This reflective narrative emphasizes the significance of self-awareness and intellectual integrity in transcending self-deception and attaining true comprehension.

o   **Example: Personal Growth and Reflection**

Imagine a researcher who believes their hypothesis is always correct, much like the prisoners in Plato's Allegory of the Cave who mistake shadows for reality. This researcher overlooks potential flaws in their methodology and dismisses conflicting data, seeing only their perspective as the truth. A real-life example is the initial resistance to the idea that Helicobacter pylori bacteria cause stomach ulcers. For years, the medical community believed that stress and lifestyle were the primary causes of ulcers. When researchers Barry Marshall and Robin Warren proposed that H. pylori was the culprit, their findings were initially met with skepticism and resistance. Many researchers clung to the established belief, dismissing the new evidence.

Through the practice of introspection and the pursuit of candid insights from peers, this researcher can begin to see beyond the shadows on the cave wall. By seeking honest feedback and critically evaluating their work, they can cultivate a clearer understanding of their research, much like the prisoner who escapes the cave and sees the world in its true form. This journey of self-discovery fosters scientific integrity and enhances the quality of their contributions to the field, leading to more robust and reliable findings.

Religion: The Art of Humility and Authenticity

Numerous spiritual paths highlight the significance of humility and the quest for truth as safeguards against the pitfalls of self-deception. In Christianity, humility is about acknowledging our limitations and turning to a higher power for guidance. This approach cultivates a deep sense of integrity and introspection, guiding individuals to harmonize their aspirations with authentic realities.

o **Example: Spiritual Reflection**

Engaging in spiritual reflection through practices such as Salah in Islam or meditation in Buddhism enables individuals to seek clarity and truth by acknowledging their biases and desires. For example, the practice of daily prayers (Salah) among Muslims incorporates a sequence of physical movements and recitations from the Quran, creating an opportunity for reflection and a deeper connection with the divine. This practice fosters a deep sense of mindfulness and awareness, encouraging individuals to recognize their inner biases and harmonize their actions with core Islamic principles.

Similarly, meditation is a fundamental practice in Buddhism that cultivates mindfulness and insight. Through meditation, Buddhists seek to understand the nature of their thoughts and emotions, recognizing the impermanence and interconnectedness of all things. This reflective process helps individuals confront difficult ideas and develop a deeper understanding of the Dharma, leading to spiritual growth and harmony.

Both approaches foster a deeper connection with one's values and beliefs and promote an openness to interacting with challenging concepts. Spiritual reflection becomes a potent instrument for enlightenment and personal growth, whether achieved via the structured rituals of Salah or the meditative practices of Buddhism.

Defense Mechanism: Engage in the Cultivation of Self-Awareness

1) **Recognize Inherent Biases:** Understand that each individual possesses biases and desires that shape their understanding of reality. Recognizing these biases marks the initial stride toward alleviating their impact.

2) **Embrace Challenging Insights:** Intentionally immerse yourself in perspectives confronting your established beliefs. This approach fosters a harmonious view and mitigates the effects of confirmation bias.

3) **Reflect and Examine:** Consistently engage in introspection regarding your thoughts and convictions. Examine if their assertions are rooted in factual support or motivated by individual aspirations. This introspective approach fosters a commitment to truthfulness in thought and action.

4) **Embrace Intellectual Honesty:** Prioritize authenticity over ease. Embrace the opportunity to reassess your convictions when confronted with new information, even if it disrupts your ambitions.

Final Thoughts

Self-deception, fueled by the alignment of desires masquerading as truths, presents a considerable risk to the integrity of the CgX system. By developing self-awareness, recognizing our intrinsic biases, and committing to intellectual honesty, we can diminish the seductive pull of self-deception. This structured methodology allows the CgX system to foster a balanced and authentic narrative, steering us toward true comprehension and sound convictions. Utilize these instruments to protect yourself from self-deception, maintaining harmony between your thought processes and the objective truth through rational exploration.

6. The General Information Maze: Sifting for Melodies of Truth

Fact Elusiveness

The complex terrain of general information offers a multitude of possibilities for the CgX system, yet effectively traversing this domain requires thoughtful and persistent engagement. Facts, those precious elements that create the beautiful melody of reality, can often be hard to grasp, often hidden beneath the veils of distortion. While general information provides a starting point, it requires careful examination to discern its authenticity and accuracy. The journey of purification may demand considerable time, yet it remains profoundly vital.

Science: Information Literacy

Understanding the nuances of information is essential. Information literacy encompasses the capacity to discern, seek out, assess, and adeptly utilize information. This ability is crucial for traversing the expansive realm of information. Exploration within the realm of library and information science highlights the crucial need for cultivating robust information literacy skills, enabling individuals to discern credible sources from those lacking reliability. Information literacy encompasses comprehending how information is generated, being aware of the context in which it appears, and critically assessing its trustworthiness.

o **Example: Academic Research**

In educational environments, learners are encouraged to thoughtfully assess the credibility of sources for their research assignments. This entails evaluating the author's reliability, the integrity of the publication, the rigor of the methodologies employed in research, and corroborating information with other trustworthy sources. This meticulous method guarantees their efforts are grounded in precise and trustworthy data.

Philosophy: The Quest for Truth

The Journey Towards Understanding Reality. Thinkers such as Aristotle and Bertrand Russell have highlighted the necessity of thorough examination in the pursuit of truth. Aristotle's principle of pursuing the "golden mean" emphasizes the importance of achieving a balanced and nuanced comprehension of information. Russell's focus on logical scrutiny and observable evidence underscores the importance of thorough and thoughtful evaluation of information to reach sound conclusions.

o   **Example: Logical Positivism**

Proponents of logical positivism, particularly those within the Vienna Circle, championed the verification principle. This principle posits that only statements that can be confirmed through empirical observation or logical reasoning hold significance. This perspective highlights the importance of thorough examination and validation in differentiating between truth and falsehood.

Religion: Discernment and Wisdom

Numerous spiritual paths highlight the significance of discernment and wisdom in the pursuit of truth. In Christianity, the essence of prudence encompasses thoughtful discernment and insight into the choices we make. This principle invites individuals to engage in thoughtful analysis of information and pursue spiritual insight in discerning truth from deception.

o **Example: Scriptural Interpretation**

In biblical studies, researchers use exegesis to precisely determine the texts' underlying meanings. A thorough examination of the historical background, linguistic nuances, and theological motifs is required to understand the underlying meaning. This systematic methodology ensures that interpretations are grounded in a profound and complex understanding of the text.

In Christianity, this rigorous exegesis ensures that biblical interpretations are firmly grounded in a thorough understanding of historical and cultural contexts. For instance, interpreting Jesus's parables involves examining the socio-political environment of first-century Palestine, understanding the nuances of the original Greek or Hebrew text, and discerning the theological implications. This deep dive into scripture helps believers apply timeless truths to their modern lives with wisdom and clarity.

Similarly, in Islam, scholars engage in Tafsir to interpret the Quran. Tafsir involves analyzing the historical context in which verses were revealed, understanding the classical Arabic language's intricacies, and exploring the Hadith (sayings and actions of the Prophet Muhammad) for deeper insights. This process ensures that Quranic interpretations are accurate and meaningful, guiding Muslims in their faith and daily practices precisely.

In Christianity and Islam, the disciplined practice of scriptural interpretation fosters a profound connection with the divine message, nurturing spiritual growth and wisdom.

Defense Mechanism: Elevate Your Research Capabilities

1) **Develop Information Literacy:** Cultivate your capacity to discern, seek out, assess, and adeptly apply information. Grasp the framework surrounding the information provided and evaluate its trustworthiness with a discerning eye.

2) **Assess Source Credibility:** Evaluate the credibility of information sources. Reflect on the author's expertise, the credibility of the publication, and the substantiation behind the assertions.

3) **Cross-Reference Information:** It is essential to validate facts by consulting various credible sources to ensure accuracy and reliability. This method helps to confirm accuracy and consistency.

4) **Engage in Critical Thinking:** Interact with information through a discerning lens. Challenge your beliefs, assess the information, and explore different viewpoints.

Final Thoughts

Traversing the labyrinth of general information demands a thoughtful and meticulous approach to discern truth from falsehood, ensuring genuine insights are uncovered amidst the noise. By refining your research abilities with an emphasis on thoroughness and insight, you can cultivate the skills to identify trustworthy sources and validate information. Utilize these resources to traverse the intricate terrain of data, reshaping it into a basis for cultivating a balanced synthesis of validated insights within the CgX framework. This structured method enables you to build solid conclusions and make thoughtful choices, safeguarding the clarity of your thinking.

7. Fanaticism: The Distorted Melody of Obsession

Sound Judgment

Those who possess fervent passions and unwavering convictions can act as conduits for the spread of misinformation. Their assertions, often laden with exaggeration and emotional nuances, can lead individuals to misguided interpretations. Evaluating the author's neutrality and recognizing signs of a comprehensive discussion is essential.

Science: The Impact of Emotions on Decision-Making

Exploration in cognitive psychology reveals emotions' profound impact on our decision-making processes and judgments. When we allow our emotions to dictate our conclusions, we risk clouding our perception and straying from objective reality. The fervor of fanaticism, marked by deep emotional engagement, often amplifies this distortion, resulting in biased and exaggerated statements. Understanding how emotions shape our perception of information enables individuals to assess the trustworthiness and validity of various sources with greater discernment.

o **Example: Social Movements**

Think about societal movements like advocacy against climate change or the anti-vaccine campaign. Even while these movements are driven by passionate advocacy and have good intentions, the fervor of their feelings can occasionally lead to inaccurate representations of the truth. An ardent opponent of vaccinations, for example, may exaggerate the dangers of vaccinations while downplaying their advantages, which could result in widespread disinformation and hazards to the public's health. In a similar vein, a climate change activist may exaggerate facts or images to highlight how urgent the problem is, which could skew the complex scientific consensus.

These instances show how emotional passion may occasionally obscure factual data despite its ability to rally support. An ardent supporter may use hyperbolic language to emphasize their point, which could skew perceptions of the fundamental facts. Critical evaluation necessitates a harmonious interaction between emotional resonance and empirical proof to ensure that the movement's central message is factually sound and emotionally compelling to its audience. This well-rounded strategy encourages supporters to make educated decisions and upholds the integrity of the cause.

Philosophy: The Dangers of Fanaticism

Exploring the Perils of Extreme Beliefs. Throughout history, thinkers have cautioned against the perils of extreme devotion. Søren Kierkegaard, a Danish thinker, posited that unbridled passion devoid of thoughtful consideration may result in harmful consequences. Fanaticism frequently overlooks the complexities of understanding and the value of diverse viewpoints, leading to a limited and skewed perception of reality. Highlighting the importance of rational thought and analytical reasoning reduces the dangers linked to extreme beliefs.

o **Example: Political Extremism**

Political extremism poignantly illustrates the perils inherent in unwavering fanaticism. Those who hold extreme views frequently utilize emotionally charged language and oversimplified stories, overlooking the intricate realities and diverse perspectives that exist. Through a thoughtful examination of rhetoric and the pursuit of balanced viewpoints, one can navigate the complexities of discourse and steer clear of the pitfalls of extremism.

Religion: The Need for Moderation

Numerous spiritual paths highlight the significance of balance, urging followers to be wary of extreme zealotry. In the teachings of Islam, the principle of "wasatiyyah" embodies the essence of moderation, promoting a harmonious and measured approach to behavior. This principle invites individuals to embrace a balanced perspective, promoting a reflective and nuanced engagement with their beliefs and relationships.

o   **Example: Fanatical Beliefs**

When beliefs are elevated to the point of fanaticism, the dangers associated with religious extremism become profoundly concerning. Individuals with extreme views often manipulate religious doctrines to rationalize their radical behaviors, resulting in significant harm and societal fragmentation. Individuals can cultivate a balanced and genuine expression of their beliefs through moderation and thoughtful examination of extreme perspectives.

Defense Mechanism: Assess Impartiality and Seek Well-Rounded Expositions

1)   **Evaluate the Emotional Tone:** Examine the emotional undertone of the information presented. Expressions laden with exaggeration and emotional resonance might suggest an absence of impartiality.

2)   **Identify Author's Impartiality:** Delve into the author's history and possible influences on their perspective.

Reflect on whether their perspective is well-rounded or if it leans towards extremism.

3) **Seek Diverse Perspectives:** Interact with various sources to cultivate a well-rounded comprehension. Embracing a range of viewpoints mitigates the sway of extreme beliefs.

4) **Reflect on Evidence:** Analyze the evidence with a discerning eye. It is essential to ground conclusions in objective data, steering clear of emotional reasoning.

In Conclusion

Fanaticism, characterized by fervent emotions and unwavering convictions, has the potential to skew the harmonious essence of truth. By evaluating the author's neutrality, recognizing emotional nuances, and pursuing comprehensive analyses, one can adeptly traverse the intricate terrain of information with discernment. Adopt these approaches to protect your mental faculties, allowing your thought processes to remain anchored in well-rounded and trustworthy information. This methodical approach enables the CgX system to produce trustworthy and sophisticated insights, leading to a more profound comprehension of existence.

8. Zealotry: The Distorted Melody of Fanaticism

Wild Imagination

The phenomenon of wild imagination, particularly among fanatics, individuals inclined towards exaggeration and fanciful thinking, and those prone to embellishment and whimsical thought, presents a notable obstacle to the credibility of information within the CgX system. Often marked by a rich imagination, their claims can lead one away from the quest for truth. Approach information that is presented with heightened emotional intensity or lacks sufficient evidence with a discerning mindset.

Science: Emotional Appeal and Cognitive Biases

The interplay between emotional resonance and cognitive distortions in our understanding of the world. Studies in cognitive psychology reveal the profound impact of emotional appeals on shaping our perceptions and judgments. When we allow our emotions to guide our reasoning, we risk drawing conclusions that may not align with objective reality. Intense devotion frequently heightens emotional resonance, utilizing rich imagery and overstated assertions to engage and enthrall audiences. Understanding these strategies empowers individuals to thoughtfully assess the reliability of the information presented to them.

o **Example: Sensationalist Media**

Reflect on media that thrives on emotional resonance and captivating narratives. Such sources frequently emphasize striking and embellished stories to capture interest, which may undermine the reliability of the information presented. Through a thoughtful examination of the evidence and pursuit of balanced narratives, individuals can effectively navigate emotional influences and distinguish factual information.

Philosophy: The Pitfalls of Imaginative Excess

The Dangers of Overactive Imagination in Philosophical Thought. Thinkers such as David Hume have delved into the perils associated with an overactive imagination. Hume warned us about the dangers of letting our vivid imagination overshadow reason, suggesting that this can result in superstition and irrational beliefs. Engaging in critical thinking and reasoned analysis is vital for addressing the distortions that arise from unchecked imagination and fervent beliefs.

o **Example: Conspiracy Theories**

Imagination and exaggerated claims are common components of conspiracy theories. Without any empirical support, these theories tell complex, emotionally stirring tales. According to the conspiracy theory known as "chemtrails," for example, the persistent trails that airplanes leave behind are chemical or biological agents that are purposefully sprayed for evil intentions. The theory endures because of fanciful and inflated claims, even though several scientific investigations refute these claims and clarify that contrails are just water vapor condensing in the chilly upper atmosphere.

The Me Too campaign also demonstrates how emotional passion can occasionally result in exaggerated portrayals, even while it is necessary for rallying support and increasing awareness. For instance, although the movement has been successful in drawing attention to the widespread occurrence of sexual harassment and assault, some cases of unsubstantiated allegations have resulted in misunderstandings and confusion, overshadowing the campaign's main point.

By carefully considering the information and conducting a critical examination, one can avoid the dangers of extravagant exaggeration. By examining sources carefully, considering larger contexts, and striking a balance between emotional resonance and empirical substantiation, people can gain a more accurate and nuanced understanding of complex situations.

Religion: The Call for Discernment

Numerous spiritual paths highlight the significance of careful judgment while warning against the perils of extreme devotion. Within the framework of Christianity, the essence of prudence encompasses the art of discerning judgment and steering clear of extremes. This principle invites individuals to engage in thoughtful analysis of teachings, steering clear of interpretations that are overly dramatic or laden with emotional intensity.

o   **Example: Apocalyptic Predictions**

Predictions of an apocalyptic nature frequently encompass striking and amplified scenarios that resonate deeply with our emotions. Spiritual guides who prioritize discernment inspire their followers to thoughtfully assess various assertions and pursue nuanced understandings of sacred writings. This method fosters a reflective and balanced engagement with one's beliefs.

Defense Mechanism: Exercise Caution and Seek Evidence

1) **Evaluate Emotional Appeal:** Examine the emotional quality of the content. Expressions that heavily rely on emotional resonance often suggest a deficiency in impartiality and substantiation.

2) **Identify Supporting Evidence:** Carefully consider the evidence provided to support the claims stated. Verifiable facts must be used to support the information rather than depending solely on vivid imagination.

3) **Seek Balanced Perspectives:** Interact with various sources to cultivate a well-rounded comprehension. Equitable representation and a variety of perspectives serve to mitigate the effects of extreme ideologies.

4) **Reflect on Reasoning:** Continuously examine your thought processes. Examine the extent to which conclusions are grounded in objective evidence versus those that may be swayed by emotional resonance and creative thought.

Final Thoughts

The fervor of zealotry and the boundless nature of imagination present considerable obstacles to the credibility of information in the CgX system. Through the practice of discernment, assessing emotional resonance, and pursuing corroborative evidence, one can adeptly maneuver through the sway of fanaticism with clarity and wisdom. Adopt these approaches to protect your mental faculties, allowing your thought processes to be anchored in reliable and factual data. This structured methodology enables the CgX system to produce trustworthy and substantiated insights, leading to a more profound comprehension of existence.

9. The Discordant Notes: Enemies of Sound Thinking

The path to developing a strong CgX framework requires a deep understanding of particular forces that hinder our ability to think critically. These adversaries, much like discordant notes in a grand composition, can destabilize the foundation of our understanding. Let us engage in a thoughtful examination of various significant influences:

a) **Intimacy and Passion: The Alluring Forces of Emotion**

Overcoming Reason

Emotions and desires can significantly cloud rational thought within the CgX framework. Approach their influence with discernment, prioritizing rational thought and empirical evidence in your choices.

Science: The Impact of Emotions on Judgment

Social and cognitive psychology studies reveal that deep and fervent emotions can obscure our judgment and influence our decision-making processes. Emotional attachment often clouds our judgment, making it challenging to engage in objective analysis. By acknowledging the significance of these emotions, one can endeavor to cultivate a balanced viewpoint and emphasize rational thought over emotional sway.

o   **Example: Exploring Relationship Decisions**

Reflect on the ways in which romantic emotions shape our choices in relationships. Emotions play a crucial role in our lives, yet they can occasionally cloud our judgment, causing us to miss important warning signs or to make decisions that may not serve our best interests. Through the harmonious integration of emotions and reason, one can navigate the complexities of decision-making with greater clarity and insight.

Philosophy: The Role of Rational Control

Thinkers like Plato and Aristotle highlighted the significance of exercising rational control over our emotions. Plato's tripartite theory of the soul emphasizes the essential role of reason in guiding the spirited and appetitive dimensions of our human experience. According to Aristotle, the essence of virtue lies in the delicate balance between extremes, a balance that is navigated through the guidance of reason. The essence of these philosophical principles highlights rational control's crucial role in preserving sound judgment.

o   **Example: Ethical Dilemmas**

In real-life scenarios, ethical dilemmas often present themselves in various professional and personal contexts, adding layers of complexity to the decision-making process. Consider a healthcare professional faced with the decision to allocate limited resources, such as ventilators, during the COVID-19 pandemic. Emotions, like empathy and guilt, can cloud judgment, leading to potentially biased decisions. By emphasizing logical reasoning and reflecting on the moral consequences, healthcare professionals can approach these challenges with enhanced understanding and authenticity. They must balance their emotional responses with ethical principles and clinical guidelines to ensure fair and just outcomes for all patients involved. This disciplined approach helps navigate the complexities of ethical dilemmas, ensuring sound and balanced decision-making.

b)   **The Distorting Symphony of Negative Emotions**

Distorting Perception

Negative emotions like hatred, anger, jealousy, and fear profoundly shape our perception, often clouding our grasp of the facts within the CgX system. These emotions act as dissonant elements, disrupting the balance of logical reasoning.

Science: Negative Emotions and Cognitive Biases

The interplay between negative emotions and cognitive biases is a fascinating area of exploration. It invites us to reflect on how our emotional states can shape our perceptions and judgments, often leading us to skewed interpretations of reality. Understanding this relationship can empower us to navigate our thoughts and feelings with greater awareness and intention.

Unpleasant feelings can activate mental shortcuts that skew our understanding and decision-making. Anger can manifest as a hostility bias, causing individuals to perceive ambiguous situations through an aggressive lens. Fear has the potential to heighten our awareness of risks, often resulting in responses that may be disproportionate to the actual threat. Understanding these biases empowers individuals to navigate their emotions and uphold a balanced perspective in their analyses.

o **Example: Workplace Conflict**

Anger and jealousy are two unfavorable emotions that frequently skew our perception of our coworkers' actions and motivations in workplace disputes. Imagine a situation in which two workers are competing for the same promotion. Jealousy and anger can cause people to misinterpret one another's behavior, creating a poisonous work atmosphere. A constructive critique from a coworker could be interpreted as a personal assault, which would intensify the argument.

However, one can handle disagreements more effectively by controlling negative emotions and seeking objective facts. This entails stepping back to evaluate the circumstance impartially and attempting to comprehend each party's underlying motives and viewpoints. People can address the underlying reasons for the dispute by promoting open communication and a cooperative approach.

Effective emotion management can result in more fruitful and peaceful working relationships. Methods like emotional intelligence training and mindfulness can also help.

Philosophy: The Stoic Approach to Emotions

Stoic philosophy emphasizes the importance of navigating negative emotions by employing rational thinking and exercising self-discipline. The Stoics posited that our emotions stem from our judgments, suggesting that by transforming these judgments, one can attain a state of tranquility. This perspective highlights the significance of logical reasoning in transcending the misleading influences of adverse feelings.

o **Example: Personal Resilience**

In practical situations, a person adhering to Stoic ideas may encounter several personal and professional obstacles with a calm and controlled demeanor. Envision a professional who, following an unforeseen termination, encounters a heightened sense of worry and ambiguity. Rather than yielding to panic, they utilize Stoic techniques such as cognitive reframing to manage these negative feelings. They acknowledge that the layoff is beyond their influence and concentrate on what they can govern: their reactions and subsequent actions.

The individual contemplates earlier achievements and qualities, reaffirming their capacity to surmount challenges. They actively pursue employment opportunities, cultivate professional connections, and enhance their skills while retaining a balanced perspective. By adopting the Stoic idea of concentrating on the present and perceiving setbacks as chances for development, they foster resilience and skillfully navigate life's adversities.

This method sustains emotional equilibrium and fosters personal development and adaptation, enabling individuals to prosper despite challenges.

c) **Fantasy and Self-Deception: The Dangerous Melody of Make-Believe**

Uncontrolled Enthusiasm and Imagination

While unrestrained enthusiasm and creativity are undeniably valuable human qualities, they can, if not properly managed, lead us away from our intended direction within the CgX system. The complex relationship between unrestrained fantasies and a propensity for self-deception can create a misleading sense of coherence in our beliefs, which often strays far from the truth of objective reality.

Science: Self-Deception and Cognitive Dissonance

Exploring the intricacies of self-deception and the phenomenon of cognitive dissonance reveals profound insights into human behavior and thought processes.

Self-deception represents a fascinating interplay between our perceptions and the truths we choose to embrace, often skewing reality to fit our innermost desires or convictions. The theory of cognitive dissonance elucidates how individuals navigate and reconcile conflicting information, striving to uphold a sense of internal harmony. Awareness of self-deception and the navigation of cognitive dissonance are crucial for fostering clear and truthful perceptions.

o   **Example: Unrealistic Entrepreneurial Plans**

In practical situations, a motivated entrepreneur, propelled by excessive excitement, may develop business strategies based on overly optimistic assumptions, which could result in unrealistic expectations. Consider an entrepreneur who establishes a software startup, confident that their groundbreaking app would transform the market instantaneously. Despite initial enthusiasm and early achievements, they neglect essential market research and consumer input, concentrating only on their vision.

This self-deception, fueled by cognitive dissonance, inhibits their recognition of possible deficiencies in their business model. They may overlook indicators of diminished user involvement or disregard feedback that contradicts their expectations. By meticulously evaluating the feasibility of their goals and soliciting constructive input from mentors, advisors, and prospective consumers, the entrepreneur can acquire a more realistic viewpoint.

This approach entails consistently reassessing their assumptions, performing comprehensive market analysis, and being receptive to adjusting their plan based on facts. By synchronizing their aspirations with the concrete environment, entrepreneurs can reconcile their enthusiasm with achievable objectives, thus enhancing their prospects for sustained success.

Philosophy: The Importance of Intellectual Honesty

Thinkers such as Jean-Paul Sartre and Friedrich Nietzsche highlighted the significance of intellectual honesty and self-awareness. Sartre's notion of "bad faith" encapsulates the intricate dance of self-deception, a mechanism employed to evade the confrontation of unsettling realities. Nietzsche emphasized the importance of developing a deep understanding of oneself while discarding the soothing falsehoods that often cloud our perception. Exploring these principles underscores the importance of intellectual honesty in fostering a clear and objective understanding.

o **Example: Personal Reflection**

Participating in consistent self-reflection and pursuing candid insights from reliable sources can empower individuals to identify and transcend self-deception. This approach fosters a commitment to truthfulness and harmonizes one's convictions with the empirical world.

In Summary

The path to achieving clarity of thought within the CgX system demands a keen awareness of certain forces that threaten our capacity for critical analysis. One can sustain a harmonious and rational viewpoint through the acknowledgment and regulation of the dynamics of closeness and fervor, as well as adverse feelings and unchecked creativity. Adopt these approaches to protect your mental faculties, allowing your reasoning to stay anchored in logical thought and unbiased evaluation. This methodical approach enables the CgX system to produce trustworthy and precise insights, leading to a more profound comprehension of existence.

Achieving Reliable Truth

Amidst the cacophony of conflicting voices, the pursuit of reliable truth is the ultimate quest. Embrace the kaleidoscope of diverse perspectives, recognize the echo chamber's deception, and sharpen your critical thinking skills. Seek the mantle of recognized authority, unmask ulterior motives, and question the seductive strains of propaganda. Navigate the tangled web of self-interest and fanaticism, ensuring that your symphony of thought is founded on verifiable facts and logical coherence.

1. Embracing the Kaleidoscope: Unveiling Diverse Perspectives

The CgX system functions like a kaleidoscope, revealing a rich tapestry of viewpoints. Interacting with concepts that challenge conventional wisdom is crucial for identifying our blind spots and fostering a deeper understanding of the intricate nature of our reality. Imagine a scholar wholly committed to exploring ancient texts from a specific civilization. Embracing a variety of cultural viewpoints enables the scholar to attain a deeper and more comprehensive grasp of historical narratives. Similarly, the CgX system benefits from integrating various perspectives before arriving at any conclusions.

Science: Cognitive Diversity and Problem-Solving

Exploring the interplay of cognitive diversity and its impact on effective problem-solving. Cognitive science insights reveal that a variety of viewpoints can significantly improve our ability to solve problems and foster innovation. The richness of varied thought processes, knowledge bases, and problem-solving strategies empowers groups to address intricate challenges with greater efficacy. Research conducted by Scott

Page and others reveals that groups enriched with varied viewpoints excel beyond uniform groups in producing innovative solutions and making informed decisions.

o **Example: Multidisciplinary Teams**

Envision a collaborative group of experts from various fields tackling the pressing issue of climate change. The team formulates holistic strategies that consider environmental, economic, and social dimensions by synthesizing knowledge from various disciplines, such as climatology, economics, sociology, and political science. Fueled by varied viewpoints, this collective methodology results in stronger, more impactful resolutions.

Philosophy: The Exploration of Dialectical Thought

Thinkers like Georg Wilhelm Friedrich Hegel highlighted the significance of interacting with various perspectives via the dialectical approach. This method encompasses the integration of opposing concepts to reach elevated understandings. The dialectical method proposed by Hegel—comprising thesis, antithesis, and synthesis—illustrates the profound impact of engaging with contrasting viewpoints, enhancing comprehension, and fostering intellectual advancement.

o **Example: Debates in Philosophy**

Engaging in philosophical discussions frequently requires a deep exploration of opposing perspectives. Through the thoughtful examination of contrasting viewpoints, thinkers enhance their concepts and cultivate deeper understandings. This dynamic interplay highlights the importance of varied viewpoints in the quest for understanding and insight.

Religion: Interfaith Dialogue

Exploring the nuances of faith through open conversation. Interfaith dialogue underscores the significance of connecting with various religious viewpoints to cultivate a deeper sense of mutual understanding and respect. By examining shared values and distinctions, individuals cultivate a richer understanding of their own convictions and those held by others. This conversational method fosters harmony, acceptance, and personal development.

o **Example: Interfaith Initiatives**

Interfaith initiatives, exemplified by the Parliament of the World's Religions, unite representatives from diverse faith traditions to engage in dialogue about common concerns and work together on social issues. These conversations deepen our comprehension of one another and foster a more inclusive and harmonious existence.

Practical Steps for Embracing Diverse Perspectives

1) **Explore various viewpoints:** Immerse yourself in insights drawn from diverse cultural, academic, and ideological backgrounds. This endeavor will expand your perspective and challenge your beliefs.

2) **Promote Dialogue:** Cultivate an environment where open and respectful exchanges can occur with those who possess differing perspectives. Active listening and fostering constructive dialogue can reveal fresh perspectives and diminish preconceived notions.

3) **Reflect on your Biases:** Make it a habit to examine your own biases and consider their impact on your thought processes. Recognize areas where awareness may be lacking and work towards transcending them by welcoming a variety of viewpoints.

4) **Integrate Insights:** Combine perspectives from various angles to cultivate a deeper comprehension of intricate matters. This holistic method strengthens the validity and dependability of your findings.

In Summary

Welcoming diverse viewpoints is crucial for enhancing the CgX system and paving the way to a trustworthy understanding of reality. Exploring concepts that question conventional wisdom fosters a deeper and more integrated understanding of our reality. This method deepens our thinking, improves our ability to tackle challenges, and fosters intellectual and spiritual development. Allow a variety of viewpoints to illuminate your journey toward understanding, ensuring that your thought process is thorough, inclusive, and multifaceted.

2. The Echo Chamber's Deception: Recognizing Confirmation Bias

The Echo Chamber's Deception

The human mind naturally tends to pursue information that reinforces its established beliefs. The occurrence of confirmation bias fosters an echo chamber, amplifying pre-existing beliefs and obstructing the pursuit of intellectual growth. The CgX system ought to acknowledge this bias and actively seek out information that questions its current understanding. In the spirit of inquiry that seeks to provoke thought rather than simply confirm existing beliefs, the CgX system should embrace dissonance as a pathway to stronger, more robust conclusions.

Science: Cognitive Psychology and Confirmation Bias

The study of cognitive psychology reveals the intricate ways in which our minds operate, particularly through the lens of confirmation bias. Research in cognitive psychology reveals the profound impact of confirmation bias on our perceptions and choices. People often gravitate towards information that aligns with their existing beliefs while overlooking or rejecting evidence that challenges those views. This widespread bias can result in a skewed perception and suboptimal choices. Recognizing confirmation bias is essential for cultivating a mindset that values objectivity and critical analysis.

o **Example: Medical Diagnosis**

Envision a medical professional to evaluate a person's health status. When a medical expert is resolutely convinced that a patient has a particular ailment, there is a propensity to focus on symptoms that corroborate this belief, perhaps overlooking signals that may suggest another diagnosis. A physician who suspects pneumonia may concentrate on validating symptoms such as a prolonged cough and fever, perhaps neglecting signs of an alternate diagnosis like heart failure, which can manifest with analogous symptoms.

To alleviate this bias, medical personnel are instructed to investigate multiple potential diagnoses, diligently seeking information that refutes their initial assumptions. This method is termed differential diagnosis, wherein physicians evaluate several potential illnesses and systematically exclude them based on clinical data. They may also pursue second opinions, consult with specialists, and employ diagnostic testing to guarantee a thorough assessment.

By remaining receptive to alternate explanations and meticulously scrutinizing all available evidence, healthcare personnel can enhance the precision of their diagnoses and boost patient outcomes. This methodical approach mitigates the risk of confirmation bias undermining the quality of medical care.

Philosophy: Exploring the Significance of Dialectical Reasoning

Philosophical traditions highlight the significance of interacting with contrasting perspectives to deepen comprehension. Hegel's dialectic illustrates the process where opposing ideas come together, leading to a more profound comprehension. This approach fosters exploring opposing perspectives, enhancing cognitive development and fortitude.

o **Example: Philosophical Debates**

In practical situations, dialectical reasoning is essential for enhancing philosophical dialogue and comprehension. Envision a public discourse on ethical dilemmas related to artificial intelligence and privacy. Intellectuals and specialists with varied perspectives actively engage with opposing viewpoints, endeavoring to understand and integrate their insights. One philosopher may advocate for the advantages of AI in augmenting human talents, while another expresses apprehensions over privacy and ethical considerations.

This dialectical thinking process, characterized by the rigorous challenge and defense of ideas, enhances theories and fosters remarkable insights. By accepting dissonance and recognizing the legitimacy of contrasting viewpoints, participants might enhance their comprehension of intricate matters. This method enhances their positions and fosters a more intricate and thorough dialog, highlighting the significance of engaging with varied perspectives.

Such discussions promote open-mindedness and critical analysis, cultivating an atmosphere conducive to genuine intellectual development. Dialectical thinking ensures that conclusions are comprehensive and based on a meticulous analysis of all pertinent factors.

Religion: Challenging Faith and Spiritual Growth

In spirituality, engaging in inquiry and confronting one's convictions can foster personal development and deepen one's comprehension of one's beliefs. Numerous spiritual paths invite followers to confront uncertainties and pursue profound understanding through contemplation, inquiry, and conversation.

o **Example: Theological Inquiry**

In practical contexts, scholars and adherents frequently engage in rigorous examination and inquiry of their spiritual convictions to augment their understanding and intensify their faith. Consider a theologian examining the intricacies of sacred books like the Bible or the Quran. This theologian may initially engage with these texts via the lens of preconceptions shaped by their upbringing or community.

Through thorough theological inquiry and engagement with many interpretations and critiques, they question their basic convictions and encounter alternative perspectives. This endeavor may encompass examining historical circumstances, language subtleties, and diverse commentary from various churches or intellectual traditions. By actively pursuing and contemplating ideas that diverge from their own, the theologian acquires a more nuanced and thorough knowledge of their faith.

This process of inquiry and introspection not only strengthens their belief but also fosters a more sophisticated and resilient spiritual outlook. It illustrates the significance of liberating oneself from the echo chamber of confirmation bias, promoting a rigorously scrutinized and deeply cherished belief.

Defense Mechanism: Proactively Seek Challenging Information

1) **Recognize Confirmation Bias:** Be aware of the inclination to prioritize information that aligns with your pre-existing beliefs. Recognizing this bias is the initial move toward alleviating its impact.

2) **Seek Diverse Perspectives:** Deliberately seek knowledge that questions your beliefs. Connect with diverse sources and individuals with varying beliefs to expand your understanding.

3) **Embrace Dissonance:** Consider contradictory information as a chance for deeper understanding and personal development. Embrace dissonance as a pathway to cultivate more resilient and comprehensive insights.

4) **Reflect and Analyze:** Consider how fresh insights influence your convictions. Examine the data and reflect on how it aligns with your current perspective.

In Summary

Identifying and addressing confirmation bias is crucial for promoting intellectual growth and maintaining an objective mindset. The CgX system can reach more robust and comprehensive conclusions by actively pursuing challenging information and welcoming dissonance. This structured method fosters analytical thinking and encourages a richer, more intricate comprehension of our surroundings. Allow these approaches to assist you in maneuvering through the intricacies of information, ensuring that your mental processes stay adaptable, impartial, and focused on development.

3. The Skeptic's Eye: Sharpening Critical Thinking Skills

The Skeptic's Eye

The cultivation of critical thinking abilities stands as the essential cornerstone of the CgX system in its quest for truth. By developing the capacity to identify logical fallacies in arguments and nurturing a strong sense of skepticism, the CgX system is prepared to maneuver around and avoid the traps of erroneous reasoning. It is essential to recognize a strawman fallacy, where an opponent's argument is misrepresented to make it easier to challenge. Enhancing critical thinking capabilities strengthens the CgX system's resilience to manipulation and sharpens its ability to distinguish between fact and fiction.

Science: The Exploration of Cognitive Psychology and the Intricacies of Logical Fallacies

The exploration of cognitive psychology delves into the intricacies of human thought processes, learning mechanisms, and the nuances of memory retention. Grasping the nuances of prevalent logical fallacies is essential for cultivating robust critical thinking abilities. Reasoning errors that compromise an argument's integrity are known as logical fallacies. Various fallacies have been identified, including the strawman fallacy, ad hominem attacks, and false dilemmas, which can distort our understanding and lead to poor decision-making.

o **Example: The Strawman Fallacy**

A strawman fallacy arises when an individual distorts an adversary's argument, simplifying it for the sake of easier criticism. In a discussion surrounding environmental policy, one might misrepresent their opponent's stance by asserting, "They aim to eliminate all industries and ruin the economy." In contrast, the true argument focuses on the adoption of sustainable practices. Identifying and steering clear of these fallacies is crucial for maintaining clarity and rationality in thought.

Philosophy: Exploring the Socratic Method and the Essence of Critical Inquiry

The Socratic Method, rooted in the teachings of the ancient Greek thinker Socrates, highlights the importance of critical questioning and engaging dialogue. Socrates employed inquiries to provoke thought, elucidate ideas, and reveal foundational convictions. This approach nurtures analytical thought by prompting individuals to scrutinize their beliefs and those of others, guaranteeing that their reasoning is sound and substantiated.

o **Example: Socratic Dialogue**

In a thoughtful exchange, individuals partake in a sequence of inquiries and responses to delve into profound ideas. In a dialogue about justice, one might ask, "What is justice?" and then delve deeper with inquiries that explore the nuances and complexities inherent in the responses. This journey aids in deepening comprehension and cultivating more cohesive reasoning.

Religion: The Significance of Discernment

Many spiritual traditions emphasize the importance of discernment—the ability to evaluate judiciously—when contemplating beliefs and viewpoints. In Christianity, discernment is considered a significant spiritual skill that allows humans to differentiate between truth and deception, frequently influenced by the Holy Spirit. Christians are urged to discern the spirits (1 John 4:1) and pursue wisdom via prayer and contemplation.

In Islam, discernment, referred to as "Furqan," is deemed essential for differentiating good from wrong, as informed by the Quran and Hadith. Muslims are urged to deeply contemplate their faith and pursue knowledge to prevent deception (Quran 17:36).

In Buddhism, discernment (Panna) is an essential component of the Eightfold Path, fostering the knowledge required to perceive reality accurately. Buddhists engage in mindfulness and meditation to cultivate insight and clarity, allowing them to confront life's obstacles lucidly.

This method encourages profound contemplation and careful evaluation of information via the perspective of spiritual principles.

o **Example: Exploring Religious Doctrines**

An individual may conduct a critical examination to evaluate diverse interpretations of religious texts. For example, a Christian may examine the Bible, taking into account the historical context, authorship, and theological ramifications of chapters such as the Sermon on the Mount. They develop a more profound and nuanced understanding of their beliefs by analyzing many comments and translations.

A Muslim may examine diverse readings of the Quranic verse "There is no compulsion in religion" (Quran 2:256), contemplating its context and significance through Tafsir (exegesis) by various scholars. This insightful examination aids in comprehending the verse's ramifications for religious liberty and tolerance.

A Buddhist may contemplate the Buddha's teachings, examining the context and importance of ideas such as "Anatta" (non-self) through meditation and the study of the Pali Canon. This process enhances their comprehension of self and world, promoting spiritual development.

By employing rational thought and active participation, individuals can enhance their understanding of their beliefs, fostering spiritual development and knowledge.

Defense Mechanism: Enchase Critical Thinking Abilities

1) **Recognize Logical Fallacies:** Cultivate the ability to identify prevalent logical fallacies, including strawman arguments, ad hominem attacks, and false dilemmas. Grasping these fallacies enhances our ability to critically assess arguments.

2) **Embrace a discerning mindset:** Nurture a balanced sense of skepticism. Examine beliefs, question assumptions, scrutinize proof, strive to grasp the logic underlying discussions, and seek to understand the reasoning behind arguments.

3) **Engage in Socratic Dialogue:** Explore and refine your beliefs using the Socratic Method. Utilize a questioning approach to delve into and enhance your convictions. Participate in meaningful conversations with others to deepen and refine your comprehension.

4) **Reflect and Analyze:** Consistently engage in introspection regarding your thought processes. Examine

your reasoning for clarity, alignment, and rational integrity.

Final Thoughts

Enhancing critical thinking abilities is vital for the CgX system's quest for truth. Through the identification of logical fallacies, the cultivation of skepticism, and the practice of critical inquiry, the system strengthens its defenses against manipulation. It enhances its capacity to discern fact from fiction. Adopt these approaches to enhance your mental faculties, guaranteeing that your thought processes are anchored in reason, transparency, and sound judgment. This structured method enables you to traverse the intricacies of information with assurance and understanding.

4. Recognized Authority: The Mantle of Expertise

Recognize Authority

To begin evaluating information's reliability, one must thoughtfully analyze its origin. Is the information sourced from a reputable and acknowledged authority in the discipline? Envision them as conductors guiding a harmonious ensemble; their deep understanding ensures a seamless and accurate performance. Assessing qualifications, connections with reputable organizations, and a proven track record of achievement in the specific field is crucial.

Science: The Roel of Expertise in Establishing Credibility

The credibility of scientific claims frequently relies on the qualifications and knowledge of the individual presenting them. Individuals with advanced degrees, significant experience, and connections to esteemed institutions tend to offer more trustworthy insights. Publications that undergo thorough assessment by fellow specialists in the discipline act as a standard for establishing trustworthiness. This vetting process guarantees that the information adheres to elevated standards of precision and dependability.

o   **Example: Scientific Research**

Reflect on a transformative study regarding climate change published in a peer-reviewed journal by a group of scholars from a prestigious university. The researchers' qualifications, connection to a respected institution, and rigorous peer-review process enhance the study's trustworthiness. This meticulous method guarantees that the conclusions are grounded in robust evidence and informed scrutiny.

Philosophy: The Fallacy of Appealing to Authority

The impact of authority on reasoning has always intrigued philosophers and intellectuals. Utilizing proven knowledge can surely bolster the credibility of an argument; nevertheless, it is equally essential to circumvent the "appeal to authority" fallacy. This fallacy occurs when a statement is considered valid purely due to the endorsement of an authoritative figure without assessing the supporting evidence.

Critical thinking necessitates a comprehensive analysis of the evidence and logic supporting individuals' assertions in authoritative roles. It is imperative to interrogate and evaluate their claims rather than accepting them without question. By doing so, we cultivate a profound and resilient comprehension, guaranteeing that our convictions are anchored in reasonable examination rather than uncritical acceptance.

o **Example: Philosophical Analysis**

Imagine a current intellectual referencing Aristotle's ethical theory in a contemporary discussion on morality. While Aristotle's authority enhances the discourse, the thinker must furnish facts and robust reasoning to validate their claims. For instance, in a discourse on ethical dilemmas about artificial intelligence, merely referencing Aristotle's virtue ethics is inadequate. The philosopher must illustrate the relevance of these ancient concepts to modern technological dilemmas, correlating them with facts and current ethical frameworks.

Relying solely on Aristotle's authority, without critical scrutiny or contextual analysis, would weaken the argument's validity. An effective discourse necessitates the incorporation of credible viewpoints, current research, and sound reasoning to construct a comprehensive and compelling argument.

In a practical situation, contemplate a healthcare practitioner promoting a specific treatment regimen exclusively based on the endorsement of a distinguished authority. Although the expert's judgment holds significance, the practitioner must also assess contemporary clinical trials, patient outcomes, and peer-reviewed research to substantiate their suggestion. This guarantees that the proposed treatment is based on extensive evidence rather than just authority, augmenting their argument's credibility and efficacy.

Religion: The Importance of Religious Scholars

In spirituality, scholars' and theologians' insights are pivotal in deciphering sacred texts and shaping belief systems. Those dedicated to studying religious traditions, possessing profound knowledge and a nuanced grasp of their beliefs, offer significant perspectives and interpretations. Their profound understanding illuminates intricate theological ideas and connects them to modern challenges.

○ **Example: Islamic Jurisprudence**

In Islam, the scholars referred to as "ulama" hold a position of great esteem. They are recognized for their profound understanding of the Quran, Hadith, and the intricacies of Islamic law. The insights and rulings provided are a compass for individuals seeking to comprehend and engage with their spiritual beliefs. The credibility of these scholars stems from their profound research, deep devotion, and connection to esteemed religious organizations.

Defense Mechanism: Assess the Credibility of the Source

1) **Evaluate Credentials:** Consider the credentials and knowledge of the person or entity offering the information. Seek out higher education, specialized credentials, and relevant professional experience within the discipline.

2) **Check Affiliations:** Reflect on the associations with respected institutions or organizations. Esteemed organizations frequently maintain rigorous standards in both research and ethical conduct.

3) **Review Track Record:** Assess the history of achievements and contributions made by the individual or institution within the field. A proven track record of trustworthy work bolsters the credibility of their insights.

4) **Analyze the Evidence:** Even in the presence of authority, it is essential to thoughtfully assess the evidence and logic that support their assertions. Engage critically

with the essence of their argument rather than simply accepting it based on who is presenting it.

5. Beyond the Facade: Unmasking Ulterior Motives

Ulterior Motives

It is essential to acknowledge that the motivations behind those who disseminate information can vary significantly, and not all are purely rooted in a sincere desire to impart knowledge. It is crucial to engage in a thoughtful examination of the author's potential hidden agendas that may impact the authenticity of the information presented. Is a deeper motive at play, or are they advocating for a particular principle? Although this does not necessarily compromise the credibility of the information, it undeniably invites a more critical and thoughtful examination. It is crucial to thoughtfully examine potential biases and scrutinize the information.

Science: The Influence of Persuasion and Cognitive Bias

The study of persuasion delves into the intricate ways in which individual motivations and inherent biases shape communication and behavior. Studies in psychology and communication reveal that people often convey information in a manner that serves their objectives, potentially engaging in selective data usage or framing narratives to resonate with their intentions. Grasping these persuasive strategies enables us to thoughtfully assess the underlying intentions of the information presented.

o   **Example: Political Messaging**

Political campaigns frequently employ various persuasive strategies to influence the public's perceptions and beliefs. Through the careful framing of issues and the selective presentation of data, individuals in positions of power seek to advance their agendas. Engaging in a thoughtful analysis of political messaging requires an awareness of these strategies and a commitment to exploring a variety of sources to cultivate a well-rounded understanding.

Philosophy: Exploring the Moral Dimensions of Communication

The discourse surrounding communication ethics has been a longstanding focus, emphasizing the imperative to share information with honesty and clarity. Kant's categorical imperative underscores the importance of actions that can be universally adopted, highlighting the necessity of honest communication. This ethical framework invites individuals to reflect on the underlying motives of the information they engage with while also promoting a commitment to integrity in their own expressions.

o   **Example: Ethical Journalism**

Journalists must uphold the principles of accuracy and impartiality in their reporting of news. Engaging in ethical journalism necessitates a commitment to transparency regarding sources and intentions, clarifying conflicts of interest, and ensuring a balanced representation of perspectives. Assessing news reports through the lens of ethical standards enables individuals to uncover the trustworthiness and underlying intentions of the information presented.

Religion: Discernment in Guidance

In the realm of spirituality, discernment requires a thoughtful examination of the intentions and trustworthiness of those who guide us and the teachings they present. Numerous spiritual paths highlight the significance of pursuing insight and comprehending the motivations behind direction to guarantee it resonates with fundamental values and beliefs.

o **Example: Spiritual Leadership**

Envision a guiding figure imparting wisdom to their followers on the principles of virtuous existence. Assessing a leader's direction requires a deep exploration of their intentions—do they truly aim to elevate those they lead, or does self-interest drive them? Discernment empowers individuals to navigate these influences and arrive at thoughtful decisions.

Defense Mechanism: Critically Evaluate Potential Biases

1) **Recognize the possibility of underlying biases:** Acknowledge that authors' perspectives can shape the way information is conveyed, potentially reflecting their own agendas. Reflect on the underlying context and intention that shape communication.

2) **Examine the Evidence:** Carefully analyze the evidence presented to substantiate the assertions made. Seek out coherence, trustworthiness, and pertinence in the information presented.

3) **Cross-Reference Sources:** Thoroughly explore diverse sources to substantiate the information presented. Embracing a variety of viewpoints fosters equilibrium in our understanding, mitigating biases and enriching our comprehension of complex issues.

4) **Reflect on Impact:** Ponder the possible effects of the information and the intentions driving its spread. Contemplate how these elements could influence your understanding and reaction.

Final Thoughts

Revealing hidden intentions is crucial for thoroughly assessing information and safeguarding its authenticity. By acknowledging inherent biases and thoughtfully evaluating the evidence, we can adeptly traverse the intricate landscape of information with clarity and insight. Adopt these approaches to protect your mental faculties, allowing your thought processes to be anchored in reliable and impartial data. This structured methodology enables the CgX system to produce a coherent and trustworthy depiction of reality, steering you toward insightful and substantiated conclusions.

6. The Siren Song of Propaganda: Questioning Paid Persuasion

Questionable intention

Individuals who manipulate public sentiment for monetary benefit deserve a thorough analysis within the CgX framework. Their statements, much like jarring notes in a symphonic arrangement, have the power to disrupt the very nature of truth. Approach their conclusions with an elevated sense of scrutiny and thoughtful examination. It is crucial to examine the sources of their financial support and any potential conflicts of interest that could emerge.

Science: The Impact of Propaganda

Studies in communication and psychology reveal the profound impact that propaganda can have on shaping public perception. Techniques of persuasion, including emotional appeals, selective fact presentation, and repetition, are crafted to influence and shape audiences' perceptions. Grasping these techniques enables individuals to thoughtfully assess the motivations underlying the information and identify possible biases.

o **Example: Advertising and Consumer Behavior**

Reflect on how advertising shapes consumers' choices and actions. Organizations frequently employ compelling strategies to advocate for their offerings, highlighting advantages while minimizing potential downsides. Through a thoughtful examination of advertisements and an awareness of the underlying financial incentives, individuals can empower themselves to make more discerning choices in their purchasing behavior.

Philosophy: The Ethical Dimensions of Persuasion

The discourse surrounding the ethics of persuasion and the obligation to convey truth has been a longstanding topic of contemplation among thinkers. Aristotle's rhetorical exploration of ethos, pathos, and logos highlights the significance of establishing credibility, evoking emotional resonance, and constructing logical arguments. Engaging in ethical persuasion requires a delicate equilibrium of these components, all while upholding a commitment to honesty and integrity. Understanding the ethical dimensions of persuasion enables individuals to thoughtfully evaluate the intentions underlying the information presented.

o **Example: Political Campaigns**

In political campaigns, aspirants employ various persuasive strategies to cultivate and attract support from the electorate. By carefully examining the rhetoric and understanding the candidates' underlying motives, individuals can arrive at more enlightened choices when casting their votes. In political discourse, ethical communication must uphold the values of transparency and truthfulness, steering clear of any manipulation that serves individual interests.

Religion: Discernment and Integrity

Various spiritual traditions emphasize the importance of discernment and integrity in our interactions. In Christianity, the concept of expressing truth with compassion, as articulated in Ephesians 4:15, underscores the moral need to communicate with integrity: "But speaking the truth in love, we will grow to become in every respect the mature body of him who is the head, that is, Christ." This ethical framework encourages individuals to critically evaluate the motives behind information and to prioritize veracity.

In Islam, the principle of honesty (sidq) is fundamentally established in the Quran and Hadith. The Quran advocates for believers to uphold the truth, even when it conflicts with their personal interests (Quran 4:135). This focus on integrity and honesty in communication highlights the necessity of assessing the reasons and credibility of the information provided.

Buddhism's Right Speech, a component of the Noble Eightfold Path, underscores the need for accurate communication, refraining from slander, and promoting harmony. Buddhists are urged to contemplate their speech and intentions, guaranteeing that their communication is truthful and consistent with the tenets of wisdom and compassion.

o **Example: Spiritual Teachings**

Religious leaders prioritizing transparency and candor in their communications foster trust and dependability among their followers. A Christian pastor who openly addresses the church's financing and philanthropic endeavors can cultivate a stronger bond with their congregation. Likewise, an Imam who transparently discloses the sources of financial backing for mosque initiatives and community programs fosters trust within the Muslim community.

In a Buddhist environment, a monk who exemplifies Right Speech by candidly discussing the financial support for the temple and community programs fosters a culture of transparency and trust. This method aids followers in comprehending the genuine motives behind their spiritual guidance and guarantees that teachings are grounded in sincerity and integrity.

By critically assessing the motivations and financial backing of religious groups, individuals can foster a faith grounded in authenticity and ethical integrity. This practice guarantees adherence to the principles of discernment and integrity, safeguarding against the distortion of spiritual messages by external influences or monetary motives.

Defense Mechanism: Critically Evaluate Financial Backing and Conflicts of Interest

Examine the underlying motivations and potential biases associated with financial support and competing interests.

1) **Investigate Financial Backing:** Examine the sources of financial support. Delve into the origins of the funding behind the information source. Reflect on the potential impact financial support could have on how information is conveyed and structured.

2) **Recognize Conflicts of Interest:** Evaluate possible conflicts of interest stemming from financial or personal relationships. Consider how these conflicts may influence the trustworthiness and impartiality of the information presented.

3) **Analyze Persuasive Techniques:** Cultivate awareness of the strategies employed to shape and influence perceptions. Analyze the effectiveness of emotional appeals, the strategic use of selective facts, and the role of repetition in the conveyed information.

4) **Seek Transparency:** Value sources that openly disclose their funding and any possible biases. Openness fosters trust and enables a deeper understanding for more thoughtful assessment.

In Summary

Examining the dynamics of compensated influence and acknowledging the power of propaganda is crucial for upholding the integrity of the CgX system. Through a thoughtful examination of financial support, recognition of potential conflicts of interest, and a careful analysis of persuasive methods, one can adeptly traverse the intricate landscape of information with clarity and insight. Adopt these approaches to anchor your thinking in reliable and impartial information, protecting yourself from the alluring pull of propaganda and fostering a balanced understanding of reality.

7. Profit and Bias: The Tangled Web of Self-Interest

Financial Stake

The impact of financial motivations and individual investments on how information is conveyed is essential to contemplate in discussions about any topic. Is the author possibly reaping financial rewards from a particular viewpoint? This does not automatically deem the information false; instead, it highlights the potential for bias to shape how the data is understood. It is crucial to stay aware of this aspect and to adjust your acceptance of their conclusions with careful consideration.

Science: The Role of Conflicts of Interest

Investigations within the social and behavioral sciences realm illuminate the profound effects of conflicts of interest on the flow of information. Research indicates that financial motivations can shape the results and how findings are communicated. In academia and science, conflict of interest policies serves as essential mechanisms to address potential biases, emphasizing the importance of transparency and the disclosure of financial relationships. Grasping these dynamics enables individuals to thoughtfully evaluate the possible biases in the information they come across.

o **Example: Pharmaceutical Research**

Reflect on the implications of pharmaceutical research that drug companies finance. Although the research offers significant insights, the financial connections to the sponsoring entity can potentially skew the findings. Research indicates that trials funded by industry tend to present more favorable results. By carefully analyzing financial support disclosures and pursuing independent research, one can enhance one's ability to evaluate the conclusions' reliability.

Philosophy: The Ethical Dimensions of Self-Interest

Engaging in deep discussions about ethics and self-interest highlights the importance of transparency and integrity in our interactions. Thinkers such as John Stuart Mill and Immanuel Kant have delved into the moral dimensions of self-interest in making choices. Kant's categorical imperative emphasizes the importance of actions that can be universally embraced, fostering a culture of honesty and transparency. Mill's utilitarianism emphasizes the importance of the greatest good for the greatest number, prompting individuals to reflect on the wider consequences of their actions and intentions.

o **Example: Ethical Journalism**

In journalism, reporters must uphold ethical standards by transparently disclosing any conflicts of interest and steering clear of financial entanglements that may jeopardize their impartiality. By embracing these foundational principles, journalists cultivate a sense of credibility and foster public trust. Assessing news reports through the lens of ethical standards empowers individuals to recognize underlying biases and the impact of personal agendas.

Religion: Integrity and Altruism

Various spiritual traditions emphasize the importance of integrity and altruism, urging followers to partake in unselfish and honest conduct.

In Christianity, the principle of integrity is highlighted by the teachings of Jesus Christ, who stressed the importance of living authentically and loving others unconditionally. In Matthew 6:1-4, Jesus instructs on the need to give to the needy discreetly, emphasizing the value of genuine intentions and altruism: "Be careful not to practice your righteousness in front of others to be seen by them." Failure to do so will result in no reward from your Father in heaven. When you provide assistance to the impoverished, refrain from proclaiming it ostentatiously, ensuring that your generosity remains discreet. This ethical framework encourages Christians to critically assess their behaviors and reasons, ensuring they are devoid of self-serving interests.

In Islam, the principle of sincerity (ikhlas) emphasizes the importance of nurturing pure intentions and performing actions free from ulterior motives. The Quran underscores that actions must be performed exclusively for the purpose of Allah, devoid of any aspiration for material reward or acknowledgment. Surah Al-Baqarah (2:261) exemplifies this by stating: "The example of those who spend their wealth in the way of Allah is like a seed of grain that sprouts seven ears; in every ear, there are a hundred grains." This principle urges Muslims to examine their activities and confirm they are motivated by authentic faith and benevolence.

By meticulously analyzing information and behaviors through the prism of these spiritual ideals, individuals can circumvent the dangers of self-interest and guarantee that their conduct embodies authentic integrity and generosity. This method alleviates the impact of financial and personal prejudices, fostering a more ethical and transparent lifestyle.

o   **Example: Principles of Ethical Commerce**

Contemplate an entrepreneur operating an organic food enterprise driven by ethical and spiritual principles. This leader prioritizes honesty and integrity in all business dealings. The company transparently discloses its sourcing policies, guaranteeing that all suppliers comply with sustainable and ethical agricultural processes. They explicitly reveal any possible conflicts of interest, including affiliations with significant retailers, and continuously adhere to ethical standards in their operations.

Upon introducing a new product, the corporation engages third-party auditors to validate their assertions, confirming that the organic designation is legitimately obtained. They interact with their clientele via open forums and social media, soliciting input and addressing complaints transparently. This dedication to transparency establishes a robust foundation of trust and credibility with consumers and stakeholders.

By examining corporate processes from this viewpoint, consumers can evaluate the veracity of the company's information and activities. Stakeholders can observe the authentic dedication to ethical business practices, bolstering their trust in the company. This strategy enhances the brand's reputation and cultivates a devoted consumer base that appreciates integrity and authenticity.

Defense Mechanism: A Critical Evaluation of Financial Stake

1) **Identify Financial Interests:** Delve into possible financial advantages that could shape the author's viewpoint. Reflect on how financial connections might shape the way information is conveyed.

2) **Assess Disclosure Statements:** Seek out those that illuminate financial connections. Being open about where funding comes from and any potential conflicts of interest significantly boosts trustworthiness.

3) **Seek Independent Verification:** Ensure unbiased sources corroborate the information you encounter. Integrating insights from studies or reports produced by impartial organizations effectively mitigates potential biases.

4) **Examine Motivation:** Analyze the fundamental motivations that propel the information presented. Examine the potential impact of financial interests on the interpretation and representation of information.

In summation

Understanding the impact of financial motivations and individual investments is crucial for a thoughtful assessment of information. By recognizing possible biases and thoughtfully adjusting your acceptance of conclusions, you can skillfully traverse the intricate landscape of self-interest with clarity. Adopt these approaches to anchor your thinking in trustworthy and impartial information, preserving the integrity of the CgX system and steering you toward sound and dependable conclusions.

8. Avoiding Confirmation Bias: A Harmonious Orchestra of Perspectives

Mitigating Bias

It is a prevalent aspect of human nature to gravitate towards information that resonates with our pre-existing convictions. The aspiration to participate is admirable; however, it is crucial within the CgX framework to maintain awareness of the dangers posed by confirmation bias. During the journey of verifying facts, it is crucial to avoid imposing your desires onto the other person. It is quite frequent for people to subtly modify their reactions to meet your anticipations, even when such modifications require straying from objective truth. Embrace the collection of knowledge with an open mind, ready to interact with various viewpoints.

Science: Cognitive Psychology and Confirmation Bias

Confirmation bias represents a significant aspect of human cognition, illustrating how individuals prioritize information that aligns with their existing beliefs while disregarding or minimizing opposing viewpoints. This bias may result in a skewed perception and impede the process of thoughtful analysis. Recognizing confirmation bias is the initial stride toward alleviating its impact. To mitigate this bias, it is proposed that one might explore various strategies, including the contemplation of alternative hypotheses, the pursuit of disconfirming evidence, and the engagement with a range of diverse perspectives.

o **Example: Empirical Inquiry**

In scientific inquiry, the tendency to favor information that aligns with preexisting beliefs can significantly shape the interpretation of data and the structuring of experiments. Researchers must implement double-blind studies, engage in peer review, and replicate experiments to address this bias. Such practices guarantee that our conclusions are grounded in objective evidence and free from the influence of preconceived notions.

Philosophy: Exploring the Socratic Method and the Essence of Critical Inquiry

The Socratic Method, originating from the teachings of the ancient Greek thinker Socrates, highlights the importance of critical questioning and engaging dialogue. By examining underlying beliefs and exploring diverse perspectives, one can confront personal biases and cultivate a deeper, more intricate comprehension of the world. This reflective perspective resonates with the ideals of reducing confirmation bias by embracing open-mindedness and engaging in critical thinking.

o **Example: Philosophical Thoughtful Discourse**

In a discourse on ethics, individuals may articulate contrasting perspectives regarding a moral dilemma. By thoughtfully analyzing each argument and being open to diverse viewpoints, one can achieve a deeper and more nuanced understanding. This approach mitigates confirmation bias while fostering intellectual development.

Religion: The Art of Discernment

In spirituality, discernment denotes a deep and contemplative examination of one's ideas and teachings. Various spiritual paths encourage individuals to undertake a journey of discernment, seeking elevated understanding and insight to confront complex ethical and spiritual challenges. This method aligns with the principles of analytical thinking and objective assessment.

o **Example: Navigating Ethical Dilemmas in Christianity and Islam**

In Christianity, adherents are urged to participate in contemplative meditation and pursue heavenly direction when confronted with moral dilemmas. A Christian may contend with the ethical ramifications of a business choice, such as whether to prioritize profit over equitable treatment of employees. Through contemplation of biblical principles, soliciting guidance from spiritual authorities, and introspecting on the tenets of compassion and justice, people can identify the most ethical course of action.

In Islam, the practice of Istikhara (praying for guidance) is crucial for making important decisions. A Muslim with a multifaceted ethical dilemma—such as reconciling professional duties with personal religious commitments—may engage in Istikhara, contemplate Quranic principles, and seek counsel from erudite scholars. This technique enables them to approach the circumstance with a clear conscience, harmonizing their actions with spiritual values.

Through these practices, individuals can develop a deeper and more thorough understanding of their faith, promoting ethical and spiritually aligned decision-making.

Embracing Varied Perspectives: The Influence of Interfaith Discourse

Interfaith discussion functions as an effective mechanism for enhancing understanding and appreciation of the world's varied religious systems. Engaging in substantive dialogues with individuals from diverse religious traditions allows for the exploration of differing perspectives and the examination of common principles. This dialogue enables individuals to challenge their assumptions and get a deeper comprehension of their own and others' convictions. From this inclusive viewpoint, interfaith discourse fosters cognitive and spiritual growth, encouraging mutual tolerance and harmony within a pluralistic community.

o   **Example: Interfaith Dialogue**

In practical situations, interfaith discussion acts as an effective instrument for enhancing understanding and appreciation of the world's varied religions. For instance, contemplate a communal gathering where leaders and adherents from many religious traditions—such as Christianity, Islam, Judaism, Buddhism, and Hinduism—convene to deliberate on their spiritual practices and theological doctrines.

Participants engage in discussions to investigate diverse perspectives and analyze common concepts. A Christian may comprehend the importance of Ramadan in Islam, whilst a Muslim may acquire an understanding of the value of Lent in Christianity. This dialogue enables individuals to challenge their assumptions and develop a deeper comprehension of their own and others' convictions.

Interfaith discourse promotes inquiry, active listening, and contemplation of shared ideals that surpass individual religious traditions, including compassion, justice, and the quest for truth. This inclusive viewpoint fosters cognitive and spiritual growth, enabling individuals to establish connections of understanding and respect among diverse faiths.

Engaging in such talks enables individuals to cultivate a more nuanced and empathic perspective, thus fostering a more harmonious and inclusive society.

Defense Mechanism: Engage with Diverse Perspectives

1) **Recognize Confirmation Bias:** Be aware of the inclination to prioritize information that supports your pre-existing views. Recognizing this bias represents the initial stride toward alleviating its impact.

2) **Seek Disconfirming Evidence:** Actively pursue information that contradicts your beliefs. Interacting with information that challenges our beliefs fosters a more nuanced understanding and mitigates the influence of bias.

3) **Consider Alternative Hypotheses:** Delve into various interpretations and understandings. This approach fosters a spirit of inquiry and thoughtful analysis.

4) **Engage with Diverse Perspectives:** Actively pursue and interact with various informational sources. This method expands your comprehension and nurtures cognitive development.

In summation

It is crucial to steer clear of confirmation bias and welcome a symphony of diverse viewpoints for the CgX system. Acknowledging bias, pursuing disconfirming evidence, and engaging with various perspectives can alleviate the impacts of confirmation bias and cultivate a deeper, more sophisticated comprehension. This structured methodology fosters analytical reasoning and a harmonious and comprehensive viewpoint. Allow these strategies to illuminate your path through the intricate information landscape, fostering an objective and receptive mindset.

9. The Chorus of Science: The Melody of Verifiable Facts

Testing Facts

The systematic characteristics of scientific inquiry, characterized by organized methods of exploration and classification, serve as a powerful instrument inside the CgX framework for evaluating material. Whenever feasible, seek academic sources that can corroborate the facts presented. The empirical basis of scientific evidence serves as a structural framework akin to the cohesive pieces that underpin a symphony, ensuring that the work is firmly rooted in verifiable facts.

Science: The Significance of Peer Review and Bibliometrics

In scientific research, peer review and bibliometrics are essential methods for evaluating the credibility and importance of information. Peer review is an essential process wherein specialists in a specific domain evaluate research, confirming that the results are credible and reliable. Bibliometrics, encompassing citation counts and impact factors, provides quantitative evaluations of the importance and quality of scientific publications. Analyzing peer-reviewed literature and assessing bibliometric indicators enables the evaluation of the reliability and significance of scientific knowledge.

o **Example: Evaluating Research Studies**

Examine a practical situation in which a medical researcher evaluates the effectiveness of an innovative cancer therapy. The researcher would commence by examining peer-reviewed studies, confirming that cancer experts had evaluated and authenticated the results. A study published in a prestigious medical journal such as The Lancet signifies thorough peer review.

The researcher will after that analyze bibliometric markers, including citation counts. A frequently referenced study indicates that the research has significantly impacted and gained widespread acknowledgment worldwide. Furthermore, the researcher would examine the journal's impact factor, which reflects its repute and the average citation frequency of its articles.

By anchoring their assessment in these empirical metrics, the researcher guarantees that their judgments regarding the new treatment are founded on solid, dependable evidence. This systematic methodology adheres to the tenets of scientific investigation, fostering a comprehensive and reliable evaluation of medical innovation.

Philosophy: The Importance of Empirical Evidence

Philosophical discourse emphasizes the essential role of empirical evidence in validating assertions and arguments. Observations and experiments provide empirical evidence, establishing a solid basis for our comprehension of the world. By anchoring conversations in visible evidence, philosophers guarantee that their findings are not merely hypothetical but substantiated by credible data. This method corroborates theoretical findings and improves their relevance to practical situations.

o **Example: Empirical Philosophy**

Contemplate a diligent researcher who methodically examines concepts and collects data to substantiate their theoretical frameworks. In cognitive science, a researcher may examine the impact of mindfulness meditation on attention and emotional regulation. The researcher offers empirical evidence for their idea through controlled experiments and the collection of quantifiable data.

By meticulously analyzing empirical facts, the investigator develops a more profound and dependable comprehension of the studied phenomena. This method encapsulates the fundamental principles of thorough investigation, guaranteeing that conclusions are firmly based on verified data. Scholars might achieve a cohesive amalgamation of theory and practice by synthesizing empirical evidence with philosophical reasoning, thus enhancing our collective understanding.

Religion: The Integration of Faith and Reason

In spirituality, reconciling religion with rational reason is essential for a comprehensive and meaningful understanding of spiritual reality. Many spiritual traditions promote the quest for comprehension and enlightenment through the balanced integration of religion and reason. This combination cultivates a belief system grounded in transcendent understanding and empirical evidence, enabling individuals to engage with spiritual experiences using heart and mind.

o **Example: The Catholic Church**

The Catholic Church represents a profound tradition of harmonizing faith with reason, as shown by the works of theologians such as St. Thomas Aquinas. Aquinas asserted that faith and reason coexist harmoniously, with reason providing a logical foundation for religious beliefs. He contended that reason and scientific investigation are vital instruments for comprehending and elucidating divine truths, augmenting religion rather than contradicting it.

Aquinas' Five Ways, which serve as justifications for God's existence, depend on rational evidence and logical inference while upholding essential theological tenets. This method guarantees that religion is not unreasoning but is grounded in critical analysis and empirical facts. By integrating faith with reason, individuals can develop a more profound and nuanced understanding of their beliefs.

o **Example: The Integration of Faith and Reason in Islam**

Islam encompasses a profound tradition of integrating faith with reason, a concept beautifully exemplified by the works of scholars such as Al-Ghazali and Ibn Rushd (Averroes).

i. **Al-Ghazali,** recognized for his influential work "The Incoherence of the Philosophers," posited that although reason holds significance, divine revelation requires illumination to truly guide it. He held the view that faith and reason coexist harmoniously, enhancing one another rather than standing in opposition. His writings highlight that authentic understanding arises from the interplay of logical reasoning and profound spiritual awareness.

ii.   **Ibn Rushd,** also known as Averroes, presented a compelling argument in his work "The Incoherence of the Incoherence," asserting that reason and faith coexist harmoniously. He suggested that rational inquiry and philosophical reasoning can unveil a more profound comprehension of religious truths. Ibn Rushd's endeavors to harmonize Aristotelian philosophy with Islamic theology illuminate the vibrant relationship between faith and reason within Islamic intellectual tradition.

iii.   **Qur'anic Guidance:** The Qur'an invites us to engage in thoughtful contemplation and rational inquiry. Passages like Surah Al-Imran (3:190-191) and Surah Al-Zumar (39:9) encourage individuals to reflect deeply on the signs of the divine within the cosmos and to pursue understanding.

The dynamic relationship between faith and reason has enabled Islamic scholars to develop a richer and more nuanced understanding of their beliefs, akin to the explorations found within the Christian tradition.

In Conclusion

Integrating faith with reason allows believers from various spiritual traditions to enhance their comprehension and practice, resulting in a deeper and more enlightened experience of their faith.

Defense Mechanism: Seek Scientific Literature and Verify Facts

1)   **Consult Peer-Reviewed Sources:** It is essential to consult scholarly articles and publications whenever feasible, as this practice guarantees the reliability and credibility of your information.

2) **Evaluate Bibliometric Indicators:** To gauge the information's importance and quality, consider citation counts, impact factors, and various bibliometric measures.

3) **Verify Empirical Evidence:** Seek empirical evidence substantiating the presented assertions. Grounding our understanding in careful observation, rigorous experimentation, and verifiable evidence is essential.

4) **Integrate Faith and Reason:** In spiritual discussions, strive to blend belief with rational thought, ensuring that convictions are rooted in transcendent wisdom and observable reality.

In Summary

The harmonious blend of empirical evidence is a fundamental component in the CgX system for assessing information. Exploring scientific literature, engaging with peer-reviewed sources, and validating empirical evidence can help one ascertain that one's conclusions are grounded and trustworthy. This methodical approach enriches the authenticity and dependability of the information, steering you toward a more profound comprehension of existence.

Cultivating a Discerning Approach

In the final movement of our journey, we delve into cultivating a cautious and discerning mindset. The eternal question mark guides your relentless inquiry, while the dual role of active listener and critic sharpens your perception. Strengthen the vital instruments of willpower, reason, and conscience, and remain wary of the treacherous trio: senses, emotions, and memory. As you rise from a passive spectator to the conductor of your cognitive orchestra, wield the baton of critical thinking with precision and intent, orchestrating a harmonious quest for truth that resonates with clarity and insight.

1. The Eternal Question Mark: A Melody of Inquiry

Embrace a continuous quest for understanding. Embrace the boundless nature of your curiosity. Approach the information you come across with a discerning mindset, avoiding a simplistic skepticism that rejects all assertions. Instead, cultivate a dedication to deepening your comprehension and attaining clarity in your cognitive frameworks. Imagine your mind as a conductor, constantly refining the harmony of your thoughts and ensuring that every idea rings with precision. Delve deeply into the information at hand, allowing yourself the time to ascertain its factual soundness before arriving at any conclusions.

Science: The Significance of Inquiry in Scientific Exploration

The essence of scientific inquiry lies in an insatiable curiosity and an unwavering quest for understanding. Inquisitive minds delve into the complexities of existence, crafting inquiries and orchestrating experiments to illuminate the intricacies of our natural surroundings. This method of exploration guarantees that our conclusions are grounded in a thorough examination and observable facts.

o **Example: The Empirical Approach**

Consider a researcher in the field of environmental science investigating the impact of a new pesticide on local bee populations. The scientific method guides their systematic exploration, beginning with the formulation of a hypothesis: "The new pesticide decreases the bee population."

The researcher designs and executes a series of experiments to test this hypothesis. They establish control and experimental groups of bee colonies, ensuring all variables are controlled except for the presence of the pesticide. Over several weeks, they meticulously observe and record changes in the bee populations.

Next comes the data analysis. The researcher uses statistical tools to compare the populations of the control and experimental groups. They might discover a significant decline in the experimental group, supporting their hypothesis. They also review the data for anomalies or patterns that suggest alternative explanations.

Each step of the empirical approach enhances the researcher's understanding, solidifying their knowledge base. By continually refining their hypothesis and methodology, the researcher gains deeper insights into the pesticide's environmental impact. This systematic inquiry bolsters their findings and contributes to the broader scientific community's knowledge, ultimately informing policy decisions and conservation efforts.

This real-world application demonstrates how the empirical approach in scientific exploration cultivates a discerning and robust understanding of complex issues, ensuring that conclusions are reliable and well-founded.

Philosophy: Socratic Questioning

Exploring the depths of thought through the art of inquiry. The method of inquiry attributed to Socrates highlights the significance of engaging in deep questioning to delve into intricate concepts and reveal foundational beliefs. This approach fosters deep reflection and enables individuals to attain enhanced clarity in their cognitive frameworks.

o   **Example: Socratic Dialogues**

In the tradition of Socratic dialogues, individuals engage in a dynamic exchange of questions and answers, delving into the depths of philosophical ideas. By challenging beliefs and scrutinizing information, individuals enhance their comprehension and attain profound realizations.

2. The Dual Role: Listening with a Critical Ear

Embrace the duality of your existence by fully immersing yourself in the art of active listening. Immerse yourself in the conversations of others, utilizing a thoughtful approach to evaluate the ideas shared. Reflect on your position as an observer and a discerning evaluator, analyzing the harmony and unity of the piece.

Science: Active Listening and Critical Thinking in Communication

Exploring the nuances of communication through the lens of active listening and critical thinking reveals profound insights into human interaction.

Engaging in active listening and employing critical thinking are fundamental elements that enhance the quality of communication. Through the practice of deep listening and thoughtful analysis of differing viewpoints, one can foster enriching conversations and arrive at well-considered conclusions.

o   **Example: Peer Review in Academia**

The peer review process is essential for preserving the integrity and quality of academic work. Envision a researcher presenting a manuscript on the effects of climate change to a prestigious scientific magazine. The manuscript is subjected to peer review, during which specialists in the domain rigorously evaluate the research.

The reviewers critically examine the arguments, analyzing the data and methodology employed. They assess the corroborative evidence, confirming its strength and pertinence. For example, they may assess the accuracy of the climate models employed and the credibility of the data sources utilized. Reviewers evaluate the clarity and consistency of the article, ensuring that the findings are reasonable and well-substantiated.

The reviewers offer constructive feedback intended to promote the author's development. They may propose supplementary experiments, advocate for more thorough data analysis, or emphasize alternative interpretations of the findings. This input assists the author in enhancing their work, rendering it more comprehensive and reliable.

Compliance with the peer review procedure enhances the rigor and trustworthiness of academic pursuits. The outcome is a paper that provides significant insights to the scientific community based on rigorous assessment and ongoing enhancement.

Philosophy: The Role of Dialogue in Critical Inquiry

Philosophers have long recognized the value of dialogue in critical inquiry. It has been acknowledged for ages that engaging in dialogue is essential for deep exploration and understanding. Participating in meaningful dialogue enables individuals to explore their thoughts, reflect on different viewpoints, and enhance their comprehension.

o Example: Philosophical Debates

In philosophical discourse, individuals articulate their viewpoints while thoughtfully examining opposing perspectives. This conversation and thoughtful evaluation journey reveal profound insights and foster the evolution of our intellect.

3. The Vital Instruments of the Mind: Willpower, Reason, and Conscience

Strengthen Your Tools

Three fundamental faculties—willpower, reason, and conscience—serve as the instruments in your cognitive orchestra. Through consistent practice, structured training, and a commitment to discipline, one can hone these skills to become reliable tools for perceiving the truth of existence. Encourage individuals to critically evaluate all information before accepting it as truth. Trust in their ability to discern the delicate balance of truth amidst the overwhelming noise of misinformation.

Science: Cognitive Control and Decision-Making

The interplay of cognitive control and decision-making processes is a fascinating area of exploration. Understanding how we regulate our thoughts and actions can illuminate the complexities of human behavior and the choices we make.

Exploration within cognitive science underscores the pivotal roles of willpower, reason, and conscience in the intricate decision-making process. The capacity for willpower, often referred to as self-control, empowers individuals to manage their impulses and focus on their long-term aspirations. Logical analysis and critical thinking form the foundation of reason, whereas conscience serves as the compass for ethical decision-making. The interplay of these faculties fosters a foundation for sound judgment and precise perception.

o **Example: Academic Study Habits**

A student may harness determination to fend off distractions and concentrate on their studies, employ rational thought to grasp intricate ideas, and rely on their moral compass to uphold academic honesty. The learner can attain scholarly achievement and individual development by enhancing these resources.

Philosophy: Rationalism and Ethical Reasoning

Philosophers such as Immanuel Kant and John Stuart Mill highlight the significance of rational thought and moral deliberation. Kant's deontological ethics emphasizes the importance of duty and moral principles, whereas Mill's utilitarianism prioritizes achieving the greatest good for the greatest number of people. These frameworks illuminate the significance of rational thought and moral awareness in making ethical choices.

o **Example: Moral Dilemmas**

In navigating moral dilemmas, one must engage in thoughtful reasoning to assess the potential outcomes of one's choices while also attuning to one's inner conscience to uphold ethical integrity. By enhancing these abilities, individuals can approach intricate ethical dilemmas with lucidity and moral steadfastness.

4. The Treacherous Trio: Senses, Emotions, and Memory

Faulty Origins

One must approach the information derived from sensory experiences, emotional responses, and recollections within the CgX system with a discerning mindset. Like delicate instruments prone to discord, these sources can produce inaccuracies if not carefully observed. Consistent self-discipline is essential to ensure their reliability. Recognize the potential unreliability of these sources and engage in a thoughtful evaluation of the information they provide.

Science: The Reliability of Sensory Perception and Trustworthiness of Memory

Research in psychology and neuroscience reveals that our sensory perceptions, emotional reactions, and memories may not be as dependable as we presume. Sensory illusions, emotional biases, and memory distortions frequently influence our views and judgments. By recognizing these limitations, we can meticulously analyze material to ensure its veracity.

o **Example: Eyewitness Testimony**

The reliability of eyewitness evidence is often scrutinized in real-life situations, especially within legal contexts. For instance, an eyewitness may assertively remember observing the defendant at the crime site in a criminal trial. Psychological studies indicate that stress, lighting conditions, and weapon presence can substantially diminish recall accuracy. Emotions like fear and anxiety might further impair memory retrieval. In light of these limitations, legal systems frequently mandate corroborative evidence, such as DNA or video recordings, to guarantee accurate conclusions. This method underscores the necessity for a rigorous assessment of sensory and memory-derived information, recognizing the fallibility of human perception.

Philosophy: The Role of Skepticism

Philosophers like David Hume and René Descartes have emphasized the importance of skepticism in evaluating our sensory perceptions and recollections. Hume thoroughly examined the reliability of our sensory impressions, scrutinizing the foundation of our knowledge and comprehension. Descartes utilized a stringent process of skepticism, systematically questioning all that could be disputed to uncover certain facts.

o   **Example: Cartesian Doubt**

Descartes' methodology of skepticism, termed Cartesian Doubt, entails rigorously evaluating the reliability of our sensory perceptions to reveal indubitable truths. This strategy encourages individuals to critically evaluate material and ascertain its authenticity. For example, contemplate a scientist who faces unforeseen outcomes in an experiment. Instead of taking these conclusions at face value, they utilize Cartesian skepticism to scrutinize every facet of the experiment—reassessing the approach, verifying data, and eliminating alternate hypotheses. This meticulous examination guarantees that the conclusions reached are sound and dependable, reflecting Descartes' quest for certainty.

By synthesizing these philosophical and scientific concepts, we can develop a critical approach to knowledge, acknowledging the constraints of our senses, emotions, and memories. This perspective not only improves our comprehension but also protects the integrity of our judgments.

In Conclusion

In the grand orchestration of exploration, the CgX system transitions from a mere observer in the theater of knowledge to the esteemed position of the conductor. Guided by the principles of critical thinking, it embarks on a harmonious journey toward truth, welcoming a symphony of varied viewpoints while challenging the discord of confirmation bias. This transformation allows the CgX system to traverse the intricate symphony of understanding, emerging as a genuine orchestrator of wisdom and a creator of resonant choices amidst ambiguity. With a thoughtful demeanor, the system transforms into a robust tool—its components finely attuned to the resonances of credible insights, enabling us to discern the subtle harmonies of truth amid the overwhelming noise of information. Consequently, the CgX system possesses a unique blend of discernment and understanding, resulting in a robust, imaginative synergy that echoes with lucidity and profound awareness.

Conclusion: The CgX System – A Robust Tool for Cognitive Engagement

The CgX system fundamentally acts as a powerful instrument for enhancing cognitive interaction. The effectiveness of this approach hinges on our ability to identify and eliminate sources of misinformation. By employing critical thinking, emphasizing factual evidence, and safeguarding against cognitive biases, we can enable the CgX system to create a unified and harmonious portrayal of truth.

By recognizing the subtle intrusions into our thinking—such as opinions, unsolicited advice, the relinquishing of critical thought, gossip, self-deception, and pervasive misinformation—we equip ourselves with the essential tools to uphold the purity of our cognitive functions. Embrace the principles of thoughtful analysis, genuine inquiry, and thorough investigation to effectively navigate the intricacies of the information landscape.

By cultivating a disciplined and discerning mindset, we can fully leverage the CgX system, anchoring our thoughts and decisions in verified insights and dependable truths. Allow this method to steer you in your quest for understanding and reality, nurturing a comprehensive, educated, and illuminated viewpoint of existence.

Closing Remarks: The Conductor of Your Symphony of Thought

In this intricate dance of ideas, where outside forces and inner dialogues intertwine, you hold the reins of your fate. With the instrument of analytical reasoning at your fingertips, compose a symphony that resonates with both elegance and depth. Align your mind with your aspirations, crafting your existence and steering you toward a realm brimming with potential. Delve into the intricacies of the psyche, forge unwavering self-control, and foster a resilient framework of beliefs. As you craft your intricate tapestry of awareness, allow it to echo with authenticity, intention, and steadfast lucidity.

a.   Discerning the Melody: Cultivating a Critical Ear

We must stay vigilant in the organization of our thoughts. Knowledge from the outside world, much like distant echoes, reverberates through our senses. Yet, what truly matters is the ability to dissect the very core of the music being encountered. The stories we weave in our minds hold the power to uplift and mislead, often blurring the lines between truth and illusion.

Cultivate a sharp awareness of your internal monologue, consistently probing the origins and logic that underpin your thoughts. Is their foundation anchored in logic or propelled by transient feelings? Just as a maestro meticulously orchestrates each note to create a flawless performance, we must confront and dismantle any destructive or unfounded thoughts that jeopardize our mental harmony.

b. **The Mind as Amplifier: Recognizing the Power of Our Thoughts**

The faculties of our mind—reasoning, memory, intuition—act as formidable amplifiers. They exchange ideas without concern for their origins. Envision the mind as an expansive symphony, where each thought resonates with its own unique tune, weaving together the intricate fabric of our awareness. These instruments possess the power to conjure harmonious melodies that mirror intellect and imagination, or they might unleash dissonant echoes of dread and uncertainty. The core truth is found in understanding that the mind, by its very nature, fails to distinguish between these ideas. It simply magnifies their core nature. As the creators of our inner worlds, it is crucial to sharpen our awareness to evaluate the value of every thought we decide to elevate.

c. **The Paradoxical Mechanism of Time: Welcoming Complexity as a Catalyst for Development**

The depths of the human psyche unfold a captivating enigma, defying all efforts to unravel its intricate layers. It transcends simple logic, exploring the intricate layers of cognition—both creative and harmful. Identify the fundamental paradox. Delve into the complexities of the psyche, where true metamorphosis awaits. Like a skilled artisan reviving a delicate instrument, we hold the power to refine our minds, reshaping harmful thoughts into pathways of meaningful action.

d. The Composer and Captain: Orchestrating Your Destiny

William Ernest Henley's profound words echo through this intricate web of contemplation: "I am the master of my fate; I am the captain of my soul." To carve out our destinies, we must grasp the moment with intention. The ideas we hold close feed the depths of our soul. Remove the shadows of doubt, anxiety, and despair. Let us weave together intricate tapestries: echoes of strength, purpose, and possibility. We are both the architect and the analyst in this complex dance of consciousness. We hold the power to choose the mental symphonies that echo within us, guiding our inner voyage toward a future teeming with possibilities.

Final Thought: Illustrations and Anecdotes

As you contemplate the ideas laid before you, take a moment to immerse yourself in the complex composition of thoughts that dwell within your mind. What kind of haunting tune are you weaving into existence? Do your thoughts resonate with your deepest desires, or is there a dissonance lurking in the shadows that demands your scrutiny?

Imagine the human mind as a vast, mysterious celestial orchestra, where each neuron plays its part in a hauntingly beautiful arrangement, weaving together the complex and often unsettling choruses of existence. Across the annals of time, we meet extraordinary intellects who have deftly woven their thoughts into a tapestry of brilliance—Einstein's revolutionary theories of relativity echoing through the hallowed halls of physics, da Vinci's visionary sketches forging an intricate connection between art and science, and Ramanujan's mathematical revelations, a hauntingly beautiful manifestation of numerical elegance. Envision, if you dare, a vast concert hall nestled within the shadows of your psyche, a realm where your thoughts and emotions intertwine in a haunting symphony of creativity. What echoes in the depths of the soul? What kind of haunting melodies linger in the air?

In acknowledging the complex web of thoughts that dwell within, we unveil the power to forge a narrative that resonates with meaning, shaping our experiences and guiding us toward a brighter future. In the shadows of the psyche, where chaos often reigns, the cultivation of self-discipline emerges as a beacon. Through the forging of a steadfast belief system, one can navigate the labyrinth of existence, orchestrating the mind's tumultuous symphony toward a life rich with meaning and profound satisfaction. In the shadows of existence, where the echoes of profound thought linger, you hold the power to conjure a hauntingly beautiful melody within you. This melody, born from the depths of your being, guides your every action and shapes the uncertain path of your future.

May you delve into the depths of thought with a keen eye and clarity, weaving a tapestry of ideas that resonates with truth and insight?

THE DYNAMICS OF COGNITEXIS: SHAPING THE MIND'S LANDSCAPE

ᔍᔎᔍᔎ

I n the haunting depths of the human mind, the realm of Cognitexis unfolds—a dynamic landscape where thoughts and emotions swirl like mist in the night. Within the shifting sands of consciousness lies the untamed power to shape our reality. This journey through Cognitexis is an exploration of the forces that etch our mental tapestry, a quest to uncover the hidden mechanisms driving our thoughts and actions.

Amidst the shadowy dance of habitual thought and the whispers of the unconscious, we confront the tempest of our inner monologues, striving to master the dualities within. Anchored by guiding principles and archetypal whispers, we navigate the labyrinth with an unyielding will, forging our minds in the crucible of experience.

As we delve deeper, the harmony and disharmony of thought and action reveal themselves, challenging us to tame the echoes within and educate the murmurs of our psyche. This odyssey is not for the faint-hearted; it demands a fearless seeker ready to unveil the profound mysteries of their own Cognitexis. Will you dare to venture into this enigmatic landscape, where the mind's darkest secrets lie in wait?

Ready to journey into the dynamic realms of Cognitexis and shape the very landscape of your mind?

First Sub realm: Habitual and Dynamic Thought Processes

These concepts explore the patterns and changes in our thought processes, examining how habits form and evolve and how knowledge and experience shape our thinking.

1. Etching the Tapestry: The Power and Peril of Habitual Thought

The human mind is not only a sculptor of every form of exterior creation; it is a sculptor of its own interior labyrinth. The chisel it wields? Well, habitual thought. We foster one kind of thought, take care of it with pointed attention, and leave an impression on the cognitive canvas. Repetition makes this impression deeper, and the voluntary thought now turns into an invisible puppeteer, silently shaping our perceptions and behaviors from behind the scenes. The question this begets is, is it the power of realizing the true inner potential of Cognitexis or our yielding ourselves to some unseen forces lurking in the labyrinthine passages of the mind?

Scientifically, habitual thoughts function like well-worn paths. These grooved tracks become the superhighways on which information travels faster and faster in the brain. In time, it becomes easy for similar thoughts and performances to follow the path. With repetition, the electrical impulses coursing along the pathways increase in strength, thus solidifying the thought pattern. In due time, these ingrained patterns run smoothly in the diaphragm and build our reality with no conscious effort.

But the mystery of the mind deepens when we consider the echoes of past experiences and whispers from the subconscious. These forgotten memories and deeply ingrained beliefs can act as unseen puppeteers, pulling the strings of our habitual thoughts. Are we truly in control, or are we merely elaborate dance puppets on the stage of our own minds?

The longer we allow these habitual thoughts to etch themselves like malignant vines across the cognitive landscape, the harder it becomes to break free from their control. Cognitexis, once a vibrant and ever-shifting terrain, risks becoming a rigid, predictable expanse. Therefore, new thoughts and experiences take root more difficultly in such hardened soil of our already-entrenched patterns. These might derail many people in adapting to and evolving in a fast-changing world. The sense of urgency creeps in: the more we give in to comfortable autopilot, the greater the risk of living like prisoners of our own minds. In a manner of speaking, the tendrils of inbuilt patterns tend to rise and choke the cognitive flexibility we really need, turning the once-expanded Cognitexis into a mental cage.

This transforms into a quest to uncover the deep-seated beliefs that serve as both a formidable foundation of our existence and a dangerous relinquishment of power. Listening to the enigmatic echoes from within through the lens of knowledge that reveals the fundamental principles governing our deep-seated behaviors while remaining vigilant against the chains of our own thoughts—with these, the force of routine thinking can be harnessed to shape Cognitexis into a realm of expansion and potential.

2. The Ever-Shifting Sands of Thought: A Dynamic Landscape

The human mind is not a monolithic slab etched with preordained programs. Instead, it resembles a vast desert of ever-shifting sands sculpted by the relentless winds of experience. Our thoughts are not static entities but rather **evolving responses** to the constant barrage of stimuli we encounter. The external world bombards us with sensory symphony–sights, sounds, emotions–and Cognitexis acts as a complex filter, processing this information and generating thoughts in response. These thoughts, in turn, shape our perception of reality, creating a feedback loop where experience informs interpretation, and interpretation colors future experiences.

Scientifically, Cognitexis can be understood through the lens of neuroplasticity. This remarkable property of the brain allows neural pathways to strengthen or weaken based on our experiences. The constant flow of information bombarding our senses stimulates the creation of new neural pathways and the reinforcement of existing ones, shaping the ever-shifting cognitive landscape. Imagine the wind whipping across the desert, carving new channels, and sculpting the dunes into ever-changing formations. Like the sands, our thoughts are constantly in motion, influenced by the ever-present sensory stimuli.

But the mystery deepens when we consider the whispers of the subconscious and echoes of past experiences swirling beneath the surface. These unseen forces, like hidden currents beneath the dunes, can subtly influence our interpretations. A forgotten memory or a deeply ingrained belief might nudge a thought in a particular direction, adding an element of intrigue to the perception process.

The ever-shifting nature of our thoughts can be both exhilarating and unsettling. The constant flux presents exciting opportunities for growth and adaptation, but it can also create a sense of uncertainty and disorientation. As the dunes of thought slip beneath our feet, shall we ever be able to solidify our hold on reality? And this inherent changeability keeps us on the edge of our seats, uncertain of what the next gust of experience will bring.

A sense of danger lurks within the shifting sands. Greater external forces-malicious propaganda, for example, or techniques of social manipulation-could take advantage of this dynamic aspect of Cognitexis to plant deceitful thoughts and make our view of reality far different from what it has been. Walking across such a shifting landscape- a landscape akin to an eternal desert-needs one's permanent vigilance to keep notions from unwanted intrusion, just as a lonely traveler through the open desert should be aware of an enemy group's appearance.

By being aware of the scientific underpinning of this dynamic system, listening to the mysterious whispers from within, and being alert to external manipulation, one can negotiate the shifting sands of thought with full awareness and determination. The everlasting landscape of Cognitexis offers the same share of challenges and opportunities, and by embracing its fluidity, one can build a more decent reality in shaping our thoughts and perceptions.

3. The Mutable Mind: A Dance with Knowledge and Experience

The mark of a truly resilient mind lies in its adaptability. Education is not merely the passive accumulation of knowledge but an ongoing dance with experience. Bookish learning provides the foundation, the sheet music for the orchestra of Cognitexis. This initial knowledge serves as the cognitive scaffolding, a framework upon which understanding is built. However, it is through the crucible of experience, the act of putting knowledge into action and refining our understanding of the world, that the mind truly transforms. This adaptability allows us to reshape our thoughts and behaviors and rewrite our lives' scores in the face of new information and unforeseen challenges.

Scientifically, the concept of the mutable mind can be explored through the lens of neuroplasticity. This principle states that the brain is not a static organ but rather retains the ability to form new connections and modify existing ones throughout life. Experiences trigger these neuroplastic changes, allowing the mind to adapt and learn from its encounters with the world. Imagine a sculptor constantly molding and refining a piece of clay based on their evolving vision. Similarly, experiences act as the sculptor's tools, shaping and reshaping the neural landscape of the mind.

Dance with experience can also unlock hidden aspects of the mind. Experiences can trigger the emergence of implicit knowledge, a form of understanding that is not readily articulable but shapes our actions and intuitions. A seasoned athlete might possess an implicit understanding of complex physical maneuvers, even if they struggle to explain them in words. Imagine a pianist who can play a piece flawlessly based on muscle memory, even without consciously thinking about each note. Dance with experience can also activate whispers from the unconscious, unearthing hidden talents or long-forgotten memories. A traumatic childhood experience, for instance, might leave behind implicit emotional responses that influence behavior, and through therapy and self-reflection, these whispers can be brought to light and integrated into a more coherent understanding of the self.

Dance with experience is not without its risks; negative experiences can scar the mind by engraving unhealthy thoughts and behavioral patterns. Overcoming such experiences and rewriting the limiting stories they create becomes part of the process of mental resilience. Consider the case of the musician whose confidence was once shredded by a harsh critic, with the result that he never played again. With the elements of self-compassion and reframing negative experiences, the score can be rewritten to rediscover the joy in the music. Can we learn to take these jarring notes of past experiences and create a more harmonious symphony of thought and action?

A sense of danger also lurks within the external world. Deceptive experiences, carefully contrived by malicious actors, might be used to manipulate our perceptions, rewriting the score of our lives for their own gain. Disinformation campaigns and social engineering leveraging our thirst for experience in an attempt to throw us off track is also conceivable. For example, a social media feed of curated experiences churning out feelings of inadequacy or insecurity. Critical thinking thus becomes important to distinguish between real experiences and illusory, manipulative ones. By understanding the science of neuroplasticity and accounting for hidden knowledge and whispers from the unconscious, we would be aware of external manipulation so that this dance with experience furthers growth, resilience, and deeper knowledge of ourselves and the world.

Second Sub realm: The Subconscious and Inner Dialogue

These concepts delve into the subconscious mind and the internal conversations we have with ourselves, highlighting the importance of understanding and managing these inner dialogues.

1. The Whispers in the Machine: Unveiling the Unconscious Mind

While it is excellent to consider conscious thought as particularly important, the real truth about Cognitexis is even more interesting. Beneath the surface, an ocean churns, literally bubbling from the very depth of our unconscious mind. These thoughts that are created automatically, outside of our awareness, are the bedrock upon which our mental world rests. They influence our decisions and shape our emotions, guiding our behaviors in subtle yet profound ways. Can we learn to harness this hidden wellspring, or must we always be at the mercy of these unseen mental machinations?

Scientifically, the unconscious mind can be explored through the lens of implicit memory and implicit bias. Implicit memories are those that we have formed outside of our conscious awareness but are often related to experiences we've had. Sometimes, these can affect our thoughts and behaviors. For example, an advertisement for a neutral product can produce a positive response due to a positive association with a childhood experience that we no longer consciously remember. Implicit bias refers to a form of unconscious prejudice where there are subtle influences on perceptions and decisions. Sometimes, we implicitly hold a bias against members of a particular group, or rather, a preconception about how its members act or behave. This is without being aware of it, and such implicit biases then come out in subtle influences on our interactions. By the same token, in understanding such processes, we are able to start identifying and perhaps mitigating the influence of the unconscious mind.

The mystery deepens when we consider the vast, unexplored territory of the unconscious. Is the unconscious but a repository of all past experiences, or does it well from an even deeper spring of intuition and creativity? Flashes of inspiration seemingly from nowhere are well-documented by artists and inventors alike. Might these be whispers from the unconscious? Might it even be a bridge to the collective unconscious, the realm of shared human experience extending beyond the individual? These questions add an extra layer of intrigue to our quest into unseen mental machinations.

The power of the unconscious mind can be both a source of empowerment and a potential threat. By harnessing its wellspring of creativity and intuition, we can unlock hidden potential. A scientist may suddenly come up with a breakthrough inspired by an unconscious connection, while an artist plunges deep into the well of emotions in order to create a masterpiece. Yet, it is in the subconscious that negative prejudices and emotional provocations reside, which take us along paths that are not desirable. We jump to unwarranted judgments because unconscious biases or some negative experiences from the past fire up subconscious anxieties that work against us one way or another. The key lies in a deep understanding of its influence and developing the ability of conscious control.

A sense of danger lurks within the shadows of the unconscious. External forces, like manipulative advertising or social conditioning, can exploit our implicit biases to influence our behavior for their own gain. Targeted marketing campaigns, for example, might trigger positive associations with a product based on our past experiences, subconsciously nudging us toward a purchase. We must remain vigilant, recognizing the potential for the unconscious mind to be hijacked by external forces, and develop strategies to mitigate their influence.

By understanding the scientific underpinnings of the unconscious mind, acknowledging its mysterious depths, and remaining vigilant against external manipulation, we can begin to navigate the whispers in the machine. This hidden realm holds the potential for both empowerment and danger; by harnessing its power with awareness, we can unlock the full potential of Cognitexis.

2. Taming the Tempest: Mastering the Inner Monologue - A Dance with Duality

The most powerful, however, need not be the most inflexible of masters—the great storm of whispers and echoes reside within Cognitexis. We do have the sensational capacity to regain control from our unstoppable inner voice, which is called thought discipline. Discipline of the mind is at the core of one's mastery of Cognitexis.

Pruning the Electrical Storm: Through the intentional, volitional allocation of our attention and focus, we can take what happens within Cognitexis-electrical storms and take that tempest from chaos into precisely guided currents. This moves us beyond mere automaticity to deliberate choice. However, such mastery requires commitment: a laser beam-like focus upon a certain purpose. Can we cognize one thought and amplify it to such a degree that it becomes the very driving obsession of one's existence, a guiding star against which all greater disturbances are inconsequential? For some, this focused thought is how one taps into the true potential of Cognitexis. But one must beg the question, do we substitute one form of control for another?

It can be **scientifically explained** within the scope of executive function. This important brain function is, in a way, treated as the control center for planning, paying attention, and making decisions. In this way, we practice meditation or other mindfulness exercises geared toward reinforcing our executive function; we build the psychic muscles that will allow us to control the inner monologue. As we train our brains to filter out distractions and remain focused on a chosen thought, we gradually build the mental stamina to weather the storms within Cognitexis.

The tempestuous Cognitexis, however, holds mysteries that extend beyond conscious control. Within the storm, whispers of intuition and echoes of past experiences can intertwine with our chosen thoughts. While focus amplifies the chosen path, can we completely silence the undercurrents of the unconscious? Does true mastery lie in acknowledging and integrating these whispers rather than complete domination? Perhaps the key lies in a delicate dance—amplifying the chosen thought for direction while acknowledging the whispers of the unconscious for a more nuanced understanding.

The path to mastering the inner monologue is fraught with challenges. The relentless barrage of external stimuli, from social media notifications to the allure of a half-remembered song, can threaten to pull our focus away from the chosen thought. Can we maintain the necessary focus to navigate the storm, or will the tides of distraction sweep us away? Here, the role of executive function becomes paramount. As we strengthen this cognitive muscle, we develop the ability to filter out distractions and maintain our focus on the chosen path, even amidst the chaos.

A sense of danger lurks within the quest for mastery. Might the obsessive focus on a single thought become a mental prison, constraining our creativity and flexibility? Could external forces, like manipulative messaging or social conditioning, exploit our heightened focus to control our thoughts and actions for their own gain? By remaining vigilant and recognizing the potential pitfalls of overzealous control, we can navigate the path to mastery with awareness.

Taming the tempest within requires a delicate balance. By harnessing the scientific tools of thought discipline, acknowledging the mysteries of the unconscious, and remaining vigilant against external manipulation, we can transform the inner monologue from a relentless storm into a powerful tool for navigating the complexities of Cognitexis. This dance with duality, between conscious control and unconscious whispers, is the essence of mastering the inner world and unlocking the mind's full potential.

3. Taming the Whispers: Educating the Echoes Within

The human mind is not a monolithic entity but a vibrant ecosystem teeming with voices. Whispers and echoes dance through the labyrinthine halls of Cognitexis. Some whispers originate from our conscious will, fueled by desires and goals. Others, more enigmatic, rise from the depths of the unconscious, carrying the weight of past experiences and primal urges. All vie for dominance, shaping our thoughts and actions. The ability to navigate this cacophony lies not in silencing the whispers but in educating the echoes within.

Speaking scientifically, we could take it one step ahead by examining the echoes in terms of cognitive reappraisal- a process in which there is activity considering how to reappraise or reframe thinking and feeling. If a thought or anxiety becomes an echo, it's through cognitive reappraisal that we are equipped with the ability to take this echo and make it an exceptionally empowering narrative. Consider an echo flickering, whispering doubts to one's capable mind. Through cognitive reappraisal, the echo is thus turned to remind us of our past successes and, in effect, change the influence within Cognitexis to strengthen our confidence.

The echoes within could also hold the key to unlocking hidden aspects of ourselves. Jungian psychology suggests the existence of archetypes, universal patterns that reside in the unconscious. These archetypes might manifest as echoes, influencing our behaviors and motivations. For instance, an entrepreneur might be haunted by the echo of the "creator" archetype, urging them to bring their innovative ideas to life. By understanding these echoes and their potential connection to archetypes, we can gain a deeper understanding of our inherent potential.

The process of educating the echoes is fraught with challenges. Unrecognized negative thought patterns can be built on past experiences or biases that distort the echoes to take unproductive paths. It's like laying a distorting filter over the echoes to warp their message. The unrecognized biases serve as this kind of filter, allowing the echoes of doubt to become deafening while whispers of potential remain still faint. Can we be aware of such distortions, clear them, and make the echoes guide us toward a better future?

A sense of danger also lurks within the external world. The echoes within can be manipulated by outside forces, such as advertising that manipulates or algorithms of social media. They could control our ideas and activities to their benefit with contrived messages that key into our most profound desires or insecurities. Imagine a social media feed teeming with distorted echoes designed to cultivate feelings of inadequacy and steer us towards impulsive purchases. Discerning genuine echoes from manipulative distortions becomes crucial in this psychological thriller. By understanding the power of cognitive reappraisal, acknowledging the potential for archetypal echoes, and remaining vigilant against internal biases and external manipulation, we can cultivate the skill of educating the echoes within. This mastery allows us to transform the cacophony of whispers into a symphony of intention, guiding us toward a life of purpose and fulfillment.

Third Sub realm: Anchoring and Guiding Principles

These concepts focus on the core principles and guiding thoughts that provide stability and direction in the mind's labyrinth.

1. The Anchoring Thought: A Beacon in the Labyrinth

Not all thoughts come into the world equal. Some-impelled by a sharp purpose-are unstoppable. Feeding an energized thought infused with a well-defined purpose takes root in Cognitexis and becomes an anchoring thought. **An anchoring thought** isn't any ordinary thought; it's that beacon casting our life force inwards, thereby saving us from the tides of distraction. The more we can impregnate that thought with meaning and passion, the stronger its anchoring power. Imagine a lighthouse that cuts through the fog of the brain, not just a flicker but a brilliant beam guiding one through the rocky shoals of impulsive thought to calmer waters of focused intention.

Scientifically, the anchoring thought can be understood through the lens of attention bias. Our brains are wired to prioritize certain types of information over others. This inherent bias allows an anchoring thought, fueled by a strong purpose, to capture and hold our attention. The more emotionally charged or personally relevant the anchoring thought, the stronger its hold on our attentional spotlight. Think of a student fueled by the desire to excel in a challenging course. The anchoring thought of academic success becomes a powerful magnet, drawing their focus towards studying and learning, even amidst social media distractions or the allure of a weekend getaway.

The anchoring thought, however, might not be solely a product of conscious intention. Does it purely stem from our deliberate choices, or are there deeper forces at play? Could whispers from the unconscious, longings buried deep within, influence the formation of a truly captivating anchoring thought? Perhaps the most potent anchors are those that resonate with a deeper purpose, a sense of calling that transcends conscious awareness. An artist might find themselves inexplicably drawn to a particular theme, a creative urge welling up from the depths of their being, and this becomes the anchoring thought that guides their artistic exploration.

The journey through the labyrinth of the mind, even with the anchoring thought as a beacon, is not without its challenges. Competing distractions, both internal and external, constantly vie for our attention. The internal chatter of self-doubt, the lure of social media notifications, or the enticing aroma of freshly baked cookies all threaten to pull our focus away from the anchoring thought. Can we sustain the intensity of the anchoring thought and resist the siren call of distractions, or will we lose our guiding beacon and become lost in the mental maze? Meditation or mindfulness training could be very effective tools for enhancing our capability to filter out distractions and focus on the chosen path.

A sense of danger also lurks in the external world. Malicious actors could exploit the power of the anchoring thought to manipulate our focus. Deceptive narratives, disguised as purposeful goals, could lure us towards actions that serve their agenda, not our own. Critical thinking becomes paramount in discerning genuine purpose from manipulative illusions. For example, social media algorithms might craft personalized narratives that exploit our insecurities, creating a false sense of purpose that ultimately keeps us glued to our screens. By remaining vigilant and recognizing the potential pitfalls of manipulation, we can safeguard the integrity of our anchoring thought.

The anchoring thought offers a powerful tool for navigating the complexities of Cognitexis. By harnessing the scientific understanding of attention bias, acknowledging the potential influence of the unconscious, and remaining vigilant against external manipulation, we can transform this thought into a radiant beacon, guiding us through the labyrinth of the mind and toward fulfilling our true purpose.

2. The Unyielding Will: A Beacon in the Storm

The hallmark of a mature Cognitexis is not just the vastness of its knowledge but the unyielding will, a potent force that transcends mere knowledge accumulation. This unwavering determination acts as a beacon in the storm, a guiding light that propels us forward even amidst the turbulence of distractions and doubts. It allows us to focus our mental energies with unwavering focus, relentlessly pursuing our goals and aspirations. A powerful trio powers this unwavering determination:

a) **A Definite Motive:** A clearly defined purpose acts as the anchor, tethering our intentions and preventing them from being swept away by the currents of indecision.

b) **A Burning Desire:** Passion ignites the spark of intention, transforming a nebulous thought into a compelling force. This emotional fuel propels us forward, pushing us to overcome obstacles and persevere through setbacks.

c) **The Unyielding Power of Determination:** Inner strength serves as the foundation, enabling us to transform ambition and purpose into relentless pursuit. It grants us the strength to fend off distractions, endure through trials, and stand firm against the challenges that arise.

Without this potent trio, even the most meticulously crafted plan crumbles in the face of adversity. The most perfectly composed symphony of structured cognition–the sheet music for the orchestra of the mind–becomes meaningless without the conductor's unwavering will to bring it to life.

The Science of Unwavering Will. Scientifically, the concept of the unyielding will can be explored through the lens of executive function. This set of cognitive processes allows us to plan, prioritize, and control our thoughts and actions. A strong will taps into these executive functions, enabling us to maintain focus and overcome obstacles in the pursuit of our goals. Imagine an orchestra conductor wielding the baton with unwavering determination, ensuring the musicians stay focused and deliver a flawless performance. The conductor's will acts as the central command, directing the orchestra towards a unified goal. Unwavering will shall ignite within the hearts of those who possess among the most cherished human attributes.

a) **Deeper connection with one's purpose.** The unyielding will might also tap into a deeper reservoir of human potential. Perhaps it connects us to a sense of archetypal purpose, a whisper from the collective unconscious that resonates with our deepest desires. This connection fuels an almost mystical sense of determination, urging us to persevere even when the path seems shrouded in uncertainty. For instance, an artist driven by the archetypal "creator" might experience an unyielding will to express their vision, even in the face of rejection or setbacks. Understanding this potential connection allows us to harness the power of these deeper whispers to fuel our unwavering determination.

b) **Overcoming Challenges.** The journey towards our goals is rarely smooth sailing. Imagine a fog rolling in, obscuring the path forward and tempting us to abandon our journey. Internal challenges, such as self-doubt or procrastination, can threaten to derail our progress. External forces, like social pressures or unexpected obstacles, can also test the strength of our will. Can we maintain our resolve in the face of these challenges, or will our unyielding will crumble under pressure?

A sense of danger also lurks in the external world. Malicious actors might attempt to exploit weaknesses in our will, using manipulation tactics to steer us away from our goals. Deceptive advertising or social engineering campaigns can chip away at our resolve, subtly swaying our desires and undermining our sense of purpose. Imagine a siren song luring sailors off course. Critical thinking and a healthy dose of skepticism become crucial in safeguarding the integrity of our will. By understanding the science of executive function, acknowledging the potential connection to a deeper purpose, and remaining vigilant against internal and external threats, we can cultivate an unyielding will that serves as a beacon, guiding us toward fulfilling our aspirations.

Fourth Sub realm: Archetypes and Intent

The following concept stands alone to emphasize the profound impact of archetypal figures and intentionality within the cognitive landscape, acting as deep-rooted influences on our thoughts and actions.

Archetypes and Intent: The Deep Whispers of Cognitexis

No matter how transient, every thought would seem to emanate from the seed of intention- a nascent murmur in Cognitexis. This mysterious spark, so some describe it, sets an ensuing chain reaction that crafts the electrical tempests raging across our minds. Whence, though, do these murmurs arise? Do they well up from conscious will- that is, a deliberative act of choice to focus attention on this or that thought? Or is it a far more sophisticated dance kind of quantum puzzle in which free will becomes closely intermingled with whispers from some deeper place?

Scientifically, the birth of intent can be explored through the lens of decision-making models. These models posit a complex interplay between conscious deliberation and unconscious processes. While we might sit down and consciously weigh options, underlying biases, past experiences, and even subconscious emotional responses can all play a role. These hidden factors can subtly influence our final decision, whispering a particular direction into our ears. Imagine the conscious mind as a conductor, attempting to orchestrate the symphony of Cognitexis. Yet, beneath the surface, subtle melodies from the unconscious—echoes of past experiences or ingrained biases—can subtly influence the overall composition.

The whispers of intent could originate from the depths of the unconscious, echoes from a collective unconscious that transcends the individual. This concept delves into the realm of Jungian psychology and the idea of archetypes, universal patterns that influence our thoughts and behaviors. Perhaps these whispers represent a deeper intelligence, a pool of shared human experience that guides us in subtle, often imperceptible ways. Entrepreneurs might be drawn to the whispers of innovation, a dormant archetype of the "creator" stirring within their Cognitexis. Or an artist might be haunted by the whispers of longing, an echo of the collective human desire for beauty and self-expression.

The source of the whispers remains a mystery, and this very mystery creates a sense of suspense. Are we truly in control of our intentions, or are we merely puppets on the strings of unseen forces? The whispers, originating from the unconscious, could harbor positive and negative influences. A creative spark might ignite a masterpiece, but a buried fear could manifest as self-sabotaging thoughts. We might dream of starting a business, yet a whisper of doubt rooted in a past failure might hold us back. Understanding the nature of these whispers becomes crucial in harnessing their power for good.

A sense of danger also lurks within the whispers. That is to say, intent whispers are usually subtle, and any external manipulative mechanisms would most definitely be able to make use of that subtlety in nudging us toward intent that would benefit them rather than ourselves. Targeted marketing campaigns may perhaps be mobilizing whispers of desire for the latest gadgets, unknowingly molding our intentions. We may not even consciously notice these influences from without, yet they sneakily turn the course of our intentions in certain directions. In this shadowy realm, the essence of critical thinking emerges as an indispensable tool, enabling us to discern the genuine murmurs of our inner selves from the insidious echoes of external influences.

Decision-making using scientific models, consideration of collective unconsciousness, or social manipulation are the threads through which the enigma birth of intent can be unraveled. Whispers within Cognitexis, which were mysteries, may now become ways that guide and empower us in learning to navigate the intricate dance between conscious will and the whispers from within.

Fifth Sub realm: Harmony and Integration of Thought and Action

These concepts explore how thoughts and actions harmonize or clash and how our mental processes are refined and integrated within the broader cognitive framework.

1. The Conductor and the Orchestra: The Harmony and Disharmony of Thought and Action

The human mind is a magnificent orchestra, a complex symphony of thoughts and actions. At the center of this symphony stands Cognitexis, the conductor wielding the baton of intention. Structured cognition serves as sheet music, a meticulously crafted blueprint that guides the orchestra toward a specific outcome. This intricate score is informed by accumulated knowledge, allowing us to initiate and control ingrained habits. Habits become the instruments—the physical expressions of our intentions played out on the real-world stage.

However, the performance is not always harmonious. Disharmony can arise when the conductor struggles to maintain control, the sheet music becomes muddled, or the instruments fail to resonate in unison.

Scientifically, structured cognition can be understood through the lens of habit formation. Habits are like well-rehearsed pieces of music requiring minimal conscious effort. Think of a musician effortlessly playing a familiar tune. Similarly, our habits are encoded in the "sheet music" of our mind, allowing the conductor (our conscious mind) to initiate them with ease. This process works beautifully when our habits align with our goals. But what happens when they don't? Imagine the habit of checking social media every five minutes—this behavior might have become deeply ingrained in your mental sheet music. When it's time to focus on a demanding task, this habit creates disharmony, interrupting the flow of concentration.

Though seemingly in control, the conductor might be influenced by whispers from the subconscious. These whispers, like echoes from past experiences or emotions, can subtly alter the interpretation of the sheet music, leading to unexpected improvisations within the symphony. A musician might suddenly introduce a melancholic flourish into a joyful piece, reflecting a subconscious emotional state. Does the conductor truly lead, or is there a deeper intelligence at play? Understanding the potential influence of these whispers can help the conductor maintain a more harmonious performance.

The performance is fraught with challenges. External distractions can easily disrupt the conductor's focus, like a sudden noise from the audience startling an orchestra mid-performance. This distraction can lead to a missed cue and a discordant note. Additionally, the sheet music itself might contain flaws—biases or outdated beliefs that disturb the harmony. Consider the outdated belief that multitasking is an effective strategy. This belief can lead to a chaotic performance if encoded into the mental sheet music as the conductor attempts to juggle multiple instruments simultaneously. Critical thinking becomes crucial here, enabling us to identify and revise these errors to achieve a more balanced performance.

A sense of danger lurks within the performance. External forces, like manipulative advertising or social conditioning, could attempt to hijack the conductor's control, altering the sheet music to serve their own agendas. Targeted marketing campaigns, for example, might introduce deceptive notes into the sheet music, subtly manipulating our desires and leading us to pursue actions that benefit the advertiser, not ourselves. We must remain vigilant, recognizing the potential for external manipulation and safeguarding the integrity of the internal symphony.

By understanding the science of habit formation, acknowledging the influence of the subconscious, and remaining vigilant against external manipulation, the conductor can lead the orchestra of the mind toward a more harmonious performance. Through this process, we can transform the symphony of thought and action into a beautiful expression of intention, achieving a flow state and fulfilling our true potential.

2. The Forged Mind: Echoes in the Labyrinth

The true test of a forged mind lies not just in its theoretical knowledge but in its ability to navigate the labyrinthine depths of Cognitexis. Here, within the swirling storms of thought and emotion, theory meets its crucible. Practical experience acts as the searing heat that tempers the theoretical into the practical. Through the crucible of trial and error, we learn to navigate the whispers and echoes within our own minds, to distinguish the whispers of intention from the shadows of doubt. This mastery allows us to translate knowledge from the abstract realm of theory into the tangible world of action.

The echoes within the labyrinth can be both allies and adversaries. The whispers of intuition, honed by experience, can guide us towards wise decisions. Conversely, the echoes of past failures or self-doubt can become insidious saboteurs, leading us astray. **Scientifically,** this process can be understood through the lens of experiential learning. This theory posits that knowledge is best acquired through active engagement with the world. Experience provides a laboratory for testing theories and developing practical skills. As we navigate the labyrinth of Cognitexis, each experience becomes a data point, refining our understanding of ourselves and the world. Imagine a scientist meticulously conducting experiments and refining their theories based on the observed results. Similarly, we navigate the labyrinth, experiencing an experiment that shapes our internal map.

The echoes within the labyrinth could also hold the key to unlocking hidden aspects of the mind. Jungian psychology posits the existence of archetypes, universal patterns that reside in the collective unconscious. These archetypes can manifest as echoes within the labyrinth, influencing our thoughts, behaviors, and even dreams. By deciphering these echoes, we can gain a deeper understanding of our own motivations and unlock hidden potential. For instance, an entrepreneur might be haunted by the echo of the "creator" archetype, urging them to bring their innovative ideas to life. Understanding these echoes allows the forged mind to harness its power for positive outcomes.

The path through the labyrinth is not for the faint of heart. It is fraught with challenges, both internal and external. Cognitive biases, ingrained patterns of thought that can lead to errors in judgment, lurk in the shadows. These biases can distort the echoes within the labyrinth, leading us down misleading paths. Imagine a map shrouded in fog, with landmarks obscured by distortion. Cognitive biases act like fog, obscuring the true nature of the echoes and making navigation difficult. Can we recognize these biases and navigate around them, or will they lead us astray?

A sense of danger also lurks within the external world. Malicious actors might attempt to manipulate the echoes within the labyrinth, using social engineering tactics or targeted messaging to steer us towards actions that benefit them. Discerning genuine echoes from manipulative illusions becomes crucial in navigating this treacherous landscape. Imagine a siren song echoing through the labyrinth, luring us towards a dead end. We can avoid these manipulative traps by remaining vigilant and critically evaluating the echoes we encounter.

By understanding the power of experiential learning, acknowledging the potential for archetypal echoes, and remaining vigilant against internal biases and external manipulation, the forged mind can navigate the labyrinth of Cognitexis with skill and purpose. This journey of self-discovery allows us to transform theory into action, shaping our thoughts and behaviors into a powerful force for good.

THE COGNITEXIS CONTINUUM: EXPLORING THE BOUNDARIES OF COGNITION

᪥᪥᪥

I n the shadowy expanse of Cognitexis, the boundaries of cognition stretch and morph like an elusive specter. This journey through Cognitexis Continuum is an exploration of the extremes of human thought, from its origins and mechanisms to its control and darker potentials.

We begin by igniting the spark of the electrified mind, delving into cognition's dual nature and the vulnerable seeds of thought before the walls take form. As we progress, we uncover the hidden gateways of habits, the whispers of intellect, and the distortions of the echo chamber that shape our realities.

The Odyssey demands mastery of the narrative, constructing formidable defenses within the walled garden of the mind and deciphering the unconscious tales that echo through the labyrinth. Yet, as we journey deeper, we encounter shadowy incursions where thoughts become weapons and the dangers of a corrupted Cognitexis emerge.

Are you prepared to explore the farthest reaches of Cognitexis, to confront both the brilliance and the darkness within? The journey through the boundaries of cognition awaits, fraught with peril and profound insight.

First Enigma: Foundations and Origins of Thought

These concepts explore the foundational elements and origins of thought, examining the initial sparks of cognition and the dual nature of Cognitexis.

1. The Electrified Mind: A Spark Ignited

Imagine the mind as a vast, complex universe, a web of innumerable neurons poised to ignite with purpose. When stirred by the whispers of the mind or the shadows of the world, these neurons awaken in a dance of synchronization, releasing a jolt of electricity—the spark that births a thought. The electrical fluctuations pulse at the core of thought, weaving the primal threads from which our perceptions and experiences are meticulously forged.

Reflect on the instant when a crucial task resurfaces in your mind or when the solution to a perplexing dilemma crystallizes in the shadows of your thoughts. This flicker of understanding courses through your mind like a jolt of electricity, illuminating the shadows and revealing hidden truths. It is these subtle, almost imperceptible electrical activities that form the very foundation of our cognitive existence, allowing us to ponder, absorb knowledge, and navigate the labyrinth of choices that define our lives.

Finally: the unseen currents that pulse through our consciousness form the very core of our reflections and encounters. Understanding this fundamental aspect of our cognition is essential for deciphering the intricate layers of Cognitexis. By delving into the essential nature of these neural impulses, we can uncover the complex interplay of thought that molds our perceptions and directs our choices.

2. The Duality of Cognitexis: Origin and Destination

Cognitexis, cloaked in its mysterious intricacies, fulfills a dual role in the grand narrative of the mind. It serves as both the origin and the ultimate sanctuary of electrical energy within the depths of the mind. Within the shadowy corridors of the mind, the complex dance of neurons sparks the initial glimmer of a thought. This initial spark ignites a tumultuous surge of neural activity, conjuring the essence of thought from the shadows. Yet, the journey does not find its end there.

Cognitexis serves as a formidable conduit, an intricate web within that sifts through and refines these nascent ideas, shaping them into the conscious realities we ultimately grasp. Imagine the instant when clarity pierces through the fog of confusion and the intricate puzzle of thought aligns into a singular, illuminating truth. This awakening marks the apex of Cognitexis' dual existence, where the primal flicker of thought is meticulously honed through relentless scrutiny, culminating in a profound and deliberate awareness.

In the shadows of existence, this duality manifests in the intricate dance of learning and memory. Upon the first brush with unfamiliar knowledge, your mind conjures an instinctive reaction. As time unfolds, through the relentless cycle of repetition and the weight of reinforcement, this knowledge seeps into the very fabric of your mind, transforming into a steadfast and ever-present element of your cognitive terrain.

The Final Word: Cognitexis serves a crucial dual role in cognition, functioning as both the source and the ultimate endpoint of electrical energy. This revelation unveils the complex interplay between our neural pathways and the striking realities they summon into existence. Grasping this duality deepens our insight into human thought's intricate and ever-shifting nature.

3. The Vulnerable Seed: Before the Walls Take Form

The thought generation process within Cognitexis unfolds in a manner that is anything but uniform. A fragile moment of exposure unfolds—the embryonic phase, where ideas are on the cusp of emergence. In this fragile twilight of conception, Cognitexis's safeguards remain in a state of incompletion. In this nascent phase, peril lurks, vulnerable to the insidious touch of outside forces and cunning manipulations.

Are there individuals adept at bending these delicate constructs of thought, quietly steering the course of our consciousness before the defenses can solidify? Reflect on the influence of media and advertising, which frequently prey upon the fragile seeds of individual thought to manipulate consumer behavior. They can manipulate our inclinations and choices in these pivotal instances through a relentless barrage of compelling narratives before our discerning minds are fully awakened.

In the shadows of emerging consciousness, the fragile nature of thought stands exposed, ripe for the hands of those who seek to twist and control it. Understanding this fragility may lead us to foster a more deliberate and autonomous form of contemplation. By recognizing the forces that seek to mold our perceptions, we can fortify our mental fortresses and guarantee that our cognitive routes are crafted through intentional and contemplative endeavors.

Second Enigma: Mechanisms and Influences of Thought

These concepts delve into the mechanisms and influences that shape our thinking, highlighting the dual nature of thought, the impact of habits, and the spectrum of intellectual potential.

1. The Bifurcated Blade of Thought: A Force to Wield with Care

Deep within the recesses of the human psyche lies a formidable weapon, deftly manipulated by the intricate dance of opposing thoughts. This power can serve as the final harbinger of virtue or unleash devastating turmoil. By channeling disciplined thought, the focused mastery of this electric force allows the mind to achieve remarkable feats. Envision a relentless drive, a sharpened intellect that pierces the shadows, revealing the path to victory amidst the chaos. Profound truths and extraordinary creations emerge from the depths of this harnessed power.

Reflect on the monumental strides made by brilliant minds such as Albert Einstein, whose unwavering intellect birthed the theory of relativity, forever altering our perception of the cosmos. His intense intellectual fervor shattered the confines of tradition, casting light upon uncharted realms of understanding.

Untamed, the raw power of the mind can spiral into a harbinger of its own demise. The chaotic tempest of our thoughts can spiral into a maelstrom of hopelessness—a shadowy presence that shrouds understanding and leads us down a treacherous road to destruction. These unbridled thoughts resemble a potent force; their destructive power can obliterate our dreams and perceptions.

In the shadows of the human psyche, one can observe the haunting reality faced by those ensnared by anxiety or depression. Here, unbridled thoughts twist and turn, spiraling into a vortex of despair, ultimately plunging the mind into a chasm of emotional and psychological chaos. The relentless grip of these unchecked thoughts can stifle the journey of self-discovery and the pursuit of true well-being.

Concluding Reflection: The power of thought possesses a dual essence, capable of igniting either blinding illumination or devastating shadows. To navigate the shadows that threaten to engulf us, one must forge a disciplined mind, harnessing our energy with precision to fend off the insidious grip of unbridled negativity. In the shadows of our minds, where thoughts twist and turn, lies a profound potential waiting to be unleashed. By delving into the depths of meditation, grappling with cognitive behavioral techniques, and engaging in intense intellectual pursuits, we can manipulate the very fabric of our consciousness, steering it toward a realm of positive and transformative possibilities.

2. Habits: Gateways to the Unseen

Intentional habits rise above simple routines; they channel the wild currents of thought and bring them forth into existence. Imagine a web of glimmering pathways winding through Cognitexis, where each path symbolizes a distinctive behavior. By cultivating and intentionally infusing a thought with unwavering attention, we unleash a potent force that courses through the labyrinth of our consciousness.

As a particular route unfurls through the relentless cycle of a selecting process, the power of Cognitexis arises, metamorphosing this deliberate decision into an instinctual and unthinking pattern of conduct. At our core, we intertwine with and forge our own destinies, carving the intricate designs of thought we yearn to internalize within the depths of our being.

An exemplary manifestation resides within the realm of mindfulness. In the shadows of existence, each fleeting moment draws one deeper into the labyrinth of thought, where the act of observing without bias or judgment becomes a silent rebellion against the chaos of the mind, strengthening the fragile threads of awareness and presence. This may lead to a deeper mastery of one's inner turmoil, heightened clarity of thought, and a significant alleviation of the burdens that weigh heavily on the mind.

Imagine a scenario steeped in tension: a professional, ensnared by the relentless grip of workplace stress, embarks on a journey to weave mindfulness into the fabric of their daily existence. Every dawn, they dedicate a fleeting ten minutes to the quiet depths of meditation, anchoring themselves in the rhythm of their breath while casting aside the shadows of distraction. As time unfolds, this endeavor sinks deep into their psyche, morphing their once tentative attempts into a sanctuary of tranquility, a dark solace amidst the chaos of existence. This conscious journey weaves into their daily toil, granting them the fortitude and lucidity to confront each challenge that lies ahead. By mastering this transformative practice, they enhance their mental acuity and vitality, revealing the profound impact that deliberate habits can have on the fabric of our consciousness.

Does this lead to the revelation of that limitless knowledge whispered about in shadows, or is it merely a way to unknowingly yield authority to the mysterious powers lurking within Cognitexis?

In the end, the deliberate actions we embrace carve the intricate routes of our consciousness, guiding our deeds and convictions. By embracing transformative practices, we can ascend the labyrinth of our minds and invigorate our very essence.

3. The Whispers of Intellect: A Spectrum of Potential

Thoughts transcend the mere flicker of electrical impulses; they are the profound imprints of the immense potential hidden deep within the human psyche. Some thoughts resonate with piercing clarity, exuding a potent intellectual force, while others waver in the shadows, their whispers cloaked in mystery and intrigue. Mastering the art of attuning oneself to these subtle murmurs of thought is essential in traversing the intricate maze of the mind.

Contemplate the chasm that separates a sudden, piercing revelation—akin to a revolutionary scientific breakthrough—from a transient, nearly instinctual intuition regarding another's feelings. Each type of thought possesses its own significance, yet it is the ability to unravel their distinct nature that reveals their true power. We can unearth profound insights about our existence and the enigmatic world that envelops us by attuning ourselves to these shadowy murmurs.

Illustration: Navigating Challenges in Creativity

Envision a solitary engineer, ensnared in the labyrinth of a complex design challenge, where shadows of doubt loom large, and the weight of existential questions hangs heavy in the air. In the shadows of countless possibilities, certain notions emerge with piercing clarity, their intellectual weight undeniable, while others linger in the murky depths, elusive and hauntingly subtle. Through the mastery of perceiving these subtle murmurs, the engineer unveils the most compelling solutions, shaping them into groundbreaking designs that challenge the very fabric of reality. This endeavor not only sharpens their ability to unravel complex dilemmas but also propels advancement within their domain.

Finally, The profound nature of each thought unveils the depths of our unique potential. By unraveling these murmurs, we can unveil profound truths and traverse the intricate maze of consciousness with greater precision. Embracing this skill can unlock a labyrinth of personal and professional transformation, allowing us to tap into the shadowy depths of our cognitive potential.

4. The Echo Chamber: A Distortion of Reality?

The integrity of our thoughts, the precision of our mental echo chamber, rests upon a vital element—the caliber of information that we nourish it with. As a cracked mirror distorts reality, an untrustworthy source and a barrage of messages warp the mind, leading to twisted perceptions and errant conclusions. Cognitexis, as the harbinger of our thoughts, magnifies these distortions, drawing us deeper into the abyss of misinformation and the paralysis of intellect.

Consider the profound effects of social media on the labyrinth of our minds. In a world where algorithms meticulously curate our experiences, we find ourselves ensnared in echo chambers that amplify our convictions and systematically erase opposing viewpoints, leaving us to ponder the implications of such a reality. This may result in a distorted view of existence, where deception and partial truths reign supreme. During election cycles, one is often engulfed by a relentless tide of politically charged narratives, images, and perspectives that resonate with their pre-existing beliefs. This relentless conditioning can warp their perception of political events and issues, obscuring the broader reality that lies beyond their immediate grasp.

Example: Traversing the Shadows of Information

Envision a world where a solitary news source feeds individuals' minds, carefully curated to echo their own political convictions, creating a labyrinth of confirmation obscuring the broader truth. As time unfolds, they may discover their thoughts and beliefs drifting towards extremes, shaped by the confines of a limited array of viewpoints. In the shadows of information, one must navigate the labyrinth of diverse news sources, daring to confront the unsettling narratives that challenge their beliefs and relentlessly pursue truth through critical evaluation of the information that unfolds before them. In this pursuit, they may uncover a more nuanced and profound comprehension of the unfolding realities around them.

Ultimately, the caliber of the information we allow into our minds profoundly shapes the precision of our reflections. One must tread carefully through the shadows of bias and misinformation, for they weave a deceptive tapestry that can ensnare the mind within its echoing confines. In the shadows of our existence, the pursuit of varied and trustworthy sources of knowledge becomes a vital endeavor, allowing us to weave a richer tapestry of understanding while protecting the fragile essence of our minds.

Third Enigma: Control and Defense of Thought

These concepts focus on strategies for controlling and defending the mind, emphasizing the importance of narrative control, mental defenses, and the role of unconscious cues.

1. Taming the Tempest: Taking Control of the Narrative

As enigmatic energies churn in the abyss of Cognitexis, we remain steadfast, not simply as observers in this odyssey of the mind. In the shadowy recesses of our minds, an epic struggle unfolds, vying for dominion over the relentless tide of inner whispers. Through a discerning lens, we can direct the currents of our perception and sift through the insights that feed the evolving tale of Cognitexis, ultimately crafting its fate.

It is a formidable challenge, for the mind is akin to an expansive galaxy, frequently swept by storms of confirmation bias and erratic emotions. Envision a realm where a person navigates the turbulence of workplace politics, each decision grounded in fog and consequence. By deliberately honing in on meaningful insights and trustworthy perspectives, one can sift through the clamor of rumors and prejudice, guiding one's mind toward fruitful resolutions.

With unwavering determination and an unyielding commitment, we can navigate the tumultuous currents of our minds, steering our consciousness toward a realm of profound insight and clarity. Envision an athlete, ensnared in the labyrinth of their own mind, grappling with the shadows of doubt as they prepare for a pivotal competition. Each thought, a potential adversary, must be subdued to preserve the fragile balance of focus and unwavering confidence. Through the shadows of uncertainty, they forge a tale of resilience and triumph, battling the specters of self-doubt and harnessing their inner strength to pursue their ambitions.

Final Thoughts

While Cognitexis looms ominously, we hold the power to steer our thoughts and narratives through deliberate focus and a thoughtful engagement with the ocean of information surrounding us. Through the cultivation of mental fortifications and the mastery of our inner dialogues, we can traverse the labyrinth of our consciousness, uncovering deeper truths and a more profound sense of direction.

2. The Walled Garden of the Mind: A Formidable Defense

Cognitexis is a realm of enigmas and intrigue, where every corner hides a truth waiting to be uncovered. It harbors an intricate self-preservation system akin to a mental firewall that meticulously controls the influx of information. This mechanism serves as a sentinel, warding off outside forces and safeguarding the purity of our cognitive landscapes. At the very least, that is the dominant hypothesis. The full measure of Cognitexis' defenses lies cloaked in an enigma. Are these barriers genuinely unassailable, or do hidden vulnerabilities exist that might permit sinister entities to breach the sanctity of our innermost reflections?

Ponder the shadows of our reality, where the tendrils of advertising and media weave their intricate web, shaping perceptions and desires in subtle and profound ways. Corporations invest staggering amounts in weaving narratives that slip past our cognitive barriers, embedding insidious suggestions deep within our psyche. With its calculated machinations, the digital realm preys upon our weaknesses, molding our convictions and actions in ways we scarcely perceive. Much like a sinister virus breaching the defenses of a digital fortress, these external forces can seep into Cognitexis, insidiously reshaping the very fabric of our thoughts.

The Bottom Line: The safeguards of Cognitexis stand as a crucial barrier, preserving the sanctity of our innermost reflections. Grasping these defenses unveils the shadows lurking within our psyche, urging us to confront our vulnerabilities and fortify the fragile bastions of our mental well-being. Through the relentless pursuit of critical thought, an acute awareness of the origins of our knowledge, and a continuous examination of our convictions and prejudices, we can strengthen our mental defenses and assert dominion over the intricate terrain of our minds.

3. The Unconscious Tell: Echoes in the Labyrinth

Though Cognitexis stands as a guardian over our fundamental thought processes, its defenses are not without their vulnerabilities. Whispers of our inner turmoil seep through the cracks of our facade—manifesting in unguarded expressions, fleeting facial tics, and the very way we carry ourselves, revealing the shadows that dwell within. These unconscious tales serve as portals into the intricate maze, revealing fleeting insights into the concealed workings beneath the surface. One must ponder: Is it possible to master the subtle art of concealing our tells, to become the architects of our own facades, safeguarding the enigmatic truths of Cognitexis?

Reflect on the intricate dance of reality, akin to a high-stakes poker game, where participants relentlessly pursue mastery over their own expressions and movements, striving to conceal the truth of their intentions. Masterful poker players grasp the significance of mastering these hidden signals, wielding them as a weapon to secure their edge in the game. Through cultivating mindfulness and self-awareness, they master the art of regulating their responses, cloaking their expressions in an impenetrable veil of neutrality.

In the invisible realm of high-stakes business negotiations, those who possess an acute awareness of their hidden signals can navigate the treacherous waters of interaction with greater mastery. Consider a CEO poised at the precipice of a monumental deal, meticulously calibrating their body language. In the recesses of tension, they craft an image of unwavering confidence and serene composure, a façade that belies the turmoil beneath. By delving into and mastering these subtle signals, they can cultivate a more profound exchange and achieve outcomes in negotiation that resonate with deeper truths.

Final Thoughts

Subtle signals can unveil the shadowy corners of our psyche, exposing the concealed layers of our thoughts and emotions. By recognizing these subtle signals, we unearth profound truths about our own nature, paving the way for deeper connections with others. Cultivating acute self-awareness and mastering the delicate nuances of our expressions empower us to traverse the intricate web of social and professional realms with greater finesse, preserving the sanctity of our innermost thoughts and feelings.

Fourth Enigma: The Dark Side of Thought

These concepts address the darker aspects of cognition, exploring how thoughts can be weaponized and the dangers of a corrupted Cognitexis.

1. The Shadowy Incursion: When Thoughts Become Weapons

A moment of vulnerability in Cognitexis unleashes a cascade of severe and catastrophic repercussions. The mind stands as a fortress, yet when its walls weaken, unbidden yearnings seep in, entwining themselves within the very fabric of thought. These may transform into insidious thoughts, nourished by the manipulations of the outside world or the anxieties that dwell within, evolving into relentless tormentors that lead one toward the abyss of despair and self-destruction.

Even more unsettling is the prospect of an entire mind being seized against its will. Imagine a master of deception, one who possesses an intricate knowledge of Cognitexis' frailties, infiltrating the most intimate recesses of our existence—the essence of our being. The implications are substantial. Imagine a realm where the essence of our minds is stripped away, where malevolent murmurs manipulate our choices and distort our understanding of existence. This scenario may unravel through intricate maneuvers of psychological manipulation or the insidious spread of deceitful narratives.

Example: Social Engineering and Cybersecurity

In the shadows of reality, the cunning maneuvers of cybercriminals reveal the lurking peril of social engineering tactics. Through the cunning exploitation of cognitive biases and the subtle manipulation of emotional triggers, assailants can ensnare individuals, compelling them to reveal sensitive secrets or take actions that betray their own best interests. Consider the insidious nature of a phishing email, masquerading as a communication from a trusted source, luring an unsuspecting individual into a web of deceit. One-click on that malevolent link could unravel the very fabric of their personal data, leaving them vulnerable in a world where trust is a fragile illusion.

Moreover, the vulnerability of Cognitexis to external forces unveils yet another peril lurking in the shadows. Abandoned thoughts, the detritus of others' minds, may yet take root in the depths of our own consciousness. Intrusive ideas, like propaganda or subliminal cues, can warp our perception and guide us toward choices we may never have contemplated.

To traverse this treacherous terrain, one must grasp the essence of Cognitexis—its formidable strengths and, crucially, its vulnerabilities. By strengthening our mental barriers and mastering the art of distinguishing allies from adversaries within the intricate maze of consciousness, we can protect the sanctity of our minds. Sharpening our critical thinking, cultivating an awareness of the media's hidden agendas, and embracing mindfulness are essential defenses against the insidious influences that lie in the darkness around us.

The Bottom Line: in moments of vulnerability, Cognitexis reveals its fragility, opening the door to manipulation and corruption. Guarding our mental sanctum demands a keen awareness of lurking threats and the courage to confront them head-on, ensuring our thoughts remain untainted. Through unwavering vigilance and intentionality in our thoughts, we can assert dominion over our mental realm and fend off the sinister forces that loom over our sacred inner space.

2. The Corrupted Cognitexis: When Thought Becomes a Weapon

The human mind operates as a labyrinthine, self-perpetuating enigma. Recent investigations suggest the existence of an internal fail-safe mechanism—a mental self-correcting system embedded within Cognitexis. It could be contended that this mechanism is triggered when Cognitexis is wielded for sinister ends, yet its true essence eludes complete comprehension. Envision a sinister force, insidious and relentless, gnawing away at the very core of Cognitexis. This decay reveals itself through a gradual unraveling of critical thought, a pervasive negativity that clouds judgment, and a chilling decline in the faculties of reason.

Reflect on the consequences of enduring engagement with brutal narratives or radical beliefs. As time unfolds, these pervasive influences can corrode one's capacity for critical thought, nurturing a psyche ensnared by hostility and an unyielding intolerance. This gradual unraveling of the mind may reveal itself through a heightened vulnerability to falsehoods, a distortion of sound judgment, and an inclination towards self-destructive actions.

Another compelling inquiry raised by this theory of self-correcting Cognitexis is whether this inherent failsafe was crafted to shield the mind from becoming a harbinger of destruction. In the shadows of reality, those who find themselves ensnared by destructive thought patterns often spiral into psychological turmoil or crippling anxiety. This turmoil can ignite a profound internal reckoning, compelling a deep reassessment of their beliefs and actions.

Example: Rehabilitation Initiatives

In reality, this notion manifests within rehabilitation initiatives aimed at those harboring extremist ideologies. These programs frequently delve into the intricacies of cognitive-behavioral therapies, seeking to unravel and reconstruct the very fabric of thought patterns. By confronting destructive ideologies and cultivating analytical thought, these initiatives seek to reclaim mental clarity and mitigate the peril of self-inflicted intellectual demise.

Final Thoughts

A deeper inquiry beckons to unveil the shadows of these enigmas. Yet, one truth stands resolute: the human mind is not a tool to be manipulated without consequence. The reckless wielding of

Cognitexis' power could exact a dire toll, possibly spiraling into a profound intellectual demise. Grasping and confronting these perils is essential for protecting our mental clarity and nurturing a more profound and reasoned perspective.

THE ALCHEMY OF COGNITEXIS: TRANSMUTING EMOTIONS INTO REALITY

ಶಿತಿಶಿತಿಶಿತಿ

In the shadowy depths of Cognitexis, emotions are the crucible where raw passion is transmuted into tangible reality. This journey through the Alchemy of Cognitexis is an exploration of the profound power and purpose of emotion, the art of managing and harnessing desires, and the enigmatic dynamics and paradoxes that define our emotional landscape.

We begin by delving into the crucible of emotion, where passion forges its purpose, and the spectrum of emotional charge stokes the flames of action. As we navigate further, we confront the dual nature of the emotional shield and the diverse symphony of desires that color our experiences.

The odyssey then leads us into the realm of paradox, where the elusive spark of emotion wields immense power yet dances on the edge of contradiction. We witness the fading flame of passion, understanding our most intense desires' fragile and fleeting nature.

Are you prepared to embark on this alchemical journey to transmute the raw materials of emotion into the gold of reality? The exploration of the Alchemy of Cognitexis awaits, revealing the hidden secrets of our emotional depths.

First Riddle: The Power and Purpose of Emotion

These chapters explore the transformative power of emotions, emphasizing how passion and desire can forge purpose and drive action.

1. The Crucible of Emotion: Where Passion Forges Purpose

Within the labyrinth of Cognitexis, a captivating alchemy unfolds. Raw thoughts, wisps of intention, are transformed into potent forces for action. The catalyst for this transformation? Emotion. Our emotional landscape acts as the crucible, a vibrant forge where desires, fears, and aspirations collide. Within this crucible, thoughts are imbued with passion, becoming the driving force behind our every move.

Scientifically, neurological research sheds light on this intricate dance between emotion and thought. The amygdala, our emotional core, plays a crucial role in assigning value to thoughts. It prioritizes those aligned with our desires and filters out the rest. Imagine a skilled blacksmith meticulously selecting the right tools for the job. The amygdala acts similarly, choosing thoughts that resonate with our emotional state and discarding those that don't.[2]

For instance, when we encounter a potential threat, the amygdala triggers a fear response, preparing us to either confront or flee the situation. This emotional evaluation influences our thoughts and actions, prioritizing those relevant to our survival and well-being.

However, the full extent of this emotional alchemy remains shrouded in mystery. Are emotions merely the product of biochemical reactions, or is there something more at play? Could a deeper connection exist between our emotions and the unseen forces that may influence Cognitexis? Perhaps these emotions tap into a wellspring of archetypal drives, universal patterns that reside in the unconscious, influencing our desires and shaping our actions in mysterious ways.

The potential for manipulation lurks within this realm. External forces, like manipulative advertising or social media algorithms, can exploit our emotional vulnerabilities. By crafting messages that resonate with our deepest desires or insecurities, they can distort our emotional landscape and steer our actions for their own gain. Imagine a skilled deceiver whispering promises of grandeur into the ear of the blacksmith, subtly manipulating their focus and leading them to forge weapons instead of life-saving tools. Discerning genuine emotional echoes from manipulative distortions becomes crucial in navigating this psychological thriller.

By understanding the science of emotional cognition, acknowledging the potential for archetypal influences, and remaining vigilant against external manipulation, we can become masters of the crucible. We can harness the power of our emotions to forge a path driven by purpose, transforming wisps of intention into a life of passion and fulfillment.

2. The Spectrum of Emotional Charge: Stoking the Flames of Action

Emotions exist on a vast spectrum, each with its unique power to stoke the flames of action within the furnace of Cognitexis. A flicker of hope can ignite a spark of determination, while a surge of anger can fuel relentless pursuit. The key to wielding the power of emotional alchemy lies in understanding this spectrum and harnessing its energy.

A clear intention transforms into a powerful force when charged with an all-consuming passion. This searing fervor ignites our minds, transforming elusive ideas into the stark reality of decisive movement. Envision the blacksmiths, their relentless ambition to shape a legendary sword driving each strike of the hammer, echoing with a haunting intensity. In a world shrouded in shadows, a meticulously crafted purpose, ignited by an intense desire, transmutes mere thoughts into tangible actions.

Scientifically, the research delves into the intricate dance of motivation, revealing the pivotal influence of dopamine, that intriguing neurotransmitter tied to our deepest rewards and pleasures. Studies reveal that the brain releases dopamine when faced with rewarding stimuli, a mechanism that reinforces behaviors and fuels motivation. By igniting an intense yearning for a particular result, we can unleash the flow of dopamine, intensifying our concentration and drive.

Moreover, research into the neurobiology of motivation reveals a compelling connection: elevated dopamine levels correlate with heightened effort and unwavering persistence in pursuing goals.[3]The depth of our emotional engagement wields a powerful influence over our performance and resolve, as the dopamine-fueled reward mechanism strengthens our dedication to achieving our goals.

However, the shadows that dance at the edge of the emotional spectrum pose a significant threat. Here, the thriller within the furnace unfolds. Malevolent forces could exploit vulnerabilities within the emotional landscape. They might manipulate our fears, stoke the flames of anger beyond constructive purpose, or twist our desires into distorted reflections. Imagine a skilled manipulator whispering anxieties into the ear of the blacksmith, warping their desire to create a magnificent sword into a need to forge a weapon of destruction. Discerning these manipulative whispers from the embers of genuine desire becomes paramount.

Social media algorithms, for instance, can act as these manipulative whispers, bombarding us with content that triggers fear, outrage, or envy. These carefully crafted messages can hijack our emotional furnace, fueling the flames with a distorted sense of purpose. A genuine desire for connection can be twisted into a yearning for social validation, and a healthy dose of ambition can morph into a relentless pursuit of fleeting recognition. Critical thinking becomes our shield, allowing us to discern the whispers that serve our true purpose from those who seek to exploit our vulnerabilities and steer us down a destructive path.

By understanding the science of emotional motivation, harnessing the power of a burning desire, and remaining vigilant against external manipulation, we can become masters of the emotional furnace. We can learn to stoke the flames with the right fuel, transforming the spectrum of emotions into a potent force that propels us toward achieving our goals and fulfilling our deepest desires. In this way, we navigate the thriller within the furnace, emerging with the strength and clarity to forge our own path.

3. The Alchemical Symphony: The Power of Amplified Desire

The true power of the emotional alchemist lies not just in wielding individual emotions but in orchestrating a symphony of desires. Through the principle of desire augmentation, we become conductors, fusing multiple emotional states into a potent force that propels us toward a singular envisioned aim.

Imagine the burning ember of ambition intertwined with the deep love for one's family. This potent emotional cocktail fuels relentless effort and unwavering focus, ensuring the fulfillment of financial goals and the deeper desire to bring joy to loved ones. It transcends mere wealth accumulation, becoming a pursuit driven by a genuine desire to uplift and secure the well-being of those we hold dear.

Science offers a fascinating score to this symphony. Research on motivation highlights the power of intrinsic versus extrinsic motivation. Intrinsic desires, fueled by emotions like love and purpose, lead to greater persistence and satisfaction than extrinsic motivation, which might solely focus on achieving financial security. The symphony thrives on the internal drive for contribution and the fulfillment it brings, creating a more sustainable and enjoyable journey.

However, the echoes within Cognitexis can play a role here as well. Perhaps these echoes act as a resonant chamber, amplifying certain emotional combinations that align with our ancestral goals or the whispers of the collective unconscious. Imagine a descendant of explorers with a deep-seated yearning for adventure subtly amplified by the echoes of their forebears. This intrinsic pull, resonating with the echoes of the past, could fuel a powerful desire to explore and discover.

Desire augmentation intensifies the potential for manipulation. Sinister influences might manipulate this mechanism, quietly steering us to merge our aspirations in ways that fulfill their selfish motives.

- Envision a reality where the deep-seated desire for safety morphs into a relentless chase for riches, ultimately sacrificing the bonds we hold dear. Maintaining a healthy skepticism and a clear understanding of our true desires is essential for mastering the alchemical formula with precision. We must navigate the fine line between a true yearning for security that nurtures our safety and the well-being of those we cherish and a distorted chase for wealth driven by deceit. We can discern genuine harmony from discordant manipulations by maintaining a clear awareness of our core values and motivations.

- The possibility of manipulation looms larger, yet it remains within the realm of control. These sinister forces can sow insidious seeds, twisting our deepest yearnings. They could subtly steer us to intertwine our deep-seated desire for safety with a distorted perception of justice, igniting violent actions under the guise of safeguarding. Yet, by keeping a sharp focus on our fundamental values and drives, we can unravel the true symphonies from the jarring deceptions.

By understanding science, acknowledging the whispers of the unseen, and remaining vigilant against manipulation, we can become masters of our own Alchemical Symphony. We can learn to blend the vibrant hues of our emotions with intention, composing a life rich in purpose, meaning, and the unwavering pursuit of our deepest desires. This is not a solitary act but a collaborative masterpiece, a testament to the power of our emotions working in concert.

Second Riddle: Managing and Harnessing Emotions

These chapters focus on the complexities of managing and harnessing emotions, highlighting the dual nature of emotional defenses and the diverse array of desires.

1. The Emotional Shield: A Double-Edged Sword

In the case of successful use, emotions can become staunch defenders of Cognitexis. When filled with a well-defined purpose and powered by an emotional charge, a human mind can hardly be interrupted by sidetracking thoughts. Intrusive thoughts whisper around and echo inside to fall on such an unpopulated ground where they can take root so easily. The emotionally driven force acts as a shield, sending off the unwelcome intruders and keeping their concentration on the current work.

Scientifically, the "attention filter" concept aligns with this idea. Our brains can only process so much information at one time, and our emotions direct our attention. We filter out superfluous stimuli by directing our emotional energy toward our goal. Like a laser beam, its strength depends on the level of our emotions. The more emotional the charge, the stronger a laser beam our attention becomes, effectively filtering out distractions.

The notion of an "attention filter" emerges from the intriguing theory of selective attention. It suggests that our minds possess a finite ability to process information, compelling us to sift through the noise and hone in on what truly matters. Emotions wield a powerful influence in this intricate dance, guiding our focus toward stimuli that resonate deeply within us. This intense focus sharpens our capacity to hone in on what truly matters, allowing us to dismiss the noise that seeks to divert our attention.[4]

Studies reveal that emotional triggers possess a unique power to seize and maintain our focus far more compellingly than neutral cues. A Dixon et al. (2017) study revealed that emotional images trigger more intense and prolonged attentional reactions than their non-emotional counterparts. This intensified concentration resembles a piercing beam, where the depth of our feelings dictates the clarity of our gaze. The intensity of our emotions sharpens our focus, allowing us to sift through distractions and hone in on what truly matters.[5,6]

However, the emotional shield can be a double-edged sword. While it protects us from distractions, it can also become a barrier that isolates us from valuable information. Here, the mysterious element comes into play. Could there be a deeper purpose at play? Perhaps emotions act as a filter not just for external distractions but also for internal whispers that don't serve our current goals. The emotional alchemy might be a process of selection, choosing the whispers that propel us forward and quieting those that might lead us astray. However, this filtering process can become overly selective, silencing essential warnings or gut feelings in favor of the emotionally charged narrative.

The potential for manipulation lurks within this labyrinthine landscape. Malevolent forces could exploit emotional vulnerabilities to create a distorted shield. Consider a social media campaign that actually builds an extremely high level of emotive charge around a particular narrative- in other words, one that feeds into your existing biases and shuts out the presence of any voice in opposition. The kind of mind this would create is a purely obsessed conviction- a shield if you would like, absolute to the point it blinds us from all outside threats and inside truths. Meanwhile, we have to take care of our emotional bodies so that the shield will protect us and not insulate us against the external world. We must be aware of what emotional stories we are creating and make sure those emotional focal points are not too narrow, so they blind us from the whispers of truth and worldly realities.

By understanding the science of the attention filter, acknowledging the potential for emotional over-selection, and remaining vigilant against manipulation, we can transform the emotional shield from a double-edged sword into a powerful tool. We can harness its focus to achieve our goals while remaining open to vital information, ensuring the shield protects us without compromising our ability to navigate the complexities of Cognitexis.

2. The Alchemist's Palette: A Symphony of Desires

Forget the limited metaphor of a fiery furnace. Within the depths of Cognitexis lies a far more captivating workshop. Emotions aren't mere fuel; they're a vast palette of vibrant hues, each corresponding to a fundamental human desire. Security whispers in calming blues, ambition blazes as fiery orange, and the yearning for connection glows with a warm yellow. We, the alchemists of our own minds, wield the brush, meticulously blending these emotional colors to paint the landscape of our thoughts and experiences.

Science offers a fascinating glimpse into this workshop, unveiling the intricate dance between emotions and brain activity. Neuropsychology points out the sections of the brain that govern our emotional responses. For example, fear is generated in the amygdala. Its stimulation, in response, then creates a chain reaction of chemical messages, which in turn results in the secretion of stress hormones such as cortisol and adrenaline. It is a crucial response, mainly because the surge in hormones increases our attention and alertness, thereby supposedly preparing us to be better equipped against perceived threats. Simply put, the amygdala acts like a conductor, urging the orchestra of our physiology to express more response toward danger.[7]

This intricate interplay extends beyond individual emotions. Social psychology delves into the connection between our fundamental desires and our social behavior. Take the desire for connection, for example. When this drive is dominant on our emotional palette, it will trigger pathways associated with the secretion of oxytocin, sometimes even referred to as the "love hormone." Oxytocin induces a disposition toward confidence and bonding and makes us more approachable for social contact and the basis for good relationships. Knowing the above neurochemical links helps us recognize our emotional palette's large impact on our social lives.

Science doesn't stop there. Studies on decision-making reveal the interplay between emotions and the prefrontal cortex, the area responsible for rational thought and planning. When emotions run high, they can temporarily hijack the prefrontal cortex, clouding our judgment and leading to impulsive choices. However, with conscious effort, the prefrontal cortex can exert its own influence, helping us regulate our emotions and make well-considered decisions. This delicate dance between emotion and reason allows us to leverage the power of our emotional palette while maintaining control over our thoughts and actions.

But the whispers within the workshop extend beyond scientific explanations. Echoes from the collective unconscious, or perhaps even forgotten ancestral desires, may subtly influence our chosen colors. Imagine a yearning for adventure, passed down through generations, subtly nudging an individual towards a life of exploration. Do these unseen forces truly guide our hand as we select the emotional hues that paint the canvas of our minds?

Beware the shadows that lurk in the corners of the workshop. Malicious entities or rogue thoughts can exploit vulnerabilities, twisting our desires into warped reflections. Security can morph into paranoia, connection can become a suffocating dependence, and noble ideals can be weaponized into blind fanaticism. Maintaining a healthy emotional state and a critical eye toward our motivations are essential for effectively wielding the alchemist's palette.

By understanding the science of emotional motivation, acknowledging the whispers of the unseen, and remaining vigilant against manipulation, we can become masters of our inner symphony. We can learn to blend the vibrant hues of our emotions with intention, composing a life rich in purpose, meaning, and the unwavering pursuit of our deepest desires.

Third Riddle: The Dynamics and Paradoxes of Emotion

These concepts delve into emotions' dynamic and sometimes paradoxical nature, exploring how powerful sparks can fade and the contradictions inherent in emotional experiences.

1. The Elusive Spark: A Symphony of Power and Paradox

In the recesses of Cognitexis lies the elusive spark: the emotions. These are not mere transient feelings but lifebloods that set the alchemy between thought and action aflame. Positive emotions are buoyant feelings of joy or hopeful anticipation of that dream, which drive us forward in an unstoppable manner with unbridled enthusiasm. On the other hand, even negative emotions, like the desperate drive of fear or the focused intensity of anger, can be just as powerful in motivating us toward avoiding a threat or overcoming an obstacle.

The key to wielding this power lies in understanding the paradox—that all emotions, regardless of their valence (positive or negative), can be harnessed to serve a desired purpose. Imagine a musician not just mastering joyful melodies but also wielding the power of a mournful cello to evoke a depth of emotion. Similarly, we can learn to utilize the full spectrum of our emotional palette to create a symphony of action that propels us toward our goals.

Science offers a fascinating score to this symphony. Studies on emotional intelligence highlight the importance of recognizing and managing emotions effectively. By understanding the physiological and psychological effects of different emotions, we can leverage their power strategically. For instance, channeling the focus and alertness heightened by fear can be instrumental in overcoming a challenging task, while the surge of energy from anger can fuel unwavering determination.[8]

Consider the intricate dance of the mind when fear takes hold; the amygdala ignites a cascade of adrenaline and cortisol, hormones that prime the body for an instinctual battle or a desperate escape. This intense awareness and concentration can prove crucial when facing daunting challenges, like executing a pivotal presentation or competing in a high-pressure athletic event. By harnessing this response, individuals can elevate their performance in high-stakes situations, transforming fear into a driving force instead of a debilitating one.[9]

In a striking parallel, the onset of anger ignites a rapid escalation in heart rate and blood pressure, unleashing a powerful surge of energy. This intense physiological response can be channeled to ignite an unyielding resolve and relentless perseverance when confronted with challenges. An athlete might harness their fury from a sensed injustice, channeling it into relentless training, thereby elevating their performance to new heights. When harnessed and channeled effectively, this intense emotional force can transform anger into a powerful driver for constructive change and unwavering strength.

But the whispers within Cognitexis raise intriguing questions. Where do these emotions come from? Do they truly begin with chemical reactions in the brain, or is something else at work? Might the echoes of our ancestors or the collective unconscious influence the emotional palette we draw from? A descendant of warriors, perhaps with a quickened capacity for bravery and unwavering determination, his subtle inclinations were the echoes of his forebears.

The potential for manipulation intensifies with this complexity. Malevolent forces can exploit emotional vulnerabilities, twisting perceptions and manipulating situations to evoke specific responses. Imagine a political regime that weaponizes fear, using propaganda and disinformation to control populations. By flooding media channels with images of chaos, they cultivate a constant state of anxiety, prompting people to accept oppressive policies in exchange for a false sense of security. Or consider how anger can be stoked on social media. Algorithms amplify polarizing content, nudging users into echo chambers that fuel outrage. With emotions running high, people may be driven to actions they wouldn't have considered on their own, sometimes even inciting violence for an agenda they don't fully understand.

Discerning the true source of our emotions in such environments becomes paramount. Is the surge of hope you feel from a motivational message a genuine spark of possibility, or is it a cleverly crafted illusion designed to fuel blind obedience to a charismatic leader or a commercial product? The line between authentic emotion and manufactured sentiment can blur, making it vital to examine what stirs our feelings.

By understanding science, acknowledging the whispers of the unseen, and remaining vigilant against manipulation, we can become masters of our own emotional symphony. We can learn to harness the power of all emotions, positive and negative, composing a life rich in purpose, meaning, and the unwavering pursuit of our deepest desires. This is not a solitary performance but a collaborative masterpiece, a testament to the power of our emotions working in concert.

2. The Fading Flame: Where Passion Withers

Cognitexis, that mighty engine within us, feeds not merely upon raw thought and emotional fuel but upon a heady elixir: definiteness of purpose. The burning flame ignites intention and puts direction upon our thoughts. Without this passion, the spark flickers and dwindles. This lack, this aimless drift, is a self-imposed limitation. While one wanders aimlessly without some radical goal, one's thoughts become weak and lose their potential to emerge in reality.

Science offers a roadmap to reignite this flame. The studies on goal setting emphasize the specific use of SMART goals: Specific, Measurable, Achievable, Relevant, and Time-bound.[iii] These kinds

---

iii **SMART** represented as:

of goals give a clear direction and tangible target for our thoughts and activities. Integrate this into your everyday life by identifying a single area where you feel you're drifting. Then, break this down into one clear, actionable goal.

Take, for instance, the desire to have improved health: exactly define what you will do, such as "I will exercise for 30 minutes, five days a week." This framing turns general intention into concrete action, raising drive and the chances of success. Writing down these goals and frequently revisiting them can also serve to remind one of the purposes that drive one forward with energy.

But the embers of passion—where do they ignite? Is it purely a rational process, or do whispers from deeper wells guide us? Sometimes, in the echoes within Cognitexis, the sparks of purpose lie from our past or the collective unconscious. Take some time to reflect on your personal history and what helped you. Something from a childhood fascination or ancestral legacy might hint toward some higher calling. Give adequate time to explore your interests and passions, journaling on some past experiences that seemed most meaningful. By acknowledging these whispers, you will be able to outline some hidden desires that perhaps are waiting to be fanned into a bright flame.

The potential for manipulation intensifies with this vulnerability. Malevolent forces can exploit this lack of purpose, creating seductive distractions and fostering a pervasive sense of

---

- **Specific** goals are well-defined and unambiguous. For example, instead of setting a goal to "get fit," a specific goal would be "run three times a week."
- **Measurable** goals include concrete criteria for tracking progress. For instance, "increase running distance by 0.5 miles every week" provides a way to measure improvement.
- **Achievable** goals are realistic and attainable, considering the individual's current capabilities and constraints. Setting a goal to "run a 5K in two months" might be achievable for someone who already runs regularly.
- **Relevant** goals align with broader life objectives and values. If improving health is a priority, the running goal directly supports this relevance.
- **Time-bound** goals have a clear deadline, creating a sense of urgency and helping to prevent procrastination. "Complete a 5K race by the end of the summer" sets a specific timeframe for achievement.

apathy. Imagine a world where entertainment becomes a meticulously crafted labyrinth designed to keep us tethered to the mundane. Instant gratification becomes a weapon, lulling us into a comfortable numbness, preventing us from forming our own ambitions and wielding the power of Cognitexis. Maintaining a burning passion and a clear vision for the future becomes crucial in this battle for control.

By understanding the science of goal setting, acknowledging the whispers of the unseen, and remaining vigilant against distractions, we can reignite the flame within. We can cultivate a definitive purpose, a guiding light that ignites our thoughts and translates them into meaningful action. This is not a solitary journey but a focused pursuit, a testament to the power of a burning passion within.

THE HIDDEN COMPASS: SUBCONSCIOUS ANCHORS IN COGNITEXIS

ୡ୶ ୡ୶ ୡ୶

In the enigmatic depths of Cognitexis, hidden compasses guide us through the uncharted realms of the subconscious mind. Here, where thoughts whisper and desires burn like ancient flames, we embark on a journey to uncover the anchors that shape our inner landscape. As we navigate through the cultivation of the subconscious garden, the automatic mechanisms of thought, and the transformative power of desire, we confront the shadows and light that dwell within.

This odyssey demands mastery of the harmonious dance between thought and action, urging us to embrace imperfection and practice with unwavering resolve. Along the way, we craft the mental frameworks that lead to success, guided by the hidden architect within. Are you ready to uncover the hidden compass and navigate the labyrinthine depths of your own subconscious? The journey awaits, fraught with peril and promise, as we seek the anchors that define our very being.

First Challenge: Cultivating the Subconscious Garden

These concepts focus on the metaphorical garden of the subconscious mind, emphasizing the cultivation and maintenance of thoughts and curiosity while also addressing the dangers of neglect.

1. Weaving the Tapestry: Cultivating the Subconscious Garden

The human mind is an expansive realm, not a limited stronghold, a deep ocean teeming with enigmas hidden beneath its depths. In the depths of its currents, the subconscious pulsates—a vibrant domain brimming with instinctive reactions, habitual behaviors, entrenched patterns of understanding, and the profound insights gleaned from lived experiences. The notion of thought embedding implies that by nurturing—deliberately sowing seeds in the guise of particular thoughts—this concealed domain can undergo a profound transformation.

With time, these reaffirmations, like seeds nurtured with intention, begin to take root within the subconscious. They evolve from acts of conscious will into set patterns, eventually blooming into the fruits of our inner labors. Yet the process still remains shrouded in mystery. It would almost seem that an unseen principle is at work, some sort of hidden gardener tending the soil, cementing these whispers into fast-set fixtures within the subconscious tapestry.

Science offers a fascinating lens through which to view this unseen gardener. Research on neuroplasticity highlights the brain's remarkable ability to form new connections and strengthen existing ones through repeated experiences. This aligns beautifully with the concept of thought embedding, suggesting that deliberate repetition can solidify specific pathways within the brain. By consistently planting the seeds of our desired behaviors, we cultivate neural pathways that make them easier and more natural to express in our actions.

Whispers in Cognitexis raise other questions, though. Is this a case of pure neural reinforcement, or is something more at play? Might the echoes of our past or the collective unconscious somehow alter the depth with which we embed thoughts? Perhaps those whispers that fall in line with our inherent tendencies or echo from our ancestry will vibrate a little bit more inside the subconscious, easily taking root versus those that do not. Think of a descendant of builders, born to create, for whom affirmations about overcoming and never losing concentration proved particularly fertile ground in his subconscious garden.

This vulnerability intensifies the potential for manipulation. Malevolent forces could exploit this fertile ground, bombarding us with deceptive whispers, seeking to plant the seeds of harmful habits or manipulate our subconscious desires. Imagine a world where social media algorithms become insidious gardeners, subtly planting seeds of insecurity or dissatisfaction, steering our actions for unseen agendas. Guarding the gates of the subconscious, ensuring only the chosen seeds take root, becomes crucial in this ongoing battle for control.

By understanding the science of neuroplasticity, acknowledging the whispers of the unseen, and remaining vigilant against manipulation, we can become skilled cultivators of our own subconscious garden. We can plant the seeds of desired behaviors with intention, nurturing them into flourishing habits that shape our thoughts and actions. This is not a solitary task but a continuous process of growth, a testament to the power of mindful cultivation within the vast landscape of the human mind.

2. Fertile Ground: Cultivating Curiosity's Garden

The depths of the mind are not barren wastelands but vibrant fields teeming with potential; certain regions thrive more abundantly than their counterparts. Certain plots or areas are more open to the seeds of thoughts, much like a gardener's carefully tended spaces. Our individual passions serve as compelling anchors, attracting particular thoughts and increasing their chances of taking root in the rich depths of the subconscious. When topics ignite our curiosity or passion, they create an instinctive openness; consequently, the assimilation of these thoughts can evolve into profound habits.

Science unveils a captivating perspective on this hidden realm within. Investigations into attention and memory reveal a chilling truth: the profound impact of interest and engagement can shape our perceptions and realities. We instinctively draw toward the information that resonates with our desires, and this concentrated focus weaves those thoughts more intricately into the fabric of our minds. This intricately weaves together the notion of personal interests serving as anchors for the deep recesses of subconscious thought embedding. Envision an individual captivated by the reverberating allure of melodies. Their intrigue surrounding music theory or a specific instrument cultivates an environment where these thoughts can fester, possibly evolving into the compulsion of daily practice.

The whispers echoing through Cognitexis undeniably ignite a cascade of compelling questions. What ignites our intrigue regarding specific topics? Do these fascinations stem purely from our current interactions, or might they be reverberations of our past experiences or a collective unconscious that pulls at the strings of our curiosity? Could it be that age-old skills or societal norms weave a web of lingering shadows that echo within individuals, irresistibly drawing their focus?

Envision descendants of renowned mathematicians, irresistibly captivated by the intricate web of puzzles and logic. They discover this as particularly rich terrain in the expansive realm of inquiry, hinting that specific inclinations may be intricately embedded in our cognitive legacy. This exploration ignites deep inquiries into the roots and impacts of our cognitive endeavors.

The opportunity for manipulation looms greater in this rich terrain. External forces may cunningly exploit our personal interests, shrouding manipulative suggestions in the guise of content that resonates with our deepest passions. Envision a reality where digital platforms meticulously tailor information to deepen our entrenched beliefs, yet rather than melodies, they inundate us with an unending flow of unsettling conspiracies. Or educational materials, instead of fostering a genuine passion for science, are infused with insidious propaganda that advances a particular ideology. Scrutinizing the origins of information and shielding oneself from deceit becomes crucial when traversing this rich terrain of the mind.

By understanding the science of attention and memory, acknowledging the whispers of the unseen, and remaining vigilant against manipulation, we can become skilled gardeners of our own curiosity. We can cultivate the seeds of our genuine interests, nurturing them with focused attention and critical thinking. This allows them to blossom into vibrant habits that enrich our lives and shape our subconscious in a way that aligns with our authentic selves. This is not a passive stroll through the garden but a continuous process of exploration and mindful cultivation, a testament to the power of curiosity in shaping the fertile landscape of our minds.

3. The Forsaken Garden: Where Weeds Take Root

The human mind is an active garden; like any garden, it requires constant care. Left untended, it can become fertile ground not for our desired crops but for the insidious growth of destructive thoughts. An idle mind, bombarded by the random stimuli of the environment, is particularly susceptible to this. These stray thoughts, like weeds, can take root and choke out the more desirable mental flora we strive to cultivate.

Science offers a glimpse into this neglected garden. Research on the Default Mode Network (DMN) sheds light on the brain's activity when not engaged in a specific task. The DMN is associated with mind-wandering and self-referential thought. While this can be beneficial for sparking creativity, excessive DMN activity can also lead to rumination and negative thought spirals. Imagine an unchallenged mind, left to its own devices, dwelling on past failures or anxieties about the future. These weeds of negativity, if left unchecked, can quickly take root and crowd out the more positive and productive thoughts we wish to cultivate.

But the whispers within Cognitexis raise a haunting question. Are these destructive thoughts entirely random? Could echoes from our past or the collective unconscious influence the content of these weeds? Perhaps ancestral anxieties or societal fears leave behind faint echoes that resonate more readily within the idle mind. Imagine a descendant of survivors with a heightened awareness of potential threats. Left unchecked, these echoes could manifest as a constant undercurrent of worry or suspicion within the garden of their mind.

In this forsaken garden, the shadows of deceit loom larger, waiting to ensnare the unsuspecting. The neglect of such a garden could spiral into something darker, where cunning narratives twist and turn, preying on unsuspecting minds, sowing seeds of negativity, and fanning the flames of discord within society. Imagine a world where the very algorithms steering social media are designed to cultivate anger and despair, an unending cycle of hostility, and a stark division between "us" and "them." Or orchestrated settings that instill dread and unease, overwhelming individuals with a relentless stream of pessimism that flourishes in the receptive soil of their unoccupied thoughts.

A mentally active lifestyle and a sense of purpose are the keys to the gardening of the mind. In so doing, by stimulating our minds' growth and nurturing direction, we leave less room for weeds to set in. This is not to say that one must lead an existence that does not allow for quiet; rather, it implies an awareness on the part of the individual to ensure that the time spent in quiet indeed nourishes and does not suffocate the states that we want to achieve in our mind.

Knowing the science of the DMN, heeding the whispers of the unseen, and keeping the manipulative tactics at bay make us skilled gardeners of our minds. We can tend more consciously to our thoughts, sprouting seeds of positivity and purpose while uprooting weeds of negativity before they choke out our mental well-being. Rather, it is not a seasonal chore but an unyielding development process stimulant to what the power of mindful attention can do to shape this thriving garden that our thoughts are.

Second Challenge: Subconscious Mechanisms and Desires

These concepts explore the subconscious mind's automatic processes, deep-seated desires, and the internal conflicts that arise from them.

1. The Mind on Autopilot: When Thoughts Take the Wheel

One of the more interesting, probably unsettling aspects of the human psyche is how it can take thoughts repeated long enough and make them automatic behaviors. Though not fully understood, the process acts like a kind of mental autopilot, where these ingrained thought patterns take the wheel of our behaviors. It is as if, through strident thought, a groove is cut within the mind, a well-worn path within the subconscious. This passage turns into a fast lane, funneling certain behaviors into one's subconscious and automatic responses.

Science offers a glimpse into the inner workings of this autopilot. Research on the basal ganglia, a brain region associated with routine behaviors, sheds light on habit formation. As we repeat an action or thought, the basal ganglia become more efficient at carrying it out, allowing it to transition from a conscious choice to an automatic response. Imagine a morning routine–setting the alarm, making coffee, checking your phone. Once requiring conscious thought, these actions become ingrained in the basal ganglia, allowing you to function on autopilot while your mind wakes up.

But the whispers within Cognitexis raise intriguing questions. What determines how deeply a thought carves its path within the subconscious? Is some sort of thought inherently "stickier" than others, or perhaps echoes from the past or racial unconsciousness create this effect? Perhaps ancestral habits or social norms leave behind faint whispers that vibrate more readily with certain thought patterns. Now imagine the child of a couple of marathon runners, practically born to run, and how ideas of physical activity could very well cut deeper paths into that subconscious than they would into the mind of someone not so liberated.

This vulnerability intensifies the potential for manipulation. External forces could exploit this process, bombarding our minds with repetitive suggestions designed to create harmful or controlling habits. Imagine a world where social media algorithms are weaponized to embed addictive behaviors, constantly reminding you to check your phone or buy the latest product. Once relegated to the realm of conspiracy theories, subliminal messaging could become a tool to steer our subconscious toward specific actions. Understanding how our minds form autonomous behaviors becomes paramount in safeguarding our mental autonomy.

Understanding science, listening to the whispers of the unseen, and then keeping watch against the manipulative are how we become aware of the autopilot tendencies of our minds. We can learn to be more mindful about which thoughts deepen the most grooved paths and consequently shape our behavior with deliberateness instead of by default. This is not a passive voyage but an active traversal of the inner landscape, one that itself constitutes evidence of the power of conscious choice in peremptorily sculpting the autopilot of our minds.

2. The Fuel of Desire: Kindling the Flame of Subconscious Absorption

Motives and burning desires act as the potent fuel that propels thoughts into the fertile ground of the subconscious. Fueled by a strong emotional charge, a well-defined goal creates the ideal conditions for subconscious absorption. These desires act as a catalyst, accelerating the process by which repeated thoughts take root and transform into ingrained habits.

The realm of science unveils a captivating insight into this blazing crucible. Exploration into dopamine, a neurotransmitter intricately tied to the concepts of reward and motivation, unveils profound insights into this intricate process. In moments when we yield to the pull of our deepest desires, a surge of dopamine courses through us, illuminating the intricate dance between our motivations and the very essence of our being. The relentless waves of dopamine serve to solidify the behavior, weaving it into the fabric of routine until it emerges as an instinctual part of one's existence. This resonates with the notion that profound yearnings can inscribe thoughts deep within the recesses of the subconscious mind. It evolves into an endless loop: the deeper the longing, the more entrenched the corresponding thoughts become.

Imagine an individual driven by an intense yearning to unlock the intricacies of a new language. Driven by the exhilarating exercise of dialogue and the profound bonds it forges, this dynamic interplay fuels a relentless pursuit of mastery in vocabulary and the intricacies of grammar. As time unfolds, these practices evolve into deeply rooted habits shaped by the compelling influence of dopamine's reinforcement.

But the whispers within Cognitexis raise a captivating question. Where do these powerful desires originate? Are they merely the products of our conscious minds, or do echoes from our past or the collective unconscious influence the birth of these burning desires? Perhaps ancestral dreams or societal expectations vibrate inside us, shaping the motive that drives our thoughts and behaviors. Imagine a member of a family of explorers with an innate curiosity about adventure subtly magnified by the echoes of his or her globe-circling ancestors. This intrinsic tug, initiated and developed in life by whispers from beyond the grave, may lighten an overwhelming compulsion to explore the unknown.

The potential for manipulation intensifies with this vulnerability. External forces might manipulate the process by bombarding our minds with manipulative suggestions aimed at cultivating certain desires. Imagine a world in which advertising preys on your insecurities, creating an unrelenting pursuit of the latest trends- or a world in which political propaganda fuels divisive desires for power. The battle of the subconscious requires discernment in how to differentiate genuine desires from manipulated ones. We must understand how to distinguish the embers of our genuine passion from the manufactured flames of manipulation.

Knowing the science of dopamine and reward, giving a head to the whispers of the unseen, and watching out for manipulation here, one can consciously master the art of kindling the flames of subconscious absorption. We can deliberately feed our minds with robust desires, for example, those that have been born in our most intimate longings and true aims. These desires will catalyze the rocket of thoughts and actions and help create a life enriched with profound habits and an eternal pursuit of the authentic self. It is not merely an act of reaction; it is one continuous process of self-realization and an empowered act-testimony of desires shaping up in the subconscious mind.

3. The Colosseum of the Mind: Gladiatorial Thoughts in Mortal Combat

The human mind is not a tranquil meadow but a dynamic Colosseum where thoughts clash in a relentless struggle for dominance. In this gladiatorial arena, only the most resilient ideas emerge victorious. Through a process akin to natural selection, repetitive thoughts, fueled by potent emotions and backed by consistent action, carve deeper grooves within the subconscious. These "thought warriors" push aside their weaker rivals, those flimsy notions lacking the conviction of consistent reinforcement. This highlights the crucial role of self-discipline—the conscious effort to cultivate the thoughts we desire and uproot those that hinder us.

Science provides a strategic blueprint for navigating this psychological warfare. Exploring the depths of Cognitive Behavioral Therapy (CBT) unveils the intricate web connecting thoughts, emotions, and actions, revealing the complex interplay that shapes our experiences. The premise of CBT suggests that our feelings can shift through carefully adjusting our thoughts and behaviors. Through unwavering self-discipline, the ability to choose transforms specific thoughts into a relentless cycle, crafting a formidable shield that positions them at the heart of the mental arena. Imagine this: shattering the paralyzing dread of speaking in front of others and transforming it into a powerful conviction of "I have valuable insights to offer," continuously honed and solidified through deliberate practice: becoming a member of a public speaking group. The gradual ascent of a powerful notion begins to overshadow the paralyzing grip of fear, establishing a new hierarchy within the mind.

But the whispers within Cognitexis raise a fascinating question: are these "fittest ideas" entirely self-made champions, or might they echo from our past, for example, or the collective unconscious influence which thoughts do rise to prominence? Maybe ancestral survival instincts or societal norms leave some ghostly whisper that finds resonance so much easier with certain thought patterns. The descendants of warriors already had an inborn predisposition to courageous, enduring thoughts; hence, for them, the very idea managed more easily to cut through all obstacles to dominance in their mental Colosseum.

The likelihood of manipulation escalates within this competitive environment. External influences can exploit competition, inundating our minds with deceptive or manipulative thoughts that often overshadow our own reasoning. What if education itself was employed as weaponry to instill a particular ideology? Alternatively, what if propaganda had been utilized as a device to promote a specific set of "fittest ideas" within a population? Algorithms, originally designed to foster connections among individuals, have the potential to be manipulated, embedding addictive thought patterns into our consciousness as we find ourselves ensnared in seemingly infinite cycles of negativity and envy. In this contest for dominance within the realm of cognitive engagement, the cultivation of robust self-discipline and the enhancement of critical thinking skills are not only advantageous but essential.

Knowing the science of CBT, giving heed to the whispers of the unseen, and keeping vigil against manipulation, we can be great trainers in this mental coliseum. We can breed the thoughts we want and give them discipline and action to make them champions in our minds. This is not a single fight but an ongoing self-mastery process, in essence, testimony to the strength of conscious choice that shapes our thoughts' gladiatorial landscape.

Third Challenge: Transformation and Action

These concepts delve into the transformative power of thoughts and the journey from ideation to action, highlighting the importance of practice and the acceptance of imperfection.

1. The Alchemist's Forge: From Thought to Tangible Reality

The shift from mere thought to ingrained behavior is far more than a simple mental maneuver. It demands the intense forge of experience to take shape. Even the most intricately designed thought, forged in the depths of the mind's workshop, remains elusive and unanchored, unable to transform into a dependable habit until it is manifested in the tangible realm. Orderly thought, devoid of the spark of urgency, lingers as an elusive notion. Only through the transformation of thought into deliberate action can we create a habit that endures, lurking in the shadows of our psyche, waiting to be unleashed.

Science offers a guiding principle in this alchemical process. In this intricate dance of transformation, a singular principle emerges from the shadows, illuminating the path forward. Exploring the depths of neuroplasticity reveals a chilling truth: the power of action is crucial in fortifying the fabric of our neural connections. As we engage in physical actions aligned with particular thoughts, the connections within our minds deepen, weaving a more intricate web of understanding and influence. Picture the desire to weave a thread of daily meditation into the fabric of your life. Through the deliberate act of sitting down and engaging in daily meditation, we reinforce the intricate neural connections tied to concentration and awareness, deepening our understanding of the mind's labyrinth. As the days unfold, this relentless pursuit transforms into a seamless ritual, embedding meditation deep within the psyche.

But the whispers within Cognitexis, the subconscious depths of our minds, raise a captivating question. What compels us to take action? Is it purely a rational decision driven by logic, or are there deeper forces at play? Could echoes from our past or the collective unconscious influence our urge to act? Perhaps ancestral patterns or societal expectations nudge us towards specific actions that reinforce certain thought patterns. Imagine a descendant of builders with a natural inclination towards taking action and creating something tangible. These echoes might manifest as a constant hum of motivation, urging them to take their thoughts and transform them into the physical world through acts of creation.

The whispers lingering in the depths of Cognitexis reveal the hidden forces, often unrecognized, that manipulate our deepest desires and drive our motivations. They could encompass deep-seated convictions, haunting emotions, vivid memories, or even the faintest signals from our surroundings. These whispers can subtly steer us toward specific actions, lurking in the shadows of our consciousness, their influence felt yet unrecognized. A fear of failure can creep in, planting insidious doubts that hold us back from embracing risks and chasing our ambitions. Conversely, an intense drive for purpose or connection can propel us into action, urging us to pursue something profoundly significant.

The potential for manipulation escalates in this intricate interplay of mind and movement. External forces may exploit this connection, subtly orchestrating circumstances to dissuade constructive choices or steer us toward destructive paths. Envision a reality where the very fabric of societal expectations is twisted into a tool of control, stifling the spark of creativity and paralyzing the will to act on one's own visions. Or a digital realm designed to ensnare individuals in a relentless loop of activity, stripped of any significant purpose, where participants are constantly engaged yet never truly construct anything of substance in reality. Unraveling the hidden motives that drive our choices is essential in this intricate interplay of mind and action. We must unravel the intricate web of our true desires, separating them from the insidious whispers of outside influences.

By understanding the science of neuroplasticity, acknowledging the whispers of the unseen, and remaining vigilant against manipulation, we can become skilled alchemists of our own habits. We can take our carefully crafted thoughts and put them to the test in the fires of action. Through consistent action, we can transform these thoughts into lasting habits that shape our reality and solidify the path toward a meaningful life. This is not a solitary experiment but a continuous process of refinement, a testament to the power of action in transforming the ephemeral into the tangible.

2. The Alchemical Formula: Theory and Praxis - Unraveling the Threads of Potential

In truth, the path to uncovering one's potential is not a straightforward, smooth journey but rather a complex weave of theory and practice, fraught with twists and turns. Just as the alchemist delves into the depths of ancient texts and harnesses the searing heat of the furnace, we, too, must intertwine knowledge with action, navigating the shadows of understanding to uncover hidden truths. Deep understanding serves as the underlying framework—the intricate design for growth. Yet, only through the shadows of practical experience—the fervent application of knowledge in the realm of reality—can we genuinely transform potential into a chillingly realized ability.

Imagine musicians armed with the complex framework of music theory—this knowledge serves as their very foundation, a silent force guiding their every note. However, it is only through unwavering dedication and the careful embodiment of that theory that they can transform simple notes on a page into a glorious symphony.

Science offers a guiding light in this tapestry-weaving process. Investigations into the skill acquisition process reveal an unwinding truth: the necessity of intentional and focused effort. Merely holding knowledge resembles a forgotten tome gathering dust on a shelf—it teems with possibilities yet lies dormant, waiting for the right moment to awaken. We are compelled to immerse ourselves in relentless, concentrated practice, the deliberate enactment of our understanding, to sharpen our abilities and unlock our true potential. Envision an artist on the brink of discovery, deeply aware of the intricate dance of colors yet consumed by the relentless pursuit of perfecting their craft, immersed in a complex network of brushstrokes and yet-to-be-explored techniques. This meticulous endeavor enables them to transform abstract concepts into an overtaking creation with vivid shades and intricate details.

Yet, the whispers within Cognitexis beguile with one tantalizing question: how do we bridge this chasm from theory to effective action? Is it only a matter of conscious exertion, or could echoes of our past or the mass unconscious influence such processes? Perhaps ancestral knowledge or the practices of society leave behind faint echoes guiding us in applying our knowledge in practical ways. Think of a descendant born of inventors with the innate drive to experiment and tinker. The echoes can show up as an innate curiosity about how things work, urging them to read about inventions and build them to understand through praxis.

The possibility of deceit looms in this unsettling chasm between theory and practice. External forces might manipulate this vulnerability, crafting a reality where knowledge is tightly controlled, and practical experience is rendered insignificant. Envision a reality where the very fabric of education is woven with the threads of mindless repetition, producing individuals steeped in abstract theories yet utterly devoid of the ability to navigate the complexities of the real world. Or social media echo chambers that deepen delusions, ensnaring users in a relentless barrage of falsehoods that disguise themselves as reality. Unraveling the truth from a web of deception and relentlessly pursuing chances to utilize our insights becomes essential in mastering the enigmatic formula for unlocking our true potential.

However, it's important to note that external influences are not always negative. Positive societal influences, such as supportive communities or mentors, can also play a significant role in fostering the development of skills and knowledge. While manipulation and misinformation pose challenges, it's essential to recognize the potential for positive external forces to enhance our growth and development.

Moreover, it's important to acknowledge that while external forces can influence our ability to apply knowledge, humans also possess agency and can actively resist manipulation. By cultivating critical thinking skills, being aware of biases, and seeking diverse perspectives, we can counter the effects of manipulation and make informed decisions about how to apply our knowledge. Building a strong support network can provide encouragement and guidance, helping us overcome obstacles and stay focused on our goals.

By understanding the science of skill acquisition, acknowledging the whispers of the unseen, and remaining vigilant against manipulation while considering the influence of internal motivations and critical thinking, we can become skilled weavers of our own potential. We can gather the threads of sound theory and, with focused practice, weave them into the vibrant tapestry of our realized abilities. This is not a passive process but a continuous act of creation, a testament to the power of theory and praxis in transforming potential into the masterpiece of ourselves.

3. The Spark of Action: Embracing the Imperfect Start

The proverb, "A journey of a thousand miles begins with a single step," resonates with deep meaning and invites contemplation. It underscores the profound significance of that initial stride—the instant of decision, the spark of purpose that stands as the most powerful precursor to success. Action stands as the vital bridge connecting the intricate pathways of the mind to the tangible reality we experience, manifesting our deepest desires into forms we can perceive. While meticulous planning certainly has its merits, there is an undeniable power in taking that first step, even when shrouded in ambiguity. Arthur Ashe profoundly remarked, *"Begin from your current position."* Utilize the resources at your disposal. Engage in the actions within your reach. This quote underscores the necessity of initiating action with the resources available to you, highlighting the notion that remarkable accomplishments frequently emerge from beginnings that are far from perfect. Furthermore, individuals who accomplish remarkable feats frequently embark on their journey even when the full array of resources remains just out of reach. As the saying goes, *"Those who accomplish anything of true importance frequently embark on their journey before all essential resources are within reach."*

Science unveils the shadows lurking in the corners of this journey of awakening. Exploring the depths of self-efficacy reveals a compelling revelation about the nature of action-taking. According to Albert Bandura's theory of self-efficacy, our belief in our ability to achieve goals significantly influences our motivation and behavior (Bandura, 1997). Through the pursuit of a goal, the experiences we encounter within our minds amplify our belief in our abilities, driving us deeper into the labyrinth of motivation.

Imagine a scenario where an individual harbors the ambition of crafting a novel. Writing that initial line and embarking on that first journey holds a satisfaction all its own. This initial success compels them to write the next line and then the one that follows, quickening the pace as it dismantles larger challenges.

Research supports this idea, showing that individuals with high self-efficacy are more likely to embrace challenges and persist in facing obstacles (Schunk & DiBenedetto, 2020). This cycle of setting goals, achieving them, and building confidence further reinforces the drive to pursue even more significant tasks.[10]

Yet, the murmurs echoing through Cognitexis pose a chilling inquiry. What drives one to take that initial leap into the unknown? Is it solely a logical choice, or do remnants of our past or echoes from the collective psyche exert their influence to drive us forward? Perhaps it is the primal instincts of our ancestors to venture forth or the societal emphasis on action rather than reflection that compels us to take that initial step into the unknown. Envision a lineage born from trailblazers, inherently driven to take risks and embark on uncharted ventures. Whispers linger, an incessant hum that gnaws at their thoughts, urging them toward action, perhaps in defiance of their own skeptical minds.

The opportunity for manipulation looms larger at this pivotal moment. For instance, the dread of inadequacy can be twisted by external forces, whispering that we must remain paralyzed unless we are fully equipped to confront a scenario that may never even come to pass. Envision a reality where the pervasive influence of social media cultivates an atmosphere of relentless comparison and unattainable perfection, stifling the heart's ability to embrace courage, as it constantly falls short of the distorted ideals meticulously curated by others. Or educational systems that discourage experimentation and risk, instilling a paralyzing fear of failure that can immobilize us before we even begin. Unraveling the layers of deception and mustering the bravery to initiate the journey are crucial elements in this path to success.

Delving into the depths of self-efficacy, listening to the subtle hints of the hidden, and shielding oneself from deceit create a path to profound mastery. We will cultivate the audacity to accept an imperfect beginning, realizing that the most crucial move is merely to take that first step. It is not a leap but a relentless progression, a haunting reminder of actions' impact on aspirations.

Fourth Challenge: Harmonizing Thought and Action

These concepts focus on integrating and harmonizing thoughts and actions, creating a cohesive and balanced approach to mastery and success.

1. The Captain and the Crew: A Harmonious Dance of Thought and Action

The path to self-discovery is fraught with shadows and unexpected encounters. While structured cognition, the ship's captain, offers the map and compass, it is action, the relentless crew, that drives us into the vast expanse of possibility. These two forces—deliberate thought and purposeful action—intertwine in a captivating dance, driving the evolution of the self. Intricate patterns of behavior, the very foundation of a life steeped in meaning, emerge from this inextricable bond.

Science unveils a captivating glimpse into this dynamic duo. Exploring the depths of self-efficacy reveals a haunting connection between the mind's whispers and the choices we make. The interplay between our thoughts and actions weaves a complex web of influence, shaping our reality in profound and often unsettling ways. Acting on a particular thought reinforces the neural connections tied to that thought, increasing the chances of its recurrence in the future. Envision the desire to master the art of public speaking, a journey fraught with inner turmoil and self-doubt. By stepping into the realm of a public speaking club and engaging in consistent practice, you weave a complex web of neural connections that bolster your confidence and enhance your communication skills. This, in turn, deepens your conviction in your capacity to address an audience, weaving a web of confidence that compels you to take the next step. This relentless loop of contemplation and execution fortifies both confidence in oneself and the pursuit of the intended behavior.

Yet, the hidden depths of the mind, often described as the whispers within Cognitexis, provoke a haunting inquiry. What ignites the first spark of action? Is it merely a deliberate choice, or might hidden forces, like previous encounters or societal pressures, be at play? Perhaps deep-seated instincts for discovery or cultural pressures that prioritize action over reflection compel us to make that initial move. Envision a scion of pioneers driven by an instinctive urge for boldness and movement. The unseen forces at play may reveal themselves as an incessant whisper of unease, compelling them to transform their inner musings into tangible actions.

The potential of manipulation intensifies within this intricate interplay of thoughts and actions. Outside influences may manipulate the gap that exists between thought and action, planting insidious doubts or fears that immobilize our capacity to act.

Envision a reality where the very frameworks of education are crafted to stifle ambition while social media platforms become tools of manipulation, inundating us with insidious messages that erode our sense of agency. Holding onto a sharp focus, the captain's role becomes pivotal while instilling the bravery to take action in the crew, which transforms into an essential element in maneuvering through this ever-shifting landscape.

By delving into the intricacies of self-efficacy, recognizing the hidden forces that mold our yearnings, and staying alert to the subtle art of manipulation, we can seize control of our own destinies with calculated precision. We can harness the power of organized thinking to navigate our path, summon the bravery to act, and develop a robust set of habits that drive us toward a life rich with meaning. This is not merely a fleeting journey; it is an ongoing investigation, a chilling reminder of the intricate dance between thought and action, each step revealing deeper layers of intrigue and consequence.

2. The Harmonious Tapestry of Mastery: A Strange Overture of Mind, Body, and Unified Essence

The journey of skill development unfolds like a haunting narrative, where the mind and body intertwine in a delicate dance, revealing hidden depths and unexpected twists at every turn. At its core lies the foundation of meticulously crafted habits embedded deep within the subconscious, echoing like the notes of a consuming melody played by a masterful hand. The mind, a master conductor, orchestrates every movement with calculated precision, weaving a tapestry of deliberate thought. The body, a masterful instrument, reacts with instinctive precision and, through an intense familiarity, offers insights that sharpen the mind's composition. This complex web of thought, action, and response weaves a narrative that sharpens our abilities with an unsettling clarity.

Moreover, the principle of intellectual synergy hints at a compelling connection that emerges when we abandon the notion of solitary endeavors. Through the intricate dance of collaboration, where each mind intertwines with another, we can tap into a powerful force that propels us toward achievements that eclipse the capabilities of any solitary effort. Picture a group of virtuosos, each one a genius in their own right, but it is in the moments of spontaneous creation and shared energy that their true artistry emerges, weaving a tapestry of sound that eclipses any single performance.

Science unveils the shadows of this complex interplay. Exploration into motor learning reveals the unsettling intricacies of the feedback loops that intertwine the mind and body. As we engage in any particular skill, our minds absorb the subtle cues from our bodies, allowing us to sharpen our actions and elevate our capabilities. Envision a dancer, her every movement a calculated response to the subtle whispers of her muscles and the shifting shadows around her. The essence of cultivating adept habits lies within an unending cycle of guidance, action, and meticulous improvement.

Yet, an intriguing question emerges from the murmurs within Cognitexis. What lies behind the curtain of possibility? Is this merely the result of deliberate thought, or might the reverberations of our history or the shared psyche influence this intricate performance? Perhaps the haunting remnants of ancestral movements or the relentless grip of societal continuity cast subtle shadows, steering the intricate dance of physical coordination. Envision a lineage steeped in athletic prowess, where the very essence of balance and agility courses through their veins, shaping their every move with uncanny precision. That could emerge as an innate rhythm and physical expressiveness, rendering many intricate movements instinctual in certain forms of dance.

The possibility for manipulation looms large in this elaborate spectacle: the web of connections can be exploited by outside influences that disrupt the seamless exchange between thought and action or fracture vital social ties. Imagine a reality where individuals are lured into isolation by the allure of virtual realms, their abilities in the tangible world fading away. Picture a landscape where social media algorithms are twisted into tools of manipulation, sowing discord and stifling any chance of unity. In this intricate web of skill development, the foremost concerns shift to the fragile bond with the physical realm and the elusive nature of social ties. Just as every orchestra requires a conductor to maintain its delicate harmony, we must remain vigilant of the external forces that threaten to disrupt the fragile equilibrium between our mind, body, and social ties.

When one possesses knowledge of the intricacies of motor learning, attunes to the subtle whispers of the unseen, and remains vigilant against the forces of manipulation, the potential arises to cultivate skills that empower us to master our own orchestrators. We will embed within ourselves the essential habits, sharpen our movements through intentional practice, and harness collaboration to achieve a level of skill and artistry that transcends the abilities of any one person. It's not merely an individual act but a haunting journey through existence, a testament to the intricate dance between mind and body, where the interplay of unity weaves the chilling melody of our true potential.

Fifth Challenge: Navigating and Crafting Success

These concepts emphasize the principles of navigation and discipline and the mental frameworks necessary to achieve success.

1. The Captain's Compass: Navigating with Unwavering Resolve and Discipline

Self-discipline serves as the foundation from which the ship of our lives charts its course. One of its most vital elements is the capacity to make swift and resolute choices. This transcends mere impulsive recklessness; it embodies a calculated and sharp mental acuity that keeps one on the edge of uncertainty. It's the capacity to analyze circumstances, evaluate possibilities, and decisively select a path forward, all while maintaining a sharp focus and intent. Indecision, on the other hand, can leave us floundering, the wind of opportunity whisking past our sails as we remain anchored by doubt.

Science casts a shadowy glow on the treacherous paths of decision-making. Exploring the depths of decision-making reveals the critical role of cognitive flexibility as one navigates the treacherous waters of analysis paralysis. In the shadows of decision-making, the ability to weigh options becomes a double-edged sword. Yet, those with unwavering self-discipline navigate the labyrinth of information with precision, arriving at both calculated and timely choices. Envision a captain facing an unexpected tempest, the skies darkening as chaos unfolds around him. They move forward, avoiding the trap of overthinking every potential outcome. Their experience and discipline enable them to dissect the situation, arrive at a lucid conclusion, and execute a bold maneuver to navigate through the chaos.

Yet, the whispers echoing through Cognitexis pose an intriguing dilemma. What is the source of this unwavering determination? Is it merely the result of deliberate thought, or might shadows from our history or the shared psyche shape the way we make choices? Perhaps the shadows of ancestral experiences or the weight of societal norms linger, subtly influencing our willingness to embrace risk and our strategies for confronting challenges. Envision a lineage steeped in conflict, where instinctual boldness intertwines with a penchant for meticulous strategy. These reverberations could emerge as a relentless drive and an unsettling ease in confronting difficult decisions, even amidst the shadows of doubt.

At this pivotal moment, the art of manipulation can amplify our dread of inadequacy. External forces can loom over us, stifling our resolve and leaving us in a perpetual state of waiting for a readiness that may remain forever elusive. Envision a reality where the very fabric of social media is woven with threads of anxiety, ensnaring us in a web of uncertainty as we grapple with the relentless tide of ever-changing trends. Or educational systems that overlook the importance of critical thinking rendering us susceptible to the machinations of those who wish to dictate our decisions. Establishing a robust base in critical thinking and nurturing the bravery to make decisive choices becomes crucial for maneuvering through the intricate web of life's dilemmas.

By delving into the intricacies of choice, recognizing the subtle nudges from the shadows, and staying alert to the forces that seek to sway us, we can navigate the treacherous waters of our own destinies with skill and precision. We can sharpen our minds, make decisive choices in the face of uncertainty, and traverse the tumultuous waters of existence with relentless determination. This is not merely a solitary voyage; it unfolds as an intricate journey of growth, revealing the profound influence of a disciplined mind in guiding us through the shadows toward our chosen destinations.

2. The Hidden Architect: Crafting the Mental Framework for Success

Success is a shadowy figure lurking in the corners of ambition, not merely a trophy earned through knowledge or chance. The mind's attitude shapes the very essence of our accomplishments, lurking in the shadows of our thoughts. The intricate dance of our thoughts, meticulously organized and channeled towards deliberate action, serves as the unseen catalyst for this triumph. Just as a dam controls water flow to generate energy, structured cognition manipulates our thoughts and knowledge, turning them into tangible actions that drive us onward.

Science unveils a crucial understanding of this intricate mental framework. The exploration of a growth mindset, as described by Carol Dweck, reveals a deep-seated conviction in the potential for transformation and the relentless pursuit of self-betterment (Dweck, 2006). Those with this mindset perceive challenges as gateways to development rather than barriers to progress. Their unwavering conviction drives them to navigate through challenges, pushing them ever closer to triumph.

Imagine a student, driven by ambition, confronting a series of perplexing math challenges that seem to lurk in the shadows, waiting to unravel their mind. They remain undeterred by the initial difficulties of mastery. Their belief in their capacity to learn ignites a relentless pursuit of assistance and a willingness to explore uncharted methods. Through this process, they unravel intricate ideas and advance in their understanding.

Research supports that individuals with a growth mindset are more likely to embrace challenges and persist despite setbacks, seeing effort as a path to mastery (Dweck, 2016). This mindset promotes resilience and a love of learning, essential components in the journey toward achievement.[11]

Yet the whispers within Cognitexis provoke an unsettling inquiry: from whence does it originate? Are we merely products of our upbringing and experiences, or do the whispers of our past and the collective unconscious shape our most profound convictions about success? Perhaps those ancestral values of perseverance or social norms of achievement that have outlived their discursive welcome leave haunting echoes that subtly manipulate our perceptions of challenges and aspirations. Envision a scion of architects, inherently destined to grapple and persevere. These echoes can linger in a determined mind, where the conviction that achievement arises from relentless effort takes hold.

This foundation creates an opportunity for manipulation. Every limiting belief we hold or that others seek to instill in us is surrounded by a relentless barrage of doubt, accompanied by images of success that feel just out of reach, taunting us with their unattainability. By its very nature, social media cultivates an environment steeped in comparison and envy—only the polished highlights are showcased, intensifying the gnawing sense of inadequacy that lurks beneath the surface. Or educational systems that foster rivalry instead of collaboration, setting students against one another and breeding an atmosphere of cynicism and despair.

Grasping the intricacies of the growth mindset, uncovering hidden forces at play, and shielding ourselves from manipulation empowers us to craft our own destinies. Through the careful nurturing of our faith in personal growth and the relentless pursuit of intrinsic motivation, we find ourselves constantly evolving, meticulously crafting our mindset and defining our successes.

Allow me to reiterate that cultivating a growth mindset and fostering intrinsic motivation are intertwined processes in building a psychological foundation for lasting success. Intrinsic motivation is the driving force that pushes us forward to explore, evolve, and achieve, as it offers a sense of personal satisfaction—not merely in response to the judgments of others.

THE HIDDEN HARMONY: THE COLLECTIVE COGNITEXIS UNVEILED

ໄ♣ ໄ♣ ໄ♣

I n the hidden depths of Cognitexis, where thoughts intertwine, and minds converge, lies a profound and elusive harmony. This journey through Collective Cognitexis unveils the intricate symphony of shared purpose, the moral compass that guides our collective conscience, and the delicate dance of mentorship and influence. As we navigate these realms, we uncover the hidden melodies that bind us together, the echoes of empathy that resonate within us, and the challenges that threaten to shatter our unity.

This exploration demands a keen understanding of the forces that shape our collective thought, the perils of negative associations, and the unwavering resolve to safeguard our mental wellspring. Are you prepared to unveil the hidden harmony of the Collective Cognitexis and confront the symphony of purpose and peril that defines our shared existence? The journey awaits a symphony of minds poised on the brink of unity and discord.

First Manifestation: Harmony and Unity of Minds

These concepts explore the harmonious integration of individual minds into a cohesive whole, emphasizing unity, shared purpose, and the delicate balance between harmony and discord.

1. The Unseen Melody: The Contagious Mind in Harmony and Discord

Our thoughts do not emerge from a solitary, isolated existence. They echo through a tangled web of human interactions, influencing and being influenced by the shadows of those nearby. The mind, a labyrinth of thoughts, can transmit ideas from one individual to another, particularly to those with whom we share intimate bonds. This creates a haunting interplay within the psyche, where the thoughts and emotions of others intertwine with the very essence of our being.

Science unveils the intricate mechanisms of this unseen orchestra. Exploring the depths of mirror neurons unveils a chilling glimpse into the underlying mechanisms of our conversation. Mirror neurons ignite not only when we engage in an action ourselves but also when we observe another carry out that same action. It has been proposed that our thoughts and emotions may operate in a similar manner: we seem to absorb the fervor of those around us, particularly after engaging with someone who is passionately invested in an intriguing endeavor.

Whispers in Cognitexis! Yet the whispers echoing through Cognitexis pose an intriguing dilemma. Is thought contagion merely a passive phenomenon? Do we merely absorb the thoughts of others as if we were sponges soaking in their secrets? Or are there more sinister influences at play? Could Cognitexis, serving as a potential vault of shared subconscious thought, sway our vulnerability to specific concepts or create an echo chamber that intensifies certain forms of contagion? Perhaps the echoes of ancestral experiences or the weight of societal values linger, creating an unsettling openness to those ideas. Imagine a progeny of creators, likely endowed with an instinctive affinity for artistic pursuits. Such echoes may emerge as a heightened susceptibility to infectious creativity, where the spark of another artist's ideas ignites a torrent of thoughts within his mind.

The possibility of manipulation deepens in this intricate dance of minds. Envision a reality where unseen forces orchestrate the flow of information, crafting a narrative that subtly infiltrates minds, steering collective beliefs and desires with chilling precision. Or perhaps political campaigns manipulate the shadows of the mind, weaving subtle threads of influence that guide voters toward a chosen candidate, all while remaining blissfully unaware of the unseen forces at play. Grasping the intricate dynamics of thought contagion is essential for maneuvering through this labyrinthine mental landscape.

The Antidote! By delving into the intricacies of mirror neurons, heeding the subtle hints of the invisible, and staying alert to the forces of manipulation, we can master the orchestration of our own thoughts. We have the power to select the psychological landscapes we engage in, forging bonds with those who elevate our spirits while being vigilant against the shadows of negativity and deceit that lurk around us. This is not merely an individual endeavor but an intricate dance within the vast symphony of human consciousness, a chilling reminder of how the mind can ensnare and manipulate, crafting both personal and shared experiences in unexpected ways.

2. The Orchestra in Action: A Symphony of Shared Purpose

The flow of ideas among individuals evolves beyond simple, passive exchange. It's an enthralling interplay, a delicate balance of intertwining thoughts. When individuals converge with a common goal, an intriguing dynamic unfolds—intellectual synergy. Like a carefully orchestrated symphony, the thoughts and ideas of each individual intertwine and intensify, creating a collective entity that transcends the mere sum of its components.

To unravel this intricate connection, science offers an intriguing refrain. Research into social learning reveals an unwinding truth: the mechanisms of observation and imitation play a crucial role in our understanding. We absorb knowledge not merely through solitary study but by watching and interacting with those around us, weaving a complex web of influence and insight. Intellectual synergy delves deeper, suggesting a more intricate form of learning where the alignment of thoughts intensifies the exchange and refinement of ideas, ultimately fostering the dissemination of knowledge and innovation. Imagine a gathering where each thought from one person intertwines with another, crafting a hauntingly beautiful tapestry of innovation that transcends the capabilities of any single mind.

Whispers in Cognitexis! Yet the whispers within Cognitexis provoke an intriguing inquiry. What enigmatic forces allow this unsettling harmony to emerge? Is it merely a matter of shared goals or similar histories, or is there a deeper, more enigmatic force at work? Could it be that Cognitexis operates as a resonant chamber, amplifying the aligned thoughts of various minds, creating an unsettling harmony that blurs the lines of individual perception? Is it possible for ancestral wisdom or societal norms to forge a layer of collective experience where true alignment can emerge? Envision a clandestine assembly of scientists, each hailing from distant corners of the globe, bound together by an insatiable curiosity that drives them to unravel the universe's deepest mysteries. In that realm of established knowledge, their revelations intertwine and dissolve into one another, producing outcomes that no individual mind could ever attain. In the shadows of scientific advancement, the Human Genome Project and the vaccines against COVID-19 emerge as pivotal forces, propelling humanity into a future that once lingered only in the realm of dreams for those who came before us.

Yet, within this meticulously crafted performance lies a perilous opportunity for manipulation. There exists a deep, primal urge to connect and belong, one that can be twisted by outside influences, leading to the spread of falsehoods and deceptive narratives masquerading as common beliefs. Reflect on the intricate web of social media algorithms, meticulously crafted to ensnare users in a prolonged engagement; this often leads to the formation of echo chambers, where the content served mirrors existing beliefs rather than challenging them with a spectrum of viewpoints. Consider an individual who engages with articles endorsing a specific conspiracy theory; over time, their feed becomes a labyrinth of increasingly similar narratives, drawing them deeper into a web of intrigue and suspicion. The relentless affirmation of one's convictions warps one's perception of the world around them. As time passes, this feedback can twist minds, transforming what could have been a source of intellectual synergy into a sharp instrument of division, driving people apart rather than bringing them together.

- In the shadows of society, these echo chambers reside, subtly shaping perceptions and guiding choices in ways that often go unnoticed. The COVID-19 pandemic stands as a stark reminder of the insidious ways in which algorithms and social media can distort reality, manipulating perceptions and steering public sentiment into uncharted territories. The individuals found themselves in disjointed enclaves, where only select stories were fervently upheld, deepening divides in perspectives and obliterating any trace of shared comprehension. Unity should arise from a tapestry of perspectives, but instead, it lurks in discord, orchestrated by those intent on bending the story to their will.

*   ***The manipulation of collective thought can also infiltrate educational systems,*** twisting perceptions and beliefs in subtle, insidious ways. When the demand is for uniformity rather than thoughtful analysis, the vibrant interplay of ideas will be stifled, leaving a chilling silence in its wake. Historical instances of collective delusion expose the volatile nature of such an atmosphere. A haunting example is the Bay of Pigs Invasion in 1961, where, despite clear signs of a flawed plan, President Kennedy's advisors chose silence, unwilling to shatter the illusion of consensus that cloaked their judgment. In the chilling events surrounding the Challenger disaster of 1986, the NASA engineers found themselves ensnared in a web of pressure, silencing crucial safety concerns to conform to the relentless demands of launch schedules and to sidestep potential conflict. These illustrate the chilling consequences that can arise when dissent is stifled within a group, leading to catastrophic choices.

The Antidote! Delving into these cases reveals that the essence of intellectual synergy transcends mere shared purpose; it demands an ever-watchful eye, unfiltered dialogue, and a steadfast dedication to embracing diversity. We must tread lightly around the shadows of echo chambers, guarding against the insidious pull that stifles our critical thinking. It is essential to seek out a spectrum of perspectives, lest our minds fall into a monotonous rhythm, leading us down a path paved with deception and misguided choices.

By delving into the intricacies of social learning, heeding the subtle murmurs of the hidden, and staying alert to the forces of manipulation, we can transform ourselves into adept orchestrators of our own social encounters. We can create atmospheres that stimulate the sharing of varied thoughts, igniting a tension that propels us toward shared advancement and groundbreaking discoveries. This is not merely an isolated act but a dynamic interplay, a reflection of the intricate dance of minds that weaves the fabric of our collective advancement.

3. The Hive Mind: A Tapestry Woven from Unity

As a collective mind forms, an unsettling metamorphosis takes place, revealing the depths of their shared consciousness. The distinct psyches of the group dissolve into one another, merging to operate as a singular, cohesive force. This collective consciousness harbors an unsettling strength, one that eclipses the mere addition of individual minds. Envision the calculated precision of a covert operation, where every move is meticulously planned, or the haunting beauty of a collective performance, each participant a vital thread in a complex tapestry of sound and intention.

Science serves as a steadfast guide for deciphering this unified state. Exploring the intricacies of group dynamics reveals the surprising yet fascinating power of collective intelligence lurking beneath the surface. Research shows that collectives bound by varied viewpoints and deep social cohesion often eclipse solitary efforts when navigating intricate challenges (Surowiecki, 2005). This resonates deeply with the notion of a formidable collective consciousness arising from unified thought.

Picture a group of researchers delving into the depths of a pressing crisis, their minds racing with the weight of the world on their shoulders. Every individual contributes their distinct knowledge, yet as they engage in candid dialogue and teamwork, they start to operate as a cohesive entity, uncovering answers that could have remained hidden from any solitary researcher. This process is supported by findings in social psychology, which suggest that diverse groups are more effective at problem-solving and decision-making due to their varied perspectives and expertise (Page, 2007).[12]

Whispers in Cognitexis! Yet the whispers echoing through Cognitexis pose an intriguing dilemma. What is the process behind this merging of consciousness? Is it merely the result of transparent dialogue and common objectives, or could there be more sinister influences lurking beneath the surface? Could Cognitexis serve as a conduit, enabling minds to intertwine and exchange information beneath the surface of consciousness? Perhaps the remnants of ancestral experiences of cooperation or societal values that stress collective action linger in the shadows, subtly guiding us toward this unified state. Envision a community steeped in a complex past, where the threads of collaboration weave a tapestry of shared ambitions and hidden motives. These whispers could emerge as an instinctual drive for collaboration and seamless exchange of thoughts, facilitating the group's descent into a unified mindset.

The potential for manipulation deepens in this gripping realm. It could be subtly twisted through the orchestrated fabrication of collective thought or emotional persuasion directed at masses by a hidden force, all aimed at bending the group's will. Imagine a reality where political gatherings strive to ignite fervent nationalism by tapping into raw emotions and irrationality, bypassing the rational thought of the populace. Chillingly, religious cults create an environment of isolation and fear, meticulously orchestrating a hive mind where mechanical actions prevail, leaving no room for independent thought or critical analysis. Amidst the shadows, the emergence of critical thinking skills intertwines with cultivating personal responsibility, revealing the intricate dynamics of collective consciousness.

The Antidote! We can craft an astonishingly potent collective narrative by delving into the intricacies of human interaction, tuning into the subtle cues that linger in the shadows, and remaining vigilant against the art of deception. We could cultivate a space that fosters candid dialogue, varied viewpoints, and a robust sense of personal accountability. That enables the collective consciousness to exert its influence: a collective where every strength converges, leading to accomplishments that transcend the limits of individual thought. Not merely a single act of dominance but an intricate dance of cooperation—a chilling reminder of the depths of human ambition and the shadows that linger in the pursuit of greatness.

4. The Kindred Flame: Ignited by Shared Purpose, Fueled by Synergy

What stirs the embers of synchronized minds within a group? A compelling revelation emerges from the depths of collective ambition. A shared objective, an intense desire, or a looming danger can be the igniting force that intertwines thoughts and intentions. This so-called "intellectual synergy alliance" weaves together the minds of its participants, merging their thoughts, experiences, and insights into a singular force, a collective consciousness that surpasses the capabilities of any one individual, hinting at deeper, perhaps unsettling, connections among them.

Science casts a revealing light on this enigma. Investigations into social identity theory reveal that the pursuit of common objectives intensifies collaboration and unity among groups. A singular force binds individuals together, infusing their existence with purpose; it serves as the lifeblood that fuels the flames of cooperation. Envision a team of firefighters grappling with an overwhelming blaze, each moment fraught with tension and uncertainty. The collective mission of preserving lives and controlling the blaze eclipses any personal disparities. Their collective drive allows them to anticipate each other's moves, synchronize their actions seamlessly, and reach a level of performance that surpasses the capabilities of any individual firefighter.

Whispers in Cognitexis! Yet, the whispers of Cognitexis pose a compelling inquiry: At what point does collective ambition transform into a synchronized thought? Is it merely a matter of deliberate collaboration, or is there a more profound force drawing them together? Could Cognitexis act as a conduit for intertwining emotions and motivations, allowing them to echo between minds? Perhaps the lingering effects of evolutionary pressures or societal expectations subtly shape our instincts, nudging us toward collective action in pursuit of shared goals. A firefighting team, steeped in the legacy of their ancestors who were first responders, might be tapping into these permeating echoes to forge an instinctual bond and an uncanny ability to predict the movements of others amidst the chaos of flames.

The intense interplay at hand heightens the likelihood of manipulation lurking in the shadows. External influences might manipulate the collective drive towards harmful objectives. Imagine a scenario where social media algorithms stoke the fires of anger and division, manipulating emotions and intensifying resentment towards a targeted group. Political movements that hinge on magnetic figures and stirring language, seeking to draw individuals into a divisive "us versus them" mindset, are perilous, devoid of rational scrutiny, and cultivate a dangerous conformity of thought. Cultivating media literacy and honing discernment concerning emotional manipulation becomes crucial in the depths of shared consciousness.

The Antidote! By delving into the intricacies of social identity theory, heeding the subtle murmurs of the hidden, and staying alert to the shadows of manipulation, we can master the art of igniting the fire of collective motivation. We can create settings that ignite a shared mission, promote candid dialogue, and appreciate a multitude of viewpoints. This ignites a hidden force of collective intellect, a flickering flame that casts shadows on the journey to extraordinary accomplishments, intertwined and inseparable. This is not merely a flicker but an ablaze ignited by collective ambition, a testament to how intertwined minds can forge a path toward an uncertain tomorrow.

5. The Conductor's Baton: Leading the Symphony of Minds with Discipline

The true essence of the intellectual synergy alliance lies not merely in merging minds but in a meticulously crafted collaboration that unfolds with an unsettling elegance. In this intricate tapestry, personal strengths intertwine, crafting an enchanting melody of intellect. Yet, attaining this delicate balance demands an unwavering commitment to self-control. Just as an orchestra requires each musician to master their instrument and maintain control, every member of the intellectual alliance must navigate their own thought processes with precision and awareness. Only then can they weave themselves into the intricate tapestry of shared thoughts, each thread pulling tighter in the shadows of their minds.

The complex interplay of intellects emerges as science conducts a captivating symphony for this collective pursuit. Delving into the intricacies of collaboration unveils a profound reality: the imperative of personal responsibility and the reverberating clarity of communication that has the power to either unite a collective or dismantle it entirely. Studies indicate that the essence of individual accountability weaves a tapestry of enhanced team performance and satisfaction, as it compels each member to embrace responsibility for their unique contributions (Johnson & Johnson, 2009).

Within the depths of aspiration, as each person stands resolutely devoted and intensely focused on a common goal, the complex tapestry of cooperation starts to flourish. In this intricate dance of collaboration, the art of communication emerges as a vital force, harmonizing the endeavors of team members and navigating the tumultuous waters of conflict resolution (Salas et al., 2005). This profoundly echoes the idea that self-discipline serves as the bedrock for a successful intellectual alliance, enveloped in layers of complexity and fascination.[13]

Whispers in Cognitexis! Yet, the whispers within Cognitexis pose an intriguing dilemma. What enables people to attain such profound mastery over their minds? Is it simply the result of discipline and determination, or are there more profound influences lurking beneath the surface? Could Cognitexis serve as a mysterious arena where minds engage in a delicate dance of focus, honing their skills through an intricate web of shared connection? Could it be that the whispers of our ancestors, shaped by their collaborative journeys, or the societal ideals that champion self-mastery, subtly guide us toward a deeper sense of self-discipline? Envision a group of researchers, each with their own unique story, drawn together by an insatiable thirst for knowledge and the thrill of uncovering the unknown. These reverberations could emerge as a deep-seated reverence for concentration and an instinctive knack for silencing distractions, enabling them to collaborate with pinpoint precision to unlock profound revelations.

The opportunity for deceit deepens in this joint endeavor. External forces may manipulate the vulnerabilities of self-discipline, weaving in distractions or emotional triggers crafted to unravel the delicate balance of intellectual synergy. Envision a reality where social media alerts are meticulously orchestrated to disrupt collective concentration during brainstorming or where algorithms are crafted to sow seeds of suspicion and rivalry among team members. Educational systems that overlook the importance of self-management skills and emphasize rote memorization at the expense of critical thinking may render individuals susceptible to manipulation. Crafting a deep sense of self-awareness and nurturing an environment of reciprocal respect is essential in orchestrating the intricate symphony of the mind.

The Antidote! By delving into the intricacies of collaboration, tuning into the subtle cues that linger in the shadows, and staying alert to the forces that seek to sway us, we can transform ourselves into adept orchestrators of our attention and that of those around us. We can nurture a collective sense of purpose and accountability, encouraging transparent dialogue and honoring a variety of viewpoints. This unveils the hidden depths of intellectual synergy, crafting a collaborative enigma where unique strengths intertwine, conjuring something profoundly greater than mere addition. This is not merely an individual act; it is a captivating interplay, a reflection of the profound influence of self-discipline in orchestrating a collective journey towards common aspirations.

6. The Harmonic Convergence: A Symphony of Purpose or Peril?

The notion of meticulously orchestrated mental synergy raises an intriguing inquiry: is it possible for a group, when conditions align perfectly, to descend into a shared state of heightened cognition? Envision a harmonic convergence, a moment where disparate minds resonate in unison, their thoughts weaving a powerful and unrestrained collective current. This section delves into the catalyst that sets this intricate mental orchestration in motion while revealing the lurking threats hidden within its seemingly perfect cadence.

Science reveals an intriguing equation for deciphering these transformations: The Harmony of Consciousness in Motion. Delving into the complexities of group dynamics uncovers profound truths lurking just beneath the surface. Studies suggest that shared aspirations, clear direction, and foundational trust can intertwine to create a tapestry of cooperation, revealing groundbreaking solutions that lie hidden in the obscurity of our collective endeavors (Hackman, 2002). This event echoes profoundly within the intricate dance of minds, where each individual's unique talents intertwine to form a richer, more elaborate intellectual fabric.

Imagine a gathering of specialists, each harboring their own mysteries and aspirations, coming together to tackle a baffling medical conundrum that challenges their boundaries and uncovers concealed realities. Their shared fixation on discovering a remedy, coupled with an authoritative aura and a subtle foundation of trust, allows them to blend their talents and weave a profoundly complex tapestry of concepts, potentially leading to a transformative insight. Evidence suggests that groups enriched with varied skills and a deep sense of unity possess a greater capacity for unraveling intricate challenges (Salas, Cooke, & Rosen, 2008).[14]

Whispers in Cognitexis! Echoes of Shared Resonance. But what sets this unsettling alignment into motion? Could the mysterious Cognitexis serve as a conductor, quietly intensifying collective feelings and steering the group's attention? Perhaps remnants of our ancestral past, where unity was essential for survival, linger in a haunting capacity for shared thought. Picture a gathering of primitive beings cloaked in shadows, their faces illuminated by flickering flames as they plot their next move in a deadly game of survival. Their mutual instinct for survival could have awakened a hidden capacity to align their thoughts and feelings, resulting in a more efficient pursuit.

The specter of betrayal casts an ominous shadow over this joint endeavor, A Discordant Melody. The prospect of deceit lurking within a harmonic convergence evokes an overwhelming sense of fear. Envision shadowy figures leveraging Cognitexis to incite widespread panic or twist collective actions for their sinister agendas. A magnetic figure manipulating a warped perception of Cognitexis might exploit social media or various channels to forge a collective ambition, regardless of whether that ambition is driven by deceit or animosity.

The Antidote! Maintaining Harmony. Mastering the art of critical thinking, nurturing transparent dialogue, and preserving a robust sense of self become essential in maneuvering through the intricate layers of this psychological maze. By challenging beliefs, keeping a watchful gaze, and appreciating varied viewpoints, we can guarantee that the convergence of ideas remains a formidable instrument for cooperation and advancement rather than a means for deceit and domination.

The real strength of harmonic convergence resides in its capacity to bring together varied intellects in a common quest. We can unveil a realm of potential by channeling this shared energy for positive outcomes. Yet, we must remain watchful to guarantee that the harmony stays uplifting and the orchestrator remains kind-hearted.

7. The Symphony of Success: Trust and Harmony in Every Community

Envision an orchestra where each performer embodies mastery in their unique expression. Without a guiding presence to cultivate unity and confidence, their collective effort descends into disarray. This section delves into the fundamental essence of achievement within any community or population—the intricate interplay between trust and collaboration.

The Fragile Bond – A Bedrock of Cooperation: The efficacy of any collective is fundamentally rooted in a bedrock of shared trust and harmony. The annals of history resonate with this essential truth. The trajectory of human societies, from their nascent forms to the intricate frameworks of contemporary nations, reveals a fundamental truth: without trust and cooperation, even the most noble aspirations of communities are destined to falter and disintegrate. This principle is equally relevant to families, businesses, and any collective endeavor that seeks to realize a shared objective.

The Conductor's Baton – Leading the Way to Harmony: Much like a masterful conductor orchestrates a harmonious performance, thriving communities depend on effective leadership that nurtures collaboration among their members. This form of leadership cultivates an environment of trust by establishing transparent communication, collective objectives, and an equitable allocation of rewards. When personal egos are relinquished for a collective purpose, a sense of unity arises, enabling varied perspectives to harmonize together. Envision a figure within the community that fosters transparent communication, honors the unique inputs of each member, and ignites a shared vision of meaning and direction.

Scientifically, the foundation of psychological safety holds a strong stance here. Delving into the complexities of team dynamics reveals the fundamental importance of fostering an environment where individuals feel secure and nurtured. In an environment where individuals can express their thoughts free from the shadows of judgment or mockery, the wellspring of creativity is unleashed, breathing new life into the very fabric of collaboration. Amy Edmondson's research highlights the essential role of psychological safety in fostering high-performing teams, as it nurtures an environment where open communication and innovation can flourish (Edmondson, 1999). Trust serves as the foundational pillar of a safe space, enabling individuals to embrace their vulnerabilities and engage with a multitude of viewpoints.

Envision a realm of professional engagement where the ambiguity of the future is met with confidence and every endeavor is met with acknowledgment and appreciation. This context resonates with the notion that fostering a nurturing and inclusive atmosphere significantly elevates team performance and overall satisfaction (Frazier, Fainshmidt, Klinger, Pezeshkan, & Vracheva, 2017).[15]

Whispers in Cognitexis! Is trust merely a deliberate decision, or do more profound dynamics operate within the intricacies of the human psyche? Might the mysterious domain of cognition influence the development or erosion of trust? It is conceivable that remnants of our evolutionary history, wherein collaboration was essential for survival, shape our inherent tendency to place trust in a communal context. Envision a community where a collective narrative of collaboration nurtures an inherent propensity for trust, cultivating an environment ripe for cooperative endeavors.

A dissonant composition, an exhilarating tension. In a realm where the subtleties of influence are masterfully wielded, those with ill intentions may take advantage of the inherent weaknesses found within the human psyche. The intricate interplay of subtle manipulations, misinformation campaigns, and the deliberate sowing of discord has the potential to undermine trust and disturb the fragile harmony of collaboration within a community. Envision a social media initiative crafted to create divisions among various segments of society, undermining trust and obstructing collective advancement.

The Antidote! Creating a cohesive environment, an orchestration of faith and openness. Enhancing communication abilities, nurturing an environment of openness, and staying alert to the potential for manipulation are essential for preserving equilibrium within any collective. These elements are the foundation for a community that flourishes rather than merely exists. Envision a society where connections are fostered rather than barriers erected, a collective mission binds individuals together, and an environment of psychological safety empowers each person to express their thoughts and ideas. Such an environment cultivates a harmonious blend of achievements, where the unique abilities of individuals converge to manifest something genuinely extraordinary.

This symphony unfolds through the essence of trust. Trust transcends mere conflict avoidance; it serves as the essential catalyst for unleashing the collective genius of a group. Much like a conductor orchestrates a symphony, the cultivation of trust weaves individual contributions into a cohesive and beautiful whole. Those in positions of leadership who engage in transparent communication, confront issues with sincerity, and take responsibility for their actions lay the groundwork for a profound sense of trust. In an environment characterized by openness, communities gain strength against deceit, allowing the harmonious symphony of collaboration to persist.

Second Manifestation: Navigating Collective Thought and Morality

These concepts delve into collective thought's moral and ethical dimensions, examining how shared beliefs and social dynamics shape our conscience and moral compass.

1. The Collective Conscience: Navigating the Moral Compass of Shared Thought

In the shadowy depths of collective contemplation, where notions entwine like twisted vines, a captivating notion surfaces at the Intellectual Synergy Alliance. This mysterious collective serves as a guiding force, protecting its members from the lurking shadows of moral decay.

- **The Power of Unity:** The essence of this alliance pulses with an undeniable force, a collective strength that binds them together. It taps into a deep reservoir of shared strength, a force beyond solitary thought's confines. This power teeters on a razor's edge—each individual offers a sliver of their reality, intricately entwining a web of collective consciousness. Any disruption or attempts at control loom ominously, fracturing the delicate ties that hold the alliance together. Envision a performance where one voice seeks to dominate the collective, unraveling the delicate balance and plunging the scene into a chaotic clash of jarring sounds. In a parallel manner, the collective psyche unravels when the bond fractures, exposing the group to unseen threats.

- **The Enigma of the Shared Mindscape:** The intricate web woven by the alliance eludes simple understanding. It delves deeper than simple neural processes; it surpasses the confines of the physical realm. This collective consciousness, distinct to the group, eludes the grasp of genetic inheritance. No solitary successor can claim the vast knowledge it holds within. It's an enigmatic interplay of thoughts echoing in a confined realm, a chilling reminder of the depths of collective influence. Envision a team of researchers, their minds consumed by the pursuit of knowledge, locked in a relentless quest that has spanned years, unraveling the mysteries of the unknown through their daring experiments. The intricate web of knowledge and understanding they have woven cannot be easily transferred to an unsuspecting new researcher. It's the result of their intertwined paths, the fusion of their minds, and the distinct energy that has arisen from their partnership.

- **Guardians of Collective Power:** The alliance stands as the enigmatic guardian of this formidable force. Each thought, a thread in the intricate web of our shared psyche, weaves the fabric of our collective strength together. Yet, while appearing powerful, those self-serving thoughts harbor a concealed threat—a negativity that can seep into the very fabric of the group. Kind intentions, however, create an enduring and profound effect. Envision a group delving into a project that seeks to alter the fabric of society. When an individual becomes engulfed in their selfish ambitions, prioritizing personal gain over the shared objective, it can sow seeds of discord and suspicion among the members. On the other hand, an individual who persistently introduces groundbreaking concepts and fosters teamwork amplifies the shared strength of the group.

- **Crafting Our Destiny Through Actions:** Our actions shape the very fabric of our fate. As if wielding a hidden power, we shape the fabric of existence through our actions. Yet, the temptation of a self-serving journey can be misleading. History murmurs warnings: those driven by ambition, who placed their own desires above the welfare of others, ultimately witnessed their empires disintegrate, having built nothing to support the weight of their fleeting triumphs. They transmitted whispers of their greed, failing to provide the tools to safeguard their legacies.

- **The Unfading Echo:** Yet, within the remnants of empires constructed on selfish desires, an alternate legacy emerges— the triumphs of those who harnessed their intellect for noble purposes. Their gains endure, a chilling reminder of the powerful extent of shared knowledge. They grasped that the bond surpasses mere existence, that its power resides in togetherness, and that the echoes of our deeds reach far into the future. These lasting shadows loom large, urging us to harness the enigmatic force of the Intellectual Synergy Alliance for a purpose that transcends the ordinary.

By embracing The Power of Unity, adhering to the principles outlined in The Enigma of the Shared Mindscape, and recognizing the importance of our roles as Guardians of Collective Power, we can shape our future through Crafting Our Destiny Through Actions. With an awareness of The Unfading Echo of our choices, we each become guardians of a collective awareness, carving out a more luminous tomorrow.

In the intricate world of neuroscience, mirror neurons – those enigmatic brain cells that activate upon witnessing or executing actions – have sparked a captivating theory. Could these very neurons serve as the bedrock for a phenomenon far more enigmatic, a collective consciousness that surpasses the confines of the individual mind? Step into the shadows of the Intellectual Synergy Alliance (ISA). This mysterious collective wields its influence with a chilling intent: to serve as a guiding force, protecting its members from the creeping abyss of moral decay.

Shadowy murmurs reverberate through Cognitexis, an enigmatic vault of shared subconscious musings. Could these subtle ancestral whispers be the remnants from which the ISA's collective consciousness emerged? Our ancient ancestors possibly had a primitive version of this skill, a bond that faded as personal awareness took center stage. Or is the psychic resonance encountered by the ISA something entirely unprecedented, a revolutionary evolutionary shift that reveals the hidden depths of the human psyche?

A truly terrifying vision arises from this deep abyss, demanding one's focus. Sinister manipulators, weaving through complex webs, could easily distort the very essence of the groups' minds at will, with the Intellectual Synergy Alliance (ISA) exposed in all its vulnerability. Imagine a malevolent entity stealthily breaching the ISA's communication channels, unleashing a relentless stream of insidious messages crafted with precision to sow chaos and mistrust among its ranks. This calculated instigation of strife threatens to dismantle the delicate equilibrium of the ISA, casting them into a vortex of chaos, distrust, and the erosion of their collective power.

In the end, safeguarding the core of this shared awareness is the fundamental reality of the ISA's being. The peril lies in the depths of their being and the world beyond, an ever-watchful specter that shadows their every step. A sinister presence casts a shadow over the ISA, its intentions shrouded in mystery. The fragile equilibrium of their partnership—their combined power—is disintegrating into turmoil. Will they find the strength to confront their innermost fears and realize their true potential in unison, or will they fall prey to the sinister forces that conspire to tear them asunder?

2. The Siren's Song: A Symphony of Belonging, Discordant with Dissent

The alluring call of conformity beckons, promising a deceptive sense of security wrapped in the warm cocoon of the masses. It's a haunting tune, stirring a profound longing for connection that countless souls relentlessly pursue. Yet, social psychology unveils a chilling dichotomy—the insidious yet formidable influence of social pressure on our choices. Though conformity to societal expectations can offer a semblance of belonging, it also has the potential to extinguish the flame of creativity and the core of individuality. This conjures a haunting discord—suppressing one's creative musings, leading to an oppressive burden of self-contempt. This battle echoes deeply within the soul, reflecting the torment of those who grapple with their authentic selves, as anyone who has silenced their own voice to fit in can attest.

Scientific Element: The Subtle Manipulation of Societal Expectations. Years of investigation reveal the dark undercurrents of social pressure and its subtle yet powerful grip on our actions. We are inherently social beings, instinctively driven by a deep-seated desire for acceptance and a sense of belonging among others. This deep-seated urge can emerge as an insidious influence, quietly directing our behaviors and choices to conform to the expectations of others in our midst (Cialdini & Goldstein, 2004).

Consider the example of Sarah, a young scientist who recently joined a research team. Initially excited to contribute her ideas, she quickly found herself feeling hesitant to speak up. She worried her colleagues might perceive her as a troublemaker or dismiss her ideas. As a result, Sarah began to self-censor, keeping her thoughts to herself and conforming to the group's consensus. This internal struggle between her desire for acceptance and her urge to contribute her unique perspective led to a growing sense of self-doubt and frustration.[iv]

Research indicates that social conformity can significantly impact individual decision-making and behavior, often leading to self-censorship and reduced innovation (Asch, 1956; Janis, 1972). Understanding these dynamics is crucial for fostering environments where diverse perspectives are valued, and individuals feel safe to express their ideas. [16]

Conformity, nonetheless, wields a dual nature. Though it may cultivate a sense of unity and collaboration, it can equally suffocate the spark of creativity and the essence of individuality. Research such as the Asch conformity experiments reveals the unsettling power of influence over individuals, showcasing how easily they can be led to conform, even when confronted with clear evidence of falsehood. The relentless urge to conform can spiral into a disquieting reality where the sharp edges of critical thought are dulled in the pursuit of superficial unity. The stifling of creative ideas, those flickers of originality and rebellion, can lead to profound and unsettling repercussions. Picture a group of scientists teetering on the edge of an unsettling revelation. When a single individual holds back a contrary thought, gripped by the dread of

---

[iv] **Real-World Example: The Suffragette Movement:**
- In the late 19th and early 20th centuries, women's suffrage movements advocated for women's right to vote. Despite the clear logic and justice of their cause, many women faced immense social pressure to conform to traditional gender roles. They feared being labeled as radicals, troublemakers, or unfeminine. This fear of rejection led many women to remain silent or even to oppose the suffrage movement.
- **Impact:** The suppression of women's voices due to fear of rejection delayed the progress of women's rights for decades. It limited their participation in political and social decision-making, perpetuating harmful stereotypes and inequalities.
- **Conclusion:** Just as Sarah's fear of rejection hindered her ability to contribute to the research team, the societal pressure faced by women in the suffrage movement hindered their progress toward equality. This example demonstrates how fear of rejection can have far-reaching and detrimental consequences, both for individuals and for society as a whole.

being ostracized, the entire trajectory of the investigation may be irrevocably hindered.

- **Galileo Galilei,** a celebrated figure in astronomy and physics, embodies the haunting reality of how the dread of rejection can stifle the advancement of science. In the 17th century, Galileo's brilliant mind unveiled a groundbreaking theory that would challenge the very fabric of understanding: the Earth, it turned out, revolved around the Sun, a notion that would come to be known as heliocentrism. This challenged the dominant belief that placed Earth at the center of the cosmos, unraveling the fabric of understanding that had long been accepted.

  Galileo's theory unraveled the fabric of the accepted reality, casting shadows on the power held by the Catholic Church. A haunting dread of rejection and the looming threat of persecution compelled him to silence his discoveries for a period. He ultimately unveiled his work yet encountered fierce resistance from the Church. Galileo found himself confined within the walls of his own home, compelled to renounce the revolutionary ideas that had once set his mind ablaze.

  This incident reveals the insidious grip of fear, a force that can suffocate creativity and hinder the pursuit of understanding. The delay in Galileo's groundbreaking work cast a long shadow over his personal life, ensnared as he was by the relentless pressure to conform to the dominant beliefs of his era.

This scientific evidence intertwines seamlessly with the notion presented in the narrative: stifling positive thoughts can spiral into a debilitating wave of self-resentment. The conflict within, torn between the longing for belonging and the compulsion to reveal one's distinct viewpoint, can create a profound sense of unrest.

Whispers in Cognitexis! Yet, an enigmatic resonance lingers deep within Cognitexis. Is it possible that a social echo chamber intensifies the prevailing ideas within a group, rendering any opposing views dangerously uncomfortable? What drives us to yield, even when it clashes with our deepest instincts? Is it merely a longing for belonging, or is there an enigmatic influence lurking beneath the surface? Could Cognitexis serve as a sinister social echo chamber, intensifying the prevailing thoughts within a group and rendering dissent a treacherous endeavor? Perhaps the remnants of ancestral experiences in communal existence or societal values that stress compliance linger subtly, urging us toward uniformity.

The Peril of Crafted Uniformity: A Realm Designed for Muted Existence. In this suffocating orchestration, the possibility of control deepens. Imagine a reality where the fabric of communication is manipulated, stifling opposition and weaving a tapestry of uniformity that suffocates the essence of self. Educational systems that enforce compliance rather than encourage independent thought risk transforming into breeding grounds for conformity, extinguishing the spirit of creativity that fuels advancement.

The Antidote! Fostering a deep understanding of oneself is essential to withstand the alluring pull of conformity. We must sharpen our senses to perceive the subtle murmurs of Cognitexis, acknowledging the haunting remnants of history that could lead us into the shadows of unquestioning belief. Encouraging a climate of candid conversation and instilling the bravery to question established norms are the tools required to forge a new, more cohesive arrangement. It's time to unearth our genuine voices and recognize that real advancement arises not from unquestioning obedience but from the clash of varied thoughts. In this haunting composition, each note contributes to the unsettling harmony.

3. The Echo Chamber Effect: Shaping Minds Through Social Circles

Our social circles are not merely companions; they intricately intertwine, crafting a complex web of influences that mold our perceptions and understanding of reality. Envision our minds as a labyrinth, shaped by the shadows of knowledge and the whispers of perspectives we confront. With varying degrees of intimacy and emotional weight, these social connections serve as gardeners and cultivators, shaping the intricate landscape that flourishes within our minds. Let us plunge into these intricate social realms and uncover their significant impact on our mental odyssey.

a) **Family Connections:** The Imprint of Identity. The intricate dynamics of family relationships carve out the very essence of who we are. The outcome of our resilience or fragility, confidence or hesitation, is deeply entwined with the complexities of familial connections. From the moment we enter the world, the ties of family carve a lasting mark, echoing through the corridors of our existence. Nothing compares to the intricate web of connections we share with our family. In the depths of our formative years, we are molded, often in ways we cannot fully comprehend, for better or worse. The intricate interplay within a family circle can profoundly impact our sense of tranquility and overall well-being.

b) **Professionals or Occupational Associates:** Architects of Ambition. The intricate web of our professional relationships—colleagues, mentors, and business partners— creates a subtle yet powerful atmosphere where our deepest ambitions begin to unfold. These connections serve as a framework, allowing us to ascend and achieve our goals. A mentor who provokes and ignites our thoughts can unleash a wave of creativity that drives us toward achievement. Though family lays the foundation, our professional circles meticulously construct the towering structure of our aspirations.

c) **Social Friends:** Weavers of the Social Fabric. Social friends weave through the fabric of our everyday encounters, their presence both subtle and profound. Whispers over coffee, fleeting moments of laughter, and the weight of late-night conversations—these are the echoes that linger in our thoughts. These connections distort our reality and influence our emotional state. The subtle influence of social friends intricately weaves through the fabric of our perceptions, shaping them in ways we may not fully comprehend. They can serve as a source of support, provoke our perspectives, and fundamentally influence how we navigate the social realm's complexities.

d) **Casual Associates – The Echoes of Fate:** Casual acquaintances, chance meetings, and passing encounters are the subtle hints of fate lurking in the shadows. Yet, despite their delicate nature, these fleeting connections etch themselves into the depths of our minds. A fleeting exchange with a passerby on a desolate platform or a brief smile shared with an unknown face. These seemingly insignificant moments can surge through your consciousness, igniting fresh thoughts or etching their mark deep within your psyche. A flawless social circle creates a delicate equilibrium where the influences of family, colleagues, close friends, and even fleeting acquaintances intertwine in unexpected ways.

The Dangers of Isolated Realities. The notion of echo chambers unveils a lurking threat. Contemplate the insidious ways social media algorithms and cunning individuals can forge echo chambers, intensifying the shadows of negativity that lurk within. In this realm, the social garden risks becoming suffocated by the creeping vines of negativity and the insidious spread of misinformation.

The Antidote! Sharpening one's perception, encouraging candid dialogue, and cultivating diverse social ties emerge as essential strategies for maneuvering through the intricate web of the social echo chamber. By nurturing a varied social network and embracing a critical mindset, we can guarantee that our environment thrives with a rich tapestry of ideas and viewpoints.

4. The Empathy Enigma: Unraveling the Labyrinth of the Mind

Empathy delves deeper than mere comprehension. It's an entrance into the twisted corridors of human thought, a domain teetering on the edge of the uncanny. We unveil a cache of concealed thoughts, driving forces, and unspoken yearnings by delving into these complex terrains. This intricate puzzle of understanding, a compelling fusion of intellect and an elusive essence unveils a formidable instrument. It enables us to create bonds, unravel tensions, and alter fates. It's the hidden dialect that murmurs through souls; a connection forged not from iron and concrete but from intertwined experiences and the echoes of feeling.

Science unveils a captivating blueprint for the intricate hold of our inner reflection. Explorations in social cognition unveil a thought-provoking tale about the deep impact of empathy on human connections. Mirror neurons, those complex webs of brain cells, awaken within us as we observe the actions or emotions of others, acting as a biological foundation for our capacity to empathize (Rizzolatti & Craighero, 2004).

Exploring the intricacies of another's mind reveals profound insights into their worldview. Viewing the world through another's lens reveals deep interconnections, sparking fervent collaboration and intricately weaving a fabric of communal harmony. The adept negotiator, finely attuned to the subtle emotional currents and the nuances of physical expression, wields an extraordinary talent for traversing complex scenarios, revealing common ground even amid discord (Iacoboni, 2009).[17]

Yet, what lurks beneath remains hauntingly elusive. What about the unsettling ability to not just understand but also profoundly experience the emotions of another? Is there a hidden bond lying in the shadows, an obscured route intertwining our minds? Could Cognitexis, that shadowy domain of entwined consciousness, serve as a portal for us to delve into the profound emotional abysses of others? Perhaps the echoes of our ancestral past, where existence depended on interpreting fragile social cues, persist in our consciousness—a chilling instinct for unveiling the hidden language of emotions.

Envision a mother, her instincts sharp and unyielding, perceiving the silent anguish of her child from a distance, an unsettling consciousness unfurling within her as barriers of walls loom between them. This deep connection may persist as a shadow of our ancestral past. Imagine a deeply attuned soul weaving through the chaotic throngs of a marketplace, suddenly engulfed by a surge of dread as an unforeseen clash reverberates in the air. This may serve as a chilling contemplation of our innate drive to discern the dangers woven into the very essence of our existence, where the stakes of survival teeter precariously.

The Empathy Arms Race; a perilous game of shadows. The empathy enigma, a potent instrument for forging bonds, reveals a haunting duality that can ensnare the unaware. Envision a realm where the very essence of empathy is twisted into a tool for manipulation, expertly exploited by those who possess an unsettling understanding of the human psyche. These puppeteers could delve into weaknesses, twist perceptions, and create chaos on an unprecedented level. Meticulously crafted Social media algorithms to exploit emotional vulnerabilities can potentially forge echo chambers of fury and discord, deepening the fractures within societal connections. Political campaigns could transform into a battleground of the mind, weaving intricate narratives that exploit a voter's innermost fears and desires, manipulating empathy into a weapon of manipulation.

The Antidote! Nurturing Authentic Bonds. In a world where emotional landscapes shift unpredictably, mastering the nuances of emotional intelligence, perfecting the skill of active listening, and fostering authentic connections emerge as vital strategies in this intricate game of empathy. By deliberately nurturing empathy, we can tap into its profound influence for positive change. Envision a realm where those in power engage in negotiations, fully aware of the profound psychological toll of conflict on individuals and society. By cultivating authentic relationships and transparent dialogue, we can forge pathways of insight and traverse the intricate labyrinth of human existence. Ultimately, the true essence of the empathy enigma resides not in deceit but in our capacity to forge connections, grasp understanding, and collaboratively construct a more promising future.

Third Manifestation: Mentorship and Influence

These concepts focus on the dynamics of mentorship and influence within the collective mind, highlighting these relationships' positive and negative impacts.

1. The Spark and the Flame: A Mysterious Dance of Mentorship

Mentorship is a shimmering flame, igniting a hidden spark of imagination within the mentee and leading them down a path of discovery and intrigue. A sudden flash of inspiration and exchanging ideas can propel individuals into spectacular realms of thoughtfulness. It encapsulates the essence of collaboration, as this fundamental principle of the Intellectual Synergy Alliance ignites minds, fostering an environment ripe for the incubation of innovation and progress.

Science presents a compelling formula for deciphering such transformations; it operates through the Catalyst of Social Learning. Exploring the depths of social learning reveals the intricate dynamics of mentorship's influence. Watching and engaging with those who have achieved success serves as a powerful trigger. It ignites a deep-seated urge within us—a compelling drive that propels us to chase our ambitions. Envision a young scientist, captivated by their mentor's unwavering commitment and revolutionary breakthroughs, as shadows of ambition and obsession intertwine in a delicate dance of intellect and intrigue. This revelation stirs a deep-seated obsession for unraveling the mysteries of science within the mentee, thrusting them into a labyrinth of their exploration. This undeniable reality intertwines seamlessly with the notion of mentorship serving as a powerful force for the evolution of thought.

Whispers in Cognitexis! Yet, does true, enigmatic ballet happen in the shadowy corners of Cognitexis? Or is it a haunting connection, that enigmatic link that permits thoughts and fervor to surge effortlessly from mentor to apprentice? The truth might lie hidden in the shadows, resonating from the depths of our ancestral history. Gaining wisdom from those who came before held an immeasurable significance, as societal structures fostered a deep reverence for educators. Could these subtle echoes forge a connection in mentorship that transcends mere knowledge sharing? Imagine a music student profoundly influenced by the haunting brilliance of their teacher's artistry. The connection would go beyond mere technical guidance; an undercurrent of creative energy would pulse between them. This enigmatic component could underpin the revelation that an exceptionally impactful mentor ignites a flame far more intense than mere guidance.[v]

A shadow looms over this intricate interplay, infusing the atmosphere with a haunting sense of unease. History reveals unsettling narratives of accomplished figures who, entranced by their triumphs, lose sight of the essence that fueled their ambition. Envision a world where alluring yet cunning individuals twist the concept of mentorship to serve their hidden agendas. These individuals, lacking true zeal for fostering potential, may exploit social media to craft an illusion of achievement, spinning tales that ensnare the unsuspecting and desperate. In a world shrouded in deception, honing a discerning perspective is essential, safeguarding against the seductive pull of hollow assurances. Holding onto a sharp sense of doubt and nurturing an environment of candid dialogue serve as the perfect countermeasures to this looming deception.

This exploration of mentorship unravels the complex interplay between motivation and manipulation. We will unveil the shadows of the past that influence our perception of mentorship, delve into the enigmatic connections within Cognitexis, and arm you with the insights needed to traverse the intricate dynamics of this potent relationship in a realm filled with vast opportunities and concealed threats.

2. The Tangled Web: Unveiling the Peril of Negative Associations

The Intellectual Synergy Alliance pulsates with the intensity of intricate social connections, where every interaction holds a deeper

---

[v] Effective mentorship yields a multitude of benefits. Mentees can gain a deeper understanding of philosophy, develop a more positive and effective personality through a process of "mimicking," and cultivate a strong and resilient mental attitude through guidance and shared experiences. This aligns with the principle that close associations influence our worldview, personality, and mental approach. We are shaped, in part, by those we choose to spend time with.

significance. Connections that ignite curiosity and transformation carve a path toward advancement. Yet, beneath the surface of the social landscape lies a sinister undercurrent - a complex maze of harmful connections that can ensnare individuals, guiding them toward a perilous descent. This section delves into the insidious ways toxic relationships can distort our behavior and perception, leading us down a dark path of manipulation and confusion.

Science reveals a chilling blueprint for the insidious influence of social learning. Delving into the realm of social learning and modeling uncovers a chilling reality: the influence of our peers is profound and unavoidable. Interacting with individuals who embody detrimental traits heightens the risk of us reflecting those very traits within ourselves. This disquieting occurrence, commonly known as "contagious traits," uncovers the sinister dynamics of both inspiring and harmful forces that dwell within our existence (Bandura, 1977).

Imagine a nascent creator caught in the intricate snare of a world that flourishes on despair and skepticism. The artist's creative flame wanes, besieged by the unyielding tide of despair, suffocating their path of artistic transformation. This scenario reveals the profound influence of the social environment on our behaviors and attitudes, echoing the insights of research on social learning theory (Bandura, 1986).[18]

Whispers in Cognitexis! Yet, the whispers echoing through Cognitexis pose an intriguing dilemma. What are the mechanisms behind this unsettling spread of influence? Is it merely a matter of deliberate mimicry, or could a more enigmatic force lurk in the shadows? Perhaps Cognitexis serves as a mirror, revealing the dominant traits that lurk within those surrounding it. It might be the haunting remnants of ancestral experiences and societal values that stress conformity, leaving subtle echoes that render us susceptible to the sway of others.

In a community steeped in fear and mistrust, a young person may find themselves haunted by the shadows of their upbringing. These echoes can twist into a deep-seated cynicism, warping their perception of reality and creating barriers that prevent the formation of genuine, trusting connections with others. This phenomenon aligns with theories in social psychology, which suggest that our past experiences and social environments significantly shape our perceptions and behaviors (Tajfel & Turner, 1986).[19]

A world of Echoing Realities. In this treacherous terrain, the threat of deceit looms larger than ever. Envision a reality where the intricate web of social media algorithms and cunning manipulators weave echo chambers of despair, tightening their grip on your psyche and amplifying your darkest impulses, leaving you ensnared and powerless to escape their influence. Individuals enveloped in relentless negativity remain trapped in their insecurities, ultimately becoming pawns in the hands of a manipulative force. Establishing a compelling sense of distinction is crucial in these scenarios. We must delve into the shadows of our surroundings, dissecting the myriad influences that shape our perceptions.

The Antidote! It is essential to cultivate an environment steeped in scrutiny and reflection while simultaneously fostering genuine and resilient connections. The latter serve as shields against the dangers woven into the intricate tapestry, offering a sanctuary where development can flourish in every crucial dimension.

Fourth Manifestation: Safeguarding and Cultivating Thought

These concepts emphasize the importance of protecting and nurturing collective thought, fostering cooperation, and transforming individual differences into collective strength.

1. The Pristine Pool: Safeguarding the Wellspring of Thought

The mind is like a pristine ocean, mirroring pure thought's depths, clarity, and essence. This section explores the most effective strategies for safeguarding this source from the shadowy currents of despair. As the ocean becomes clouded by unwanted debris, so too can our minds be tainted by external negativity. The significance of safeguarding that mental sanctuary intensifies, allowing for the emergence of clear thought and the formation of fruitful intellectual connections.

Science reveals an enthralling design for the wicked grasp of the Cloud of Cognitive Dissonance. The journey into the disquieting realm of cognitive dissonance uncovers the deep scars left by negative influences on our capacity for reason. In the shadows of revelation, when truths collide with our constructed realities, our thoughts ignite, fervently striving to restore a sense of coherence amidst the chaos.

Such processes may give rise to a haunting phenomenon marked by cognitive dissonance—a disquieting mental state born from the collision of opposing beliefs or actions that sharply contradict our deeply held values. In a desperate bid to quell the turmoil within, the mind frequently contorts reality or clings to familiar convictions, hindering the birth of new thoughts and inviting the shadows of flawed logic to take root.

Envision scientists ensnared in the throes of a pivotal investigation, besieged by an unyielding wave of doubt and derision from those who relentlessly underscore the pointlessness of their pursuit. They will gradually discover themselves unknowingly rejecting contradictory evidence, fervently striving to protect their foundational beliefs from the encroaching, disquieting realities. This scenario reveals the unsettling nature of the human psyche, where the struggle for internal harmony drives individuals to twist reality, dismissing any unsettling truths that clash with their established convictions (Aronson, 1992).[20]

Whispers in Cognitexis! But what are the mechanisms behind this psychological "contamination"? Is it merely a straightforward act of denial, or could there be a more intricate mechanism at work beneath the surface? Could Cognitexis serve as a filter, enhancing positive thoughts while unintentionally magnifying the darker ones, too? Perhaps remnants of our ancestral history, where conformity bolstered survival, linger as a susceptibility to the weight of social influence. This may render us vulnerable to the shadows of negativity that deepen the roots of our entrenched beliefs, even when those beliefs obscure the light of rational thought. Picture a group of minds tangled in a web of thoughts, each idea a shadow lurking in the corners, waiting to be uncovered. When a single individual voices doubt or negativity, and the collective quickly embraces that sentiment, it can trigger a chain reaction, stifling creative exploration and obstructing the stream of uplifting ideas.

The chance for treachery looms ever larger in this shared quest. In this darkened landscape, the capacity for deceit looms increasingly ominous. Envision a realm where hidden influences distort our realities, intricately entwining sinister strands of shadow into the core of our minds. These sinister "pollutants" emerge as biting critiques, narratives fueled by outrage, and the unsettling distortion of negativity bias—where the emotional burden of negative information looms far larger than the positive.

In this unsettling environment, whispers of uncertainty and mistrust creep into the thoughts of the oblivious, fracturing intellectual alliances and planting the roots of conflict. The capacity for critical thought becomes entangled in a labyrinth of lies as shadows creep further in, obscuring clarity and breeding an unsettling sense of distrust. In this realm, the boundary separating reality from illusion fades, prompting a deep inquiry: what constitutes truth, and what is merely the shadowy art of deception?

The Antidote! Preserving a Sharp Mind. In such a world, the ability to perceive the truth becomes a crucial necessity. We must navigate the labyrinth of information flooding our consciousness, scrutinizing and contemplating with a discerning mind. Fostering meaningful social connections is a crucial barrier, as these interactions allow the mind to access an unfiltered stream of ideas, inspiration, and exchanges that elevate and uplift rather than taint the wellspring of thought. Clarity of thought, the pursuit of knowledge, and connections forged through genuine respect and comprehension can be achieved when one maintains a pristine mental landscape.

2. The Alchemist's Circle: Transmuting Differences into Collective Brilliance

The Intellectual Synergy Alliance transcends mere collaboration; it embodies alchemists assemble, a dynamic arena brimming with a kaleidoscope of intellectual treasures waiting to be unearthed. Every individual contributes a distinct viewpoint, an abundance of precise insights, and a range of psychological and emotional triggers. This shared intellect serves as a potent force, enhancing personal reflections, igniting creativity, and, as the narrative implies, lifting individuals to a deeper level of comprehension. In this realm, shared insights pierce through the confines of individual thought.

There exists a compelling framework within science that elucidates the intricacies of such transformation. Exploring the dynamics of team diversity reveals intriguing benefits that emerge when varied backgrounds and experiences converge. The intricate interplay of diverse viewpoints could unravel innovative solutions, unveil profound insights into intricate dilemmas, and forge a collective intellect that transcends mere individual contributions. Imagine a design team intertwined with engineers and marketing specialists, collaboratively unraveling the complexities of a new product. Every individual contributes their distinct skills, and through transparent dialogue and teamwork, they can forge something far more groundbreaking and significant than any single person could achieve alone.

Whispers in Cognitexis! Echoes within Cognitexis provoke a captivating inquiry: how could such a creation emerge from such a varied tapestry of collective intelligence? Is this merely a matter of exchanging information, or is a deeper, more sinister motive lurking beneath the surface? Could Cognitexis act as a universal translator, bridging the gaps between minds of varied backgrounds and facilitating the leaps across the chasms of communication and understanding? It could be that the remnants of our ancestors' encounters with multiculturalism or the subtle influences of societal values promoting tolerance gently guide us to embrace and weave together a tapestry of diverse viewpoints. Envision a collective of brilliant minds, hailing from diverse corners of the globe, united by an insatiable curiosity and a singular mission to unravel the mysteries of science. These echoes may emerge as an intriguing obsession with the myriads of methods and the ability to grasp the overarching narrative, enabling them to intertwine their varied insights into a groundbreaking creation.

The opportunity for manipulation looms larger in this dynamic arena. External forces may take advantage of the fundamental difficulties in navigating varied perspectives, creating an atmosphere of discord and suspicion within the alliance. Envision a reality where the very fabric of social media is woven with threads that intensify cultural divides, crafting echo chambers that ensnare users in a web of uniformity, shielding them from the richness of diverse viewpoints. When educational systems fail to cultivate critical thinking and the ability to evaluate sources, they unwittingly expose individuals to the lurking dangers of misinformation and manipulation, leaving them defenseless in a world rife with deception. Creating an environment where inclusivity thrives and the skill to embrace various viewpoints is essential in revealing the hidden power within the alchemist's circle.

The Antidote! We can become masterful creators when we grasp the intricacies of diversity, heed the subtle cues of the unseen, and shield ourselves from the art of deception. We can create a space that nurtures a thirst for knowledge, celebrates differences, and fosters open dialogue. In this intricate dance of minds, the true enchantment of the Intellectual Synergy Alliance unfolds disparate perspectives that converge into a singular collective consciousness, illuminating paths to profound revelations and a deeper, more intimate grasp of the world that envelops us. This was a collective triumph, a testament to the power of collaboration, revealing how diverse perspectives can intertwine to forge something far more extraordinary than any single vision could achieve.

3. The Foundations of Thoughtful Cooperation: Building the Fortress of Focus

Envision a collective of brave individuals confronting a relentless blaze, where every movement is imbued with tension and uncertainty. The result is determined not solely by personal abilities but by a profound comprehension of the context and a steadfast commitment to their collective goal. This section delves into the essential elements of intellectual collaboration, uncovering the vital principles that allow a collective of thinkers to cultivate and sustain a keen, shared consciousness.

The Primal Spark, A Purpose Beyond the Individual. One such foundation is the unified intention, the fate-driven mission. Much like the primal urge for survival compels firefighters to come together against the ferocity of flames, a powerful, common goal can foster a profound collective concentration within an ISG. Across the expanse of history, one can observe many examples—

from wartime codebreakers unraveling the complexities of enemy communications to pioneering scholars collaborating to reveal transformative discoveries. In moments where the stakes reach their zenith, and the very essence of humanity teeters on edge, the relinquishment of individual aspirations emerges as a haunting imperative. A shared aspiration, a concerted effort towards a common objective, evolves into a formidable force that sustains and nurtures focused engagement.

Science reveals a fascinating framework for the Neurochemical Cocktail of Collaboration. Researchers exploring the complexities of group interactions have revealed an intriguing occurrence referred to as collective effervescence. This concept, introduced by sociologist Émile Durkheim, describes the communal bonding experience that occurs when people come together with a shared purpose (Durkheim, 1912). The convergence of individuals towards a common goal catalyzes a profound release of dopamine and oxytocin, neurochemicals intimately associated with feelings of pleasure and the bonds of connection (Baumeister & Leary, 1995).

This powerful combination enhances focus and fosters a shared sense of self, merging individual desires with the expectations of the collective. Imagine an Intellectual Synergy Group (ISG) radiating with a profound, collective energy. Ideas intertwine in a vigorous ballet, driven by an unquenchable desire to attain their common goal. This dynamic interplay underscores the importance of social bonds and collective effort in achieving extraordinary outcomes.[21]

Whispers in Cognitexis! Yet, does the profound and enigmatic dance reveal itself in the hidden depths of Cognitexis? Yet, might this shared fervor conceal a deeper, more serious truth? Can Cognitexis, that mysterious domain of the human psyche, enhance not only the uplifting emotions that inspire us but also the darker sentiments that remain concealed beneath the surface? Imagine a collective consumed by deep-seated anxiety or fervent indignation—might it be that Cognitexis unwittingly fosters an environment that amplifies these feelings, obstructing the quest for understanding and reasoned contemplation?

This unsettling phenomenon may stem from a deep-seated cognitive dissonance, the mental turmoil that emerges when individuals grapple with conflicting beliefs or attitudes. Amidst the boundaries of an ISG, a palpable tension arises as individuals grapple with the unsettling urge to align with the prevailing groupthink, even when it sharply contradicts their convictions. This could result in the stifling of divergent viewpoints and an overwhelming urge to preserve social cohesion, ultimately overshadowing the vital exercise of critical thought.

It may be that the essence of reality lies hidden beneath the fundamental drives that shape our shared behaviors. The decisions made by our ancestors, who prioritized harmony over personal gain, might have unintentionally introduced a weakness in the structure of Cognitexis, exposing it to the subtle dangers of shared beliefs.

The Intricacies of Cognitive Distractions and the Struggle for Concentration! Imagine a domain where malevolent entities might exploit the vulnerabilities of Cognitexis. Disinformation campaigns, algorithms designed to provoke outrage on social media, and diverse methods of psychological manipulation may be strategically utilized to undermine intellectual collaboration. In this scenario, "cognitive pollutants" may sow seeds of discord and mistrust within an ISG, potentially undermining the collaborative endeavors that could otherwise lead to transformative advancements. This scenario mandates the creation of robust mental defenses: the nurturing of analytical thought, the welcoming of open discourse, and an unwavering commitment to diverse perspectives become vital in this struggle for intellectual supremacy.

The Antidote! Fostering an Environment of Unfettered Dialogue. The remedy for these cognitive pollutants lies in cultivating a space for open dialogue among the ISGs. Foster an environment where diverse perspectives converge, engage in spirited discussions, and maintain a critical awareness of the information presented. May the relentless pursuit of truth and the connections of collective accountability shape ISG's direction, guaranteeing that the quest for understanding remains transparent and pure.

The Journey Towards Shared Brilliance. The enduring foundations of collective understanding—a common goal, the intrinsic satisfaction derived from cooperation, and a steadfast commitment to transparent communication—create the essential framework of a powerful partnership. By utilizing these elements, ISGs can emerge as wellsprings of collective insight, pushing the limits of human understanding and achieving accomplishments that no individual intellect could aspire to realize in isolation. The genuine power of collective intellect resides not solely in the separate inputs of each individual but in the remarkable transformation that occurs when dedicated minds, aligned with a shared purpose, come together. Their unwavering commitment and collective aspirations serve as the foundation for the emergence of new insights and the realization of remarkable objectives.

Fifth Manifestation: Challenges and Perils of Collective Thought

These concepts address the challenges and pitfalls of collective thought, exploring the factors that disrupt harmony, and the delicate balance required to maintain focus and unity.

1. The Discordant Chorus: A Symphony of Sins That Shatter Harmony

The intrinsic yearning for interpersonal bonds is undeniable. However, cultivating and sustaining meaningful connections can often resemble traversing a perilous landscape. This section delves into the seven transgressions that undermine harmonious relationships, highlighting the detrimental actions that can fracture trust and disturb the fragile balance of human connection.

The Seven Deadly Sins of Human Connection

1. **The Discord of Self-Interest.** Imagine a symphony in which each player is solely focused on their individual acclaim, disregarding the conductor's guidance and the group's collective harmony. This discordant symphony poignantly reflects the vice of self-centeredness. When self-interest dominates, authentic connection eludes us. Genuine harmony necessitates an openness to understanding the needs and viewpoints of others.

   - **Scientifically!** The fascinating realm of mirror neurons reveals a profound connection within our biology, as these brain cells activate not only during our own actions but also when we witness others in motion. This intriguing phenomenon underscores the essential role of empathy, a vital component in transcending our inherent tendencies toward selfishness.

   - **Whispers in Cognitexis!** Is it possible that Cognitexis possesses an intrinsic inclination towards self-preservation, presenting a formidable obstacle to transcending our innate selfish tendencies? It is conceivable that remnants of our evolutionary history, characterized by intense competition for resources, shape the manner in which Cognitexis navigates social interactions.

- *Envision a reality where cunning individuals take advantage of this inherent predisposition.* The mechanisms of targeted advertising and social media algorithms, crafted to ignite feelings of envy, may intensify our inherent inclinations toward self-interest.

- **The Antidote!** Enhancing emotional awareness, nurturing a supportive environment, and staying alert to deceptive strategies are essential for building meaningful connections.

2. **The Destructive Power of Greed:** Avarice, marked by an unquenchable thirst for possessions, acts as a corrosive agent on the fabric of human relationships. It breeds hostility and fosters competition, replacing assurance with uncertainty. Genuine connections thrive when anchored in mutual respect and compassion rather than driven by an unyielding quest for personal gain.

- **Scientifically!** Investigations into the brain's reward mechanisms reveal a compelling narrative about the significance of social rewards. In the intricate dance of human connection, where cooperation and generosity intertwine, the brain unveils its secrets, releasing dopamine—a powerful neurotransmitter that heralds pleasure and satisfaction. This deepens altruistic actions and fortifies connections among individuals in a collective. The experience tied to it evokes a profound, enduring memory of fulfillment and a sense of achievement. Conversely, the insatiable desire may only provide a fleeting surge of neurotransmitters. Without the accompanying memories and social connections, one is exposed to emotional fragility and long-term despair.

- **Whispers in Cognitexis!** Might Cognitexis be intertwined with the seductive nature of greed? Does it function as a self-preservation mechanism, intensifying the perceived worth of material possessions and steering us to elevate them above the significance of human relationships? The whispers of our forebears, who understood the essence of resources for survival, may shape how Cognitexis perceives value in today's complex landscape.

- *In a gripping twist, in a landscape dominated by insatiable desires, cunning entities can prey upon our weaknesses, twisting them into instruments of avarice.* Strategically crafted marketing efforts that ignite feelings of envy and highlight scarcity can drive individuals to chase after material goods, often sacrificing deeper, more significant connections in the process.

- **The Antidote!** Fostering gratitude, embracing experiences rather than material wealth, and nurturing a balanced connection with finances emerge as vital defenses against the seductive pull of greed.

3. **The Envy that Blinds:** A dark yearning for what others hold can taint the very essence of meaningful connection. It weaves a persistent thread of unease, obstructing the capacity to revel in the achievements of those around us. In the intricate dance of human connection, celebrating one another's victories while providing unwavering support in times of adversity is essential.

   - **Scientifically!** In human behavior, the concept of social comparison theory reveals a compelling truth: we are instinctively drawn to measure ourselves against the lives and achievements of those in our vicinity. When these comparisons spiral into a sense of inadequacy, the seeds of envy can begin to take hold. Yet, studies reveal that directing attention toward another individual's growth mindset, path, and dedication can diminish feelings of jealousy and ignite a sense of inspiration.

- **Whispers in Cognitexis!** As an enigmatic factor, could Cognitexis be designed to foster a mentality of competition and comparison with others? Does it heighten the perceived worth of others' belongings, igniting a sense of envy? It is conceivable that the relentless forces of evolution, driving the struggle for resources, have honed Cognitexis to possess an acute awareness of social comparisons.

- *Envision a realm where digital landscapes are meticulously crafted to ignite the flames of envy,* drawing you deeper into a web of intrigue and psychological manipulation. Devious individuals might exploit this flaw, presenting distorted images of achievement and joy, igniting dissatisfaction, and unraveling connections.

- **The Antidote!** Embracing a practice of gratitude, prioritizing personal evolution, and aligning with those who uplift you emerge as vital shields against the insidious strategies that prey on jealousy.

4. **The Lingering Echoes of Revenge:** The yearning for vengeance, the deliberate infliction of pain as a reaction to a sensed injustice, looms ominously in the background. It ensnares individuals in a relentless loop of despair, obstructing recovery and nurturing bitterness. Genuine equilibrium demands the courage to forgive and the strength to advance beyond the shadows of the past.

- **Psychologically:** Investigations into the nature of forgiveness reveal profound emotional and physiological advantages. Letting go of grudges can lower stress hormones such as cortisol and may even enhance heart health. Forgiveness is not an endorsement of the offense; rather, it serves as a pathway for the individual to escape the shadows of negativity and reclaim their peace.

- **Whispers in Cognitexis!** Does Cognitexis conceal a deep-seated desire for vengeance, echoing the remnants of our instinctual "fight-or-flight" mechanism? Could the remnants of our ancestral history, where retribution acted as a safeguard against subsequent hostility, shape how Cognitexis navigates the tumultuous waters of betrayal?

- *Envision a realm where influential figures wield intricate psychological tactics to provoke a thirst for vengeance.* Intricate manipulation schemes, deceptive narratives, and the strategic leveraging of historical wounds can be employed to create chaos and fracture connections.

- **The Antidote!** Honing sharp analytical abilities, encouraging transparent dialogue, and emphasizing healing justice is essential in countering the deceptive influences that prey on our thirst for retribution.

5. **The Inferno of Hatred:** Hatred, a fierce and consuming force, blazes with an intensity that engulfs all it encounters. It shatters trust, erodes empathy, and obliterates any possibility of meaningful connection. Connections forged in mutual respect and comprehension are fundamentally incompatible with animosity.

- **Psychologically:** Investigative findings reveal that immersing oneself in a variety of viewpoints and experiences has the potential to diminish animosity. As we delve into the narratives of individuals from diverse backgrounds, the shadows of prejudice begin to fade, revealing the complexity of their humanity.

- **Whispers in Cognitexis!** As an enigmatic element, could Cognitexis be vulnerable to emotional currents, reflecting the animosity of its surroundings? Perhaps remnants of our primal history, where allegiance and distrust of the unfamiliar reign supreme, shape how Cognitexis navigates social dynamics.

- *Envision a realm where those in power and the press manipulate the weaknesses of Cognitexis, igniting flames of animosity in a chilling game of control.* Manipulative discourse, divisive narratives, and the vilification of others can cultivate a perilous atmosphere where animosity thrives.

- **The Antidote!** Fostering empathy, embracing a variety of viewpoints, and championing comprehension emerge as vital defenses against the insidious powers that prey on animosity.

6. **The Blinding Fog of Lust:** Unchecked passions, embodied by lust, can obscure clarity and drive one toward ruinous choices. It undermines confidence and lays the groundwork for deceit and abuse. In the intricate dance of human connection, communication threads must be woven with clarity, honesty must illuminate the shadows, and respect for boundaries is the unyielding framework that holds it all together.

- **Psychologically:** Research on attachment styles reveals a compelling narrative: those with secure attachments tend to navigate their desires with a level of restraint, steering clear of the perilous paths of destructive behaviors fueled by lust. Stable connections cultivate a profound sense of self-value, empowering individuals to focus on nurturing meaningful, enduring bonds.

- **Whispers in Cognitexis!** As an enigmatic force, does Cognitexis possess an inherent urge for self-preservation, compelling us and shaping our vulnerability to lust? Perhaps remnants of our evolutionary history, where the quest for a partner was vital for existence, shape the manner in which Cognitexis interprets sexual attraction.

- *Envision a realm where the very fabric of our wants is twisted by the hands of technology, creating a suspenseful dance between control and chaos.* The rise of virtual reality encounters, coupled with precision marketing that exploits concealed emotional weaknesses, alongside the rampant spread of online adult content, may forge a landscape where desire dominates all else.

- **The Antidote!** Fostering deep emotional awareness, honing self-control, and nurturing meaningful connections emerge as vital shields against the insidious forces that prey on desire.

7. **The Crippling Grip of Fear and Doubt:** Fear and doubt, though appearing distinct, conspire together to undermine intimacy. The dread of exposing one's vulnerabilities keeps people locked away, unable to reveal their authentic selves. Uncertainty, in contrast, undermines confidence and fosters an unending atmosphere of unease. Forging deep connections demands an openness to reveal one's true self, resting on the bedrock of shared trust.

- **Scientifically:** In human connection, exploring oxytocin, commonly known as the "love hormone," unveils vulnerability's critical role in forging trust between individuals. Oxytocin is a neuropeptide that plays a significant role in social bonding and trust formation (Kosfeld et al., 2005). In the shadows of the mind, when people dare to unveil their deepest fears and insecurities, a surge of oxytocin ignites, weaving a complex tapestry of connection and intimacy that binds them together in an intricate dance of trust.

Research has shown that oxytocin can enhance trust and empathy, making individuals more inclined to open up and share their vulnerabilities, strengthening social bonds (Bartz et al., 2011). This process highlights the profound impact of neurochemicals in developing and maintaining close relationships.[22]

- **Whispers in Cognitexis!** As an enigmatic force, might Cognitexis be imbued with an intrinsic wariness, echoing the echoes of our primal survival instincts? Perhaps remnants of our primal history, where peril awaits at every turn, shape how Cognitexis navigates social dynamics, instilling a deep-seated caution towards vulnerability.

- *Envision a realm where the digital landscape manipulates our deepest insecurities,* weaving a narrative of fear and uncertainty through the very fabric of social media and targeted advertising. A relentless onslaught of pessimism, meticulously crafted narratives that amplify self-doubt, and the orchestration of digital exchanges can forge an atmosphere thick with social unease and skepticism.

- **The Antidote!** Building resilient strategies to confront fear and anxiety, nurturing a network of support, and embracing self-kindness emerge as vital shields against the cunning influences that prey on these vulnerabilities.

The Healing Melody: Cultivating Harmony in a Disconnected World

The yearning for connection pulses at the core of our existence, yet the complexities of contemporary life frequently obstruct the path to forging and sustaining profound relationships. The "Discordant Chorus" delved into the chaotic tendencies that can shatter equilibrium. This section explores antidotes—the practices and principles that can orchestrate a harmonious connection in our personal and professional realms.

1. **The Strength of Vulnerability and Openness:** Delving into fear and uncertainty, vulnerability emerges not as a flaw but as a fundamental element of deep connection. Revealing our authentic selves and deepest fears and aspirations creates a powerful bond that invites others to extend their empathy and insight. Embracing vulnerability paves the way for trust to flourish, forging a sanctuary for candid dialogue—the essence of thriving connections.

2. **The Harmony of Empathy:** Transcending mere self-interest, as explored alongside the concept of selfishness, the cultivation of empathy unveils the profound ability to perceive the world through the lens of another's experience. Delving into the depths of their emotions, motivations, and experiences unveils intricate connections and cultivates a profound sense of empathy. Picture yourself delving into a conflict with a friend, where you immerse yourself in their viewpoint, truly grasping their emotions and validating their experience. This insightful method clears the path for resolution and fortifies the bond.

3. **The Chorus of Forgiveness:** Embracing the act of relinquishing resentment, intertwined with the allure of vengeance, is essential for true healing and progression. Clinging to resentment and fury taints the very essence of our

bonds. Forgiveness is not a shield for misdeeds; rather, it serves as a powerful catalyst, freeing us from the chains of negativity and paving the way for transformative connections. Envision the act of absolving a family member for a previous wrong, creating an opportunity for the bond to mend and ensuring that the echoes of the past do not loom ominously over the now.

4. **The Rhythm of Respect:** Respect for ourselves and those around us lays the groundwork for robust connections. It involves recognizing and respecting one another's perspectives, limits, and desires. A relationship built on respect paves the way for candid conversations, stimulating discussions, and the liberty to embrace one's true self. Envision a workplace where every interaction is laced with mutual respect, creating an atmosphere ripe for collaboration and a profound sense of psychological security.

5. **The Counterpoint of Gratitude:** cultivating gratitude, in contrast to the insidious grasp of avarice, redirects our attention to the uplifting elements of our connections. Recognizing the admirable traits in those around us and articulating our gratitude deepens connections and cultivates a shared sense of value. Envision a moment where you articulate your appreciation to a significant other, highlighting the strengths that bind your connection, creating an atmosphere charged with mutual respect and understanding.

6. **The Unifying Melody of Communication:** Transparent and sincere exchanges, the remedy to the paralyzing hold of anxiety and uncertainty, are crucial for fostering trust and navigating discord. Mastering the art of communication requires a bold expression of our desires, a keen ear for understanding, and a willingness to embrace the insights of others. Envision a couple delving into their struggles, navigating the complexities of their relationship with a shared determination to uncover

answers, and fortifying their connection through profound dialogue.

7. **The Strength of Togetherness:** Humanity is inherently social, flourishing through bonds and interactions. Establishing a robust web of connections with friends, family, or colleagues cultivates a profound sense of belonging and enhances our ability to confront the complexities of existence. Envision a tightly woven community, uniting in the face of adversity, extending a lifeline of support while deepening their bonds of connection.

2. The Unruly Orchestra: A Delicate Dance of Focus

Imagine a grand symphony orchestra, every perfectly tuned instrument poised on the brink of crafting an unforgettable masterpiece. What if one violinist is determined to play a dissonant note, shattering the harmony of the ensemble? This section delves into the intricate challenge of seizing and maintaining the collective focus—a perplexing issue of achieving and sustaining group attentiveness within an intellectually charged environment.

Science reveals a chilling design for the malevolent grasp of the Symphony of Fragile Harmony within the complex interplay of group dynamics. The investigation into group dynamics uncovers a realm that is as intriguing as it is mysterious. Even though individual minds can reach remarkable depths of focus, the pursuit of creating a cohesive neural connection within a group remains an unsettling endeavor. Yet, the possible outcomes far exceed the triumphs of any single intellect. As individual egos and personal ambitions clash, concealed intentions surface, and even the faintest disruptions— from flickering lights to modest conversations—threaten to dismantle the delicate balance crucial for effective collaboration. The idea of a chaotic group resonates with these conflicts, where one "off-key" person can disrupt the fragile equilibrium of the whole.

Scientifically, Neuroscientists explore the intricate dynamics between personal psyches and the shared awareness that emerges during collaborative efforts, uncovering a web of intrigue and hidden motivations. Understanding the forces that either disrupt or enhance this delicate intellectual connection is not merely valuable but crucial for uncovering the complete possibilities of any joint intellectual endeavor.

Whispers in Cognitexis! Yet, does the true, enigmatic dance unfold in the shadowy corners of Cognitexis? Yet, what makes the recognition of this cognitive harmony so profoundly challenging? Perhaps the human mind harbors a hidden realm. This mysterious nexus acts as a conductor of a grand symphony, guiding the currents of thought and shaping the essence of how individuals within the collective engage and respond.

Perhaps remnants of our primal history, where the drive for personal survival collided with the need for collective unity, linger in palpable tension within Cognitexis. The lingering tension disrupts the delicate equilibrium essential for genuine mental unity, sending certain minds spiraling off track, much like our wayward violinist lost in the symphony. Indeed, unraveling the mysteries of Cognitexis, which shapes collective focus, could also reveal the crucial element of harmonious thought within the intellectual synergy group.

A War for the Mind's Dominion! Imagine a world where the hidden tensions within Cognitexis serve as instruments of control. Sinister intellects with a profound understanding of the human psyche may introduce nuanced disturbances—a carefully selected word, an impeccably timed interruption. The malevolent presence of these "cognitive pollutants" threatens to sow discord within an intellectual synergy group, dismantling the delicate threads of shared focus and plunging their collective endeavors into turmoil.

The Antidote! Building formidable mental fortifications—sharpening analytical abilities, encouraging transparent dialogue, and nurturing a deep sense of collective intent—emerges as vital in this battle for psychological dominance. We must remain watchful sentinels of our minds or risk becoming mere puppets in another's dark orchestration of chaos.

The Path to Harmony: The real strength of an intellectual synergy group is found not merely in the sharpness of individual intellects but in their capacity to attain a singular, intense concentration. By deliberately reducing disruptive forces, fostering transparent dialogue, and tapping into the capabilities of Cognitexis, intellectual synergy groups can evolve into finely tuned engines of intellectual collaboration. The intertwining of minds, bound by a common goal, creates a force that propels innovation and progress to heights unattainable by solitary thinkers.

The Harmony of Our Existence

Understanding these seven self-destructive behaviors and the underlying influences that may dominate allows one to navigate the intricate labyrinth of human connections with greater skill. The intricate dance of emotional intelligence, open communications, empathy, and trust weaves a captivating tapestry of human connection, revealing the depths of our shared experiences. In a landscape rife with cunning strategies, these protective measures are essential for preserving the delicate equilibrium of our interactions, enabling authentic bonds to flourish.

By embracing these practices and principles, we can orchestrate a profound connection that enriches our lives and paves the way for a more harmonious existence in the world around us. The profound necessity for human connection is an undeniable force. By approaching this need with deliberate intent, we can navigate the chasms of a fragmented existence, forging relationships that deeply nourish the essence of our being.

The true power of human connection is found not in evading conflicts but in the hauntingly beautiful harmony of hearts and minds resonating together. Every individual plays a crucial role in the intricate tapestry of humanity. When we recognize our significance and harmonize with others, we create a powerful symphony that elevates, motivates, and enhances the lives of everyone involved.

THE LABYRINTHINE DESCENT: EXPLORING COGNITEXIS CORE

ร่ะ ร่ะ ร่ะ

Introduction: A Warning to the Intrepid Explorer

The pages ahead will lead you into the heart of The Labyrinthine Descent—a journey that ventures beyond the known realms of cognition, plunging into the very core of Cognitexis. This is a domain where thoughts intertwine in an intricate web of power and peril, and where the faint-hearted dare not tread.

As you step into this enigmatic abyss, be prepared for an odyssey unlike any other. Cognitexis Core is a labyrinth of infinite twists and turns, each corridor echoing with whispers of forgotten truths and shadows of unsettling revelations. Here, the very laws of thought are laid bare, revealing their dark and unfathomable depths.

This section is not for the faint of heart. It is a place where the light of reason battles the shadows of chaos, and where each step forward may bring you closer to the edge of madness or to the pinnacle of enlightenment. As you descend deeper into the labyrinth, you will encounter the principles that govern our most profound thoughts and the hidden mechanisms that shape our perception of reality.

Be warned, intrepid explorer! The path through Cognitexis Core is fraught with danger. The echoes of ancient wisdom and the cries of cognitive dissonance will test your resolve. The forces at play within this labyrinth are powerful and unforgiving, and only those with unyielding focus and relentless curiosity will emerge unscathed.

Prepare yourself for a journey into the unknown. The secrets of Cognitexis Core await, and with them, the possibility of transformation and enlightenment. But tread carefully, for within these pages lie the keys to the most profound and unsettling truths of the human mind. Will you master the labyrinth, or will you succumb to its shadows?

Cognitexis Labyrinth Core: Navigating the Laws of Thought

In a world where the mind plays tricks and reality blurs, one must navigate the labyrinth of thought and perception. The journey is not just about unraveling the mysteries that lie within but also about confronting the deeper questions of existence and the nature of truth. Each twist and turn reveals not only the darkness that lurks in the shadows but also the light of understanding that can illuminate the path.

Cognitexis Labyrinth Core: Navigating the Laws of Thought...

The human mind serves as a relentless forge, transforming fleeting thoughts into solid, enduring intellectual prowess. Yet, this enchantment conceals a truly mysterious element: the intricate workings of the mind's core. We are all orchestrators of a mesmerizing force, an enigmatic mechanism shaping the intricate evolution of our thoughts. We embark on a daring exploration into the shadowy corners of the psyche, seeking to unveil the mysteries behind heightened awareness. We delve into the intricate frameworks that govern the amalgamation, arrangement, and interpretation of information, striving to equip ourselves for the pinnacle of cognitive mastery.

Whispers from the Superintelligent...

Shrouded in mystery, the kernel of the mind hints at a deeper, more captivating idea: Cognitexis. A vision shimmering on the horizon, emerging from a future that transcends the limitations of humanity's current understanding, hints at the rise of an extraordinary mental prowess poised for awakening. Whispers from ancient tales, carried by the currents of human potential, suggest Cognitexis hidden within the intricate folds of the mind—an elusive force pursued by those with the fervent desire to surpass the boundaries of conventional thought.

A Wellspring of Boundless Potential...

Could Cognitexis unlock a hidden reservoir of creativity, a source of profound insight that remains elusive and uncharted by humanity? Envision a mind that reshapes the fabric of existence, granting the ability to perceive and alter the world in ways that elude our current understanding, pushing the boundaries of what is conceivable. Could this hold the key to unlocking the mysteries of the mind, foreseeing the future, or even manipulating the very fabric of reality through sheer determination?

A Perilous Odyssey...

One thing is undeniable: should Cognitexis be real, it undoubtedly dwells beyond the reach of conventional understanding. It dances at the fringes of consciousness, where reality and the unimaginable intertwine and blur into one another. Only the boldest navigators of the psyche, equipped with insights from the past and glimpses of a brilliant future, will venture to cross this boundary. Prepare yourself for this journey into the depths of understanding and the potential emergence of Cognitexis, which is laden with peril and the allure of unimaginable strength.

Enter the labyrinth, where shadows twist, and whispers haunt the corridors of the mind. This is Cognitexis Labyrinth—a realm where thoughts become phantoms, and the truth is a Minotaur lurking in the depths. Every step is fraught with peril here, as the quest for ultimate conscious intelligence demands you confront the specters of your psyche. Are you prepared to face the Minotaur of truth and unravel the intricate web of existence that binds you?

FIRST SPHERE

THE FOUNDATION OF COLLECTIVE COGNITION

INTERACTION AND COLLABORATION OF THOUGHTS

In the spectral dance of existence, thoughts intertwine like phantoms in the dark. This group delves into the sinister ballet of intermingling minds, where every encounter is a shadowy waltz of influence and deception. The Cosmic Ballet beckons, revealing the haunting symphony of thoughts that converge and diverge within the labyrinth. Can you navigate this spectral orchestra and uncover the hidden truths within the dance?

1. The Cosmic Ballet: A Symphony of Intertwined Minds

(The Law of Intermingling Thoughts)

In the shadowy depths of Cognitexis, a mesmerizing spectacle unfolds—the Cosmic Ballet. This space is a metaphorical realm where thoughts dance and clash, and concepts intertwine in a captivating orchestration of cerebral dialogue. The Law of Intermingling Thoughts dictates this cosmic interplay, an exhilarating and disquieting concept.

Dismantling the Facade of Individual Genius!

This law dismantles the facade of individual genius. Even the most brilliant intellect cannot attain genuine mastery without the influence of others. Like a solitary star in the infinite universe, every mind shines with its unique light yet is forever yearning for wholeness. This suggests that true intellectual growth and innovation are products of collaborative efforts rather than solitary endeavors.

- **Collaborative Genius:** Scientific breakthroughs often emerge from the collaborative efforts of multiple minds rather than solitary genius. The Law of Intermingling Thoughts posits that intellectual synergy is crucial for significant advancements. Historical examples abound where collaboration has led to groundbreaking discoveries:

- **Watson and Crick:** The discovery of the DNA double helix structure resulted from the combined efforts of James Watson, Francis Crick, Rosalind Franklin, and Maurice Wilkins. Their collaborative work, sharing ideas and data, was essential in unraveling the complexities of DNA.

Interplay Between Male and Female Psyche!

The law explores the intricate interplay between the male and female psyche, uncovering profound insights that challenge conventional understanding. Envision them as cosmic entities, each exerting a distinct force that draws you in, compelling you to explore their depths. As they converge within Cognitexis, an unprecedented power is unleashed - a formidable alliance of intellectual synergy. This partnership breaks free from the confines of the solitary mind, unlocking a vast wellspring of boundless wisdom.

Gender Diversity in Science: The law also emphasizes the importance of integrating diverse perspectives, including gender diversity, in scientific endeavors. Historically, women have made significant contributions to science, often in collaboration with their male counterparts:

- **Marie Curie:** Her pioneering research on radioactivity was conducted alongside her husband, Pierre Curie. Their partnership exemplifies how male and female intellects can converge to achieve extraordinary scientific milestones3.

- **Lise Meitner and Otto Hahn:** Their collaborative work led to the discovery of nuclear fission. Despite facing gender-based challenges, Meitner's contributions were crucial to this breakthrough.

Historical Influences and Intellectual Synergy

Reflect on the influential individuals who have dramatically altered the course of history. Were they not players in a grand performance, their luminosity heightened by the profound dialogues with their companions? This revelation highlights the essential drive for ongoing alignment and the sharing of ideas. Historical figures often thrived in environments where intellectual exchange was encouraged, leading to groundbreaking advancements.

- **The Manhattan Project:** The development of the atomic bomb during World War II involved a massive collaborative effort among scientists from various disciplines and countries. This project exemplifies how pooling diverse expertise can lead to monumental scientific achievements.

- **"The Man Who Knew Infinity" by Robert Kanigel:** This biography of the Indian mathematician Srinivasa Ramanujan explores his collaboration with the British mathematician G.H. Hardy. Despite cultural and geographical differences, their partnership led to significant contributions to mathematical theory. This example underscores the importance of diverse intellectual collaboration.[23]

Integrating Women into Intellectual Alliances

Yet, the Law hints at an enigmatic truth lurking beneath the surface. The concept underscores the necessity of integrating women into these alliances, suggesting an intriguing potential for a deeper connection between both genders. Could the convergence of male and female intellects unveil hidden corridors within Cognitexis, offering passage to realms of understanding obscured from the alone thinker? This idea posits that gender diversity in intellectual collaborations can lead to richer, more comprehensive insights.

Navigating the Maze of Cognitexis

This journey into the Cosmic Ballet is merely the beginning. Prepare to navigate the intricate maze of Cognitexis, where teamwork transcends mere advantage and becomes essential in revealing the human psyche's full capabilities. Keep in mind that even the most exquisite performances may conceal perilous secrets. As the thoughts collide, will a captivating harmony arise, or will a chaotic dissonance loom, ready to engulf the stage?

In Conclusion

The Cosmic Ballet and the Law of Intermingling Thoughts emphasize the importance of intellectual collaboration and the integration of diverse perspectives. This concept challenges the notion of solitary genius and highlights the transformative power of collective thought. By embracing this law, we can unlock new realms of understanding and innovation, ultimately enhancing the human experience.

2. The Fabric of Minds: Weaving the Tapestry of Collective Consciousness

(The Law of Social Association)

In the shadowy depths of Cognitexis, a complex narrative emerges from the Social Web. In this realm, the strands of contemplation glisten and weave together, dictated by the intricate dynamics of social connection. This principle unveils the intricate tapestry of our minds and fates, exposing a deep revelation: we are not mere solitary architects of our existence but active players in a vast, collective design.

The Principle of Social Connection

This principle suggests that the surrounding social context shapes our mental processes. Our understanding of the world and our identity is profoundly influenced by the values, beliefs, and norms we absorb from our social groups. The socialization process plays a vital role in shaping individual growth and fostering unity within society.

Resilience: An Affirmation of the Strength Found in Relationships

The presence of robust social support systems profoundly influences the capacity to recover from challenges. In moments of adversity, our connections with others provide us with resilience and fortitude. Engaging in therapy and counseling cultivates a collaborative relationship that nurtures a safe space, enabling individuals to develop coping mechanisms and strengthen their capacity for resilience.

The Central Hub: Family

The Law suggests that our family is the central hub of our cognitive processes. Envision an expansive tapestry woven with the haunting remnants of bygone encounters—the murmuring strands of our formative years. Within this intricate family dynamic, the foundational threads of our unique identities are intricately intertwined. A nurturing atmosphere cultivates the emergence of positive thought processes woven with strength, assurance, and a profound connection to one another. On the other hand, a fractured family can etch deep scars, intertwining strands of despair and uncertainty that might demand a reckoning in the future.

Research in developmental psychology highlights the impact of early family environments on cognitive and emotional development. Studies show that children raised in supportive and nurturing families tend to develop stronger cognitive skills and emotional resilience. Conversely, those from dysfunctional families may struggle with emotional regulation and cognitive challenges (Shonkoff & Garner, 2012).[24]

Utilizing the Principles of Social Connection

Seizing this power allows us to navigate the labyrinth of our minds. Acknowledge the shadows lurking in one's familial background, where threads of self-doubt and negativity lie in wait, yearning for recognition. Ponder how these influences might be sculpting one's current thoughts and behaviors. This realization marks the pivotal first step in untangling these entrenched ties and introducing more constructive patterns. Engaging in practices like journaling, self-reflection, or therapy can become vital tools in this exploration, helping you to reveal the frayed edges that need attention and where to intricately weave in new narratives.

- **Example from Literature:** In J.D. Salinger's "The Catcher in the Rye," the protagonist, Holden Caulfield, grapples with the impact of his family dynamics on his mental state. Through his journey of self-reflection and interactions with others, Holden begins to understand and confront the shadows of his past, illustrating the importance of acknowledging and addressing familial influences.[25]

Weaving the Narrative

The family unit, while pivotal, is merely a fragment of a much larger and intricate tapestry that weaves through the Social Web. The Weaver's Guild—a network of allies, guides, and peers—persistently sharpens the intricate fabric of our thoughts. Their exchanges weave together the torn threads of existence, infusing life with bold hues and complex designs. This expansive web reveals that our thoughts emerge not in solitude but through a complex interplay of social dynamics. Thus, remain vigilant about the circles you choose to inhabit. Opt to immerse yourself in the company of those who ignite your passion and provoke your thoughts, weaving vibrant strands into the tapestry of your mind.

- **Example from Alternative Disciplines:** The notion of mastermind groups reveals the profound influence of collective human connection. These collectives unite individuals with similar thoughts, fostering an environment where ideas are exchanged, support is offered, and challenges are presented, pushing each member to realize their ambitions. In his seminal work, Think and Grow Rich, Napoleon Hill illuminated the profound impact of collective minds, suggesting that such alliances can profoundly enhance one's journey toward personal and professional evolution. In the shadows of our collective endeavors, we uncover hidden insights, navigate the labyrinth of challenges, and ultimately reach heights that elude solitary pursuits. The intricate dynamics of a mastermind group can serve as a catalyst for creativity, intensifying motivation while weaving a complex tapestry of connection among its members.[26]

Strategic Moves for Enhancing the Interconnectedness Landscape

To amplify the beneficial impact of your social circle, immerse yourself in pursuits that connect you with those who share your mindset. Engage in clubs, immerse yourself in workshops, or dive into group discussions where thoughts are shared openly and meaningfully. Furthermore, explore the possibility of connecting with mentors or engaging with communities that resonate with your principles and aspirations. These encounters will serve as the deft touch of a master craftsman, guiding you to repair fragile threads and infuse fresh energy into your intricate design.

Neuroplasticity, the brain's ability to reorganize itself by forming new neural connections, underscores the importance of social interactions. Engaging in meaningful social activities can enhance neuroplasticity, improving cognitive function and emotional well-being (Kempermann, 2019). Studies have shown that social engagement stimulates the brain, promoting cognitive flexibility and resilience against neurodegenerative diseases (Hertzog et al., 2008).[27]

Restoring Tattered Connections

When the shadows of troubled connections have frayed your mental fabric, the Law whispers that restoration is within reach. Connect with those who illuminate your path, whether mentors, friends, or therapists, as you navigate the intricate journey of reshaping and fortifying your self-image. Like skilled artisans, they provide instruments and insights that can transform past narratives and substitute detrimental habits with constructive ones.

Resilience is crucial in overcoming negative emotions and restoring mental well-being. It involves the ability to adapt and recover from adversity, and it is often strengthened through supportive social connections. Therapy and counseling can play a significant role in building resilience, helping individuals reframe negative experiences, and develop healthier thought patterns (American Psychological Association, 2022).

Neuroscience offers compelling evidence for the interconnected nature of minds. Mirror neurons, for instance, enable us to empathize with others and understand their experiences (Iacoboni, 2009). Oxytocin, often referred to as the "love hormone," plays a crucial role in social bonding and trust (Kosfeld et al., 2005). By acknowledging the profound impact of social interaction on our mental well-being, we can cultivate stronger relationships, foster empathy, and build more resilient communities.[28]

Psychological Implications:

- **Resilience and Social Support:** Strong social connections can bolster our resilience, enabling us to cope with adversity and bounce back from setbacks.

- **Social Learning and Modeling:** We learn through observation and imitation, adopting the behaviors and beliefs of those we admire or respect.

- **Groupthink and Conformity:** Social pressures can lead us to conform to group norms, even when our individual judgment suggests otherwise.

In Conclusion

Ultimately, the Social Web reveals the complex journey we navigate within the domain of Cognitexis. The complex tapestry we weave is shaped by those surrounding us, a stark reminder that our destinies are inextricably linked through each interaction we experience. Within the complex web of our minds, the choices we confront regarding which strands to hold onto and which to alter define the richness and resilience of our inner world. We are the architects of our destinies, and the connections we forge will define the strength and beauty of our complex inner worlds.

3. The Nexus of Thoughts: Where Concepts Collide and Collaborate

(The Law of Thoughts Association)

The human mind, a vast and intricate network of interconnected ideas, operates under a fundamental principle: the Law of Thought Association. This law posits that our thoughts are not isolated entities but are intrinsically linked to one another, forming a complex cognitive web. As we engage in mental processes, concepts and ideas influence each other, creating a dynamic interplay that shapes our understanding of the world.

The Cognitive Network

Imagine the mind as a vast neural network, where each node represents a concept or idea. These nodes are interconnected by neural pathways, forming a complex web of associations. When we think about a particular concept, it activates not only the node representing that concept but also the nodes of related concepts. This activation spreads through the network, influencing the thoughts and ideas that arise in our consciousness.

The Science Behind the Concept

Neurological research has provided substantial evidence to support the idea of interconnected thoughts. Studies on neural networks have demonstrated that neurons fire in patterns corresponding to specific thoughts and concepts. These patterns are not static but dynamic, constantly adapting and evolving as we learn and experience new information.

Applications of the Nexus of Thoughts

Understanding the Law of Thought Association has far-reaching implications for various fields:

- **Education:** By recognizing the interconnectedness of concepts, educators can design more effective learning experiences that foster deeper understanding and critical thinking.

- **Cognitive Psychology:** The concept can be used to explore the mechanisms of memory, creativity, and problem-solving.

- **Artificial Intelligence:** AI researchers can develop more sophisticated and intelligent systems by modeling the human mind as a network of interconnected concepts.[29]

Connecting Thoughts

Think of the Nexus as an extensive network, each node representing a concept. Connected routes, these nodes are a hive of associational energy. According to the law, every idea is impacted by the thoughts surrounding it; no thinking is independent.[vi]

The intricate workings of neural networks within the brain serve as a compelling metaphor for the Law of Thought Association. The brain's neurons, those fundamental elements of our consciousness, intertwine and converse through synapses, creating complex webs that give rise to the very essence of thought. In the intricate web of the human mind, as elucidated by neuroscientist Daniel Kahneman in his profound work Thinking, Fast and Slow, neural networks are in a perpetual state of transformation, shaped by the shadows of our experiences and the whispers of the information surrounding

---

[vi] **Note:** Just as atoms of matter are influenced by the presence of their neighbors, the same principle applies to thoughts, as they are the result of matter and energetic interactions. In a similar way that the atoms of matter are influenced by the presence of their "neighbors," people's thoughts are also shaped by the thoughts and ideas that surround them.

us. The intricate web of neural activity weaves a tapestry that dictates the potency and fluidity of these connections, echoing how ideas within the Nexus are molded by the shadows of their adjacent concepts. By exploring neural networks, we uncover human cognition's intricate and ever-shifting landscape, revealing layers of understanding that provoke profound contemplation.[30]

Impact of a Ripple

Think of a stone thrown into a calm pool and the ripples it causes to spread outward. Similarly, fresh ideas can change old ones and create new ones when they are introduced to the Nexus. Our ideas are continually changing and adapting, molded by the dance of association, as highlighted by the Law of Thought Association.

- **Example from Literature:** James Joyce's Ulysses serves as a compelling exploration of the intricate connections within the human mind. In a labyrinth of introspection, Joyce unveils the intricate web of human thought, revealing its ever-shifting and entwined essence. As Leopold Bloom traverses the shadowy streets of Dublin, his consciousness spirals into a tumultuous sea of fragmented thoughts, haunting memories, and intricate connections. The fleeting image of a flower girl evokes a haunting memory of his wife, spiraling into a profound reflection on mortality and the relentless march of time. In Joyce's haunting prose, one finds the solitary journey of a wayfaring man steeped in sorrow, grappling with a fever of his own making and striving to arrive at the city that answers his dreams. Joyce writes, *'A way a lone wayfaring man, mourning, when cursed with fever, can reach the city of his desire.'* This passage reveals how a single thought can spiral into a labyrinth of interconnected ideas, each thread pulling the mind deeper into a shadowy realm of contemplation.[31]

The Influence of Working Together

Working together is critical to the Nexus's success. By forming intellectual alliances, diverse brains can cross-pollinate ideas and propel creativity. Cooperation is essential to developing new ideas and not only a choice. We can all learn more and grow smarter when we talk to one another and share our experiences and viewpoints.

- **Example from Alternative Disciplines:** The notion of open innovation reveals the intricate dance of collaboration and the enigmatic allure of shared knowledge. By dismantling the conventional barriers that separate organizations from individuals, a realm of unsettling possibilities emerges, paving the way for profound revelations and unsettling innovations. Corporations such as Procter & Gamble have adeptly navigated the shadows of open innovation, forging alliances with academic institutions, emerging startups, and various entities to conjure new products and technologies from the depths of collaboration. Henry Chesbrough, a prominent figure in the realm of open innovation, posits that innovation is not confined to a single entity but rather permeates through a network of diverse organizations and individuals. By cultivating a shared understanding and collective effort, we may unearth the depths of human ingenuity and the shadows of our imagination.[32]

The Law guides us through human principles' murky depths

The contours of our minds shift and twist, molded by the complex interplay of our encounters, connections, and the knowledge we absorb. The individuals in our lives, the narratives we absorb, and the concepts we confront wield a profound power over our perceptions and convictions. In the shadows of the mind, where inspiration intertwines with deception, the presence of those who provoke thought can ignite a spark of creativity and foster intellectual evolution. Yet, lurking beneath the surface, the weight of negative or misleading connections can stifle the clarity of reason, plunging one into the depths of cognitive dissonance. The insidious nature of confirmation bias, the suffocating walls of echo chambers, and the relentless grip of misinformation weave a web that distorts our perceptions, ensnaring us in a labyrinth where the truth remains elusive and our grasp of intricate realities is forever hindered. The Law, shrouded in its intricate web of evidence and impartiality, beckons one to delve deeper into the shadows of critical thought, revealing unsettling truths beneath the surface of rigorous analysis. By meticulously examining the origins of our thoughts, exploring varied viewpoints, and confronting our own beliefs, we can forge a more intricate and enlightened understanding of the world around us.

In the intricate labyrinth of the human mind, as philosopher and cognitive scientist Daniel Kahneman explored in "Thinking, Fast and Slow," we find ourselves ensnared by cognitive biases that warp our perceptions and influence our choices in unsettling ways. By delving into the shadows of our biases and daring to explore alternative perspectives, we can sharpen our critical thinking and navigate the labyrinth of choices with greater clarity.[33]

- **Example from Science:** The existence of echo chambers within social media starkly illustrates the perilous nature of detrimental mental connections. When people find themselves surrounded solely by narratives that echo their own convictions, they risk falling into the abyss of cognitive biases, shackling their ability to engage in true critical thought. In their exploration book Network Propaganda, Benkler, Faris, and Roberts reveal how echo chambers weave a tangled web of perception, ensnaring individuals in a warped reality that obscures objective evaluation and stifles the contemplation of divergent viewpoints.

Just as certain physical combinations can lead to peril, so too can detrimental associations between ideas; this underscores the vital importance of critical thinking. The law compels us to delve into the shadows of our thoughts, scrutinizing the origins of our beliefs with meticulous attention, weaving a complex tapestry of notions within our Whispering Corridors.[34]

In Conclusion

The Nexus of Thoughts within Cognitexis is a labyrinthine tapestry where concepts clash and intertwine in a dance of shadows and revelations. By delving into the intricacies of the Law of Thought Association, we can unlock our minds' latent potential, weaving together threads of interconnected thinking that ignite the flames of creativity and innovation. This intricate web of ideas, woven with varied viewpoints and profound contemplation, underscores the necessity of a nurturing and thought-provoking intellectual atmosphere.

Like a ripple upon still waters can create waves that spread outward, introducing new ideas within the Nexus can disturb the surface, sending tremors through the depths of established thoughts, reshaping them in unforeseen ways. By enveloping ourselves in a tapestry of unsettling yet thought-provoking influences, we can weave a narrative of inspiration and transformation. Yet, we must stay alert to the insidious connections that can unravel the fabric of our mental clarity.

Ultimately, the Nexus of Thoughts stands as an overpowering reflection of our potential for intellectual and personal evolution. It serves as a stark reminder that through the intertwining of minds, the probing of thoughts, and the clash of varied perspectives, we can cultivate our consciousness into a vibrant and fertile landscape for startling revelations and profound understanding.

4. Intriguing Connections: The Intersection of Collaborative Thoughts

(The Law of Thought Harmonious Interaction)

In the shadowy depths of Cognitexis, an enigmatic power thrums with an invisible pulse—the Law of Thoughtful Interaction, a principle of Harmonious Engagement. In this mysterious domain, thoughts transcend the ephemeral, becoming vivid strands intricately interlaced within the essence of reality. Envision Cognitexis as an expansive, reverberating void where the atmosphere shimmers with an array of thought waves, each one a distinct thread vibrating with its own intrinsic nature.

The Thrum of Resonance

The Law of Thoughtful Interaction reveals that these thought threads, akin to harmonious notes in a long-lost cosmic symphony, are pulled together by an enigmatic force referred to as Synergistic Attraction. When akin thought waves intertwine, they generate a pulsating resonance, an intense surge of energy that unites them inextricably. Envision a pair of ideas, each pulsating with shards of a mysterious enigma. As they draw closer within Cognitexis, their paths intertwine, creating a complex tapestry woven from the depths of their shared understanding. This freshly woven strand of thought pulses intensely, suggesting the hidden truths it now conceals.

- **Example from Science:** The idea of resonance in physics serves as a reverberating metaphor for the intricacies of collaborative thought. Just as two objects vibrating at the same frequency can amplify each other's vibrations, hence, in a world where resonance shapes reality, the convergence of minds attuned to similar frequencies can intensify the echoes of their thoughts, weaving a tapestry of ideas that transcends the individual. Collaboration becomes a powerful force, an enigmatic dance of intellects that elevates the mundane into the extraordinary.

In his exploration book Where Good Ideas Come From, Steven Johnson reveals how innovation frequently arises from the unexpected intersections of varied thoughts, weaving a narrative that delves into the intricate dance of creativity and chance. In cultivating spaces where unfiltered conversation and the unrestrained flow of thoughts are not just welcomed but essential, we unlock the potential of collective reasoning, propelling us toward advancement and unraveling the intricacies of our most daunting challenges.[35]

The Fusion of Concepts

This intriguing interplay flourishes through collaboration, a notion surpassing the tangible realm's confines. As hidden influences guide the intricate movements of the universe, the convergence of varied intellects within Cognitexis can ignite revolutionary ideas. Brainstorming sessions would unfold like a suspenseful narrative, with each idea weaving into the next, creating an intricate web of insight that keeps the mind racing. The Law suggests that this synthesis creates a connection of thought that surpasses the individual components. Envision a gathering of intellectuals, each a unique lens through which to interpret the enigmatic whispers of an age-old manuscript, their minds racing with the thrill of discovery. In a dance of intellect, as their thoughts intertwine, the markings on the page start to coalesce into a design revealing a truth that eludes any solitary mind's grasp.

- **Example from Literature:** In Plato's "The Republic," the dialogues between Socrates and other characters illustrate how collaborative thinking can lead to deeper understanding and philosophical insights. Each participant's unique perspective contributes to a richer, more comprehensive exploration of ideas.

The Transformation of Mind

The Law draws a captivating parallel between the intricate mechanisms of thought formation and the forces that shape the universe. In a manner reminiscent of celestial formations emerging from chaotic nebulas, thoughts similarly harness a blend of diverse energies and experiences, weaving together intricate perspectives to forge a more profound and resilient cognitive framework. This intricate interplay facilitates a thought transformation—converting diverse concepts into a singular, powerful entity. Envision a solitary investigator, her intellect ablaze with the fire of exploration, carefully weaving fragments of forgotten knowledge into a tapestry of understanding. These elements converge in a groundbreaking theory that transforms the essence of understanding through their intricate interplay with her insights.

- **Example from Alternative Disciplines:** Cross-disciplinary collaboration exemplifies this idea in the field of innovation. When experts from different fields come together, their diverse perspectives can lead to groundbreaking innovations that are impossible within the confines of a single discipline.

The Dark Figures that Haunt

Yet, the Law recognizes the formidable forces that can shatter this delicate equilibrium. Three pivotal elements can trigger the disintegration of these intricately spun connections:

a. **The Veil of Unawareness:** When we overlook the compelling force of collaboration and the magnetic pull of shared ideas, we forfeit the opportunity to unlock true synergy. This can render the intricate web of ideas fragile, susceptible to the looming darkness that threatens to consume it.

The notion of collective thought in the realm of psychology serves as a chilling reminder of the perils that lie in the shadows of unchecked conformity. Irving Janis[36], a figure of notable repute in social psychology, reveals a chilling truth: When the desire for group harmony eclipses the need for critical scrutiny, individuals become ensnared in a web of cognitive distortions, including a perilous sense of invulnerability and an oppressive urge to conform. Such biases can ensnare the mind, leading to flawed choices as individuals stifle opposing views and neglect to explore divergent perspectives. In cultivating an environment where voices intertwine, and thoughts are dissected, we can unravel the shadows of conformity and navigate toward choices that resonate with clarity and purpose.

b. **Chaotic Disruptions:** Intentionally embracing dark thoughts can unleash a perilous energy. These jarring currents of thought, akin to sinister murmurs from hidden realms, can shatter the seamless stream of ideas, obstructing innovation and advancement. They function as tattered strands, undermining the intricate weave of ideas and leaving them vulnerable to intrusion.

- **Example from Literature:** J.R.R. Tolkien's The Lord of the Rings presents a powerful allegory for the disruptive influence of negative associations, an intense exploration of the insidious effects of dark connections that twist the fabric of reality. The One Ring, an embodiment of unrestrained authority and moral decay, ensnares its bearers, spiraling them into chaos, brutality, and the disintegration of bonds. In the analysis presented by Tolkien scholar Tom Shippey in The Road to Middle-Earth, the sinister influence of the Ring serves as a stark reminder of the perilous nature of unbridled ambition and the critical necessity of resisting the allure of temptation. By meticulously exploring the Ring's insidious grip, we uncover the profound implications of harmful connections and the critical necessity of nurturing uplifting forces in our existence.[37]

c. **The Antagonistic Mind:** More than just a shadow of negativity, sinister forces lurk within Cognitexis—the Antagonistic Mind. These enigmatic entities relentlessly strive to undermine peaceful connections, twist perceptions, and incite chaos. They revel in the disintegration of the fabric, seeking to cast Cognitexis into turmoil and darkness.

The shadowy landscape of cybersecurity compellingly reflects the internal struggles that define the human psyche. Devious individuals lurking in the shadows manipulate weaknesses within systems to sow discord, pilfer secrets, and unleash turmoil. In a haunting manner, detrimental thoughts can prey upon our minds' frailties, spiraling us into the depths of anxiety, despair, and a myriad of psychological afflictions.

Bruce Schneier unveils a chilling truth in his work Liars and Outliers: The intricate dance of deception employed by malicious actors reveals the unsettling nature of our vulnerabilities. By delving into their tactics and strategies, we can forge a path toward crafting defenses that stand resilient against the lurking dangers, both from without and within. By integrating the tenets of cybersecurity into our psychological well-being, we can fortify our mental barriers and shield ourselves from the insidious influence of detrimental thoughts.[38]

The Tapestry of Balance

Fortunately, we are not mere spectators in this intricate interplay of ideas. The Weavers of Harmony, those deeply connected to the Law of Thoughtful Interaction, serve as vigilant protectors of Cognitexis. Through sharpened instincts and profound insight into the complexities of the human mind, they can uncover and heal the fractures inflicted by chaotic influences. They can create an environment ripe for dynamic interactions, promoting teamwork and facilitating sharing varied viewpoints. The Weavers of Harmony operate as masterful craftsmen, stitching together the torn strands and safeguarding the fabric of ideas, keeping it alive and resilient against the looming darkness.

By grasping the principles of Thoughtful Interaction, we can metamorphose Cognitexis from a disordered mass of ideas into a dynamic weave of collaboration and connection. Through the art of collaboration, nurturing uplifting connections, and staying alert to the subtle echoes of doubt, we can shape the intricate melody of our thoughts, crafting a formidable shield against the mysterious entities that dwell in the shadowy realms of Cognitexis.

In Conclusion

The Law of Harmonious Interaction within Cognitexis reveals the profound potential of collaborative thought and the delicate balance required to maintain it. By understanding and applying this law, we can harness the power of synergistic attraction to create resonant ideas that transcend individual capabilities. This principle underscores the importance of collaboration, diverse perspectives, and the fusion of concepts to achieve deeper understanding and innovation.

However, we must remain vigilant against the dark figures that haunt this delicate equilibrium. By recognizing the threats posed by unawareness, chaotic disruptions, and the Antagonistic Mind, we can take proactive steps to safeguard our mental environment. The Weavers of Harmony, with their profound insight and skill, guide us in maintaining the integrity of our cognitive tapestry.

Ultimately, the Intersection of Collaborative Thoughts serves as a testament to our intellectual and personal growth capacity. It reminds us that through the power of harmonious interaction and vigilant protection, we can weave a tapestry of understanding that reveals hidden truths and propels us toward greater knowledge and innovation.[vii]

5. The Symphony of Energy: Where Thoughts Dance and Collide

(The Law of Thought as an Energetic Interaction)

In the shadowy depths of Cognitexis, a pulsating energy hums with both exhilarating possibilities and lurking threats: the collision points of mental forces. In this realm, the core of cognition reveals itself through an exhilarating interplay of allure and aversion, a captivating display that evokes profound wonder. This intricate dance is dictated by the Law of Thoughts Energetic Interaction, a principle that suggests thoughts are not simply illusions of the mind but vibrant fields of energy that engage with one another in captivating and occasionally dangerous manners.

Picture Cognitexis

Picture Cognitexis as an enormous room where innumerable thought waves glisten in the air. Every wave has its own distinct frequency, symbolizing a distinct thinking. The same universal laws of attraction and repulsion, as stated in the Law of Thoughts Energetic Interaction, also apply to these thought waves.

The notion of quantum entanglement in physics offers an interesting framework through which to explore the intricate web of human consciousness. In a world where unseen connections bind us, much like the mysterious dance of entangled particles can

---

[vii] Both the **Harmonious Interactions** (The Nexus of Synergistic Thought and **The Shadowy Dance** (Repulsive Thoughts and the Mind's Defenses) concepts serve as a reminder of the delicate balance within Cognitexis. Just as a harmonious symphony requires careful orchestration, so too does a healthy mind require the ability to manage the interplay of thoughts. By understanding the potential for repulsive clashes and harnessing the power of directed attention, we can transform Cognitexis from a battleground of discord into a vibrant symphony of thought.

influence each other instantaneously, regardless of distance, our thoughts weave an intricate web that influences our very essence, molding our experiences and guiding our actions in ways we scarcely comprehend. In the reflections of scientific inquiry, physicist John Bell unveiled a haunting truth: quantum entanglement challenges our conventional grasp of reality, hinting at eerie, non-local connections that weave through the fabric of the universe.[39]

In a striking revelation, neuroscientists have unveiled the intricate web of our brains, where disparate regions engage in a silent dialogue, their exchanges woven through the enigmatic tapestry of electrical impulses. According to cognitive neuroscientist Michael Gazzaniga, these intricate neural networks allow us to weave complex thoughts and ideas, casting enigmatic influences that shape our emotions, decisions, and actions. Through the exploration of connections between the realms of quantum mechanics and the complexities of neuroscience, we uncover a profound understanding of the enigmatic and ever-shifting essence of human consciousness.[40]

The Harmonious Thrum and the Law of Harmonious and Repulsive Interaction

A force known as the Law of Harmonious Interaction can bring together ideas in the same way that opposing charges attract in the physical world. Picture two harmonic thrums, each generated by resonating two thought waves of a comparable frequency. The amplified energy of both ideas when they combine in harmony results in deeper knowledge and the possibility of revolutionary ideas. This idea is fundamental to collaborative brainstorming, as when people contribute their ideas, the result is a harmonious whole that exceeds the individual contributions of its members.

- **Example from Literature:** "William Shakespeare's The Tempest presents a haunting exploration of the influence of focused intention." Prospero, the enigmatic protagonist, wields power over the island and its denizens, orchestrating a series of events to fulfill his own intricate designs. The capacity to mold existence through the sheer force of contemplation reflects how synchronized mental currents can converge to unveil deep revelations.

As literary critic Harold Bloom suggests, Prospero's final gesture of forgiveness and renunciation embodies the profound complexities of human understanding and the haunting potential for reconciliation. Examining Prospero's essence reveals the profound capacity of human intellect to mold reality and foster transformation, inviting us to ponder the darker intricacies of our existence.[41]

The Law of Repulsive Interaction and the Discordant Clash

The Law of Repulsive Interaction governs the coexistence of opposing forces within Cognitexis, which leads to the Discordant Clash. Think of it as two completely different waves of thought coming together like two notes in a musical composition. Cognitive dissonance, perplexity, and even the death of original thought can result from such an unpleasant collision. Such repellent forces include disinformation and negativity, which can obstruct the free flow of constructive ideas.

The unsettling nature of cognitive dissonance in psychology is a haunting illustration of the Law of Repulsive Interaction. When people confront ideas that challenge their established convictions, it stirs a profound unease, igniting a tumultuous conflict within their minds. Leon Festinger's pioneering exploration into the intricacies of cognitive dissonance reveals a haunting truth: People frequently use myriad strategies to alleviate the unsettling tension within. They may twist reality, craft rationalizations for conflicting information, or delve into the shadows of their minds, seeking only those fragments of truth that reinforce their pre-existing convictions. By delving into the intricate psychological mechanisms that fuel cognitive dissonance, we can uncover strategies to alleviate its detrimental impacts, fostering a landscape where open-mindedness and critical thinking can thrive amidst the shadows of the mind.[42]

The Shadow Legion's Whisper

Nevertheless, Cognitexis is not all sunshine and rainbows; it harbors the Shadow Legion. The Law of Thoughts Energetic Interaction could be manipulated by such constant, malevolent influences, whispering sinister thoughts. Discordant confrontations are the lifeblood of this Shadow Legion, which uses them to their advantage, sowing doubt and chaos within Cognitexis. Shadow Legion sabotages Cognitexis and exposes people's weaknesses by capitalizing on the negativity that might arise from two primary places:

a. **Harmful Associates**

The Shadow Legion can take advantage of harmful associates by the company we keep. One may associate with pessimists, cynics, or even malicious people. These externally disruptive thought-waves can throw a person's mental equilibrium off, leaving them open to the Shadow Legion's hushed murmurs.

b. **Unhealed Wounds**

The Shadow Legion can also take advantage of wounds that have not yet healed, such as past trauma or suffering. An individual battling post-traumatic stress disorder, for instance, might be more susceptible to the Legion's influence. When we let our emotions fester, it can lead to a downward spiral of negativity and cognitive dissonance, which the Shadow Legion can use to their advantage.

The realm of mental health unveils a profound understanding of the necessity of addressing detrimental influences. In the shadows of the human psyche, an approach emerges that acknowledges the haunting effects of trauma on mental well-being. It beckons us to delve deeper, to confront the hidden sources of anguish that linger beneath the surface. In the shadows of the human psyche, where past traumas linger and haunt, mental health professionals emerge as beacons of hope. They create sanctuaries that allow individuals to confront their inner demons, fostering resilience that prepares them for the inevitable storms of existence. According to the National Center for Trauma-Informed Care, trauma-informed care emerges as a framework rooted in recognizing the profound effects of trauma and violence, emphasizing the inherent strengths within individuals and acting in accordance with the rooted understanding of rebirth and the strength to endure. Understanding trauma can reshape our mental health approaches, paving the way for profound healing and the nurturing of well-being.

A Fine Line

In the face of the Shadow Legion's influence, the Weavers of Harmony, an esteemed organization of thinkers committed to cultivating intellectual harmony, maintain vigilance. They act as mediators, directing waves of thought so that they continue to interact positively and avoid any negative consequences that could arise from unpleasant collisions. The Weavers of Harmony cultivate an environment where new ideas can flourish by using their keen understanding of human psychology and critical thinking skills.

The role of cognitive-behavioral therapists resembles that of the Weavers of Harmony. These therapists delve into the shadows of the mind, assisting individuals in reshaping their negative thought patterns and nurturing positive mental interactions, akin to the Weavers who manipulate thought waves to cultivate a haunting yet profound intellectual harmony. Cognitive-behavioral therapy (CBT) stands as a formidable method, its efficacy in addressing a spectrum of mental health challenges well-documented, inviting deeper contemplation on the intricacies of the human psyche. Through the confrontation of bleak thoughts and the gradual transformation into more grounded and optimistic perspectives, this approach can guide individuals toward a deeper emotional resilience and a more profound sense of existence. As cognitive-behavioral therapist Aaron Beck has revealed, the labyrinth of our thoughts intricately weaves the fabric of our emotions and actions, guiding us through the shadows of our psyche. Through the exploration of our inner turmoil and the unsettling shadows of our minds, we can confront and reshape the destructive narratives that bind us, ultimately reclaiming our mental sovereignty and fostering a more hopeful perspective on existence.[43]

The Unanticipated Repercussions

Having said that, there are pros and cons of using Thoughts' Energetic Interaction. When people work together in harmony, great things can happen. However, when thoughts, even good ones, are amplified too much, they can have negative effects. To upset the delicate equilibrium in Cognitexis, all you have to do is imagine a harmonizing thrumming that builds to a fever pitch. Constantly present is the risk that careless handling of even the most well-meaning ideas might lead to catastrophic outcomes.

- **Example from Literature:** Mary Shelley's Frankenstein serves as a haunting narrative that explores the perilous consequences of unbridled ambition, urging a deep reflection on the moral complexities entwined with scientific and technological progress. Though sparked by lofty ideals, Victor Frankenstein's relentless quest for understanding spirals into the birth of a creature that unleashes chaos upon the world. Literary critic Harold Bloom posits that the tragic flaw of Frankenstein resides in his overwhelming hubris, a profound conviction that he can surpass the boundaries of human comprehension and master the very forces of nature itself. By meticulously exploring the repercussions stemming from Frankenstein's choices, we uncover profound insights into the nature of repulsion and the critical necessity of harmonizing our intellectual ambitions with ethical accountability.[44]

Discouragement and Hope

There is tremendous illuminating power and, at the same time, a grim possibility of evil pulsating through the Symphony of Energy. Using one's mental force responsibly is a sobering determination between them. A symphony of ideas illuminating the world can be composed by tapping into the power of harmonious connections and promoting collaboration, critical thinking, and healthy skepticism. However, we must not lose sight of the Shadow Legion's murmurs, for even a small slip-up from Cognitexis may cause it to become discordant, and reality itself would unravel.

Consider the historical narrative: the evolution of nuclear energy reveals such a duality, where remarkable progress intertwines with the ominous shadows cast by its double-edged sword application. The endeavor in Manhattan, orchestrated by brilliant minds like Robert Oppenheimer, birthed a force that irrevocably altered the trajectory of human existence. Nevertheless, it opened the door to the serene utilization of atomic energy, like power generation, and allowed the possibility of placing such destructive power in the wrong hands, bringing catastrophe upon humanity. This duality is a haunting reminder of the profound influence we wield and the critical necessity of wielding it carefully.[45]

- **Example from Alternative Disciplines:** In mindfulness meditation, individuals learn to observe their thoughts without judgment, promoting mental clarity and balance. This practice helps prevent the amplification of negative thoughts and maintains the harmony of the mind.

In Conclusion

The Symphony of Energy within Cognitexis is a dynamic interplay of thought waves, where ideas dance and collide under the influence of the Law of Thoughts' Energetic Interaction. By understanding and applying this law, we can harness the power of harmonious interactions to foster creativity and innovation while remaining vigilant against the discordant clashes that can disrupt our mental equilibrium.

Like in a symphony, where each instrument contributes to the overall harmony, our thoughts can resonate together to create profound insights and breakthroughs. However, we must be mindful of the Shadow Legion's whispers, which seek to exploit our vulnerabilities and disrupt the balance of our cognition.

Ultimately, the Symphony of Energy is a testament to our intellectual and personal growth capacity. It reminds us that by carefully cultivating our mental environment and critically assessing our thoughts, we can transform our minds into a vibrant and harmonious space for innovation and insight.

6. The Spark Exchange: Illuminating the Labyrinthine Library

(The Law of Successful Thought Exchange Processes)

In the shadowy depths of Cognitexis, an existing library where knowledge hums like a vibrant current, weaving through the aisles like a hidden force, enacting shelves strained under the burden of myriad ideas in this realm, whispering concealed secrets to those daring enough to decipher their mysteries. Welcome to a domain where the principle of Successful Thought Exchange dominates, a concept that propels intellectual collaboration to astonishing heights.

The Principle of Successful Thought Exchange

This principle transcends simple information exchange; it delves into the transformations that occur through direct or indirect mentorship. In this realm, the guides serve as beacons, igniting a flame within the intricate maze of the mentee's psyche, transforming that flicker into a formidable force of intellect, setting an intricate engine of contemplation into action.

- **Example from Science:** The relationship between Niels Bohr and Werner Heisenberg serves as a pursuing illustration of the profound impact that the exchange of ideas can wield. Bohr, a figure of great intellect and influence as a renowned physicist and mentor, strongly influenced Heisenberg's formative years, guiding him through the labyrinth of scientific inquiry. In the shadows of their frequent intense dialogues, Bohr became a beacon for Heisenberg, illuminating the path toward the revolutionary concepts of quantum mechanics and guiding him through the labyrinth of uncertainty and profound inquiry. Heisenberg reflected on Bohr, recognizing him not merely as a towering figure in science but as a profound educator whose influence extended far beyond the confines of the laboratory.[46] He possessed a unique talent for probing the depths of the mind, igniting a spark of critical thought with each carefully crafted inquiry. Their intellectual discourse not only deepened their comprehension but also thrust the entire realm of physics into uncharted territories.

The Catalyst for Self-Evolution

Driven by a meticulously honed fixation, this mechanism transforms into the catalyst for self-evolution. Envision the master of transformation, whose fingertips convert dull musings into radiant insights within the knowledge landscape. The mentor's words and actions ignite a fierce desire within the mentee, a burning ambition rooted in a clearly defined purpose.

- **Example from Literature:** N.H. Kleinbaum's Dead Poets Society is an overpowering exploration of the profound impact of mentorship on the human spirit. The figure of John Keating, portrayed by Robin Williams, compels his students to shatter the confines of societal norms and fully realize their unique identities. Keating's unorthodox approach to education, urging his students to ascend upon their desks and perceive the world through an altered lens, compels them to engage in profound critical and creative thought. A chilling reminder lingers in the mesmerizing echoes of Keating's words: *'Carpe diem, seize the day, boys, make your lives extraordinary.'*[47] Through the relentless encouragement of his students to chase their deepest desires and embrace existence in all its complexity, Keating reveals the haunting influence a committed guide can wield over the fates of those around him.[48]

The Relentless Cycle of Refinement

This yearning ignites a relentless cycle, refining and fortifying the mind's musings. Concepts are honed and intensified through relentless dialogue and meticulous refinement within the intricate corridors of knowledge. Each encounter unfolds like a secret dialogue, where the vast expanse of understanding looms like a library, and every utterance paints a vivid picture of the intricate tapestry of thought.

- **Example from Entrepreneurship:** The dynamic between Steve Jobs and Mike Markkula reveals the intricate dance of influence and ambition within the enterprise realm. Markkula, a shrewd entrepreneur and venture capitalist, cast an extended shadow over Jobs' formative years at Apple, offering guidance and an array of support that would shape the essence of innovation. In the recesses of ambition, Walter Isaacson reveals in his biography of Jobs how Markkula emerged as a guiding force, shaping Jobs' vision for Apple. He imparted lessons on the intricate dance of business strategy and financial management, offering a semblance of stability and encouragement amidst the chaos of innovation. Their intertwined ambitions wove a complex tapestry, elevating Apple from obscurity to a towering presence in the realm of technology.[49]

Structured Cognition and the Shadow Gallery

Structured Cognition, the intricate web of thoughts that defines our essence, flourishes within this Spark Exchange. Yet, it cautions against the intricate library, filled with radiant rooms and cloaked in dark recesses. The Law cautions against the Shadow Gallery, a realm where darkness thrives, extending its grasping tendrils toward the minds of those who turn their backs on the light of reason. Within this intricate labyrinth, the seeds of growth, nurtured by aspirations of virtue and commendable actions, thrive. Conversely, the insidious grip of negativity can stealthily taint the essence of our thoughts, much like a poison that seeps in over time.

- **Example from Literature:** Oscar Wilde's The Picture of Dorian Gray presents an intriguing narrative that explores the perilous consequences of surrendering to malevolent forces. Dorian Gray becomes entranced by Lord Henry Wotton's alluring yet sinister worldview, which beckons him to embrace a life of hedonism and unrestrained desire. As Lord Henry astutely observes, *'The only way to get rid of a temptation is to yield to it.'* Dorian's gradual surrender to a world steeped in vice and crime reveals the harrowing repercussions of yielding to dark thoughts and insatiable desires. By exploring Dorian Gray's character, we uncover the insidious nature of the Shadow Gallery and the critical need to nurture uplifting forces in our existence.[50]

In Conclusion

A decision awaits us, intrepid seekers of this enigmatic realm. Shall we delve into the intricate maze of the library, guided by the flickering lights in pursuit of that elusive spark to ignite our intellectual fervor? Or shall we surrender to the shadows and allow the corrosive grip of despair to infiltrate our minds? The Labyrinth conceals immense possibilities alongside tangible dangers. Choose with care, for it is through Cognitexis that the caliber of our thoughts shapes the path we traverse.

THE CRYPTIC HEART OF COGNITION

ზ♣ზ♣ზ♣

INDIVIDUAL THOUGHT PROCESSES AND MENTAL STATES

The path through the labyrinth grows ever darker as you confront the inner tempest of your thoughts. This group explores the solitary struggle within the mind's abyss, where the currents of thought threaten to engulf you. The Inner Maelstrom demands you tame the chaos within to master the art of decision-making in the face of existential dread. Here, you must confront the shadows of your psyche, battling the darkness that seeks to consume you.

1. The Inner Maelstrom: Taming the Currents of Thought

(The Law of Thought Self-Discipline)

The Principle of Mental Self-Control

In the shadowy depths of Cognitexis, a formidable presence awaits Self-Discipline. It's not a comforting beacon but a haunting guide steering us through a perilous ocean of feelings. This Law functions on a captivating and perilous principle - the obsessional current.

The Obsessional Current

This current isn't a gentle push forward; it's a fierce pull into the depths, an unwavering fixation on a goal that teeters on the edge of obsession. It empowers us to move forward, yet the price we pay is unsettling. Envision a mariner, irresistibly lured by an enchanting melody, steering towards an unseen danger lurking beneath the waves. The relentless pull of obsession can act like a seductive whisper, enticing us toward ambitions that gleam with allure yet hide treacherous pitfalls beneath their surface.

- **Example from Literature:** Herman Melville's Moby-Dick presents an enveloping narrative that explores the perilous depths of unbridled fixation. The unyielding obsession of Captain Ahab with the elusive white whale engulfs his existence, propelling him toward the precipice of insanity. In a haunting proclamation, Ahab asserts, *'All my means are sane, my ends insane.'* This quote underscores the perilous nature of fixation, revealing how it can spiral into reckless actions and ultimately lead to one's own undoing. By exploring Ahab's character, we uncover profound insights into the significance of self-discipline and the peril that arises when our desires dictate our choices.[51]

The Role of Self-Discipline

Self-discipline empowers us to traverse these treacherous depths. It sharpens our capacity to detect the nuanced changes in emotional undercurrents, enabling us to enhance the positive flows and steer away from the negative ones. This journey, reminiscent of a dramatic metamorphosis within the depths of the mind, holds immense power yet teeters on the edge of unpredictability. A single misstep might transform our emotions into a hideous manifestation, a shadowy echo of our deepest desires.

- **Example from Science:** Marie Curie's unwavering commitment to her radioactivity exploration reveals self-discipline's profound strength. Her unyielding obsession and tireless quest for understanding culminated in the revelation of radium and polonium, a journey that granted her two Nobel Prizes. Yet, as Susan Quinn reveals in her biography Marie Curie: A Life, Curie's relentless pursuit of her work led her into the shadows of peril, where the essence of her brilliance became a harbinger of her tragic fate. Curie's obsession with her work exposed her to dangerous levels of radiation, ultimately contributing to her untimely death. Her narrative underscores the delicate interplay between fervent desires and the necessity of nurturing oneself, revealing the profound implications of establishing boundaries in our relentless quests.[52]

The Power of Decisive Action

The unsettling reality is this: decisive action is the most powerful instrument for transforming emotions. Through relentless pursuit of our passions, we forge intricate connections in the depths of our minds. These pathways can morph into an automatic drive, pushing us ahead, yet they can equally transform into confinement, ensnaring us in an unyielding chase that devours everything in its wake.

- **Example from Entrepreneurship:** Elon Musk, the visionary entrepreneur steering Tesla and SpaceX, embodies the inciting allure of unwavering resolve. His unyielding quest for the unknown and audacious embrace of uncertainty have birthed profound transformations across multiple realms. Yet, as Walter Isaacson reveals in his exploration of Musk's life, the relentless pursuit of ambition and the weight of expectation has cast shadows over his personal life and mental well-being. Musk's journey underscores the delicate interplay between resolute choices and the often-overlooked realms of self-care and emotional equilibrium. In recognizing the treacherous depths of unbridled ambition, we uncover the delicate balance between seizing the moment and safeguarding our very essence.[53]

The Dual Nature of Self-Discipline

Cognitexis is a mysterious domain where the boundaries of influence and danger intertwine. Self-discipline, once a trusted ally, can morph into a ruthless master when ensnared by the grip of obsession. The whistling compass might point the way, yet it holds no promise of a secure journey ahead. Pay close attention to its signals, as one wrong move might engulf you by the very feelings you aimed to master. Within the intricate depths of your mind lies the potential for greatness, yet lurking beneath the surface are the monstrous creations of your own psyche, poised to break free.

- **Example from Literature:** Mary Shelley's Frankenstein unfolds as a haunting narrative, exploring the perilous consequences of unbridled ambition and the shadows it casts on the human psyche. Victor Frankenstein's unyielding quest for understanding, fueled by an ambition to transcend human limitations, culminates in the birth of a grotesque being. In a moment of stark revelation, the creator confesses, *'I had worked hard for nearly two years for the sole purpose of infusing life into an inanimate body. For this, I had deprived myself of rest and health.'* This relentless commitment to his craft ultimately leads to the unraveling of his existence and the devastation of those around him. By exploring Frankenstein's character, we uncover the intricate interplay between self-discipline and the necessity of harmonizing our desires with moral imperatives.[54]

In Conclusion

The Principle of Mental Self-Control and the obsessional current highlight the dual nature of self-discipline. While it can drive us to achieve greatness, it also carries the risk of leading us into dangerous territory if not balanced with self-awareness and ethical considerations. By mastering the turbulent waves of consciousness, we can harness the power of self-discipline to achieve our goals while avoiding the pitfalls of obsession.

2. The Walled Garden: A Contemplation on Selfish Thoughts

(The Law of Selfish-Thought Process)

In the shadowy depths of Cognitexis, a lone silhouette roams the confines of a walled garden. This isn't your ordinary gardener; they cultivate not blooms and botanicals but the intricate landscape of the mind. This represents the very essence of the Law of Selfish Thought, a powerful and contentious concept. In this realm, the psyche transforms into a lush garden, where triumph relies on nurturing only the most advantageous mindsets.

The Principle of Mental Selectivity

The Law of Selfish Thought suggests that for a CgX system, a web of interconnected minds, to flourish, it must embrace a strategy of mental selectivity. Just as a strategist carefully selects the pieces on a chessboard, the mind must deftly navigate its connections and influences. Immersing oneself in negativity and embracing mindsets that stifle intellectual growth is like allowing invasive weeds to suffocate the rich soil of contemplation.

Reflect on Cognitive Behavioral Therapy (CBT), a thoroughly researched and commonly applied method that highlights the significance of mental discernment. As Beck (1979) suggests, a fundamental aspect of CBT involves recognizing and confronting detrimental thought patterns, ultimately transforming them into more positive and constructive alternatives.

During a session focused on cognitive behavioral techniques, practitioners frequently lead individuals to delve deeper into their thought patterns, encouraging a deliberate choice of thoughts that foster a healthier state of mind. This resonates with the principle of introspective cultivation, where the landscape of the mind requires careful tending to nurture only the most advantageous thought processes.[55]

The brain's capacity for neuroplasticity, its intricate ability to reshape itself through the formation of new neural connections, is fundamental to the process of mental selectivity. By delving into the intricacies of thought and experience, individuals can forge deeper connections within their minds, cultivating a more resilient and nuanced perspective on the world around them. In his exploration of the mind's malleability, neuroscientist Norman Doidge reveals how our brains are in a perpetual state of transformation, shaped by the labyrinth of our thoughts and the shadows of our experiences. Through the nurturing of an optimistic mindset, we can foster the development of neural pathways that underpin our sense of well-being and joy.[56]

The Balance Between Self-Improvement and Empathy

Though the principle of Selfish Thought encourages the cultivation of positive mental patterns, some contend it fosters a kind of self-centeredness or neglect for the well-being of others. Some may argue that an exclusively self-centered perspective risks fostering a chilling absence of empathy and a troubling neglect for the welfare of those around us.

Yet, the Law of Selfish Thought does not promote a total neglect of those around us. Rather, it implies that by nurturing an optimistic outlook and prioritizing self-improvement, individuals can play a more impactful role in the greater scheme of things. An individual with a solid grounding in constructive thinking is poised to forge deep connections, work harmoniously with others, and significantly impact the world around them.

An intriguing illustration of harmonizing personal growth with compassion emerges through the practice of Mindfulness-Based Stress Reduction (MBSR). Kabat-Zinn (1990) suggests that MBSR invites individuals to delve deeper into their own consciousness, fostering a heightened sense of self-awareness and mastery over their responses through the art of mindfulness practices. This deepened understanding of oneself not only cultivates individual evolution but also amplifies the capacity for empathy and compassion towards those around us.

In MBSR programs, individuals frequently unveil a heightened emotional fortitude and an expanded ability to connect with the feelings of others. By delving into the depths of their own psyche and nurturing a state of mental clarity, individuals unlock the potential to forge deeper connections with others and engage profoundly with their communities. This resonates with the principle of introspective contemplation, illustrating that the journey of personal growth can intertwine seamlessly with the virtues of understanding and kindness.[57]

- **Example from Literature:** Ayn Rand's The Fountainhead delves into the intricate dynamics of individualism and ambition through the enigmatic figure of Howard Roark. Roark's relentless pursuit of his architectural ideals, coupled with his steadfast refusal to yield to external pressures, positions him as an embodiment of solitary aspiration. In a moment of stark defiance, Roark proclaims, 'I don't care what you think or what anyone else thinks. I know I'm right.' Though his egocentric demeanor may drive people away, it paves the way for revolutionary architectural innovations that serve the greater good of society. By exploring Roark's character, we uncover the intricate dynamics between personal ambition and the obligations we hold towards society.[58]

The Hidden Advantages of Negative Emotions

Furthermore, some contend that the Law of Selfish Thought might neglect the hidden advantages of confronting and grappling with unsettling ideas. Negative emotions, often seen as burdens, can unexpectedly ignite the flames of personal growth and lead us down the path of profound self-discovery. We can uncover profound insights and cultivate a deeper resilience by delving into and unraveling these emotions.

Resilience, the ability to adapt and recover from adversity, is closely linked to neuroplasticity. When individuals confront and process negative emotions, they engage in cognitive restructuring that strengthens their mental resilience. This process can lead to significant personal development as individuals learn to navigate and overcome challenges, thereby enhancing their overall mental health.

The notion of post-traumatic growth, emerging from the shadows of trauma, reveals the unsettling yet profound advantages that can arise from our darkest emotions. Through the shadows of hardship, one may unearth a profound strength, a richer understanding of existence, and connections that resonate with an intensity born from struggle. In exploring the human psyche, Richard Tedeschi and Lawrence Calhoun delve into the intricate layers of resilience and transformation in their work, Post-traumatic Growth: Psychological Resources. In the aftermath of profound trauma, some individuals may find themselves awakening to a heightened sense of purpose, an intensified appreciation for the fragility of existence, and a more profound connection to the mysteries of the universe. By delving into the shadows of our experiences, we can uncover a deeper understanding of how the darker aspects of our emotions shape our existence.[59]

The Role of Selective Knowledge Acquisition

Envision a vast library, its towering shelves brimming with secrets waiting to be uncovered. The principle urges us to be astute connoisseurs rather than mindless gatherers. Some books, steeped in darkness or unhelpful notions, can be wisely ignored. Rather, we ought to pursue the architects of cognition, those tomes overflowing with motivation and mental nourishment.

- **Example from Literature:** Ray Bradbury's Fahrenheit 451 delves into the intricate dynamics of knowledge and the consequences of its deliberate assemblage. Montag, the central figure, unravels the profound and unsettling influence of delving into the pages of forbidden books. As he delves into the thoughts and feelings woven throughout these pages, he challenges the suffocating reality surrounding him. In a moment of introspection, Montag confesses, *'I don't want to burn things; I want to save them.'* This revelation signifies a pivotal moment in his existence as he ventures into profound introspection and emotional emancipation. By exploring Montag's character, we uncover the profound significance of discerning knowledge and the transformative influence of literature on our thoughts and actions.[60]

In Conclusion

The choice lies with the gardener, the intrepid navigator of this enigmatic realm. The lingering inquiry is whether they will choose to remain ensconced in the familiar confines of their curated reality, a sanctuary of reassuring monotony filled with their artfully crafted notions, or venture into the forbidden realm, risking the shadows of discontent in pursuit of that singular, transformative insight?

The response, most likely, lies in a state of balance. The enclosed sanctuary nurtures development with fierce intensity but can swiftly morph into a confining cage, stifling the mind from the myriad experiences that deepen existence. The forbidden grove harbors a treasure trove of concepts, but within its depths lurk dangers that threaten to stifle the very essence of intellectual evolution.

Ultimately, the gardener of Cognitexis must be prepared to navigate both realms, cultivating a thought garden that thrives and withstands the tests of time. In the intricate maze of the mind's library, the path you carve is shaped by the caliber of your thoughts.

3. The Mind's Quicksilver: Navigating the Crucible of Opportunity

(The Law of Prompt Decision-Making)

The Nature of the Law

In the intricate maze of Cognitexis, an enigmatic force looms, steadfastly governing the realm: the Law of Decision by Prompting. In the shadowy realm where every thought is dissected and scrutinized, the rapidity of choice emerges as the hallmark of a finely tuned mechanism of CgX.

Clarity of Intent

The clarity of intent serves as the catalyst, the spark that propels the metamorphosis of ideas into existence. The Law, an unforgiving overseer, challenges not just the intellect but delves deep into the essence of determination, scrutinizing the readiness of the mind and gauging the resolve to endure. Like a searing crucible, it tests the endurance of the mind—demanding persistence to grasp a particular goal.

The Bazaar of Chances

Envision a vibrant yet transient bazaar where chances dance like elusive shadows in the night. The quick thinker maneuvers through this intense challenge with the finesse of a master strategist. Their intellect, sharpened by rigorous discipline, can instantly grasp the essence of an idea, capture these ephemeral chances, and transform them into something concrete.

The Specter of Uncertainty

Yet, a haunting presence resides within Cognitexis: the specter of uncertainty. This hidden force embodies the repercussions of passivity, a quiet predator of possibility. A fleeting chance can dissolve into nothingness in the blink of an eye, leaving you with the haunting remnants of what could have been.

The Mind's Quicksilver

The Law of Prompt Decision-Making constantly reminds us of the lurking peril that awaits in the shadows. It beckons us to forge within the Mind's Quicksilver—a rapid and resolute stream of thought, one that effortlessly adapts to every shifting tide in Cognitexis. Every decision we make is key in this enigmatic realm, revealing the hidden doors to our true capabilities and illuminating fleeting moments that propel us toward triumph.

Examples from Science

1) The Discovery of Penicillin

In 1928, Alexander Fleming stumbled upon penicillin, a moment that revealed the profound impact of swift choices in the unfolding narrative of human progress. As Fleming observed the curious interaction of Penicillium Notatum with the bacteria in his petri dish, a profound realization dawned upon him, hinting at the transformative implications of this seemingly innocuous phenomenon. His instinctive choice to delve deeper sparked the creation of the world's first antibiotic. In the unfolding narrative of discovery, one man's swift reaction to an unforeseen revelation reshaped the landscape of medicine, ultimately preserving innumerable lives in the process. Yet, one must consider that the true capabilities of penicillin remained obscured for years, underscoring the vital role of unwavering determination and relentless inquiry.

2) The Manhattan Project

The Manhattan Project, an immense endeavor during the tumultuous times of World War II, reveals the profound impact of swift choices in unlocking monumental advancements. The pressing imperative to create a powerful weapon compelled a swift convergence of minds, drawing together some of the most brilliant scientists and engineers in a race against time. In the intricate narrative woven by Kai Bird and Martin J. Sherwin in their exploration of J. Robert Oppenheimer, the essence of triumph and tragedy unfolds through the lens of rapid, calculated choices made amidst overwhelming tension. Yet, the legacy of the project stands as a haunting reminder of the moral dilemmas entwined with scientific progress, urging us to reflect deeply on the potential ramifications of our choices.[61]

Examples from Literature

1) Hamlet

William Shakespeare's Hamlet is a profound exploration of the dangers inherent in hesitation and the complexities of the human psyche. The protagonist's paralysis in decision-making sets off a haunting sequence of consequences. In the exploration of human complexity, as articulated by Harold Bloom in his examination of Shakespeare, the character of Hamlet embodies a profound philosophical depth, where his introspective nature and trepidation regarding the repercussions of his choices lead to a state of inaction. His reluctance to seek retribution for his father's death spirals into a chain of tragic events, leading to the demise of many, himself included. This inherent weakness underscores the critical nature of swift choices and the profound repercussions that can arise from hesitation.

2) The Alchemist

Paulo Coelho's The Alchemist explores the profound impact of swift choices on one's journey. Santiago, the central figure, is propelled by an unwavering sense of intent and an audacious spirit ready to embrace uncertainty. As he navigates the twists and turns of his path, he relies on instinct and belief, uncovering unforeseen possibilities and profound transformation along the way. Through accepting ambiguity and deep faith in the cosmos, Santiago navigates challenges and realizes his aspirations. This gripping narrative reveals the profound impact of resolute choices and the necessity of heeding one's innermost desires.

Examples from Alternative Disciplines

1) Business and Entrepreneurship

Steve Jobs, the enigmatic architect behind Apple, embodies the essence of decisive action in the face of uncertainty. In Walter Isaacson's intricate narrative, we discover a figure whose uncanny knack for rapid, resolute decisions became the driving force behind Apple's ascent to greatness. His sharp insight and audacity to embrace the unknown enabled him to metamorphose daring concepts into revolutionary creations. The capacity to make swift choices, intertwined with an unyielding quest for flawlessness, has carved an indelible mark in the realm of innovation.[62]

2) Sports

In the realm of athletics, the capacity to navigate high-stakes situations with swift judgment emerges as an essential trait for achieving greatness. Figures such as LeBron James and Tom Brady embody the essence of swift decision-making, showcasing the intricate dance between instinct and strategy. The athletes find themselves in a relentless dance of perception and instinct, where every fleeting moment demands a choice that could alter the fabric of the game's reality. Research in the realm of sports psychology reveals that cognitive agility—the capacity to process information and make impactful decisions swiftly—plays a crucial role in enhancing athletic performance. By refining their decision-making abilities, athletes unlock pathways to elevate their performance and realize their potential.

In Conclusion

The Law of Decision by Prompting reveals the profound necessity of clear intent and swift choices when traversing the complex labyrinth of Cognitexis. In the shadows of existence, where choices linger like specters, the power to act swiftly can turn ephemeral chances into tangible triumphs, shaping destinies in profound and unsettling ways. This principle compels us to seize the elusive nature of thought and confront the swift currents of decision-making to reveal our authentic selves.

4. The Unbreakable Spirit: Forging an Impregnable Mind

(The Law of Thoughts Resilience)

Deep within the labyrinthine Cognitexis, where shadows writhe, and whispers echo, a citadel of obsidian rises from the swirling mists—the Obsidian Citadel. Here, under a sky perpetually choked with doubt, the Law of Thought Resilience reigns supreme. This Law explores the core of an idea's resilience, its capacity to withstand the most devastating negative criticism. Within the labyrinth, ideas are more than just notions; they are fortresses under continual attack, as this terrible fact exposes.

The Obsidian Citadel: A Representation of Your Beloved Concept

Within the realm of Cognitexis stands a formidable fortress known as the Obsidian Citadel. This grand structure symbolizes the unyielding strength and resilience of individual thought processes and mental states. Rising from the shadows, the Citadel is a testament to the power that lies within the mind—a power forged in the crucible of ambition and primal passions, forming its impregnable walls.

Your aspirations serve as the relentless force propelling you forward, much like the tireless artisans, who labor day and night, to build and maintain the Citadel. Yet, the true strength of this fortress is not merely in its physical form but in its indomitable will. The Obsidian Citadel is imbued with an unbreakable spirit, representing the Law of Thoughts Resilience. This dogged soul protects the Citadel against the relentless onslaught of the Shadow Legion, repelling their attacks with unwavering determination.

The Citadel's resilience is a manifestation of your own mental fortitude. It stands as a beacon of hope and strength, illustrating how the mind can forge an impregnable defense against doubt and despair. As you navigate the intricate corridors of Cognitexis, the Obsidian Citadel serves as a reminder of the power within you—an unyielding spirit that can withstand any challenge.

Reflect on the notion of Grit, a term brought into the limelight by the insights of psychologist Angela Duckworth. Duckworth et al. (2007) describe grit as the blend of passion and perseverance directed towards achieving long-term aspirations. This trait empowers people to endure challenges and scrutiny, reminiscent of how the Obsidian Citadel stands firm against the onslaught of the Shadow Legion.

Duckworth's exploration reveals that those who possess a deeper tenacity often navigate the labyrinth of challenges with greater resilience, ultimately reaching their distant aspirations. This illustrates the principle of mental fortitude, where the strength of one's beliefs and aspirations, akin to the unyielding spirit of the Obsidian Citadel, allows one to endure harsh judgments and persist through challenges.[63]

- **Example from Science:** The notion of mental fortitude underscores the principle of cognitive endurance. In their insightful work, Richard Tedeschi and Lawrence Calhoun, in their book Post-traumatic Growth: Psychological Resources After Trauma, delve into the complexities of human experience and explore the transformative potential that arises from adversity. Following profound experiences, those who endure significant challenges may uncover a heightened sense of meaning, a deeper gratitude for existence, and more profound spiritual ties. By delving into the complexities of growth that emerge from hardship, we can gain a deeper insight into the significance of negative emotions in our existence and foster a sense of resilience.[64]

The Shadow Legion: Obstacles, Uncertainty, and Pessimism

Every obstacle, uncertainty, and pessimism that tries to get past the fortifications of the Obsidian Citadel is symbolized by the Shadow Legion, a persistent and sinister danger in the labyrinth.[65] Insidious lies are whispered by those invisible but ever-present, and they eat away at your determination. A severe warning from the Law: the relentless onslaught of the Shadow Legion will first crush the minds of those who haven't prepared themselves mentally. The Law cautions that giving up is not an option but the ultimate capitulation, allowing the invisible adversary to triumph.[viii]

- **Example from Literature**: J.K. Rowling's Harry Potter series presents a fascinating exploration of the Law of Thought Resilience. Harry Potter, the central figure, confronts a myriad of trials and tribulations, shadowed by the ominous presence of Lord Voldemort. In the face of relentless adversity, Harry presses on, propelled by an indomitable will and a fierce resolve that defies the shadows surrounding him. As Dumbledore reflects, *'It is our choices, Harry, that show what we truly are, far more than our abilities.'* Harry stands unwavering in the face of relentless darkness, battling the malevolence that seeks to consume him. Through his struggle, he embodies hope and resilience, a flicker of light in a world shrouded in shadows.[66]

The Will-forge: A Lighthouse Within the Maze

But the Will-forge, a lighthouse within the maze, dances in the midst of the whirling clouds of uncertainty. At this point, something changes. In this place, unbridled resolve is refined into an iron fist that can endure any attack. This is not a quiet room for reflection; rather, it is a furnace where aspirations are transformed into habits of action—the very tools that fortify the will.

[viii] **Reflect on the concept of Learned Helplessness,** a state where individuals perceive themselves as powerless to influence or alter their circumstances, resulting in a sense of passivity and acceptance of their fate. As Seligman (1972) suggests, the phenomenon of learned helplessness emerges when an individual faces a series of relentless, uncontrollable adversities, leading to a profound sense of powerlessness that permeates their existence.

Seligman's research reveals a haunting truth: those ensnared by learned helplessness frequently display the shadows of depression and anxiety, trapped in a mental labyrinth that renders them ill-equipped to confront the trials that life presents. This resonates with the notion of the Shadow Legion, where the relentless and ominous threats of challenges, ambiguity, and despair can overwhelm the psyche of those lacking mental fortitude. The cautionary message from the Law emphasizes the necessity of cultivating a robust mental fortitude to endure challenges and evade the final surrender.

Examine the notion of Mental Toughness, an intricate trait that embodies resilience and the capacity to endure adversity. As Clough et al. (2002) suggest, the development of mental resilience emerges from a journey of intentional and persistent effort, reminiscent of the transformative process illustrated in the Will-forge. It transcends mere instinct, a craft that can be honed and deepened through experience and reflection.

Within this intricate landscape, resilience serves as a beacon, illuminating the path through the shadows of doubt and empowering individuals to convert their dreams into tangible practices. The imagery of the furnace resonates deeply, symbolizing the arduous journey through which resilience is meticulously crafted. Through the relentless confrontation of challenges, one cultivates the fortitude essential to endure any assault, embodying the very spirit of determination.[67]

- **Example from Philosophy:** The exploration of Stoicism unveils a profound method for cultivating an unyielding mind, navigating the shadows of existence with unwavering strength. By honing in on the elements we can govern and embracing the realities that elude our grasp, one can cultivate a profound sense of tranquility and balance amidst the chaos of existence. As Marcus Aurelius reflected in his Meditations, "You have power over your mind—not outside events. Realize this, and you will find strength." Individuals can traverse the labyrinth of life's challenges by cultivating a resilient mindset, confronting each shadow with unwavering strength and an unyielding spirit.

Testament to Willpower: Echoes of Fortitude

The Will-forge is alive with the resounding footsteps of champions long since vanquished. The stories they've told reverberate through the building, providing a continual reminder that strength of will grows not in a vacuum but in the vigorous pursuit of one's goals.

The solidification of habits and actions strengthens the walls of the Obsidian Citadel. You must act and fortify your fortifications because these echoes are more than just murmurs; they are shouts of war.

A captivating exploration of the strength of determination can be discovered within the intricate domain of neuroscience. Research into the intricacies of habit formation, particularly the work of Dr. Wendy Wood, a distinguished social psychologist, reveals the deep-seated influence that repetitive behaviors exert on our neural architecture. As we immerse ourselves in certain actions—be it the delicate guitar strumming, the serene stillness of meditation, or the rhythmic pulse of exercise—our minds weave intricate webs of neural pathways, deepening the essence of our experience. The intertwining of these connections transcends mere automation, delving into the depths of our cognitive mastery and the intricate dance of self-regulation. Consider the profound impact of consistent physical activity; it emerges as a dual force, enhancing our bodily well-being and fortifying our mental resilience. This transformation is rooted in the elevation of neurotransmitters such as dopamine and serotonin, pivotal players in the intricate dance of mood regulation and motivation.[68]

The Unyielding Commander—Will

In the heart of the Will-forge, an inscription reads: "Willpower is the boss of all other faculties." The molten letters of the inscription etch themselves into the center forge, a stubborn statement indeed. Here, will is more than just a player; it's the strategist and commander, molding and guiding the forces of motivation and action. When you have a strong will, you may gather your resources and devote all of your energy to protecting your beloved notion. With its help, you may put an end to self-doubt and transform your aspirations into tangible goals. Despite the Shadow Legion's incessant pursuit, a strong resolve guarantees that you will never be without a weapon.

- **Example from Islamic History:** The Patience and Perseverance of Bilal ibn Rabah (RA). Bilal ibn Rabah (RA), one of the earliest and most devoted companions of the Prophet Muhammad (PBUH), exemplifies the unyielding power of will. As a former slave who embraced Islam, Bilal faced severe persecution and torture for his faith. Despite the relentless physical and mental abuse inflicted upon him by his master, Bilal's willpower remained unbroken. He continued to proclaim the oneness of Allah, enduring extreme hardship without renouncing his belief.

  Bilal's strong will acted as the strategist and commander, guiding his actions and sustaining his motivation. His resolve enabled him to gather his inner resources and remain steadfast in his faith, even in the face of severe oppression. With his unwavering will, Bilal put an end to self-doubt and transformed his aspirations into tangible goals, ultimately securing his freedom and becoming the first muezzin of Islam. Despite the relentless pursuit of his persecutors, Bilal's strong resolve guaranteed that he remained resilient and committed to his belief.

  This example from Islamic history highlights how Bilal ibn Rabah's (RA) strong willpower played a crucial role in overcoming immense challenges. His story aligns with the idea of "The Unyielding Commander—Will," showcasing how an impregnable mind, forged by unyielding will, can navigate and triumph over adversities.[69]

- **Example from History:** Winston Churchill's Resilience During WWII. During World War II, Winston Churchill exemplified the unyielding power of will. Amidst the relentless bombings of London and the overwhelming threat posed by enemy's forces, Churchill's steadfast resolve became the guiding light for the British people. His speeches, marked by unwavering determination and a defiant spirit, galvanized a nation under siege. Phrases like "We shall fight on the beaches" and "Never surrender" were not just words; they were the embodiment of his unbreakable will.

Churchill's willpower acted as the strategist and commander, directing the efforts of the British government and military, and instilling hope and resilience in the hearts of the populace. Despite the relentless onslaught, his resolve ensured that the British spirit remained unbroken, providing a psychological weapon against the fear and despair wrought by war.[70]

In relation to the paragraph idea, Churchill's example illustrates how a strong will can gather resources and energy to protect and uphold cherished values and goals. It shows how willpower can end self-doubt and transform aspirations into tangible achievements, even in the face of seemingly insurmountable challenges. His steadfastness amid the Shadow of enemy's Legion threats underscores the principle that a strong resolve is an impregnable defense, ensuring that one is never without a weapon in the battle for survival and success.

There Are No Quick Cuts in the Crucible: Building Resilience through Actions

Nobody should attempt to enter the Will-forge if they are easily scared. The only way to strengthen and cultivate willpower is to turn it into habits of action. The clang of hammers striking steel muffles the Shadow Legion's murmurs at this location. The Will-forge amplifies the power of the will with every defiant deed, fortifying it with each stride forward. True strength is gained through dogged persistence in the face of adversity; there are no shortcuts in the crucible. With the help of these action habits, you may strengthen the Citadel's defenses and turn it into an unbeatable stronghold, a symbol of your unwavering determination.

The field of neuroscience unveils intriguing insights into the notion that our minds are not fixed but rather fluid constructs, ever-evolving and responsive to the world around us. The brain's remarkable capacity to reshape itself by creating new neural pathways serves as a crucial foundation for cultivating resilience. Through relentless self-examination, we can sharpen our intellect, refine our emotional responses, and cultivate an unyielding mental resilience. Dr. Norman Doidge, a distinguished psychiatrist and author, articulates a profound truth in his book The Brain That Changes Itself, *"The brain is not a fixed organ but a dynamic system that can be reshaped throughout our lives."* By immersing ourselves in pursuits that demand concentration, critical thinking, and unwavering determination, we can nurture the intricate pathways within our minds that foster strength in the face of adversity.[71]

In Conclusion

A chilling yet inspiring revelation emerges from the Law of Thought Resilience: the strength of an idea is directly linked to the intensity of the will that upholds it. To navigate the treacherous maze of the mind, it is essential to understand the significance of willpower and the ability to wield the transformative energy of the Will-forge. Remain vigilant, seize the moment, and fortify your resolve with an unyielding spirit in the face of this challenge. The decision lies within you: succumb to the shadows or rise triumphant over the turmoil of your mind? The choice lies in your hands, seeker of truth. Unravel the mystery that awaits in the shadows.[ix]

[ix] By integrating these elements, we create a narrative that emphasizes the cyclical nature of building mental resilience. Strong motives fuel willpower, which in turn manifests as action, ultimately solidifying the very ideas we seek to defend. Cognitexis becomes a training ground for the mind, where the power of will is the key to forging ideas of unyielding strength. The Obsidian Citadel stands as a testament to the human spirit's ability to overcome adversity, a fortress built not of stone, but of unwavering determination.

5. The Complex Mind: Mastering the Chaos of Multitasking

(The Law of Strategic Thought Organization and Multitasking)

Delve into the intricate depths of Cognitexis, a domain where the essence of existence transcends the physical, existing solely within the realm of the mind. In this enigmatic realm, where shadows conceal lurking threats, a profound potential awaits discovery—the Law of Strategic Thought Organization and Multitasking. This law transcends simple productivity; it is a clandestine craft, a delicate ballet teetering on the edge of mental exhaustion. Proceed with caution, as in this mysterious domain, one wrong move can plunge your thoughts into the chaotic abyss of overwhelming distractions.

The Maestro and the Mayhem

Envision Cognitexis as more than a mere chamber of thought; picture it as an expansive, resonant concert hall, where the atmosphere is heavy with the tumult of countless unfulfilled symphonies, each note a whisper of potential yet to be realized. Every jarring sound echoes a task clamoring for your focus—a pressing deadline, an unfinished report, the relentless buzz of notifications. The principle of Effective Thoughtful Multitasking reveals that harnessing a distinct cognitive approach can turn the chaos of competing thoughts into a seamless and captivating execution. Yet, the journey toward mastery is laden with peril. One misstep, one lapse in concentration, and the harmony shatters into a dissonant frenzy.

Research in Cognitive Psychology demonstrates that in a world that rushes forward relentlessly, juggling multiple tasks has become a pervasive norm. Yet, the intricate web of cognitive psychology unveils a stark truth: multitasking frequently ensnares one in a labyrinth of diminished productivity and an overwhelming cognitive burden. Dr. Adam Gazzaley reveals a haunting truth about our minds: they are ill-equipped for the relentless demands of task switching, especially when maintaining unwavering focus.

To enhance the art of juggling multiple responsibilities, one might consider "task batching," a technique that encourages the consolidation of akin duties, allowing them to be executed in a deliberate, sequential manner. This alleviates the psychological strain of perpetual task shifting, enabling us to sustain concentration and elevate our efficiency.[72]

Additionally, the intricate workings of the human mind reveal a haunting truth: the relentless pursuit of multitasking not only fragments our focus but also casts a shadow over our cognitive abilities, leading us down a path of diminished performance. Studies reveal a troubling truth: juggling multiple tasks not only saps our productivity but also invites a cascade of mistakes, all while eroding our fragile grip on our cognitive faculties, constrained as they are by the finite limits of our working memory.

To navigate these shadows, deliberate strategies for multitasking become imperative. As previously noted, task batching serves as a crucial method for diminishing the chaos of constant task switching and alleviating the burdens of cognitive strain. Moreover, the delicate art of managing time and setting priorities allows individuals to immerse themselves in a singular task, enhancing both the precision of their efforts and the caliber of their output.[73]

The Convergence of Chaos

In this intricate web of the mind, triumph emerges when Cognitexis weaves a universal framework for the CgX system. Consider this as the enigmatic maestro, the singular presence that orchestrates harmony amidst the turmoil. The Law proposes the creation of a Universal Framework—a central idea that resonates like a captivating tune, weaving together the varied tasks into a cohesive narrative. This UF allows Cognitexis to uncover the hidden connections between these seemingly disparate tasks, revealing them as components of a larger, cohesive framework. A poorly defined UF is akin to a conductor with a shattered baton, amplifying the chaos lingering in the air and deepening the dissonance surrounding him.

Cognitive scientist Allen Newell introduced the concept of Unified Theories of Cognition (UTC), which encapsulates this intriguing idea. Newell's work sought to construct an intricate model capable of unraveling the complexities of cognitive processes, weaving them into a singular, cohesive narrative. Newell (1990) suggests that a clearly articulated UTC weaves various cognitive endeavors into a unified framework, including problem-solving, memory, and learning.[74]

Within this intricate structure, the UTC serves as the Universal Framework (UF) in Cognitexis, weaving together diverse cognitive tasks into a cohesive and compelling narrative. A well-defined and resilient framework can unveil the intricate links between what may appear as disparate mental activities, deepening our insight into the complexities of human thought. On the other hand, an unclear or disjointed structure can spiral into chaos and ineffectiveness, reminiscent of a maestro with a broken baton desperately attempting to guide a disarrayed ensemble. This investigation highlights the necessity of a unified and cohesive perspective on mental processes, resonating with the principle of a universal structure aimed at attaining cognitive equilibrium.

- **Example from Literature:** Sun Tzu's enduring manuscript, "The Art of War," unveils deep insights into strategy's intricacies, tactics' nuances, and the essence of leadership. Beyond its martial implications, the tenets expressed in this age-old manuscript resonate through the labyrinth of existence, touching upon the intricacies of mental structuring[75]. Much like a cunning strategist orchestrating the intricate maneuvers of a battalion, a Cognitexis practitioner must deftly arrange and elevate tasks, navigating the labyrinth of the mind to attain profound clarity and peak efficacy. In the shadows of existence, where chaos reigns, and the mind teeters on the brink, grasping the essence of strategic planning, task prioritization, and the delicate art of time management becomes a lifeline. Through these intricate maneuvers, we can traverse the labyrinth of modern life, striving to preserve our fragile mental equilibrium amidst the turmoil surrounding us.

Intense Concentration on the Precipice

When the UF is established, a fragile sense of structure begins to take shape. The Law asserts that the machinery of Cognitexis can now channel its processing power with pinpoint precision, honing in on individual tasks with an almost unnerving intensity. Envision an orchestra where every instrument is under the intense scrutiny of a conductor. Yet, there's a twist—the conductor balances precariously on a razor's edge, where even the faintest miscalculation could send them spiraling into darkness. Cognitexis intricately carves out distinct segments of its processing prowess within the UF, with each segment singularly focused on a unique task. Yet, the peril lies in an obsessive fixation on a singular endeavor, which could lead to neglecting other vital pursuits, ultimately causing the entire orchestration to collapse into chaos.

The concept of Flow State in the realm of psychology embodies this delicate equilibrium. Research conducted by Csikszentmihalyi in 1990 reveals a captivating state of intense concentration, where individuals find themselves completely absorbed in their pursuits. In moments of deep immersion, individuals tap into an extraordinary level of concentration and output, unlocking the potential for remarkable achievements. Yet, sustaining this equilibrium demands a careful approach—becoming overly absorbed in a single endeavor may cause the oversight of other crucial pursuits, ultimately leading to diminished effectiveness and the looming threat of exhaustion.[76]

Within this intricate design, flow serves as the maestro, orchestrating attention toward each task with meticulous care. The struggle lies in sustaining this profound focus without veering into fixation, as such descent can unravel the delicate equilibrium and lead to a disarray of the entire composition. This exploration highlights the significance of deliberate mental structuring and the dangers of over-obsession, resonating with the principle of sustaining balance in the face of deep focus.

- **Example from Mindfulness:** Mindfulness meditation, a time-honored practice steeped in the wisdom of ancient traditions, invites us to delve into the depths of focused attention and the profound experience of being fully present. Through the cultivation of a focused and impartial mindset, individuals can unlock deeper cognitive insights, alleviate tension, and elevate their holistic state of being. Yet, one must consider that an intense fixation on a singular aspect can spiral into a state of hyperfocus, where the individual becomes so enmeshed in the immediacy of existence that they overlook other vital dimensions of their life. This underscores the intricate equilibrium necessary for successful multitasking: honing in with intense concentration on a singular endeavor while simultaneously grasping the wider implications at play.[77]

The Danger of a Fragmented Psyche

The Law underscores the necessity of a singular, cohesive purpose. Imagine the maestro possessing a sharp insight into the symphony's essence yet haunted by a sinister presence, sowing seeds of doubt and distraction in their mind. In a striking parallel, the principle posits that we imbue all endeavors with a collective significance by uniting all endeavors under one dominant objective. This purpose serves as the central force, orchestrating and harmonizing the myriad tasks within the grand composition. Yet, the subtle murmurs of conflicting demands and diversions can swiftly pull you

349

off course. One errant notion, one surrender to the alluring call of distraction, and the whole facade crumbles into chaos.

Sophie Leroy introduced the notion of Attention Residue, which reveals the dangers lurking within a disjointed mind. Leroy (2009) suggests that when a person transitions from task to task, a fragment of their mental energy lingers, tethered to the prior engagement. The lingering remnants of past experiences create a barrier to immersing oneself in the present challenge, resulting in diminished effectiveness and an overwhelming mental burden.[78]

Within this framework, the attention residue manifests as a shadowy force lurking in the background, planting seeds of uncertainty and diversion. In the intricate dance of purpose, where every action seeks to resonate with a greater meaning, the challenge of attention residue beckons for a deliberate and unified strategy. The inability to harness one's focus can unravel the very fabric of thought, much like a carefully constructed illusion collapsing into disarray as distractions seize control.

- **Example from Science:** The theory of cognitive load, a recognized construct within the realm of educational psychology, suggests that the human mind operates under constraints, burdened by finite cognitive resources. As the mind grapples with an overwhelming influx of information and an avalanche of tasks, the weight of cognitive burden intensifies, unraveling the threads of performance and weaving a tapestry of stress that ensnares the psyche. Sweller, van Merriënboer, and Paas (1998) reveal that by dissecting intricate tasks into smaller, digestible segments and offering precise guidance, educators can alleviate the cognitive burden and improve the effectiveness of learning experiences. This concept permeates the intricacies of existence, particularly in the realm of multitasking, where the pursuit of a singular, unified intention safeguards against the encroaching chaos of mental strain, ultimately enhancing one's capacity for productivity.[79]

The Chilling Continuum: A Waltz with Fragmentation

The Law possesses a keen awareness of the boundaries that confine human thought. Though Cognitexis possesses the ability to juggle multiple tasks, genuine expertise is attained through a pursuit that teeters on the edge of fixation. The Law now unveils a complex, layered framework. Imagine a maestro guiding his ensemble through the intricate passages of a symphony, all while teetering on the brink of chaos. You unlock extraordinary outcomes by focusing your complete attention on a singular task within the UF. In an instant, you transition to a different perspective, weighing each element carefully within the grand narrative, and so forth. Yet, allow a single thought of incomplete tasks to linger, a fleeting moment of doubt, and the delicate balance shatters, potentially leading to a complete psychological collapse.

The concept of Cognitive Load Theory, introduced by John Sweller, resonates with this complex interplay of mental demands. Sweller (1988) posits that cognitive load embodies the extent of working memory resources engaged during task execution. When the mental burden is finely tuned, people can unlock extraordinary levels of achievement and understanding. Yet, when the burden grows too weighty, overwhelmed by distractions or the chaos of juggling too many tasks, it can spiral into a state of cognitive overload, ultimately eroding one's performance.[80]

Within this intricate design, cognitive load serves as the "conductor," orchestrating focus amidst the complex interplay of responsibilities. Devoting unwavering focus to a single endeavor while deftly navigating shifts paves the way for peak performance and remarkable results. Yet, the emergence of uncertainty or unfinished endeavors can unravel this equilibrium, resulting in mental strain and the risk of disintegration. This highlights the critical need to navigate our mental capacities and sustain concentration, as the turmoil stemming from overwhelming cognitive pressures can be profound.

- **Example from Literature:** Herman Hesse's "Steppenwolf" plunges into the intricate layers of the human mind, examining the nuanced relationship between rational thought and primal urges, awareness, and the hidden depths of the unconscious. The central figure, Harry Haller, reflects the disjointed essence of contemporary existence, caught in the struggle between his quest for knowledge and his instinctual yearnings. This inner turmoil, often described as the "Steppenwolf complex," illustrates the struggle to preserve a unified identity amid a growing intricacy and disarray. Through deeply exploring his character's inner turmoil, Hesse presents a profound reflection on the essence of humanity and the necessity of harmonizing the diverse facets of our identity.[81]

In Conclusion

The intricate workings of Cognitexis unveil the unsettling depths of strategic thought organization and the eerie dance of multitasking. By exploring and implementing a profound framework for thought organization and the art of multitasking, we can tap into the essence of a unified intention, deep focus, and the intricate dance of simultaneous actions to accomplish extraordinary outcomes. Yet, we must stay alert to the insidious dangers that can draw us into chaos, disarray, and overwhelming mental strain.

In the intricate dance of the mind, where shadows lurk, and truths are obscured, one must navigate the labyrinth of thought with a vigilant awareness and a discerning intellect. In navigating the shadows of our psyche and confronting the turmoil within, we can reshape our consciousness into a fortress of resilience, where growth and profound understanding emerge from the depths of our struggles.

Ultimately, the Principle of Strategic Thought Organization and Multitasking stands as a haunting reflection of our potential for intellectual and personal evolution. It serves as a haunting reminder that within the shadows of our consciousness, a unified intent and sharpened perception can guide us through the labyrinth of our thoughts, reshaping our minds into a fortress of resilience and a sanctuary for profound understanding. Yet, we must navigate cautiously, for within the shadowy depths of Cognitexis, the line dividing genius from madness is as keen as a razor's edge.

6. Conquering the Darkness: Rising from the CgX Turmoil

(The Law of Dominating Vengeful Thought Patterns)

Embark on a harrowing journey into the heart of Cognitexis, a realm intricately woven from the very fabric of consciousness. In this shadowy domain shrouded in a haze of tumultuous emotions and echoing with the remnants of ancient grievances, a concealed conflict brews—the Principle of Surpassing a Vengeful CgX System Mentality.

This is no mere mental exercise; it is a brutal struggle for survival within the chaotic storm that has overtaken your reality. The darkness here is alive, writhing with vengeful thought patterns that seek to ensnare and dominate your mind. Every step you take must be measured, every decision precise, for one wrong turn could plunge you into the depths of an unending cycle of vengeance and despair.

In this treacherous landscape, the Law of Dominating Vengeful Thought Patterns stands as a beacon of hope and resilience. It challenges you to rise above the turmoil, to conquer the darkness that seeks to consume you. With unwavering vigilance and an indomitable spirit, you must navigate this perilous path, transforming the storm within into a source of strength and enlightenment.

Prepare yourself for the battle that lies ahead. The stakes are high, and the journey is fraught with danger, but within the depths of Cognitexis lies the power to transcend the shadows and emerge victorious.

A Beacon Through the Static

Envision Cognitexis as more than a mere battleground; it transforms into an expansive, reverberating chamber, warped by the tumult of wrathful musings. Each crackle and pop serves as a haunting reminder of past injustices, an unyielding murmur that ignites your fury. The Law of Overriding presents a thrilling gamble—a potent method to cut through the noise and uncover a glimmer of understanding. Cast aside the tumult of retribution and focus intently on a fresh vista, a singular, resolute idea—your ultimate goal. This sought-after conclusion serves as a guiding light, a delicate ember dancing in the tempest, luring you toward a horizon unburdened by the chains of bitterness.

Exploring Forgiveness Therapy within the realm of psychological practice, Worthington (2006) suggests that forgiveness therapy enables individuals to navigate and transcend their emotions of anger and the desire for retribution against those who have caused them harm. This process requires an acute awareness of the detrimental effects of clinging to past grievances, guiding one towards release and ultimately reshaping chaotic emotions into a serene and concentrated mindset.[82]

Within this intricate landscape, forgiveness emerges as a guiding light amidst the chaos, steering individuals away from the clamor of vengeance and towards a more constructive and determined purpose. Embracing the act of forgiveness enables one to liberate oneself from the shackles of former resentments, akin to honing in on a steadfast notion to navigate through the tumult of vengeful reflections. This illustrates the deep significance of redirecting attention from retribution to comprehension and reconciliation, as suggested by the principle of Prevailing Over Destructive Thought Processes.

- **Example from Science:** Cognitive restructuring, an essential element of Cognitive Behavioral Therapy (CBT), serves as a formidable tool for dismantling the chains of negative thought patterns that ensnare the mind. Through the recognition and confrontation of twisted perceptions, one can alleviate the weight of emotional turmoil and enhance their existential state. Dr. Aaron Beck elucidates the insidious nature of negative thoughts, revealing how they can weave a tapestry of self-fulfilling prophecies that ensnare the mind in a web of anxiety, depression, and anger. By confronting these shadowy thoughts and replacing them with a more nuanced and grounded perspective, individuals can escape the clutches of their minds and foster a more hopeful view of existence.[83]

Mobilizing the Delicate Allies

The Law suggests that focusing on your intended outcome initiates a precarious sequence of events. A relentless focus serves as a final plea to the last vestiges of reason that might still cling to existence. Envision shards of your consciousness stretching into a tumultuous expanse of noise, yearning to grasp the elusive signal. When you tap into those fragments of reason and drive, they transform into your companions in the urgent struggle for psychological endurance.

The concept of Cognitive Reappraisal within psychology presents a compelling illustration. Reframing one's perspective on a situation that could evoke stress transforms its emotional resonance, inviting a deeper exploration of the mind's intricate workings. Gross (2002) noted that this approach harnesses the mind's untapped potential to reframe challenging situations, diminishing adverse emotional reactions and fostering a deeper sense of mental fortitude.[84]

Within this intricate landscape, cognitive reappraisal emerges as the "Delicate Allies," skillfully harnessing shards of logic and motivation amidst the chaos of stress. By delving deeply into the nuances of their circumstances, individuals can harness their mental faculties as formidable allies in the quest for emotional resilience. This journey reflects the idea of honing in on one definitive goal to harness mental energy, transforming the chaos of conflicting ideas into a unified approach for strength and endurance.

- **Example from Literature:** J.R.R. Tolkien's epic novel, The Lord of the Rings, delves into the intricacies of human experience, revealing the haunting strength of perseverance and the fragile yet vital nature of connections forged in darkness. The seemingly ordinary hero, Frodo Baggins, encapsulates a profound resolve as he ventures into a treacherous journey to obliterate the One Ring. Amidst the shadows of relentless challenges, Frodo clings to his unwavering resolve, drawing upon the unwavering loyalty of his companions and the depths of his own resilience. This stands as a haunting testament to the notion that even the most formidable obstacles can be surmounted through the unwavering strength of a steadfast support network and an indomitable spirit.[85]

Breaking the Chains of Retribution

The delicate interplay between your concentrated awareness and the supportive thoughts you can summon forms a precarious yet powerful control system. Envision this mechanism as a makeshift fortress, pieced together from the remnants of your psyche. Every pulse of intentional thought, every wave of resolute determination, chips away at the barriers of retribution that confine you. Yet the peril lurks in the shadows, ever-present. One moment of distraction, surrendering to that faint noise, and the barriers crumble, engulfing you in a flood of relentless, wrathful reflections.

The notion of Mindfulness-Based Cognitive Therapy (MBCT) illustrates this complex interplay. MBCT intertwines classic cognitive behavioral techniques with mindfulness practices, guiding individuals to unravel the intricate web of negative thought patterns. Segal, Williams, and Teasdale (2002) suggest that this approach encourages individuals to anchor their awareness in the present, diminishing the grip of vengeful thoughts and fostering a deeper emotional strength.[86]

In MBCT, intentional thought and resolve serve as the "makeshift fortress" built from the remnants of the psyche. Every deliberate moment, every ripple of conscious reflection, unravels the confines of vengeance. Yet, as the metaphor implies, the constant threat of distraction can lead to the collapse of these defenses, underscoring the necessity of unwavering concentration and awareness to preserve mental equilibrium. This perspective highlights the importance of focused consciousness and the intricate equilibrium necessary to transcend cycles of vengeance in thought.

The Beacon of Insight: A Glimmering Promise

The Law underscores the critical need to cultivate a powerful Guiding Ambition. Envision a wavering light grasped tightly, its fragile glow piercing through the overwhelming shadows that threaten to consume everything. This driving force serves as the lifeblood of your core system, a fervent yearning for a destiny that transcends retribution. It embodies your relentless quest for tranquility, a vision of a time when chaos recedes, and your thoughts cease to be your adversary.

The concept of intrinsic motivation in psychology encapsulates this profound idea. The essence of intrinsic motivation lies in the deep-seated interest or sheer enjoyment one finds in the task at hand, serving as a pivotal component of self-determination theory. Ryan and Deci (2000) suggest that intrinsic motivation plays a pivotal role in cultivating profound learning and creativity, serving as an inner compass that empowers individuals to confront challenges and surmount barriers.[87]

Within this framework, intrinsic motivation emerges as a guiding light, illuminating a profound and lasting source of inspiration. As the flickering flame navigates the depths of encroaching darkness, the essence of inner drive empowers individuals to stay attuned to their true aspirations, rising above transient obstacles and diversions. This profound inner compulsion encapsulates the unyielding pursuit of peace and personal realization, resonating with the principle of nurturing a formidable guiding aspiration.

- **Example from Science:** Neuroplasticity, the brain's capacity to reshape its very essence through the creation of new neural pathways, unveils a profound mechanism for profound change within oneself. Through the relentless pursuit of uplifting thoughts and actions, one can reshape the very fabric of one's mind, forging a perspective that embraces hope and fortitude amidst the shadows of existence. Dr. Norman Doidge, a distinguished psychiatrist and author, reveals that the brain is not a static entity but rather a fluid construct capable of transformation at every stage of our existence. Through the establishment of precise objectives, the cultivation of awareness, and the pursuit of connection with others, one can tap into the transformative potential of the mind, liberating oneself from the shackles of destructive thoughts and striving toward a profound sense of contentment and purpose.[88]

Confronting the Dark Presence

As you advance, the Law ominously hints at a chilling outcome—the wrathful specter lurking in the shadows. Envision a terrifying force emerging from the tempest of your fury, materializing within the chaos of the unknown. This being personifies retribution, a shadowy mirror of your deepest suffering. As you press against the confines, the entity twists and shifts, its strength amplified by the darkness of your unresolved bitterness. Do not waver, for if you yield to the seductive murmurs of the unknown, it will engulf you entirely.

The concept of Rumination in the realm of psychology embodies this principle. Rumination often leads one down a dark path, where the mind circles back to troubling events and emotions, intensifying despair and heightening the likelihood of succumbing to melancholy. Nolen-Hoeksema (2000) suggests that those who dwell on their thoughts are more susceptible to enduring emotional turmoil and face an elevated risk of mental health issues.[89]

Within this construct, rumination manifests as the "wrathful specter" rising from the storm of unresolved feelings. This cognitive journey embodies retribution, ensnaring the person in a relentless loop of despair that reflects their innermost anguish. The deeper the rumination, the more potent this apparition grows, nourished by lingering resentment. To escape the clutches of this inner chaos, one must seek pathways to liberate oneself from incessant thoughts and confront one's lingering feelings meaningfully. This underscores the significance of mental tactics that can break the loop of overthinking and foster emotional strength.

- **Example from Literature:** Dante Alighieri's epic poem, The Divine Comedy, delves into the intricate labyrinth of the human soul, unraveling the haunting repercussions of moral transgressions. Dante's descent into the Inferno unfolds as a chilling odyssey through the nine circles of Hell, where he confronts the tormented souls of those ensnared by their desires—lust, gluttony, greed, wrath, and a myriad of other vices that have led them to their grim fates. This allegorical journey unfolds as a haunting narrative, revealing the insidious grip of dark emotions like anger, resentment, and hatred and the chaos they unleash upon the human psyche. Dante compels readers to examine their ethical shortcomings and aspire toward a more righteous existence by exploring these shadowy facets of human nature.[90]

A Guiding Light for the Forsaken

The Law culminates in a tantalizing hint of an elusive prize. It delves into the minds of those who engage in profound contemplation, individuals who have weathered the tempest and emerged transformed, bearing the scars of their journey. Envision a solitary soul, weathered yet liberated, poised at the precipice of the unknown, a singular, searing idea guiding their journey forward. These individuals stand as a powerful symbol of the Law of Overriding, illuminating the path for those still adrift in the chaos. They stand as a haunting testament—the struggle for your psyche is a contest you cannot afford to lose.

Contemplate the notion of Post-Traumatic Growth, a phenomenon that embodies the transformative psychological evolution that emerges from grappling with profoundly challenging life situations. As Tedeschi and Calhoun (2004) noted, those who experience transformative growth frequently discover a deeper appreciation for existence, enhanced connections with others, and a more profound sense of inner strength and spirituality.[91]

Within this paradigm, those who undergo transformative growth become the "Beacon of Hope for the Lost," having traversed their inner chaos and emerged with deep revelations. These figures, marked by their struggles yet unbound, embody the profound metamorphosis that emerges when one navigates through deep psychological and emotional trials. Their odyssey encapsulates the core of an unyielding principle, illuminating a path of hope and tenacity for those ensnared in their turmoil. This highlights the profound significance of navigating through mental challenges and ultimately rising with greater resilience.

- **Example from Cognitive Psychology:** Stoicism, an age-old doctrine, unveils a deep understanding of the human condition and the quest for true fulfillment. Those who delve into the depths of human thought highlight the necessity of forging a resilient spirit, mastering one's impulses, and concentrating on the elements of existence that lie within our grasp to transform. Embracing a stoic perspective allows one to cultivate inner strength, alleviate tension, and elevate one's sense of fulfillment in life. This perspective resonates with the path of individuals who have transcended their darker impulses, embracing a more uplifting vision of existence. By honing in on the elements within their grasp and releasing the burdens of the uncontrollable, individuals can uncover a sense of tranquility and meaning amidst the relentless trials of existence.[92]

In Conclusion

The Principle of Dominating Vengeful Thought Patterns uncovers a haunting battle lurking in the shadows of the human mind. By grasping this principle, we can traverse the tumultuous tempest of wrathful musings, channeling the force of concentrated awareness, nurturing reflections, and a resolute drive to attain serenity and fortitude. Yet, we must stay alert to the shadowy dangers that can ensnare us, driving us toward obsession, insanity, and the profound loss of our very being.

In the intricate dance of the mind, where shadows lurk, and truths are often obscured, our thoughts demand a careful orchestration of awareness and scrutiny. In navigating the shadows of our psyche and confronting the turmoil within, we can reshape our consciousness into a fortress of resilience, where growth and profound understanding can emerge from the depths of our struggles.

Ultimately, the Principle of Dominating Vengeful Thought Patterns stands as a haunting reflection of our potential for intellectual and personal evolution. It serves as a haunting reminder that with concentrated awareness and steadfast conviction, we can traverse the labyrinth of our thoughts, reshaping our minds into a fortress of resilience and a sanctuary for profound understanding. Yet, we must proceed with caution, for within the complex labyrinth of Cognitexis, the path to understanding is laden with madness.

7. The Piercing Gaze: Revealing the Invisible Matrix

(The Law of Piercing Gaze Ability)

A concealed entrance awaits in the shadowy depths of Cognitexis—the Law of the CgX System Meta-Analysis Inception Principle, or for those who dare to explore the hidden, the CgX System Piercing Gaze Ability. Envision Cognitexis as a vast, enigmatic simulation, a labyrinth of thought where every corner holds secrets waiting to be uncovered. The surfaces shimmer with extraordinary truths, and the Law of Piercing Gaze Ability reveals the path to deciphering the enigma and probing beyond the facade. Yet, the wanderer must tread carefully, for such insights demand a steep toll. One miscalculation could plunge him into an abyss of his own understanding, where reality blurs and shadows of doubt loom large.

Transcending the Illusion: An Anomaly in the Framework

The principles dictate that within the razor-sharp focus of Directed Attentiveness, a highly skilled CgX can achieve the seemingly impossible. Yet, as you delve deeper, you start to notice the cracks in the facade, revealing unsettling truths lurking just out of sight. The law asserts that Cognitexis can generate innovative analytical instruments through intense mental focus. Such transformations of our apparent analysis—what we perceive as our core grasp of reality—evolve into a more nuanced interpretation or existential exploration. Through this journey of deep exploration, one can pierce the facade of existence and uncover the intricate truths—the guiding principles—that orchestrate the grand illusion.

Consider the implications of Werner Heisenberg's uncertainty principle, which reveals the inherent limitations in our quest to measure and foresee the behavior of physical systems. This principle exposes the fissures in classical physics, hinting at the profound limitations that confine our comprehension of the universe. With profound intellectual thought and cutting-edge analytical tools, scientists have ventured into the enigmatic world of quantum mechanics, revealing the complex realities that dictate the dance of particles at their most fundamental levels.[93]

- **Example from Science:** Thomas Kuhn, a distinguished philosopher in the realm of science, unveiled the notion of a "paradigm shift," capturing the essence of a profound transformation in our perception of reality. When scientists embrace a new paradigm, they confront established beliefs and forge unorthodox methods to unravel complex dilemmas. This frequently results in profound revelations that transform our perception of existence. In a world shrouded in shadows, the act of nurturing a discerning intellect and wielding meticulous analytical instruments allows one to unveil the obscured intricacies of existence, empowering them to rise above the confines of ordinary thought.[94]

Revealing the Masterminds: A Peek Behind the Veil

The Law implies that this fresh existential examination opens doors to a domain frequently linked to ethereal, profound realizations or intuitive awareness. Envision the simulation pulsating, exposing fleeting visions of the masterminds, the hidden powers that twist the very fabric of reality. Through the use of the Piercing Gaze, we can start to uncover the concealed links, the vibrant strands that intertwine to form the essence of existence.

The Law suggests that this new exploration of existence unveils pathways to a realm often associated with transcendent insights or deep intuition. Imagine the intricate web of existence vibrating, revealing ephemeral glimpses of the architects, the concealed forces manipulating the essence of truth. By employing the Piercing Gaze, we begin to reveal the hidden connections, the vivid threads that weave together to create the very fabric of being.[95]

"Gödel, Escher, Bach: An Eternal Golden Braid," Douglas Hofstadter delves into the intricate connections between logic, art, and music, uncovering the concealed patterns that shape our perception of consciousness and the nature of reality. By exploring these hidden connections, Hofstadter penetrates the psyche of the profound intellects who have influenced our understanding of reality.

- **Example from Literature:** Philip K. Dick's work "Do Androids Dream of Electric Sheep?" delves into the intricate labyrinth of identity and reality, probing the unsettling boundaries that separate humanity from the artificial. In a bleak and unsettling future, the central figure, Rick Deckard, embarks on a harrowing mission to track down and eliminate wayward androids, grappling with the shadows of morality and existence. As he plunges further into his quest, Deckard grapples with the essence of his own being and the fabric of the world around him. This narrative unfolds as a haunting exploration of the human experience, delving into the necessity of questioning reality, embracing doubt, and seeking the elusive nature of truth.[96]

Disciplined Perception: The Firewall Against the Simulation

In the realm of the mind, the paramount principle lies in a disciplined perception, a mental resilience that teeters on the edge of obsession. Now, envision the explorer within the simulation, not just glancing behind the curtain but possessing the psychological fortitude to confront and navigate the revelations that await him. Disciplined Perception acts as a formidable barrier of unwavering mental rigor, honing Directed Attentiveness into a precise, laser-like focus. It serves as your armor against the potential anomalies and distortions that arise when delving into the essence of existence.

Consider the insights of Viktor Frankl, a distinguished psychiatrist and Holocaust survivor, who profoundly highlighted the significance of mental resilience in his seminal work "Man's Search for Meaning." Frankl's notion of "logotherapy" delves into the quest for meaning in existence, even in the face of adversity. His steadfast awareness and relentless intellectual discipline enabled him to face and traverse the terrors of the concentration camps, ultimately revealing deep insights into the nature of humanity and the core of existence.[97]

- **Example from Alternative Disciplines:** Zen meditation, a practice rooted in Buddhist philosophy, deeply intertwined with contemplative thought, highlights the importance of cultivating awareness and concentrated focus. In the shadowy corridors of the mind, a practice emerges, steeped in ancient wisdom. It beckons the seeker to delve into the depths of awareness, where every fleeting thought becomes an unsettling echo, and the stillness reveals the intricate dance of consciousness. Through cultivating a focused and unbiased mind, practitioners embark on a journey that unveils profound insights into their existence and the intricate tapestry of reality that envelops them. With unwavering focus, they can shatter the facade of deception and uncover the profound essence of existence. This approach serves as a formidable instrument for traversing the labyrinthine intricacies of contemporary existence, fostering overpowering tranquility and sharpened insight amidst the chaos.[98]

A Realm of Deception: The Weight of Awareness

The Law culminates in a chilling revelation. The universe, it implies, finds solace in the familiar boundaries of the illusion. Envision the adventurer stepping back from the shadows, irrevocably transformed by the revelations they have encountered. The Law implies that our preoccupation with the superficial aspects of the simulation obscures the deeper reality that lies beneath. In embracing the Piercing Gaze, we face the danger of dismantling the facade, laying bare the intricate layers of our genuine existence. The weight of this understanding, as the Law cautions, can be immense.

The double-slit experiment, a pivotal element of quantum mechanics, reveals existence's profound and mysterious essence. As particles like photons or electrons traverse the narrow passage of two slits, they reveal a haunting duality, behaving as waves that intertwine and clash, ultimately manifesting a mesmerizing interference pattern upon the canvas of the detector screen. This fluid essence disrupts our conventional perceptions of particles as fixed, tangible entities. Yet, the enigma intensifies as researchers endeavor to discern the path taken by the particles through the slits. At this moment, their fluidity shatters, revealing a stark reality where they manifest as distinct entities, impacting the surface at precise locations. This unsettling notion implies that the very act of witnessing shapes the reality of quantum occurrences.[99]

The double-slit experiment unveils unsettling inquiries into the essence of existence, the intricacies of awareness, and the observer's influence in molding the fabric of the cosmos. In the shadows of thought, physicist John Wheeler's assertion, "It from Bit," suggests a haunting possibility: beneath the surface of existence, information and consciousness weave the essence of reality itself. The ramifications of the experiment provoke a profound reconsideration of our instinctive beliefs about causality and determinism, urging us to delve into the unsettling notion of a reality where the observer and the observed are irrevocably intertwined.[100]

The Law of the CgX System Meta-Analysis Inception Principle

The Law of the CgX System Meta-Analysis Inception Principle unveils a captivating insight into the shadows of our understood existence. This law invites you to delve into a thrilling quest, urging you to sharpen your insight and unravel the mysteries of the illusion surrounding us. Yet, keep in mind the price of such understanding may be steep. Will you embrace the challenge and confront the weight of reality, or will you choose to linger in the soothing shadows of deception? The decision lies in your hands, yet the glimmering facade beckons, its hidden truths longing to be discovered by those bold enough and disciplined enough to seek them out.

Consider the depths of human understanding: Plato's Allegory of the Cave serves as a compelling investigation into the nature of perception and the essence of reality. In this profound narrative, individuals are bound within a cavern, their perception limited to the mere silhouettes dancing upon a surface. A solitary inmate breaks free, stepping into a reality that unveils the deceptive nature of the shadows that once confined him. This narrative explores the path to understanding and the trials faced when grappling with the essence of existence.[101]

In Conclusion

The Law of Piercing Gaze Ability unveils the deep exploration of the intricacies of the enigma waiting within our understanding of reality and our perceived existence. Through comprehending and implementing this principle, we can traverse the complex labyrinth of our minds, revealing obscured realities and attaining a profound insight into the nature of being. Yet, we must stay alert to the lurking distortions and crushing burdens these revelations may impose.

In the shadows of transformative ideas of scientific revelations and the haunting narratives of the written word of literature, our understanding demands a careful balance of awareness and scrutiny. In navigating the shadows of our psyche and confronting the turmoil within, we can reshape our consciousness into a fortress of resilience, where growth and profound understanding emerge from the depths of our struggles.

Ultimately, the Law of Piercing Gaze Ability profoundly reflects our potential for intellectual and personal evolution. It serves as a poignant reminder that with concentrated awareness and steadfast conviction, we can traverse the labyrinth of our thoughts, reshaping our minds into a fortress of resilience and a sanctuary for profound understanding. Yet, we must navigate with caution, for within the complex labyrinth of Cognitexis, the path to understanding is laden with the peril of both illumination and insanity.

8. The Spiritual Dynamo: A Spark in the Labyrinth

(The Law of Spiritual Power Driver)

Deep within the intricate labyrinth of Cognitexis lies a hidden chamber, a realm brimming with uncharted possibilities. This mystical powerhouse pulses with an elusive, enigmatic force—an ethereal energy believed to unlock the secrets of an endless well of limitless intelligence. The Spiritual Dynamo is a spark of unparalleled power within the labyrinth, representing the Law of Spiritual Power Driver. Here, the very essence of spiritual energy converges, offering a gateway to profound wisdom and boundless cognitive potential.

The Nature of the Spiritual Dynamo

The true essence of this power lingers in the shadows, evoking a sense of intrigue. Some speculate it intertwines with elusive emotions such as love and faith. Often considered the most profound and transformative human experiences, these emotions might serve as conduits for this spiritual energy. Others propose it could be a biological anomaly, an intriguing twist in the complex web of human neurochemistry. This suggests that certain brain states or neurochemical balances might unlock heightened cognitive abilities.

The Impact of the Spiritual Dynamo

The origins may be shrouded in mystery, but the impact of the spiritual dynamo is inescapable. Upon activation, it infuses the psyche with heightened vitality. Imagination ignites with intensity, ideas surge with unrestrained energy, and words resonate with an undeniable force. As trepidation and uncertainty dissolve, they make way for an exhilarating boldness. This state of heightened creativity and confidence can lead to significant breakthroughs in various fields, from science and art to personal development.

The Shadow Dynamo

Yet, Cognitexis, much like a twisted maze, conceals its mysteries within. Whispers tell of a lurking force, a sinister entity thriving on the depths of human emotion, drawing strength from the very essence of fear and animosity. This shadow dynamo could be the root of the destructive impulses that taint the narrative of human history. It represents the darker aspects of human nature, where negative emotions can lead to chaos and destruction.

Harnessing the Spiritual Dynamo

The challenge lies in harnessing the power of the spiritual dynamo without succumbing to the allure of its darker counterpart. This requires a delicate balance and a deep understanding of one's own emotions and motivations. It suggests that personal growth and self-awareness are crucial in navigating the labyrinth of Cognitexis.

The Perilous Dance

The journey into the depths of the spiritual dynamo is a thrilling venture, teetering on the edge of the enigmatic and the profound. It lures us in with the allure of boundless mental prowess while subtly hinting at the cost that may come with it. Is humanity ready to venture into this mysterious abyss and face the hidden powers that await? This question invites a reflection on the ethical and moral implications of seeking such power.

Application to Artistic Inspiration

The Nature of Artistic Inspiration. Artistic inspiration often feels like a surge of creative energy, a moment when ideas flow effortlessly, and the artist feels deeply connected to their work. This phenomenon can be likened to the activation of the Spiritual Dynamo within Cognitexis. When artists tap into this spiritual energy, their imagination becomes more vibrant, and their creative output is imbued with a powerful resonance.

Historical Figures and the Spiritual Dynamo

Throughout history, many artists have described experiences that align with the concept of the Spiritual Dynamo. Here are a few notable examples:

a. **Leonardo da Vinci:** Within the pages of this Renaissance polymath's notebooks lies an unrelenting quest for understanding, intertwined with a profound bond to the questions of the natural world. His multifaceted abilities in art, science, and engineering hint at a profound source of inspiration that seems to draw from the depths of the human experience, igniting his creativity and driving his relentless pursuit of innovation. In the pages of Walter Isaacson's biography, "Leonardo da Vinci," the artist reveals a deeply profound perspective on his creative journey, portraying it as a medium for divine inspiration.[102]

b. **William Blake:** The Romantic poet and artist perceived his creative muse as a manifestation of otherworldly visions, shrouded in mystery and profound contemplation. He recounted visions of ethereal beings and whispered dialogues with spirits, convinced that these encounters shaped the very essence of his artistic endeavors. Blake's visionary experiences are intricately dissected in Harold Bloom's profound examination, revealing layers of meaning and existential inquiry.[103]

c. **Hilma af Klint:** A Swedish artist who pioneered the realm of abstract art, af Klint asserted that her creations were influenced by unseen spiritual forces, hinting at a deeper, enigmatic connection between her art and the mysteries of existence. She was convinced that her art served as a conduit for profound truths, tapping into the whispers from higher realms. Her enigmatic creations, conceived in an era when abstraction was still shunned, reveal a profound and unsettling spiritual resonance. The book Hilma af Klint: Paintings for the Future delves into the intricate tapestry of her life and artistic journey.[104]

d. **Vincent van Gogh:** The Post-Impressionist painter frequently articulated his art as a conduit for revealing the tumultuous depths of his inner turmoil and profound insights. His letters to his brother Theo unveiled an intense exploration of purpose, intertwining a belief that his art served as a conduit to a reality far beyond his own existence. Van Gogh's profound emotional and spiritual journeys are intricately woven into his artwork, meticulously examined in Stephen Naifeh and Gregory White Smith's biography, Van Gogh: The Life.[105]

In Conclusion

The Spiritual Dynamo and the Law of Spiritual Power Driver beckon us to explore the shadowy corridors of the human mind. In this domain, the divine and the demonic merge, where a flicker of insight can either unleash a torrent of artistic brilliance or engulf us in the inferno of our own fixations. As we navigate this shadowy landscape, we must proceed with caution, for the distinction between clarity and insanity is frequently obscured. The Spiritual Dynamo, an enigmatic force that oscillates between benevolence and unpredictability, presents the allure of boundless potential while simultaneously imposing the necessity for profound self-reflection and unwavering dedication to a moral journey. To wield its force without falling prey to its darkness demands a fragile equilibrium, an unending watch, and constant vigil against the seductive pulling of the shadow self.

Ultimately, the decision lies within us: to welcome the illumination and rise to elevated realms of awareness or to yield to the shadows and become ensnared in the intricate maze of our own making.

MASTERY OVER THE TRANSFORMATIVE POWER OF COGNITION

§❦ §❦ §❦

TRANSFORMATION AND REFINEMENT OF THOUGHTS

Within the labyrinth, thoughts undergo a dark alchemy, transforming into something altogether more potent. This group reveals the sinister process of refining and cultivating the mind's raw material. The Alchemist's Crucible is a place of both creation and destruction, where thoughts are forged into mental masterpieces or twisted into monstrous forms. Can you harness this dark power and shape your thoughts into something transcendent?

1. The Alchemist's Crucible: Refining Thoughts into Mental Masterpieces

(The Law of Thoughts Entertainment and Refinery Process)

Within the intricate maze of Cognitexis, a pulsating marketplace buzzes with life: the Refinery of Thought. In this chaotic realm of concepts, the Law of Thought Entertainment and Refinery Process stands as the ultimate authority. This principle explores the profound divide between those who passively absorb ideas and the keen architect who actively shapes the terrain of their own consciousness.

The Principle of Critical Thought

This principle asserts that a finely tuned intellect does not meander through the bustling marketplace, carelessly selecting every shiny object. Instead, it operates as a skilled alchemist, wielding the Crucible of critical thought with precision and purpose. Envision a bustling marketplace within your mind, alive with a cacophony of thoughts—some shining like precious gems of undeniable truth, while others linger as mere stones of whimsical imagination. Polished, the intellect resembles a cunning trader, sifting through a multitude of ideas unbound by any single notion. The discerning mind sifts through myriad concepts, effortlessly casting aside the trivial while elevating the most valuable insights guided by a wealth of experience.

In the realm of literature, Daniel Kahneman's "Thinking, Fast and Slow" delves into the intricate dance between two modes of cognition: the swift, instinctive responses of System 1 and the measured, contemplative processes of System 2. Kahneman reveals how deeper contemplation (System 2) empowers individuals to dissect and navigate their thoughts, leading to choices steeped in reason and clarity. This intentional, methodical contemplation journey resonates with the notion of a transformative forge, where unrefined ideas are shaped into exquisite intellectual creations.[106]

The scientific method is a pivotal element of contemporary inquiry, embodying the relentless pursuit of clarity amidst the shadows of uncertainty. In obscure areas of inquiry, scientists tread carefully, never taking hypotheses at face value. They delve deep, subjecting each notion to a relentless crucible of testing and analysis, seeking the truth hidden beneath layers of uncertainty. This cyclical journey, marked by keen observation, the birth of hypotheses, rigorous experimentation, and data dissection, empowers scientists to deepen their grasp of the fascinating laws that govern the natural world. In the corridors of intellectual pursuit, Karl Popper illuminated the path of scientific advancement, revealing that the essence of progress resides in the relentless quest to dismantle and disprove hypotheses. By relentlessly examining our beliefs, we can evade the treacherous traps of confirmation bias, leading us to deeper, more profound truths that lie beneath the surface.[107]

The Transformation of Thoughts

The Law of Thought Transformation transcends simple dismissal of detrimental ideas. It embarks on the audacious journey of converting the seemingly worthless "chaff" of negative thoughts into valuable resources. Much like an alchemist, the astute thinker can reshape and elevate these unwelcome thoughts into something of worth. Through deep analysis and comprehension, the psyche unveils hidden potential, turning erstwhile adversaries into surprising allies. Imagine if a fleeting worry, once a catalyst for unease, could metamorphose into a powerful driver for strategic foresight.

The concept of cognitive reappraisal in the realm of emotional regulation embodies this principle. Transforming one's perspective on emotionally charged events can significantly reshape emotional consequences. Gross (2002) illustrates that by reshaping negative thoughts and feelings, individuals can alter their emotional landscape, diminishing suffering and fostering a greater sense of well-being. This journey of cognitive reappraisal resonates with the notion of transforming harmful thoughts into invaluable assets, transmuting fleeting worries into profound strategic understandings.[108]

- **Example from Literature:** Paulo Coelho's The Alchemist unfolds as a profound narrative that delves into self-discovery's intricate nature and the shadows accompanying personal quests. Santiago, the central figure, plunges into a profound journey to unearth his Personal Legend, a singular and deeply satisfying purpose that defines his existence. As Santiago navigates his path, he is met with a relentless array of obstacles and failures that compel him to face the darker corners of his psyche, revealing the depths of his limitations and fears. Yet, through deep reflection, relentless determination, and an openness to the lessons hidden within his trials, Santiago manages to reshape these adversities into pathways for profound growth and unveiling his true self. This narrative unfolds as a reverberating exploration of the human psyche, revealing that even the darkest trials can morph into profound insights, guiding one toward a deeper understanding of existence and a more profound sense of purpose.[109]

The Perils of a Mental Dumping Ground

The Law warns of the perils associated with the mindset of a "mental dumping ground." The discerning intellect would refrain from embracing every notion that crosses its path, regardless of how alluring the murmurs in the bustling marketplace of ideas may seem. It must take on the mantle of a discerning curator, meticulously evaluating which fresh concepts to embrace without question and which to cast aside. In the dimly lit corners of the bazaar, hidden within the shadow forge, there exist those who skillfully twist perceptions for their own gain. Your ability to see through the illusions will be your shield against these cunning manipulators.

The notion of cognitive overload, as explored by Alvin Toffler in his work "Future Shock," embodies this theme. Toffler cautioned that the relentless barrage of information in today's world might ensnare individuals in a web of indecision, ultimately eroding their mental health. He underscored the importance of individuals transforming into vigilant gatekeepers of information, meticulously scrutinizing and sifting through the noise to preserve their mental acuity and evading the shadows of manipulation.[110]

- **Example from Alternative Disciplines:** In a world drowning in a torrent of information, the skill to dissect and scrutinize what we encounter has grown ever more vital. The capacity to engage with media—accessing, analyzing, evaluating, and creating—is a vital tool, enabling individuals to traverse contemporary media's intricate and often deceptive terrain. As Neil Postman, a notable thinker on media, cautioned, *"We are engulfed in a sea of information, yet we crave the nourishment of wisdom."* Through the cultivation of robust critical thinking abilities, we arm ourselves against the insidious threats posed by misinformation, disinformation, and propaganda lurking in the shadows.[111]

The Alchemist's Codex

In the shadows of tradition lies the Alchemist's Codex, a legendary manuscript concealing the enigmatic art of transforming thought itself. Let this codex shroud itself in an enigma. Yet, the essence of the Law stands unmistakably evident: a sharpened intellect possesses the power to transform even the most trivial and insignificant notions into something of immense value. The Refinery of Thought delves into the transformative power of the human psyche, where unrefined ideas are meticulously crafted into profound intellectual creations.

Neuroplasticity, the brain's capacity to reshape its very essence by creating new neural pathways, is a profound reflection of the Alchemist's Codex. Through meticulous effort and concentrated learning, one can mold the very essence of one's being, transmuting untapped potential into remarkable abilities. Dr. Norman Doidge, a distinguished psychiatrist and author, reveals a profound truth: "The brain is not a fixed organ but a dynamic system that can be reshaped throughout our lives." Through relentless self-examination and pursuing intellectually demanding endeavors, we may unearth the depths of our capabilities and confront the shadows of our existence, leading to extraordinary revelations.[112]

- **Example from Literature:** In a world where the mind twists and turns, Edward de Bono's idea of "lateral thinking" unveils the hidden potential of innovative thought, leading to unexpected revelations. In "Lateral Thinking: Creativity Step by Step," de Bono unveils the art of transforming the mundane into the extraordinary, revealing how even the most overlooked concepts can be reshaped into groundbreaking ideas through the power of creative thought. This journey of evolving and honing thoughts mirrors the essence of a hidden manuscript, where the mind serves as a crucible, molding unrefined concepts into brilliant creations.

In Conclusion

Ultimately, the choice lies in the hands of the one who pursues Cognitexis. Will they succumb to the alluring grasp of fleeting desires, their thoughts trapped in a chaotic vortex of unrefined notions? Or will they embrace the role of the alchemist, wielding the Law of Thought Entertainment and Refinery Process to transmute the raw essence of their thoughts into a carefully constructed mental landscape, abundant in beauty and fortified with strength? Deep within the labyrinth of the mind, a hidden gem awaits, ready to emerge through the piercing clarity of scrutiny and an unwavering pursuit of intellectual dominance.

2. The Alchemist's Crucible: Where Thoughts Collide and Create

(The Law of Thoughts Admixture)

In the shadowy depths of Cognitexis, a swirling vortex of vivid energy simmers and roils: the Alchemist's Crucible. In this realm, beneath the piercing light of radiant crystals, the Law of Thought Admixture holds its dominion. It asserts that the fusion of varied ideas, akin to a masterful sorcerer mixing potent ingredients, can produce a remarkable spectrum of results, both extraordinary and treacherous.

The Birth of the Unseen

Envision two distinct, murmuring elements, each possessing its own enigmatic qualities, converging within the Crucible. This ignites the transformative essence, a pivotal moment of intellectual amalgamation that gives rise to a completely novel way of thinking. Engaging in collaborative brainstorming within the Crucible can ignite revolutionary ideas, transcending the mere combination of individual contributions.

The concept of the "Medici Effect," articulated by Frans Johansson in his work "The Medici Effect: Breakthrough Insights at the Intersection of Ideas, Concepts, and Cultures," embodies the phenomenon of ideas clashing and giving rise to something unprecedented. Johansson reveals the dark undercurrents of collaboration—where varied ideas and perspectives collide—unveiling the potential for shocking innovations. This blend of diverse concepts resonates with the principles of cognitive amalgamation, leading to profound and groundbreaking results.[113]

The idea of the Medici Effect captures the intriguing core of the Alchemist's Crucible. As the Law of Thought Admixture implies, merging various concepts can yield remarkable and life-altering outcomes. At the same time, the Medici Effect reveals how the convergence of distinct viewpoints can ignite revolutionary breakthroughs. The combination of diverse components weaves a narrative that is innovative and compelling, surpassing the mere aggregation of its parts. Through the art of collaborative brainstorming and the fusion of unique ideas, individuals can unlock extraordinary intellectual transformations reminiscent of the profound changes depicted in The Alchemist's Crucible.

- **Example from Science:** The unveiling of the double helix structure of DNA by James Watson, Francis Crick, and Rosalind Franklin serves as a profound reminder of the intricate dance between collaboration and the convergence of thought, where the power of ambition intertwines with the light of discovery. This profound revelation, which transformed the realms of biology and medicine, arose from the intricate interplay of varied viewpoints and specialized knowledge. Through the intricate interplay of theoretical musings and empirical revelations, the researchers delved into the enigmatic depths of existence, unearthing the profound mysteries that underpin life itself. This instance underscores the critical nature of collaboration across disciplines and the profound impact that varied viewpoints can have on the advancement of scientific discovery.[114]

The Enhancing Companion

Just as a secondary compound strengthens a primary element, a thought process can be enhanced by another for greater impact. The exchange of viewpoints within the crucible sharpens and strengthens established concepts. The solitary fighter, his weapon sharp, yet now protected. By intertwining his knowledge with that of a cunning tactician, he emerges from the chaos with a strategy far more formidable than before, where an invigorated defense enhances his offensive capabilities.

In the realm of commerce, collaborative synergy embodies this intriguing concept. In "Built to Last: Successful Habits of Visionary Companies," James C. Collins and Jerry I. Porras delve into the intricate dynamics of how thriving companies cultivate an environment rich in collaboration and teamwork, ultimately sharpening their edge in the competitive landscape. Through the fusion of varied talents and viewpoints, these organizations cultivate an intricate web that amplifies their fundamental strategies, paving the way for heightened creativity and achievement.[115]

The notion of working together in business resonates deeply with the essence of the Enhancing Companion. In the intricate dance of ideas, where every perspective adds a layer of complexity, thriving companies amplify their influence by weaving together collaboration and teamwork into their very fabric. The fusion of varied talents and viewpoints, reminiscent of a lone warrior collaborating with a shrewd strategist, creates a more powerful approach. This partnership sharpens both protective and aggressive tactics, reflecting how a revitalized defense amplifies offensive maneuvers in the corporate arena. In this way, the Enhancing Companion reveals how the infusion of diverse perspectives and insights can culminate in more powerful and impactful results.

- **Example from Literature:** J.R.R. Tolkien's The Lord of the Rings delves into the intricate dynamics of companionship, unwavering allegiance, and the profound impact of unity in the face of adversity. The Fellowship of the Ring, a varied assembly of souls bound by a shared purpose, embodies the essence of collective elevation. Every individual contributes distinct abilities and insights to the collective, harmonizing with one another to navigate obstacles that would be impossible to face in isolation. The journey unfolds as the wisdom of one and the courage of another intertwine, revealing that the group's success hinges on the intricate dance of their combined strengths.[116]

The Treacherous Abyss

Proceed with caution, for not every combination yields a favorable outcome. Innocuous elements, when combined, can transform into something lethal; similarly, the fusion of ideas can lead to a toxic mindset. Allowing disinformation and negativity to seep into the

Crucible without restraint can lead to the emergence of dangerous ideologies. These toxic brews could seep into the maze, distorting the very essence of Cognitexis in unforeseen ways.

Historical instances reveal the unsettling consequences of manipulating narratives, as seen in the early 20th century with the rise of propaganda and disinformation in Nazi Germany, showcasing how the fusion of certain ideas can spiral into perilous realities. The regime expertly twisted narratives, weaving a compelling yet perilous belief system that spiraled into chaos and profound human anguish. This historical example reveals how the unrestrained blend of false narratives and harmful ideologies can warp perception and result in catastrophic outcomes.[117]

The chilling instance of Nazi Germany's manipulation through propaganda and deceit resonates deeply with the notion of the Treacherous Abyss. As the paragraph ominously cautions against the insidious infiltration of disinformation and negativity into The Crucible, it echoes the chilling reality of how the Nazi regime's control over information birthed a perilous and corrosive ideology. This scenario reveals how the unrestrained fusion of dark notions can warp perception and lead to disastrous outcomes, underscoring the importance of vigilance and thoughtful scrutiny when intertwining various ideas and viewpoints.

- **Example from Cognitive Psychology:** The rise of conspiracy theories on social media platforms. The relentless spread of falsehoods and elaborate conspiracies across social media unveils the perilous consequences of information left to roam freely, unchallenged, and unverified. When individuals encounter deceptive narratives, their perceptions of reality can warp, leading them down paths of self-destruction and moral ambiguity. Elizabeth Loftus, a prominent figure in the realm of cognitive psychology, has revealed the unsettling truth that memories, once thought to be steadfast, can be distorted and reshaped through the insidious power of suggestion and the relentless echo of repetition. This highlights the necessity of keen discernment and the ability to navigate the murky waters of truth and deception.[118]

The Neutralizing Agent

The Law possesses an antidote that serves as a powerful neutralizing force. Just as a toxic substance can be countered by its remedy, a particular line of reasoning can only be subdued by an opposing perspective. In the crucible, the power of analytical thought and thoughtful discourse emerges as a formidable weapon against the shadows of doubt and deception. Renowned intellects committed to maintaining the equilibrium of the crucible, the Warden's Guild vigilantly guards against the insidious toxins being introduced. Armed with the sharp tools of logic and reason, they remain ever watchful, ready to detect and dismantle any lurking dangers that may arise.

In the realm of research, the scientific method serves as a powerful force, dismantling deceptive hypotheses and unraveling misleading theories with precision. Through meticulous observation, precise measurement, and rigorous experimentation, researchers can unravel the tangled web of errors and misconceptions, constantly refining their hypotheses in a quest for truth. Karl Popper's philosophy of science presents a gripping narrative where falsifiability emerges as the ultimate test of scientific credibility, suggesting that theories must be crafted to allow for scrutiny and the possibility of being disproven.[119]

The scientific method, articulated by Karl Popper, stands as a compelling illustration of the Neutralizing Agent. In the shadows of manipulation, where every word can twist reality, the art of analytical thought emerges as a formidable shield. With the scientific method as its ally, it relentlessly dismantles the façade of false hypotheses and deceptive theories, revealing the truth lurking beneath the surface. This meticulous approach to observation and experimentation mirrors the Warden's Guild, ever-watchful against the creeping dangers that lurk in the shadows. Equipped with the sharp instruments of analysis and insight, researchers stay alert, poised to uncover and unravel any fallacies or misunderstandings that could emerge, ensuring the purity of their findings remains intact.

- **Example from Science:** The peer review process stands as a pivotal element of scientific inquiry, functioning as an essential guardian of quality and integrity in the pursuit of knowledge. Through the relentless examination of research manuscripts by impartial experts, peer review serves as a guardian of truth, safeguarding the integrity, authenticity, and innovative spirit of scientific discovery. This journey unveils the shadows of errors, biases, and methodological flaws, fostering the emergence of research that stands resilient against the darkness. In the words of intellect, Richard Feynman, a renowned physicist and figure of profound insight, articulated a haunting truth: *"Science is the belief in the ignorance of experts."* Through the relentless examination of research by discerning peers, scientists can confront the shadows of personal biases, striving to uphold the fragile integrity of their pursuit.[120]

In Conclusion

The Law of Thought Admixture invites us to explore the dark corners of the psyche. It implies that through the convergence of conflicting concepts, we may unveil concealed possibilities and create alternate and empowering existences. However, this journey is fraught with peril. Cognitexis, a realm where the lines between genesis and annihilation blur, requires an intricate equilibrium and profound insight into the hidden currents at play. In exploring the mind's intricate layers, we must tread carefully, for the shadows of our inquiries may awaken forces that threaten to dismantle the essence of our being. The fate of our inner realms depends on our capacity to wield this enigmatic craft, intertwining the ordinary with the surreal as we navigate the shadows toward understanding.

3. The Seedling Thoughts: Cultivating the Mind's Garden

(The Law of Thought Seeding Soil)

Deep within the maze-like Cognitexis lies a sanctuary: the Seeding Soil of Ideas. Here, under the watchful eye of the Law of Thought Seeding Soil, the conditions for blossoming brilliant ideas are meticulously maintained. This Law reminds us that the ideal environment for nurturing ideas is a blend of our innate potential and the circumstances in which they are cultivated.

Within this fertile ground, intellectual synergy groups, akin to master gardeners, play a crucial role. These alliances of human mastermind thinkers assist in cultivating critical thinking and structured cognition. Together, they identify psychological impediments—thorny vines that hinder growth—and transform them into opportunities for development. They turn desires into actionable behaviors through a framework of disciplined, organized thought.

In this dark alchemy of transformation and refinement, these gardeners teach self-discipline, fostering resilience in the mind's garden. Collaborating and sharing diverse perspectives enable individuals to escape destructive thought patterns and nurture the most vulnerable seedlings into robust, resilient ideas. These think tanks ensure that even the rawest thoughts can be forged into mental masterpieces, ready to withstand the shadows of the labyrinth and thrive in the light of consciousness.

The Seeding Soil: A Representation of Mental Fertility

The Seeding Soil is a vast garden teeming with life, where the development of thought processes occurs through the delicate interplay between seed and soil. Our preexisting mental state, shaped by genetic and environmental factors, impacts the growth of our ideas, much like how soil quality affects plant growth.

The notion of a "growth mindset," brought to light by psychologist Carol Dweck, embodies the essence of nurturing one's mental landscape. Dweck's research reveals that those who embrace a growth mindset perceive their abilities as something that can evolve through commitment and effort, cultivating a rich atmosphere for discovery and advancement. This perspective starkly opposes a more rigid outlook, where people are convinced that their skills are unchangeable. The delicate balance between an individual's inner thoughts and the surrounding influences shapes the possibilities for growth and transformation.[121]

As presented by Carol Dweck, the notion of a growth mindset intertwines seamlessly with the intriguing concept of the Seeding Soil of Ideas. Just as the Seeding Soil embodies a rich backdrop where concepts can thrive, a growth mindset establishes the perfect atmosphere for exploration and evolution. The dynamic relationship between a person's thoughts (the seed) and their surroundings (the soil) shapes their capacity for development, reflecting how the richness of the soil influences the flourishing of plants. By embracing a transformative perspective, individuals can tend to their concepts and cultivate their mental landscape, resulting in the emergence of extraordinary insights.

- **Example from Science:** The realm of epigenetics has transformed our perception of the intricate dance between our surroundings and the very fabric of our genetic identity. Epigenetic modifications, like the intricate dance of DNA methylation and histone acetylation, possess the power to shape gene activity while leaving the fundamental DNA sequence untouched. Our experiences, actions, and surroundings significantly influence the evolution of our minds and overall well-being. Consider the implications of nurturing environments; research indicates that children who grow up with access to quality education and healthcare often exhibit elevated IQs and superior cognitive outcomes compared to their counterparts in less fortunate circumstances. This stark contrast invites deeper reflection on the nature of development and the factors that shape our intellect and potential.[122]

Soil fertility allows some seeds to grow to their full potential, while deficiency limits the growth of others. The law emphasizes the importance of using high-quality Seeding Soil. Caring for one's mental landscape, encouraging curiosity, and honing critical thinking skills can create a fertile environment for ideas to grow into vibrant concepts.

- **Example from Literature:** Mary Shelley's Frankenstein delves into the intricate dance between the thirst for knowledge and the shadows cast by one's surroundings. Victor Frankenstein, the central figure of the tale, finds himself enveloped in the intellectually charged environment of Ingolstadt University. His ambition ignites in this shadowy realm of intellect, where brilliant minds grapple with profound ideas, driving him to push beyond the confines of human understanding. The university's libraries, laboratories, and intellectual discourse serve as the shadowy backdrop for Frankenstein's obsessive scientific endeavors, inevitably culminating in the birth of his grotesque creation.[123]

Beneficial Pollinators for Garden Enhancement

In the Seeding Soil, flitting pollinators symbolize the alliances of intellectual synergy as they traverse from one garden to another. These partnerships unite individuals from diverse backgrounds and perspectives, disseminating fresh ideas and insights. Introducing new viewpoints acts like pollen to an established idea, nourishing it and catalyzing its transformation into a revolutionary thought.

Collaboration is pivotal for growth and can be a powerful tool in the fight for mental survival; the Law reminds us of this crucial fact. By sharing varied perspectives, we can help each other escape destructive thought patterns and cultivate a flourishing garden of innovative ideas. These beneficial pollinators, with their ceaseless activity, epitomize the dynamic exchange of knowledge and creativity that enriches the fertile ground of Cognitexis, ensuring that each seed of thought has the potential to bloom into a revolutionary idea.[124]

In business, the notion of open innovation, articulated by Henry Chesbrough in his work "Open Innovation: The New Imperative for Creating and Profiting from Technology," is a compelling illustration of the power of collaborative intellectual partnerships. Chesbrough unveils the intricate dance of companies as they seek to amplify their innovation prowess through alliances with external partners, weaving together a tapestry of diverse perspectives and ideas that could lead to unexpected twists and turns. This interplay of perspectives, akin to a subtle force igniting a spark, cultivates groundbreaking ideas and transformations.

The notion of open innovation, as presented by Henry Chesbrough, intriguingly intertwines with the captivating idea of Beneficial Insects for Garden Enhancement. Much like elusive shadows weaving through a web of intrigue, open innovation thrives on collaboration with external partners, allowing fresh ideas and perspectives to emerge and take flight. This collaboration, reminiscent of a sudden twist in a gripping narrative, invigorates and transforms established concepts into groundbreaking revelations. By cultivating varied alliances and sharing unique perspectives, organizations can break free from harmful mental traps and propel their evolution, reminiscent of how fertile ground nurtures the blossoming of creativity and groundbreaking concepts.

- **Example from Interdisciplinary Management:** The concept of cross-functional teams has emerged as a compelling force within contemporary organizations. In the convergence of divergent minds, where varied expertise intertwines, a fertile ground for creativity and innovation emerges, illuminating the outlines of complex challenges that lie ahead. As observed by Peter Drucker, a distinguished management consultant, "The paramount duty in leadership is to forge a unity among individuals centered on common objectives and principles." Through the intricate dance of collaboration and communication, cross-functional teams unravel the barriers that confine them, enhancing efficiency and steering the organization toward an enticing and captivating success.[125]

The Bitter Vine: Obstacles to Mental Fertility

But stay alert! In the Seeding Soil, vines of negativity—like thorny vines—intertwine with the vibrant flora, threatening to stifle beneficial ideas and drain vital nutrients. These insidious vines include misinformation, prejudice, and other forms of interpersonal negativity. These thorny obstacles will choke even the most promising seedling thoughts if left unchecked. The Law of Thought Seeding Soil reminds us that vigilance is crucial. We must continuously identify and uproot these destructive influences to protect and nurture the fertile ground of our minds, ensuring that positive, innovative ideas can flourish and thrive.

Irving Janis's notion of "groupthink," first presented in his work "Victims of Groupthink," is a compelling metaphor for how entangled forces can suppress valuable insights. When a collective prioritizes unity and agreement above the scrutiny of ideas, it can spiral into a web of flawed choices and stifled voices, creating an unsettling atmosphere where dissent is quietly extinguished. This unsettling occurrence can stifle creative thought and permit harmful prejudices and falsehoods to flourish without restraint.[126]

As articulated by Irving Janis, the notion of collective conformity resonates deeply with the essence of the Bitter Vine. As tangled roots entwine to suffocate promising concepts and siphon vitality from the fertile ground, a collective mindset stifles scrutiny and extinguishes the spark of originality. The yearning for unity and acceptance among peers can give rise to the rampant proliferation of harmful prejudices and falsehoods reminiscent of how entangled roots suffocate budding ideas. By remaining alert and cultivating a space that embraces varied viewpoints and analytical thought, we can avert the harmful consequences of collective conformity and guarantee the emergence of valuable concepts.

- **Example from Science:** The spread of falsehoods, especially in our current digital landscape, resembles the relentless encroachment of invasive vines, suffocating the very essence of what is genuine. In the shadow of the COVID-19 pandemic, a torrent of deceptive narratives and half-truths regarding the virus and vaccines surged through the labyrinth of social media, ensnaring the unsuspecting in a web of confusion and fear. The insidious nature of misinformation, born from a wellspring of fear and distrust, obstructed public health initiatives, sowed seeds of vaccine hesitancy and played a pivotal role in the relentless spread of the disease. Elizabeth Loftus, a leading expert in the realm of cognitive psychology, reveals the unsettling truth about the human mind's vulnerability to misinformation. This treacherous force can weave false memories and warp beliefs into a haunting tapestry of illusion.[127] Numerous studies reveal a troubling truth: the insidious spread of misinformation erodes the fragile foundation of public trust in science and health authorities, steering individuals toward perilous choices and amplifying the specter of health risks.[128]

The Gardeners: Cultivating Resilience and Structured Thinking

Together, the Laws of Thought Resilience and Thought Rescue do more than each could on their own. They are intrinsic to the Seeding Soil and are propelled by energy groups in the brain that are always building a healthy mental environment. Using the much-needed critical thinking and organized cognition, conceive of the groups as professional gardeners. They assist individuals in identifying areas of psychological impediments, such as thorny vines, and in resolving these issues through the use of a framework that promotes structured thinking in transforming desires into behavioral patterns. Another key aspect of willpower is self-discipline, which they teach to a considerable degree. These think tanks give these most vulnerable seedlings a chance.[x]

The idea of cognitive-behavioral therapy (CBT) serves as a prime example of how skilled practitioners can nurture resilience and foster organized thought processes. CBT delves into the mind's shadows, uncovering and confronting the tangled web of cognitive distortions and negative thought patterns, replacing them with brighter, more adaptive thoughts and behaviors. This method delves deep into the mind, unraveling the complexities of thought and emotion, guiding individuals to harness their inner strength and reshape their impulses into constructive actions.[129]

The notion of cognitive-behavioral therapy intertwines seamlessly with the essence of The Gardeners. Like skilled gardeners uncovering hidden issues in the soil, CBT empowers individuals to recognize and confront their negative thought patterns, cultivating

---

[x] By incorporating these elements, we can transform a dry explanation into a captivating story about the cultivation of ideas within the enigmatic realm of Cognitexis. The Law of Thought Seeding Soil becomes a testament to the power of nurturing our minds, creating a fertile ground where even the most humble thought can blossom into something extraordinary. The Seeding Soil stands as a vibrant symbol of our potential for growth, a reminder that with mindful cultivation, even the most barren landscapes within our minds can become gardens overflowing with the fruits of our imagination.

a mindset filled with healthier and more adaptive beliefs. This method delves into the depths of the mind, highlighting the importance of analytical thought, organized reasoning, and personal control, much like the enigmatic figures who nurture strength and clarity in a chaotic world. CBT guarantees that the most delicate sprouts (thoughts) are nurtured by offering a structure for reshaping cravings into constructive actions, creating a fertile ground for a robust mental landscape.

- **Example from Literature:** George Orwell's haunting narrative, 1984, delves into the unsettling realities of oppressive regimes and underscores the profound significance of independent thought. The central figure, Winston Smith, challenges the suffocating authority of the Party through subversive thoughts and acts of defiance. His battle to preserve his uniqueness and analytical abilities underscores the resilience of the human essence, capable of defying even the most suffocating forces of domination. Winston's odyssey highlights the necessity of nurturing inner strength, bravery, and an unwavering dedication to authenticity, even when confronted with challenges.[130]

The Blossoming of Ideas: Transforming Cognitexis

These components, when combined, allow us to turn a dull description of the mysterious Cognitexis into an enthralling tale of the growth of ideas. A tribute to the power of nourishing our brains, The Law of Concept Seeding Soil shows how even the humblest concept can develop into something spectacular when given the right environment. The Seeding Soil is a living representation of our capacity for development; it serves as a gentle reminder that our thoughts can transform from a desolate wasteland into a verdant garden if we tend to them with care.

Consider the notion of "constructivist learning," a theory initially shaped by Jean Piaget and further elaborated by thinkers such as

Lev Vygotsky. This concept illustrates the profound impact of the right environment on the evolution of ideas. Constructivist learning reveals that knowledge emerges through the intricate web of experiences and interactions that learners weave with their surroundings. In an atmosphere where encouragement and stimulation intertwine, even the most basic concepts can evolve into deep insights and groundbreaking creativity.[131]

The notion of constructivist learning, initially shaped by Jean Piaget and further elaborated by Lev Vygotsky, resonates deeply with the essence of The Blossoming of Ideas. Much like the Seeding Soil creates the perfect backdrop for ideas to flourish, constructivist learning highlights the critical role of a nurturing and stimulating atmosphere in the growth of knowledge. In this atmosphere, individuals engage in a captivating journey, unraveling basic ideas and morphing them into deep revelations. This process reflects how the Seeding Soil can transform even the simplest idea into something extraordinary, provided it is nurtured in the right environment. By nurturing our thoughts with precision and cultivating the ideal atmosphere, we can metamorphose our mental terrain from a barren expanse into a lush oasis of creativity.

- **Example from Science:** Consider the concept of neuroplasticity; the brain's remarkable capacity to reshape itself through the formation of new neural connections reveals the astonishing adaptability of the human psyche. By pursuing intellectually engaging endeavors—embracing new skills, immersing ourselves in mindfulness, and daring to confront our limits—we can nurture an adaptable, robust, and inventive mind. Dr. Norman Doidge, a distinguished figure in the realm of psychiatry and literature, articulates, "The brain is not a static entity but a fluid system capable of transformation across our lifetimes." By carefully cultivating our thoughts and embracing varied experiences, we can unveil the depths of our potential and reshape the very fabric of our minds.[132]

- **Example from Literature:** Paulo Coelho's The Alchemist unfolds as a profound narrative, exploring the intricate journey of aspiration and the metamorphosis of the self. Santiago, the central figure, sets forth on a quest to unearth his Personal Legend, a singular and profound purpose that promises to bring meaning to his existence. Amidst the shadows of his journey, Santiago confronts enigmatic figures and formidable trials, awakening a profound understanding of his aspirations and the dark forces of his mind. His journey unfolds as an engulfing testament to the notion that by cultivating our deepest desires and embracing the decisive steps of our actions, we may unlock the potential for the extraordinary.[133]

By integrating these examples, we can see how the Seeding Soil metaphor beautifully encapsulates the potential for growth and transformation within our minds. Just as gardeners tend to their plants, we must nurture our thoughts and ideas, providing them with the conditions to flourish. This process underscores the importance of a supportive environment, continuous learning, and the resilience to overcome challenges.

In Conclusion

Our journey through the fertile ground of concepts within Cognitexis unveils a deep investigation into the intricacies of our minds. By delving into the Law of Thought Seeding Soil's intricacies, we unveil our profound capacity to cultivate and transform our thoughts into remarkable ideas. This intricate landscape, shaped by our encounters, insights, and collective endeavors, underscores the profound impact of an encouraging and thought-provoking atmosphere.

Much like a meticulous gardener nurturing their plants, we must remain ever-watchful, cultivating the richness of our mental landscape, igniting curiosity, and welcoming many viewpoints. In this pursuit, we navigate the intricate labyrinth of doubt and deception, allowing our thoughts to blossom and play a vital role in the evolution of shared understanding and imaginative expression.

In the end, the Seeding Soil vibrantly reflects our potential for profound growth, both in thought and in self-awareness. It serves as a poignant reminder that under the right circumstances, even the simplest notion can evolve into something extraordinary, reshaping our thoughts from desolate landscapes into lush realms of creativity and understanding.[xi]

4. The Awakening of Splendid Thoughts: A Dance with the Abyss

(The Law of Splendid Thoughts Awakening)

Within the ever-changing labyrinth of Cognitexis, an enigmatic potential lurks—the Law of Splendid Thoughts Awakening. This statute whispers secrets of a power reserved for the gravest moments, a trial forged in the scorching heart of despair and ignited by the flickering glow of unwavering belief.

Envision Cognitexis not as mere contemplation but as a colossal slumbering entity sprawled across the terrain of consciousness. In the midst of dire turmoil, a formidable force begins to stir. This awakening unleashes an extraordinary torrent of intellectual prowess, defying the chaos that surrounds it. It is a dance with the abyss, where the darkest depths of the mind give rise to the most splendid thoughts, transforming despair into a crucible of profound insight and innovation.

[xi] The Traveling Pollinators: Further enriching the Seeding Soil are the traveling pollinators, a metaphor for intellectual synergy alliances. These alliances, formed between diverse minds, flit from garden to garden within the Nexus, carrying fresh ideas that cross-pollinate the fertile ground. New perspectives, like pollen, can fertilize existing ideas, leading to the blossoming of groundbreaking concepts. The Law reminds us that collaboration is not only essential for growth, but also a powerful tool for thought rescue. By sharing diverse perspectives, we can help others break free from the confines of unproductive mental loops.

The Source of Despair

The Law suggests that in the depths of overwhelming challenges, especially during moments of profound sorrow, the human spirit rises above the confines of the mundane. This transcends a simple boost in physical prowess; it is a profound awakening—a powerful surge of the mind's potential. Grief, a powerful emotional brew, serves as the spark that awakens a hidden well of resilience and unwavering belief. This intense blend stirs a concealed force within the person, a force that surpasses the limits of logic.[xii]

The field of psychology has long acknowledged the intricate dance between hardship and transformation. The aftermath of trauma often unveils a profound transformation within individuals, revealing an unsettling yet remarkable ability to evolve and adapt as they navigate the shadows of their experiences. As observed by psychologist Richard Tedeschi, those who have navigated through the shadows of adversity frequently express a heightened appreciation for existence, deeper connections with others, and an intensified sense of purpose. Through the exploration of their innermost selves and the connections forged with others, individuals can navigate the shadows of adversity, emerging not only with a sense of hope but also with a profound insight into their own existence and the intricate tapestry of reality that envelops them.[134] This personal transformation often manifests as increased resilience, a deeper appreciation for life, and a newfound sense of

---

[xii] **This awakened power draws its potency from two key elements:**

a.　**Augmented Directed Attentiveness:** Grief acts as a laser, sharpening our focus to an extraordinary degree. This hyper-vigilance creates a vast stream of thought efflux, a torrent of ideas and solutions flooding Cognitexis. Every ounce of mental energy is channeled towards solving the problem at hand, the problem of navigating the crushing weight of grief.

b.　**Unassailable Faith:** Grief, when coupled with a deep well of faith, becomes a potent force. This unwavering belief in a higher purpose, in the possibility of overcoming the seemingly insurmountable, fuels the awakened power. It acts as an anchor in the storm, preventing the individual from being swept away by the torrent of emotions.

purpose, much like the profound awakening described in Cognitexis.

- **Example for History:** Consider the narrative of Viktor Frankl, a Holocaust survivor, and esteemed psychiatrist, which illustrates the emergence of extraordinary insights amidst deep despair. In his gripping narrative "Man's Search for Meaning," Frankl reveals his journey to uncover significance and purpose amidst the chilling realities of the concentration camps. His steadfast conviction and determination propelled him beyond the depths of physical and emotional anguish, igniting a deep intellectual and spiritual power that challenged the turmoil enveloping him.[135]

The Surge of Intense Contemplation

The embodiment is a revelation into a more potent form of Focused Awareness. Imagine a vast river of contemplation winding slowly and abruptly, intensifying with clarity and purpose. Cognitexis, driven by the urgency of the moment, channels every ounce of its processing power into unraveling the dilemma before it. This surge of concentrated contemplation propels him into an expansive flow of ideas, a domain teeming with boundless concepts and unorthodox answers. Problem-solving transforms into a formidable force driven by Cognitexis's intricate mechanisms' relentless efficiency.

The concept of "flow," articulated by Mihaly Csikszentmihalyi in his work "Flow: The Psychology of Optimal Experience," embodies the essence of a powerful wave of deep reflection. Csikszentmihalyi reveals that when individuals immerse themselves in a state of flow, they unlock an intense level of focused awareness and clarity, allowing them to confront intricate challenges and conjure groundbreaking solutions. This seamless state of engagement resonates with the concept of Cognitexis, harnessing its capabilities to dissect complexities and thrust individuals into an expansive realm of limitless possibilities.[136]

As Mihaly Csikszentmihalyi presents, the notion of flow seamlessly intertwines with the essence of The Surge of Intense Contemplation. As the narrative unfolds, a deep current of introspection surges with newfound clarity and intent, revealing a realm where heightened awareness allows individuals to harness their cognitive prowess to unravel intricate dilemmas. This journey into a state of seamless creativity thrusts individuals into a world of limitless concepts and unconventional solutions, reflecting how Cognitexis navigates challenges with unwavering precision. By immersing themselves in a deep state of focus, individuals can turn their introspection into a powerful catalyst, crafting groundbreaking and impactful solutions to the obstacles that confront them.

- **Example from Literature:** Viktor Frankl's memoir, Man's Search for Meaning, explores the depths of human resilience and the enduring quest for hope amidst the darkest of circumstances. Amidst the torment of Nazi concentration camps, Frankl discovered a profound refuge and resilience within the realm of his mind. By concentrating on a future imbued with significance and intention, he managed to rise above the terrors of his circumstances and preserve a profound sense of tranquility. Frankl's narrative highlights the profound impact of deep reflection and the necessity of discovering purpose in existence, even amidst the bleakest moments.[137]

A Choreography with the Void

Yet, the Principle of Magnificent Ideas Awakening cuts both ways. This force, emerging from a place of urgency, can just as readily be twisted by that very same desperation. The reckless exploitation of this awakened potential can unleash catastrophic outcomes, possibly resulting in the very annihilation it aims to prevent. This is a captivating descent into the unknown, a dangerous choreography where the distinction between genius and insanity fades with each fleeting idea.

It teeters on the edge of brilliance and chaos, where the promise of greatness intertwines with the lurking shadows of ruin. Envision a blaze that possesses the duality to shape metal and annihilate nature. When harnessed with intention, the awakened force transforms into a luminous guide, leading one through the shadowy depths of sorrow. When wielded without caution, it has the power to devour our core, reducing our identity to mere ashes in a desolate landscape.

Artistic expression and imagination have perpetually danced on the edge of genius and insanity. Numerous creators, including Vincent van Gogh and Sylvia Plath, have wrestled with the complexities of mental health, leaving an indelible mark on their artistic expressions. Their battles frequently sparked bursts of profound creativity, yet they exacted a heavy price on their emotional health.

Vincent van Gogh, a figure of profound complexity, created some of the most iconic paintings in history, yet he grappled with the depths of severe mental illness, including bipolar disorder. His chaotic feelings and intense creativity sparked his brilliance, leading to his heartbreaking end.

Exploring the intricate dynamics between artistic expression and psychological struggles is essential for nurturing creators and cultivating an environment that prioritizes emotional well-being. By discerning the subtle indicators of turmoil and extending the right kind of assistance, we can empower creators to flourish and express themselves without sacrificing their mental health.[138]

- **Example from Literature:** Mary Shelley's portrayal of the "mad scientist" archetype in Frankenstein serves as a striking example of a dance with the abyss. Dr. Victor Frankenstein's relentless pursuit of defying mortality and forging existence culminates in the emergence of a terrifying creature. His audacious manipulation of scientific possibilities leads to disastrous consequences, creating a chilling ambiguity between brilliance and insanity. The story reveals how the allure of success can become entangled with the ominous specters of downfall when power is harnessed recklessly.[139]

Confronting the Dual Forces: A Narrative of Competing Energies

The Law recognizes how fear can shape our attention and influence our decisions. Fear, an instinctual force, undeniably sharpens our focus and awareness. Envision an individual on the brink of peril, their mind sharpened to a singular point, consumed by the urgent need to flee. Yet, the Law implies that this power, driven by fear, has its boundaries. It reveals itself predominantly in the tangible world, bestowing sudden surges of power or enhanced agility.

The fight-or-flight response, a physiological reaction triggered by perceived threats, is a powerful mechanism that can enhance our physical capabilities and alertness. The instinctual reaction to danger, a visceral response ignited by the shadows of perceived threats, serves as a profound mechanism that sharpens our senses and amplifies our physical prowess. In moments of peril, our very essence responds with a cascade of hormones, like adrenaline and cortisol, priming us for a confrontation with the unknown or a desperate escape to sanctuary. This reaction has been crucial for our existence over time, allowing us to swiftly confront looming threats.

Yet, the instinctual reaction of fight or flight is fundamentally crafted to confront immediate, tangible dangers. In the intricate tapestry of our modern existence, we find ourselves ensnared by relentless pressures that can engulf both our physical and mental realms. The continuous engagement of our primal instincts can unravel a tapestry of health issues, weaving together threads of anxiety, depression, and even heart disease.

To navigate the complexities of stress and uphold mental equilibrium, one must cultivate methods to master the primal instincts that surge within us. Engaging in mindfulness meditation, yoga, and various relaxation techniques can soothe the restless mind and cultivate a profound sense of tranquility within. Through mindfulness and the nurturing of self-care, we can adeptly maneuver through the complexities of contemporary existence, fortifying our spirits against the relentless tide of stress.[140]

The Force of Belief

The Law demands that the force unleashed by belief transcends every aspect of this earthly display. Belief, a steadfast certainty in a favorable conclusion, transcends and surpasses the ordinary boundaries of the physical world. It delves into the boundless depths of the human spirit, forging a profound connection between the individual and a force that transcends his own existence. A bond that ignites a surge of extraordinary ideas—an impact that not only endures the harshest external circumstances but also achieves astonishing feats and defies rational explanation.

Consider the story of Mahatma Gandhi and the Indian independence movement; it vividly illustrates the power of conviction. Gandhi's relentless commitment to peaceful defiance and his deep-seated faith in the strength of truth and justice captivated countless Indians, drawing them into the intense battle for freedom. Amid overwhelming obstacles and harsh oppression, Gandhi's conviction reached beyond the tangible, intertwining with a deeper, almost unseen power that ultimately catalyzed India's freedom from British domination.[141]

The narrative of Mahatma Gandhi and the quest for Indian independence intricately weaves into the concept of unwavering conviction. In a narrative that delves deep into the psyche, the essence of belief emerges as a powerful catalyst, pushing beyond the mundane confines of reality. Gandhi's steadfast faith in

401

nonviolent resistance and justice ignited a fervor within a nation, compelling it to rise against insurmountable challenges and claim its freedom. His conviction created an intense bond among people, linking them to a powerful force beyond their individual lives and sparking a wave of remarkable thoughts and deeds. Gandhi's remarkable resilience in the face of adversity and his extraordinary accomplishments driven by sheer belief highlight the profound influence of steadfast faith and conviction, echoing the core principles of the Law of The Force of Belief.

- **Example from Literature:** Paulo Coelho's The Alchemist unfolds as a profound narrative that delves into the intricate dance between faith and the relentless chase of aspirations. Santiago, the central figure, sets forth on a profound quest to unearth his Personal Legend, a singular and deeply satisfying purpose that defines his existence. As Santiago navigates the labyrinth of his experiences, he faces a series of obstacles and disappointments. Yet, his steadfast conviction in his aspirations ignites his relentless drive to continue onward. His narrative underscores the significance of nurturing a robust belief framework and the transformative influence of optimistic thought in realizing one's aspirations.[142]

The Doctrine of Magnificent Ideas Awakening

The Doctrine of Magnificent Ideas Awakening unveils the shadows of our existence, revealing a reservoir of strength poised for discovery. Yet, the journey toward this strength is laden with peril. It requires a careful equilibrium, a tension-filled interplay between longing and belief. Will you yield to the dark allure of this power, or will you master it to accomplish what others deem unattainable? The decision lies in your hands, yet proceed with caution, as the emergence of Profound Insights may lead to your redemption or your downfall.

- **Example from Entrepreneurship:** The landscape of entrepreneurship unfolds as a captivating journey, teetering between remarkable possibilities and daunting uncertainties. Visionary creators are frequently propelled by an unwavering conviction in their concepts and an insatiable quest for their aspirations. Yet, as a visionary Steve Jobs once articulated, "Innovation distinguishes between a leader and a follower." Though the allure of innovation beckons with promises of success, one must tread carefully, weaving it with meticulous planning and execution to navigate the shadows of uncertainty.

Numerous visionaries have navigated the intricate dance of success and setbacks throughout their odysseys. Elon Musk is a figure of extraordinary achievement, having navigated the tumultuous waters of innovation with ventures such as Tesla and SpaceX. Yet, beneath this veneer of triumph lies a landscape riddled with obstacles and trials that test the very fabric of ambition. His steadfast conviction in his ideals, unyielding determination, and ability to pivot has enabled him to navigate challenges and attain remarkable accomplishments.[143]

Example for History: Consider the tale of Joan of Arc, a striking illustration of the profound impact of extraordinary visions coming to life. Fueled by an unshakeable conviction in her sacred purpose, Joan of Arc guided the French forces to a series of significant triumphs throughout the Hundred Years' War. Her path was riddled with danger as she encountered overwhelming obstacles and doubt from those around her. Against all odds, her deep understanding and unwavering belief propelled her to achieve what many considered impossible. Yet, her journey took a dark turn, culminating in her capture and execution. Joan of Arc's narrative reveals the intricate interplay between desire and conviction, showcasing how the arrival of deep realizations can pave the way for both salvation and ruin.[144]

In Conclusion

The Unveiling of Remarkable Insights within Cognitexis exposes the deep capabilities of the human psyche when confronted with tedious challenges. By exploring and implementing profound concepts, we can tap into the depths of conviction, concentrated perception, and deep reflection to accomplish extraordinary outcomes. Yet, we must stay alert to the insidious dangers that can spiral into obsession, self-destruction, and the reckless misuse of our awakened capabilities.

In the intricate dance of post-traumatic growth and the cautionary narratives that echo through the ages, our minds demand careful stewardship guided by awareness and incisive reflection. By navigating the shadows of our psyche and confronting the turmoil within, we can reshape our minds into a fortress of resilience and a sanctuary for profound understanding.

Ultimately, the Splendid Thoughts Awakening stands as a profound reflection of our potential for intellectual and personal evolution. It serves as an overpowering reminder that, through the power of belief and the intensity of focused awareness, we can traverse the labyrinth of our own minds, reshaping our thoughts into a fortress of resilience and a sanctuary for profound understanding. Yet, we must navigate cautiously, for within the enigmatic realm of Cognitexis, the cost of progress could very well be the essence of our own sanity.

5. Thought Channeling: A Journey into the Weaver's Labyrinth

(The Law of Thoughts Channeling)

Delve into the intricate maze Cognitexis, a domain where the essence of existence transcends the tangible, delving deep into the labyrinth of the mind. In this dimly lit space, where secrets linger and whispers of the unknown intertwine, exists a concealed sanctum—the Law of Thoughts Channeling. Proceed with caution, for in this mysterious realm of exploration, one wrong move could dismantle the intricate tapestry of your psyche. The Law presents a formidable instrument, yet its essence is cloaked in an enigma. Will you harness its power for benevolence, or will you be engulfed by the tumult of ideas it provokes?

Harnessing the Many, Weaving the Unknown

The Law implies that the CgX system, the essence of your cognitive processes, has the potential to transform into a clandestine weaver. Envision a dimly lit workshop where shadows dance among shelves brimming with enigmatic threads, each pulsating with an eerie, ethereal luminescence. This Law suggests that the CgX system can tap into an array of thought channels—a complex web of mental and environmental currents converging within the workshop. A haunting truth lingers: these channels must intertwine to form a cohesive, singular tapestry reminiscent of crafting the essence of existence itself. The atmosphere hums with electric tension as threads of information weave together, their ultimate intent shrouded in an enigma.

The concept of neural plasticity illustrates the captivating dynamics of thought manipulation and the complex interplay of mental functions. The brain possesses a remarkable ability to reshape itself, continuously forging new neural connections as life unfolds. This capacity enables the mind to evolve with fresh encounters, absorb novel insights, and mend from setbacks. The intricate dance of neural plasticity reveals a web of connections, much like how the CgX system weaves diverse thought streams into a unified narrative shrouded in layers of complexity and intrigue.[145]

The complexities of our brains unfold like an enigmatic labyrinth, where billions of neurons intertwine in a web of deep and unsettling connections, each thread leading to unexpected revelations. As we plunge into the depths of the unfamiliar, our minds intricately intertwine, strengthening familiar threads while daring to create new pathways through the labyrinth of understanding. The complex interplay of our mind's architecture weaves a captivating narrative, urging us to explore the shadows of our own awareness and the hidden corners of our psyche.[146]

Much like a masterful creator weaving intricate patterns, our thoughts intricately blend information from various sources, crafting a deep tapestry of understanding and perception. Yet, akin to a delicate web that threatens to unravel, our thoughts can descend into turmoil and doubt if we fail to examine the stories we consume and how we perceive them.

The notion of neural plasticity, as articulated by Norman Doidge, intriguingly resonates with the theme of Harnessing the Many and weaving the Unknown. As the hidden intricacies of the mind unfold, the notion that our thoughts can shape reality takes on a darker hue, revealing the brain's remarkable capacity to adapt and forge new pathways in the shadows of our consciousness. This process demands a complex interaction of numerous neural networks and external influences, reflecting the delicate intertwining of cognitive pathways within the CgX system. The air crackles with unsettling energy as the true motives behind these interactions remain cloaked in mystery, mirroring the intricate and ever-changing landscape of the mind. By tapping into this force, individuals can manipulate their mental faculties to unlock extraordinary levels of intellect and self-discovery, as if shaping the core of reality itself. Yet, like a delicate web that threatens to unravel, failing to examine the stories and perspectives can plunge one into a realm of confusion and unpredictability.

But tread carefully, wanderer, for entangling yourself with these dark strands may unveil unexpected repercussions.

The Dual Journey: A Journey Through the Intricate Maze of the Tapestry

Journey into the Depths of the Intricate Web - In this context, the concept of Forbidden Weaving emerges as a striking parallel to the Law. Thus, the atelier not only crafts a tapestry but is intricately channeling into the very essence of thought. As Forbidden Weaving delves into concealed dimensions, Tandem Thoughts Channeling explores the intricate connections and revelations among diverse streams of thought. It reveals concealed routes within your psyche, an intricate labyrinth of knowledge that can bestow upon you nearly unfathomable strength.

The intricacies of neural networks and their operations create a fascinating parallel to the themes of the Dual Journey and Forbidden Weaving. The intricate web of connections in our brains, woven by billions of neurons linked through synapses, reveals a fascinating and unsettling depth. As we navigate life, our minds intricately craft new neural pathways, strengthening familiar routes and creating unexpected links that can lead to unforeseen revelations. This journey, reminiscent of a hidden narrative, explores the shadowy corners of our psyche, weaving together intricate threads of thought to form a complex mosaic of understanding.

Like a masterful creator weaving intricate patterns, our thoughts blend fragments of knowledge from diverse origins, crafting a deep tapestry of understanding and awareness. Yet, akin to a delicate web, our thoughts can descend into turmoil and doubt if we fail to examine the stories we consume and how we perceive them.[147]

The notion of neural networks, as articulated by Norman Doidge, intriguingly intertwines with the themes of the Dual Journey and Forbidden Weaving. As the atelier weaves a tapestry, capturing the very essence of thought, so too do the neural networks in our minds create a complex web of connections that define our thoughts, memories, and actions. The journey of forging new neural pathways and strengthening the ones already in place reflects a captivating exploration of the complex ties between various streams of consciousness. This journey uncovers hidden pathways in our minds, offering us a depth of power that is almost beyond comprehension. Yet, akin to a delicate web that can easily fray, our thoughts demand meticulous examination of the stories we embrace to avert turmoil and doubt. By delving into the depths of our neural networks, we can traverse the intricate maze of our psyche and reveal the hidden power that lies within.

- **Example from Literature:** Dante Alighieri's Divine Comedy delves deeply into the intricacies of the human spirit, navigating the shadowy corridors of transgression, redemption, and the ultimate quest for enlightenment. Dante, the central figure, ventures into a treacherous odyssey across realms of despair, redemption, and transcendence, meeting many metaphorical characters and profound terrains along the way. This symbolic odyssey serves as a reflection of the mind's inner workings and the soul's evolution.

  As Dante ventures into the abyss, he grapples with the most shadowy facets of the human mind, encompassing lust, gluttony, greed, and wrath. This journey into the abyss serves as a profound metaphor for the inner struggle of facing oneself and recognizing the boundaries and flaws that define our existence. Confronting these shadowy elements, Dante uncovers profound insights about his essence and the intricacies of human existence.[148]

As the Law cautions, the procedure possesses a chilling superiority over ordinary cognitive functions. As you grasp the hidden connections that bind existence, you must confront the price of such knowledge. The very fabric of sanity begins to fray as you confront the raw essence of thought.

Molding Your Perceptions: Sharpened Awareness, the Edge of Reality

The Law compels an individual to embrace a heightened sense of disciplined awareness. Envision the workshop, not merely brimming with threads but overshadowed by an ominous presence—a conscious framework that strains and resists the relentless surge of raw data flooding in. In this light, Disciplined Perception emerges as a shadowy force forged from the depths of mental determination, teetering on the edge of fixation. This ability empowers you to navigate the currents of information within your mind's intricate pathways. You are the architect of your own mental labyrinth, selecting the threads of information to intricately craft your narrative.

The notion of selective attention, explored by figures such as Daniel Kahneman, embodies the essence of Disciplined Perception. Selective attention is the intricate dance of the mind, where individuals hone in on particular details, skillfully filtering out the noise of the irrelevant. This mental skill enables individuals to sift through the chaotic barrage of sensory information and focus on what truly counts. Through the art of selective attention, one can enhance one's perception and sustain an intense focus, skillfully navigating the overwhelming flood of unfiltered information.[149]

The notion of selective attention, explored by Daniel Kahneman, intriguingly intertwines with the theme of shaping one's perceptions. In a world where the unseen pulls at the threads of our consciousness, the Law demands sharpened vigilance. At the same time, selective attention becomes the lens through which we discern the vital from the trivial, navigating the shadows of distraction. This mental skill reflects the journey through the swirling tides of knowledge in the mind's complex corridors, much like choosing the strands of information to weave a compelling story. Through the art of selective attention, one can hone one's perception and sustain concentration, skillfully navigating the relentless tide of sensory overload. This focused awareness allows individuals to craft the intricate designs of their minds, meticulously molding their reality with intent and resolve.

- **Example from Psychology:** The practice of mindfulness, deeply embedded in Buddhist and ancient traditions, has surged in prominence lately, captivating many with its promise to alleviate stress, sharpen concentration, and elevate the essence of well-being. Through the intricate exploration of the now, one can unravel the complexities of one's inner world, gaining profound insights into the labyrinth of thoughts, emotions, and sensations that shape one's existence.

  Yet, as one delves into the depths of self-awareness, navigating this journey with a sense of equilibrium becomes crucial. The relentless focus on mindfulness may spiral into a state of hyperawareness and incessant thought, potentially intensifying feelings of anxiety and depression. Jon Kabat-Zinn, a trailblazer in the realm of mindfulness, underscores that the essence of this practice lies not in banishing negative thoughts and emotions but in witnessing them with an open and accepting perspective.[150]

Disciplined Perception is a double-edged sword! it guards against the impending tempest of forbidden knowledge, yet it can morph into an obsession—a ceaseless quest for profound connections that threatens to unravel the very essence of your psyche.

A Realm of Possibilities: A Web of Secrets Beckons

The Law culminates in a haunting revelation of this power's dark possibilities. At the core of cognitive manipulation, the Law unveils a pathway to cultivate taboo ideations. Envision the workshop as a dynamic force, not merely crafting a tapestry but intricately altering the very essence of your thought processes. Through the meticulous crafting of diverse mental pathways and the unwavering force of determination, one can transform the very terrain of one's mind. Unlock hidden potentials as you explore the enigmatic depths of your psyche through the intriguing practice of thought channeling. But heed this warning, seeker of truth: the wisdom you pursue could very well lead to your downfall.

The concept of cognitive dissonance, first presented by Leon Festinger, highlights the intricacies of mental conflict and the unsettling avenues it reveals. The unsettling clash of conflicting beliefs, values, or attitudes can lead to a profound sense of psychological discomfort in an individual. This unease can trigger profound shifts in actions and mental patterns as people seek to reconcile their conflicting feelings. The intricate dance of conflicting thoughts can unearth concealed abilities and fresh perspectives, yet it may spiral into adverse consequences if left unchecked. People often find themselves rationalizing destructive actions or convictions to alleviate their unease, resulting in a perilous shift in their mindset.

Imagine the workshop as a powerful entity, not just weaving a narrative but profoundly transforming the core of perception itself. By intricately weaving together various mental routes and harnessing an unyielding drive, the clash of conflicting thoughts can reshape the landscape of the mind itself. Yet, this journey can unravel a tangled web of hidden truths and forbidden thoughts, exposing the chilling potential of mental influence. As people delve into the mysterious corners of their minds, they should be cautious, for the knowledge they seek might ultimately bring about their undoing.[151]

The notion of conflicting beliefs, as put forth by Leon Festinger, resonates deeply with the theme of A Realm of Possibilities: A Web of Secrets Beckons. As the shadows of the Law unveil the unsettling depths of mental influence, the unsettling nature of cognitive dissonance hints at the profound shifts that can occur within our thoughts and actions. This journey can uncover concealed abilities and fresh perspectives reminiscent of delving into the mysterious layers of the mind through introspective exploration. Yet, the unsettling nature of conflicting thoughts can spiral into adverse consequences if left unchecked, echoing the caution that the knowledge sought might ultimately bring ruin. By delving into the complexities of cognitive dissonance, individuals can traverse the labyrinth of their own minds, revealing concealed strengths while steering clear of the perils of mental manipulation.

In Conclusion

The Law of Thoughts Channeling reveals an enthralling journey, yet the price it demands is shrouded in an enigma. Delving into the practice of thought channeling feels akin to navigating the complex labyrinth of one's own psyche. Much like a powerful weapon, it possesses the inherent ability to reveal truths and unleash chaos. Through the labyrinthine corridors of our consciousness and the deep tales spun in the fabric of literature, alongside the reflective practices of mindfulness, every moment unveils the delicate balance of reaching for deeper truths.

Will you dare navigate the intricate maze of your own psyche, or will you slip into the shadows as the chance slips away? The workshop beckons, its alluring promise pulsating with hidden possibilities. Move forward with trepidation, for the cost of exposing hidden truths can be both dangerous and profound. Yet the gains from mastering this craft may lead to a profound shift, elevating one's understanding to a new dimension of awareness.

This refined exploration delves into the profound implications of mastering thought channeling, illuminating the perilous yet alluring journey that beckons the mind. It stirs a blend of trepidation and intrigue, urging a pursuit of knowledge that dances on the edge of enlightenment and danger.

6. Augmented Realities: Where Thoughts Transform into Enchanting Summons

(The Law of Thoughts Complementing Reality Inception)

Delve into the intricate depths of Cognitexis, a domain where the essence of thought reigns supreme, untamed, and unfiltered. In this realm, shadows twist, and murmurs resonate, revealing the profound influence and peril inherent in The Law of Thoughts Complementing Reality Inception. This age-old concept, cloaked in an enigma, implies that your prevailing thoughts—the relentless, haunting echoes within your consciousness—possess the power to bend the very essence of existence to your will. But proceed cautiously, for the Law wields a dual nature, offering great power while concealing a perilous, cutting edge beneath its surface.

The Alchemist's Forge - A Realm Where Identity Shapes Fate

The Law unfolds hauntingly, reminiscent of a dark and secretive transformation. Envision a blazing furnace in the depths of your mind, fueled by the intense heat of mental autosuggestion. In this intricate journey, the prevailing thoughts that occupy your mind intertwine with the actions they provoke, becoming indelible elements of your very essence. Like a sinister alchemist distorting reality, the shadows of negative self-talk and fear can construct an unyielding prison of self-doubt, ensnaring your very essence. On the flip side, relentless optimism can forge your essence into a tool of unyielding determination. Within these shadows lurks a perilous truth: the Law remains indifferent to all. Your perception is shaped by the echoes you decide to elevate.

Consider this intriguing notion: the self-fulfilling prophecy, a term coined by Robert K. Merton, illustrates how our beliefs can shape

413

the very fabric of our reality. When a person's beliefs about a scenario shape their actions, it can create a chilling cycle where those beliefs come to life, manifesting in ways they never anticipated. This intriguing occurrence reveals the power of dominant thoughts to mold our reality, either by amplifying fears and negative self-perceptions or cultivating a sense of hope and resolve.[152]

The notion of a self-fulfilling prophecy, as articulated by Robert K. Merton, intertwines seamlessly with the realm of Augmented Realities: A space were thoughts morph into captivating manifestations. As the concept of thoughts intertwining with reality unfolds, it becomes evident how our expectations can manipulate our actions, leading to a cascade of events that ultimately shape our existence. Dark whispers of self-doubt and paralyzing fear can trap the mind in a suffocating cage, while an unwavering belief in oneself can become a powerful weapon of relentless resolve. The intricate dance of thought's influence, as unveiled in the Alchemist's Forge, exposes how our understanding and the world around us are molded by the whispers we decide to amplify. By grasping this concept, one can manipulate their mindset to reshape their existence, yet they must tread carefully to evade the dangerous fallout of dark thoughts.

Lasered Concentration - A Guiding Light in the Darkness

The Law reveals the gripping force of concentrated awareness. Envision a lighthouse, its lone beam battling to penetrate a tumultuous storm of despair. Intense concentration operates in a parallel manner, yet rather than steering vessels, it hones your perception of the hidden influences that mold your existence. By honing in on a singular objective, you cast a guiding light into the chaotic depths of Cognitexis. This signal, however, has the power to draw in both allies and adversaries as the light of optimism reveals hidden paths; the shadows of negativity beckon those who thrive on your insecurities and trepidations.

Consider this intriguing concept: the idea of flow, articulated by Mihaly Csikszentmihalyi in his work "Flow: The Psychology of Optimal Experience," perfectly captures the essence of intense focus. Flow is a captivating mental state where an individual becomes entirely absorbed and fixated on one task, resulting in peak performance and a profound sense of satisfaction. This sharp focus enables individuals to maneuver through the intricate web of their own minds and behaviors, much like a beacon illuminating the darkness of uncertainty. Yet, reaching that elusive state of flow demands a careful equilibrium between challenges and skills, for an excess of negativity or distraction can shatter the delicate balance and pull you away from that immersive experience.[153]

As articulated by Mihaly Csikszentmihalyi, the notion of flow seamlessly intertwines with the essence of Lasered Concentration - A Guiding Light in the Shadows. As the paragraph reveals, concentrated awareness serves as a beacon amidst the tumultuous shadows of Cognitexis. At the same time, the state of flow embodies an intensified immersion that sharpens both perception and performance. This mindset empowers individuals to uncover the unseen forces that mold their reality, akin to a beacon illuminating the chaos of a raging tempest. Yet, the flow state draws in both uplifting and dark forces, reflecting how the glow of hope can illuminate concealed routes while the lurking shadows of despair invite challenges. By delving into the depths of focused awareness, individuals can unlock a captivating energy that guides them through shadows and obstacles, revealing their true potential.

- **Example from Science:** The profound impact of focused attention is a concept deeply rooted in cognitive psychology. As we immerse ourselves in a particular endeavor, our mind engages in a complex web of connections that effectively sifts through distractions, enabling us to hone in on the matter before us with unwavering clarity. This concentrated awareness can elevate our capabilities and ingenuity, allowing us to realize our aspirations.

Yet, an overwhelming focus can lead to unforeseen repercussions. Inattentional blindness manifests when our concentration on a singular endeavor blinds us to the significant details lurking in our surroundings. This intriguing occurrence underscores the necessity of harmonizing concentrated focus with a more expansive consciousness.

As Daniel Kahneman, a Nobel Prize-winning psychologist, has suggested, our focus is a finite asset that can be easily inundated. Grasping the confines of our focus allows us to navigate our mental resources more effectively, steering clear of the shadows cast by unseen distractions.

Ultimately, the essence of mastering attention resides in striking a delicate equilibrium between concentrated focus and a wider consciousness. By honing the skill to immerse ourselves in particular endeavors while staying receptive to fresh insights and viewpoints, we can tap into the profound potential of concentrated awareness to realize our aspirations and embrace a more enriching existence.[154]

The Intricacies of Desire - Blessing or Curse?

The Law unveils the chilling reality of Directed Attentiveness. Envision the lighthouse beam cutting through the darkness, not guiding you to safety but exposing a terrifying creature lurking in the abyss, waiting to strike. Just as concentrated awareness can summon possibilities, fixating on dark thoughts and the patterns they breed (avoidance, dread) can unleash terrifying specters. These hidden powers flourish in despair and aim to prey on your weaknesses. Your attention transforms into a haunting melody, luring you not toward triumph but into the depths of your own inner turmoil.

Consider the haunting idea of rumination, a theme explored by Susan Nolen-Hoeksema in her research, which illustrates how focused contemplation can spiral into detrimental consequences. Delving into the depths of one's mind can lead to an unsettling cycle of distressing thoughts and emotions, intensifying the shadows of depression and anxiety lurking just beneath the surface. This mental framework ensnares people in a relentless loop of despair, akin to a spotlight revealing horrifying entities lurking in the depths. By obsessing over shadowy thoughts, people cultivate a psychological landscape where hopelessness and sinister forces flourish, resulting in deeper internal chaos.[155]

The notion of rumination, explored by Susan Nolen-Hoeksema, intertwines seamlessly with the theme of The Intricacies of Desire - Blessing or Curse? As the paragraph reveals, Directed Attentiveness unveils horrifying entities lurking in the depths. At the same time, rumination ensnares the mind in a web of troubling thoughts and feelings, spiraling into dark mental states. This intricate mindset cultivates a psychological landscape where hopelessness and dark forces thrive, echoing a chilling tune that draws people into their emotional chaos. By grasping the influence of focused awareness and handling it with care, individuals can avoid the traps of overthinking and channel their cravings toward favorable results, turning possible burdens into unexpected advantages.

- **Example from Literature:** Shakespeare's Macbeth is a profound exploration of the dark consequences of ambition spiraling out of control. Macbeth, a valiant general of Scotland, finds himself ensnared by an alluring prophecy that foretells his ascent to the throne. This seemingly harmless prediction awakens a sinister longing within him, propelling him toward a chilling sequence of malevolent acts. The insatiable quest for dominance engulfs Macbeth, transforming him into a profoundly tragic entity.

- The performance unveils the perilous consequences of letting yearning obscure reason and ethical principles. The tragic unraveling of Macbeth illustrates a profound warning regarding the necessity of balance, restraint, and the quest for virtuous aspirations. In his relentless pursuit of ambition, Macbeth forsakes the whispers of his conscience, ultimately surrendering to the abyss that lies within.[156]

Contemplations - The Murmuring Designers

At the core of the Law resides a haunting notion: the magnetic force of thought. Envision your mind as a labyrinth of shadowy murmurs reverberating through a boundless, hidden void. The murmurs of thought may not take shape as tangible entities. Yet, the principle implies they reverberate through the very essence of existence, drawing in the fundamental elements required to bring them into being, whether for better or worse. Your attention serves as a powerful magnet, attracting the uplifting or challenging events that define your journey.

Consider this intriguing concept: the "law of attraction," brought to the forefront by Rhonda Byrne in her book "The Secret," illustrates the compelling power of thought as a magnetic force that draws experiences into our lives. The principle suggests that the energy of one's thoughts can manifest into real-life experiences, shaping the reality one encounters, whether uplifting or dark. This concept implies that the thoughts we dwell on—positive or negative—serve as a powerful force, attracting similar experiences and results into our reality. By honing in on particular thoughts, we can steer the direction of our path and mold our existence.[157]

The notion of the law of attraction, brought to the forefront by Rhonda Byrne, resonates deeply with the essence of Contemplations - The Murmuring Designers. As the words unfold, they reveal a captivating interplay of mental energy that pulses through reality, hinting at a powerful principle where our innermost thoughts serve as a beacon, pulling in experiences that mirror our desires. By concentrating on uplifting or dark reflections, we shape the occurrences that carve our path, much like the whispers echoing through a maze that summons essential forces into existence. Grasping this principle empowers individuals to manipulate their thoughts, crafting their reality while simultaneously acknowledging the weight of responsibility that accompanies the focus of their attention.

- **Example from Alternative Disciplines:** The Law of Attraction suggests that our mindset shapes our reality. Uplifting thoughts attract favorable outcomes, whereas pessimistic thoughts invite unfavorable circumstances. This idea has gained traction through works such as Rhonda Byrne's The Secret. The allure of the Law of Attraction captivates many, yet its empirical foundation invites scrutiny and contemplation.

  Though optimistic thought allures with the promise of enhanced well-being and diminished anxiety, the empirical foundation for its ability to conjure particular realities remains tenuous at best. Striking a delicate equilibrium between hopeful aspirations and grounded realities while taking decisive steps is essential.[158]

Clarity of Intent - The Catalyst that Ignites Destiny

Clarity of intent serves as a formidable weapon, guiding you through the perilous terrain of the Law of Thoughts Augmented Reality. Much like a meticulously crafted plan steers a skilled architect, a resolute aim channels your mind and deeds; it doesn't offer an illusion of safety from the perils of the law; rather, it arms you with the essential tools to navigate obstacles and realize your ambitions.

The notion of SMART goals—Specific, Measurable, Achievable, Relevant, and Time-bound—first put forth by George T. Doran perfectly illustrates the essence of Intentional Clarity. SMART goals create a precise and organized blueprint for defining and reaching ambitions. By establishing clear and attainable objectives, individuals can precisely direct their energy and resources, akin to a carefully orchestrated strategy guiding a masterful creator. This sharp focus acts as a spark, fueling determination and steering individuals through obstacles on their journey to achieve their dreams.[159]

The notion of SMART goals, brought forth by George T. Doran, seamlessly intertwines with the essence of Clarity of Intent - the spark that sets one's fate into motion. Much like how a sharp focus can navigate through the shadows of uncertainty, SMART goals carve out a precise and organized path for defining and realizing ambitions. This precision directs actions and assets with intent, reflecting how a carefully designed strategy guides a masterful creator. By establishing and chasing precise objectives, individuals can maneuver through challenges and achieve their desires, equipped with the vital instruments of insight and resolve. This meticulously crafted method guarantees that a clear purpose acts as a spark, fueling ambition and steering individuals toward their ultimate fate.

- **Example from Entrepreneurship:** A sharp and captivating vision is essential for navigating through the intricate maze of any endeavor. In the dimly lit corners of our lives, a clear intention rises like a flickering flame, leading us through the intricate maze of desire, determination, and strength. This concept is deeply embedded in a mental landscape highlighting the significance of well-articulated goals. It suggests that when ambitions are clearly defined, quantifiable, attainable, pertinent, and time-sensitive, they can significantly elevate both outcomes and the motivation to prevail. In the shadowy corridors of desire, we navigate our journey by dissecting lofty dreams into manageable, bite-sized steps. This approach sheds light on our path and provides opportunities for introspection and recognition as we traverse the shadows of our pursuits.

Diving into the depths of the mind, Carol Dweck's insights illuminate the power of a growth mindset—a belief in the ability to transform and learn—that plays a crucial role in chasing one's dreams. Embracing a growth mindset compels us to face challenges directly, unearth lessons hidden within our failures, and persevere through the dark corners of adversity.

Consider, for example, the intriguing narrative surrounding Elon Musk. His unyielding quest to revolutionize electric vehicles, explore the cosmos, and conquer artificial intelligence has thrust him into extraordinary heights of success. Musk's sharp focus, tireless ambition, and unwavering determination have enabled him to maneuver through a maze of challenges, creating an enigmatic presence that intrigues and motivates countless individuals worldwide. His story unravels with an intense grip, revealing the deep influence of a striking and unwavering ambition.[160]

In Conclusion

In the shadowy passages of Cognitexis, where murmurs of darkness unveil hidden truths, and the mind wields the ability to alter reality, the Law of Thoughts Complementing Reality Inception unveils its cryptic essence. This timeless notion implies that the unyielding reverberations within your mind hold the power to shape reality according to your desires. Yet, tread carefully; this strength is laced with a treacherous undercurrent.

Envision yourself poised at the edge of an infinite abyss, where the very fabric of your mind weaves the tapestry of your destiny. The shadows writhe and sway, hiding the allure of immense power alongside the ominous threats that lie in wait for the unsuspecting.

Will you have the audacity to seize this power, intertwining your deepest longings with the essence of existence itself? Or will you find yourself trapped in the depths of your own mind, a captive of your own design?

The inner crucible of your thoughts glows with an intense fire stoked by the fervor of self-induced belief. In this realm, your deepest reflections entwine with your deeds, merging seamlessly into the very fabric of your being. Destructive inner dialogue and paralyzing fear can create an impenetrable cage of uncertainty, whereas unwavering hope can elevate you into a symbol of steadfast resolve. Yet, keep in mind, the Law stands unfeeling to all—it is your interpretation that molds your fate.

As you traverse this complex labyrinth, tread carefully. The labyrinth of your thoughts beckons, its alluring whispers resonating with uncharted possibilities. However, the cost of revealing hidden truths can be both treacherous and profound. Will you dare to navigate the intricate maze of your own psyche, revealing the hidden truths that lie beneath, or will you dissolve into the shadows as the chance eludes your grasp?

The path lies before you, wanderer of the mind. Welcome the mysterious force of contemplation and allow your descent into the abyss to commence. But proceed cautiously, for the journey to understanding is laden with danger, and the boundary between success and destruction is perilously narrow.

PRESERVATION AND PROTECTION OF THOUGHTS

Withinin the labyrinth, certain routes unveil hidden sanctuaries of ancient understanding. This collective is committed to safeguarding the invaluable secrets of the psyche, concealed from the looming darkness that threatens to engulf them. The Archives of Wisdom loom as a formidable barrier against the relentless shadows that strive to obliterate our understanding. In this realm, you must fiercely protect the invaluable shards of your mental legacy, lest they slip away into the shadows of oblivion.

1. The Archives of Wisdom: Safeguarding the Mind's Treasures

(The Law of Acquired Thoughts Preservation)

In the shadowy depths of Cognitexis, a concealed chamber lies in wait: the Archives of Wisdom. In this realm, illuminated by the shimmering glow of crystals, the principle of safeguarding acquired thoughts holds an undeniable power. It safeguards the invaluable insights and connections cultivated within the psyche, whether in solitude or together, from the relentless erosion of time and chaos.

The Principle of Safeguarding Acquired Thoughts

This principle asserts that any disturbance to a synchronized mindset jeopardizes the momentum achieved through rigorous mental exertion. Envision the Archives of Wisdom as an expansive labyrinth, its corridors lined with murmuring volumes, each pulsating with the collective insights of history's thinkers and their intricate dialogues. The Law cautions that these invaluable volumes risk fading into oblivion or suffering irreparable harm without meticulous care. Intrusions, whether from within or without, threaten to unravel the fragile equilibrium of the library, putting at risk the invaluable wisdom contained within its walls.

The notion of a "memory palace," rooted in the ancient craft of mnemonics, embodies the essence of protecting cherished ideas. Envisioning a familiar space, the memory palace technique allows you to intertwine fragments of information with unique spots throughout that environment, creating a web of connections that linger in the mind's shadows. This mental visualization captivates individuals, enhancing their ability to retain and recall information, reminiscent of how the Archives of Wisdom safeguards precious insights and connections. Crafting a meticulously arranged mental sanctuary, the memory palace guards precious insights against the relentless decay of time and disorder.[161]

The notion of a memory palace, as explored by Frances A. Yates, resonates deeply with the theme of The Archives of Wisdom: Protecting the Mind's Hidden Gems. Much like the intricate web of a mind unraveling under pressure, the memory palace technique serves as a refuge for precious insights, allowing individuals to anchor their thoughts in familiar spaces, shielding them from the chaos that threatens to consume clarity. This mental visualization constructs a meticulously arranged environment, echoing the intricate pathways of the Archives of Wisdom. By carefully nurturing the secrets held within the memory palace, one can guard against the creeping shadows of forgetfulness and the potential for irreversible damage. This meticulous method guarantees that the precious insights hidden within the mind are safeguarded, preserving the delicate balance of the mental archive.

- **Example from Science:** Safeguarding knowledge and cultural legacy is crucial for unraveling the intricacies of history, influencing our current reality, and igniting aspirations for what lies ahead. The Smithsonian Institution's Cultural Rescue Initiative is a compelling illustration of the necessity for anticipatory actions in preserving cultural treasures. Following the devastating earthquake in Haiti in 2010, a team of experts from the Smithsonian embarked on a mission to safeguard and maintain thousands of cultural treasures, ensuring that these priceless artifacts would endure for generations to come.

This endeavor underscores the significance of safeguarding not just tangible artifacts but also the ethereal essence of cultural heritage, encompassing the whispers of oral traditions, music rhythms, and dance movements. Through the meticulous documentation and preservation of these cultural elements, we can safeguard their legacy for future generations.[162]

The Need for Anticipatory Actions

The Law underscores the critical need for anticipatory actions. The Archives transform into a dynamic center of perpetual discovery, where individuals and ISA members immerse themselves in the pursuit of knowledge, fostering an ongoing dialogue of ideas that keeps the intellectual pulse alive. This continuous journey deepens the entrenchment of ideas: the insights gained from previous encounters serve as a powerful catalyst for mental evolution.

The notion of "anticipatory guidance," utilized in pediatric healthcare, is a prime example of proactive measures. Anticipatory guidance is about equipping parents and caregivers with the insights and support they need to foresee and tackle potential health and developmental challenges in children. This anticipatory strategy wards off issues before they emerge, fostering a robust evolution. The ongoing exchange between healthcare providers and caregivers creates an intriguing hub of revelation, where past experiences shape future decisions and elevate children's holistic health.[163]

The notion of anticipatory guidance in pediatric healthcare resonates deeply with the imperative for proactive measures. As the paragraph unveils the Archives morphing into a vibrant hub of endless exploration, anticipatory guidance embodies the art of preemptive measures, tackling looming challenges before they surface. The relentless conversation between healthcare providers and caregivers reflects an unending quest for understanding and exchanging ideas, much like the intricate narratives explored in the Archives. Lessons drawn from past experiences act as a compelling force in enhancing the well-being and growth of children, mirroring the way deeply rooted concepts drive psychological transformation. This strategic maneuver keeps the intellectual heartbeat thriving, safeguarding knowledge for those who will come after us.

- **Example from Literature:** Ray Bradbury's dystopian novel and chilling narrative in Fahrenheit 451 offers a haunting vision of a world where books are banned and brutally destroyed, stirring unsettling thoughts about the essence of knowledge and the fragility of freedom. In this oppressive reality, a secretive group called the Book People dedicates themselves to safeguarding literature, embedding entire works deep within their consciousness. Their decisions expose a deep awareness of the need to fiercely guard knowledge and legacy, even when faced with the lurking threats of oppression and challenge.

- The pursuits of the Book People reveal the intricate layers of human resilience and the unyielding power that lies within the written word. In a world where every word could vanish, they cling to the intricate layers of meaning, ensuring that the beauty and depth of literature remain untouched, even as shadows loom over its physical existence. This dynamic strategy acts as a compelling force for psychological transformation, relentlessly intensifying the fixation on concepts. Their story reveals an urgent call to action, a suspenseful journey to safeguard precious insights, ensuring that this treasure trove of wisdom continues to be a vibrant source of revelation for those who come after.[164]

- The illustration of the Book People in Ray Bradbury's Fahrenheit 451 resonates deeply with the concept of the necessity for proactive measures. As the paragraph illustrates the Archives as a vibrant hub of endless exploration, the Book People represent a relentless commitment to preserving literature by memorizing entire works. This calculated move guarantees that precious knowledge and traditions remain intact despite relentless forces aiming to erase them. The relentless interplay of thoughts and conversations among the Book People reflects a dynamic energy that sustains and transforms understanding unexpectedly. Their endeavors underscore the critical need to safeguard and nurture cultivated ideas, propelling a continuous quest for mental transformation and revelation.

The Practice of Mental Clarity

This practice of mental clarity stands as the foundation for safeguarding wisdom within the Archives. Just as a skilled curator safeguards precious volumes, we must cultivate habits that maintain concentration and preserve this delicate mental equilibrium. Engaging in meditation, practicing critical thinking exercises, and mastering the art of clearing your mind can significantly enhance your mental landscape, fostering an optimal space for learning and retention.

The practice of mindfulness meditation, steeped in ancient traditions and rooted in Buddhist practice, has surged in popularity, captivating those seeking mental clarity, a reprieve from stress, and a pathway to holistic well-being. Through the art of embracing the now, one can sharpen one's mental faculties, honing the ability to concentrate and fend off the incessant pull of distractions. This endeavor resembles that of a careful architect, skillfully arranging and preserving an expansive collection of reflections and concepts.

The idea of mindfulness meditation, brought to prominence by Jon Kabat-Zinn, showcases the pursuit of mental clarity. Practice unfolds in the depths of the mind—an intricate dance of attention that draws you into the now. Here, thoughts, emotions, and sensations swirl around, waiting to be acknowledged without the weight of judgment. It's a journey into the self, where every moment holds a secret waiting to be uncovered. This technique sharpens focus, alleviates tension, and cultivates a clear mind. Through consistent mindfulness meditation practice, one cultivates a prime mental environment for absorbing knowledge and enhancing memory, akin to a meticulous curator protecting invaluable treasures in the Archives.[165]

The notion of mindfulness meditation, as presented by Jon Kabat-Zinn, seamlessly intertwines with the essence of The Practice of Mental Clarity. As the paragraph reveals the significance of nurturing habits to sustain focus and safeguard mental balance, mindfulness meditation emerges as a methodical pathway to attain mental lucidity. This technique sharpens focus, alleviates tension, and cultivates a perfect mental environment for absorbing and retaining knowledge. Through the practice of mindfulness meditation, individuals meticulously shield their mental realm, akin to how a master curator guards precious artifacts within the Archives. This strategic method guarantees that knowledge remains intact and easily obtainable, creating a dynamic atmosphere ripe for exploration and insight.

The Dangers Within the Archives

Yet, the Archives harbor their own dangers. Sinister figures, referred to as the Corruptors, hide in the maze, intent on creating chaos and undermining the clarity of the mind. These sinister influences can emerge as inner turmoil, external distractions, or the calculated distortion of truth. The Law serves as a stark reminder of the necessity for constant awareness. By uncovering the insidious strategies of the Corruptors, we can protect the Archives and preserve the sanctity of the knowledge we cherish.

In a chilling exploration of Cognitive Psychology, the notion of cognitive distortions, as examined by Aaron T. Beck in his groundbreaking work on cognitive therapy, serves as a haunting reflection of the Corruptors lurking within the Archives. Twisted perceptions can cloud the mind, spiraling into a web of negativity that ensnares emotions and drives unsettling actions. These distortions are the malevolent forces that erode mental clarity and truth, reminiscent of the Corruptors lurking in the Archives. By uncovering and confronting these deceptive thought patterns through a transformative process, individuals can safeguard their mental landscapes and maintain the sharpness of their insights and understanding.[166]

The exploration of cognitive distortions, as articulated by Aaron T. Beck, resonates deeply with the unsettling themes found in The Dangers Within the Archives. As the paragraph unveils the Corruptors as dark entities that thrive on chaos and cloud the mind, cognitive distortions emerge as twisted thoughts that breed negativity and skew perception. These distortions are the dark forces lurking in the psyche, poised to dismantle the essence of clarity and understanding. By delving into and confronting these mental traps through therapeutic exploration, individuals can safeguard their inner realms and maintain the integrity of the truths they hold dear. This vigilant strategy highlights the critical need for ongoing consciousness to protect the precious revelations lurking in the depths of the psyche.

- **Example from Science:** Our conscious mind often betrays us, distorting the truths we hold dear. The intricacies of the mind reveal how our inherent biases can warp our understanding of the world, steering us toward misguided choices and shadowy conclusions. Consider the allure of confirmation bias, a subtle yet powerful force that compels us to pursue information that aligns with our preconceptions while conveniently dismissing any evidence that challenges our worldview. This may result in a constricted mindset and an unwillingness to embrace transformation.

Grasping the intricacies of cognitive biases is essential for preserving mental acuity and arriving at well-founded conclusions. By acknowledging our inherent biases and intentionally exploring many viewpoints, we can diminish their influence on our thought processes.[167]

The Guild of Restorers

Within the shadowy depths of that intricate maze, hidden yet radiating from the Archives, exists a clandestine Guild of Restorers. This sanctuary safeguards the flicker of hope for brighter days ahead. In that place, a select few dedicated individuals painstakingly repair torn pages, restoring wisdom that has been lost to the shadows. In their grasp, more than in any other, the essence of the Law resonates with a powerful voice, especially in tumultuous times when shadows recede, revealing a guiding light that points the way forward.

Consider the Monastic Scriptoria of the Middle Ages; they serve as a haunting reflection of the Guild of Restorers, where secrets of the past were meticulously preserved and transformed under the watchful eyes of those who understood the weight of their craft. In secluded chambers of monasteries, monks engaged in a meticulous ritual, their hands gliding over parchment as they breathed life into ancient texts. Each stroke of the quill was a silent vow, a promise to safeguard the wisdom of the ages from the relentless grasp of oblivion. These monks operated in the shadows, meticulously piecing together fragments of knowledge, battling against the looming threats that sought to erase the wisdom of the past. Their relentless pursuit safeguarded the essence of civilizations, illuminating the shadows of chaotic eras with an unwavering brilliance.[168]

The notion of the Monastic Scriptoria in the Middle Ages intriguingly parallels the essence of The Guild of Restorers. In a world where shadows loom, and secrets linger, the devoted souls meticulously mend the frayed edges of history, echoing the relentless efforts of monks in their secluded chambers, who laboriously transcribe and safeguard the fragile remnants of wisdom, ensuring that the essence of knowledge endures against the passage of time. Their endeavors shielded the essence of civilizations, reminiscent of a clandestine group ensuring that the glimmer of hope remains alive for a more promising future. In their hold, the core of the Law echoes with intense clarity, particularly in chaotic moments when darkness fades, unveiling a beacon that directs the path ahead. The monks' unwavering commitment to safeguarding wisdom and knowledge reveals the dark undercurrents of restoration and protection, highlighting the fragile threads that hold together the tapestry of intellectual heritage.

- **Example from Literature:** Umberto Eco's historical mystery novel, The Name of the Rose, intricately explores the profound significance of monks as guardians of wisdom. The Benedictine monks of the abbey engage in a careful dance with time, preserving and restoring ancient manuscripts as if each fragile page holds the echoes of forgotten truths, waiting to be unearthed by those who dare to seek the wisdom of the past for the sake of future enlightenment. Their unwavering commitment to their art underscores the significance of safeguarding cultural legacies and the profound worth of intellectual endeavors.

The monks' work embodies a relentless quest to safeguard wisdom, a battle against the inevitable erosion of understanding by the relentless passage of time, and a battle to ensure that it is not lost to the ravages of time. In the shadows of time, the act of preserving and restoring ancient texts becomes a profound journey into the depths of human understanding, weaving a tapestry that enriches our cultural heritage in ways that echo through the corridors of thought.[169]

In Conclusion

The Archives of Wisdom, a mysterious sentinel of the psyche's concealed riches, invites us to traverse a gripping path through the intricate maze of self-discovery and the haunting reverberations of our intellectual legacy. Amidst these shadowy corridors of thought resides a force, the Law of Acquired Thoughts Preservation, capable of safeguarding the deep insights and complex interrelations intricately stitched into the very essence of our consciousness. Yet, tread carefully, for in the depths of darkness reside the Corruptors—insidious forces intent on dismantling the fragile fabric of our understanding and existence.

As we traverse this enigmatic landscape, we must stay alert, taking deliberate steps and preemptive actions to safeguard the integrity of our inner selves. The truths we unearth and the wisdom we safeguard transcend our understanding, reaching into the shadows of time that stretch before us. The destiny of our minds, and possibly the core of what it means to be human, rests precariously on our capacity to protect and nurture the wellspring of understanding.

Will you embrace the struggle, protecting the concealed riches of your psyche, or will you yield to the darkness that aims to obliterate your existence? The Archives of Wisdom beckon, their alluring whispers resonating with untapped possibilities. Advance with unwavering resolve and a fierce heart, for the path that lies before you is shadowed by danger, yet the fruits of true understanding are immeasurable.

2. The Thought Vaults: Salvaging the Mind's Treasures

(The Law of Thoughts Rescue)

The Thought Vaults are a secret cavern deep within the maze of Cognitexis. Here, illuminated crystals keep the Law of Thought Rescue in check. In doing so, it equips the mind to protect not just its own treasures but also to serve as a lighthouse for the intellectually lost.

The Power of Structured Cognition

The power to unleash this potential, according to this law, lies in a well-established mental process and Structured Cognition. Picture this: a huge library with bookshelves lined with old, worn books that have held the wisdom of many generations. Some ideas in this library, meanwhile, run the risk of becoming stuck in a rut, of becoming part of a routine that does us no good. The Law instructs us to quickly change our thinking patterns, tapping into the library's extensive collection to activate the problem-solving machinery that focuses on incidents.

The notion of cognitive restructuring, as articulated in cognitive-behavioral therapy (CBT), embodies the essence of Structured Cognition. Unraveling the mind's labyrinth, cognitive restructuring beckons you to confront those shadowy thought patterns lurking in the corners. It's a journey of transformation, where you dismantle negativity and weave in threads of resilience and clarity. This journey empowers individuals to shatter the chains of unproductive thought patterns and unleash their innate problem-solving prowess. By delving into a vast array of mental tactics, one can reclaim their thoughts and fortify their psychological strength.[170]

The notion of cognitive restructuring, as articulated by Judith S. Beck, resonates deeply with the intriguing premise of The Thought Vaults: Salvaging the Mind's Treasures. As the Law of Thoughts Rescue empowers the mind to safeguard its hidden gems and illuminate the path for those adrift in confusion, cognitive restructuring offers a methodical way to uncover and confront the shadows of negative thinking. This method empowers individuals to escape the confines of unhelpful mental patterns and unlock their innate problem-solving skills, reminiscent of delving into a vast reservoir of insight hidden within the depths of the Mind Archives. Through the process of reshaping thoughts, one can fortify their mental strength and protect their precious revelations, allowing their minds to shine with insight and lucidity.

- **Example from Science:** Cognitive restructuring, a key technique in Cognitive Behavioral Therapy (CBT) and a pivotal approach in therapeutic practices. Consider a scenario where an individual is engulfed in the shadows of anxiety before a job interview. Through the lens of cognitive restructuring, they can confront the haunting whispers of negative thoughts—like "I'm destined to fail" or "I'm inherently inadequate." In this introspective journey, these thoughts can be transformed into a more grounded reality, embracing affirmations such as "I've equipped myself thoroughly for this moment" or "I possess the necessary skills and experiences to thrive."[171]

Foreseeing and Evading Dangers

With this gear, we can foresee and evade dangers to our health and the intellectual partnerships we've built with others. A robust mental apparatus acts as a barrier, warding off both outside threats and the subtle but deadly influence of the Shadow Weaver, an evil being that tries to bring out damaging ideas from the depths of one's mind.

The notion of cognitive-behavioral therapy (CBT), pioneered by Aaron T. Beck, embodies the art of anticipating and sidestepping threats lurking in the shadows. CBT provides individuals with the mental arsenal to uncover and confront destructive thought patterns, effectively halting the rise of toxic ideas and emotions. By cultivating a strong mental framework through CBT, individuals can fend off external pressures and the insidious pull of internal cognitive distortions, which lurk like a hidden puppeteer, trying to draw forth harmful thoughts from the recesses of the mind.[172]

The notion of cognitive-behavioral therapy, crafted by Aaron T. Beck, intriguingly intertwines with the art of anticipating and sidestepping threats. As the narrative unfolds, it reveals a powerful mental fortress that shields against lurking dangers, while CBT equips individuals with sharp cognitive instruments to unearth and confront the shadows of negative thinking. This method acts as a safeguard against the rise of toxic thoughts and feelings, akin to anticipating and sidestepping threats to well-being and collaborative intellect. By honing and utilizing these mental strategies, individuals can shield themselves from the insidious yet lethal grip of internal cognitive distortions, much like resisting the manipulative whispers of a hidden puppeteer seeking to unleash harmful thoughts. This strategic mindset guarantees emotional strength and the maintenance of meaningful connections.

- **Example from Literature:** George Orwell's dystopian novel and unsettling narrative, 1984, reveals a chilling world where the very fabric of personal thought is not just suppressed but intricately manipulated, prompting a haunting reflection on the nature of control and the delicate balance of liberty. The protagonist, Winston Smith, navigates a treacherous landscape of control, pushing back against the oppressive grip of the Party with his rebellious thoughts and daring actions. The struggle to maintain individuality and sharp intellect reveals the tenacity of the human spirit, able to resist the most oppressive influences that seek to control it.

Winston's sharp perception of the Party's deceit and his boldness in confronting the dominant narrative underscore the critical need for introspection in a world often cloaked in deception. Through cultivating a curious mind and welcoming diverse perspectives, Winston embodies the art of anticipating and sidestepping threats. He fiercely guards his mental sharpness and intellectual honesty, fending off the insidious yet lethal pull of the Party's manipulation—a reflection of the Shadow Weaver's efforts to unearth harmful thoughts lurking in the recesses of the mind.

The character of Winston Smith in George Orwell's 1984 embodies the essence of anticipating and sidestepping threats with a chilling precision. As the narrative unfolds, it reveals a formidable mental shield that protects against looming threats, with Winston's keen perception and analytical prowess enabling him to anticipate and navigate the perils of the Party's deceit. By cultivating a curious mind and welcoming various perspectives, he protects himself from manipulation and makes his decisions with sharp insight. This proactive strategy reflects the necessity of cultivating a strong mental framework to guard against outside dangers and internal misperceptions, akin to fending off the Shadow Weaver's grip. Winston's narrative unfolds as a gripping exploration of the mind's strength and the ability to anticipate and navigate threats in a landscape rife with deceit and influence.

Becoming Rescuers of Thoughts

However, it is not where the Law ends. We are given the ability to become rescuers of thoughts. Structured Cognition allows us to rescue others endangered mental processes, just like an expert librarian can find a misplaced book. We can assist others in overcoming mental obstacles and achieving their goals by thinking critically and providing alternate viewpoints.

The notion of cognitive reappraisal, highlighted in studies of emotional control, showcases the intriguing journey of transforming our thoughts into saviors. Reframing a situation can alter its emotional resonance, transforming how we perceive and react to it. By guiding individuals to shift their viewpoints and engage in deeper analysis of their experiences, cognitive reappraisal can save fragile mental states and unveil new angles of perception. This journey enables people to confront their inner demons and reach their aspirations.[173]

The notion of cognitive reappraisal, as examined by James J. Gross and Oliver P. John, intriguingly intertwines with the theme of Transforming Our Inner Narratives. In the shadows of the mind, Structured Cognition emerges as a lifeline, a way to salvage the fragile threads of thought that hang in the balance. Meanwhile, cognitive reappraisal acts as a powerful tool, enabling individuals to twist and turn their perceptions, challenging the very fabric of their experiences. By presenting unexpected perspectives and guiding others to rethink their circumstances, cognitive reappraisal serves as a skilled curator, uncovering hidden truths and liberating the mind from turmoil and uncertainty. This method enables people to break free from their inner demons and reach their aspirations, acting as saviors of the mind and elevating the shared experience of wellness.

- **Example from the Field of Education:** Peer tutoring programs reveal their potency in deepening student comprehension while cultivating an atmosphere of mutual support and growth. In the intricate dance of collaboration, students unravel the threads of understanding, confronting shadows of misconception while forging a path toward profound insight. This shared journey of knowledge not only enriches those who seek assistance but also profoundly transforms those who extend their guidance. In the act of elucidating ideas to others, guides frequently uncover layers of comprehension within their own minds.

Studies reveal that collaborative learning experiences can enhance intellectual performance, foster analytical reasoning, and elevate personal confidence. Through the exchange of insights and mutual encouragement, individuals can forge a transformative environment, unlocking deeper understanding and reaching new heights of achievement.[174]

Fueling Collective Success

The scope of this capability goes beyond only individuals. A sharp intellect, according to the Law, can fuel the thought processes that propel individual and collective success. Picture a weak light, like a torch, unable to fully illuminate the way ahead. The Law instructs us to recognize when these fires are going out and to light them again by stimulating thought and discussion.

Illustration from Organizational Behavior: The idea of transformational leadership, as examined by Bernard M. Bass and Bruce J. Avolio, embodies the essence of igniting shared achievement. Transformational leadership captivates and drives team members to transcend their personal ambitions, all for the collective benefit of the organization. Through the cultivation of a space where dialogue flows freely, ideas are challenged, and creativity thrives, transformative leaders spark a renewed sense of purpose within their teams, driving them toward remarkable achievements and shared victories.[175]

The notion of transformational leadership, examined by Bernard M. Bass and Bruce J. Avolio, resonates deeply with the theme of igniting shared achievement. As the paragraph illustrates the awakening and rekindling of intellectual flames to drive achievement, transformational leadership is about captivating and energizing team members to reach shared aspirations. By cultivating a space where dialogue flows freely, ideas are scrutinized, and creativity thrives, transformational leaders spark a resurgence of intellectual passion within their teams, akin to igniting a dim flame to cast a brilliant light on the path forward. This method captivates the mind, igniting both personal and shared reflections, ultimately driving heightened achievement and a sense of unity in success.

- **Example from Software Engineering:** Collective intelligence, where shared brilliance intertwines, reveals the captivating force of intellect that drives both personal and shared success. The intertwining of intellects—a deep connection forged through the dance of personal ideas—has driven humanity to its most astonishing triumphs. In the intricate interplay of collaboration, the shared intellect reveals a web of creativity and innovation that lurks unseen in solitude. This intriguing occurrence unfolds in multiple realms, encompassing the intricacies of science, the innovations of technology, the dynamics of business, and the creativity of the arts.

Delve into the complex tapestry of open-source software development, where platforms such as Linux and Wikipedia arise from the collective efforts of numerous programmers and contributors worldwide, each thread woven with intention and intrigue. Every individual weave their distinct strand into the intricate fabric of creativity. In a web of shared insights and intricate frameworks, these collectives have crafted powerful tools that have dramatically altered the landscape of our lives and pursuits. The intense collaboration of these minds rekindles the dim flames of solitary endeavors, casting a revealing light on the journey toward shared achievement.[176]

The notion of shared intellect, as examined by Pierre Lévy, resonates deeply with the theme of Igniting Unified Achievement. As the paragraph illustrates the awakening and rekindling of intellectual flames to drive achievement, the synergy of minds reveals how their intersection fosters heightened creativity and groundbreaking ideas. In the realm of open-source software development, projects such as Linux and Wikipedia reveal a web of collaboration, where individuals from every corner of the globe weave together a narrative of innovation that eclipses solitary endeavors. By provoking deep thought and sparking intense discussions, these groups awaken dormant ideas and cast light on the journey toward shared achievement. This method captivates the mind, igniting both personal and group reflections, ultimately paving the way for extraordinary accomplishments and collective victories.

The Long-Lost Library

Word on the street is that somewhere in the maze lies a long-lost library that holds long-forgotten ideas that could hold the key to unleashing tremendous power. The very existence of the Thought Vaults—a repository of undiscovered information—attests to this possibility. Enormous power, however, is accompanied by enormous responsibility, as the Law serves as a reminder. So long as the mazelike Cognitexis is a safe haven for intellectual curiosity and collective genius, each of us must take personal responsibility for protecting our own mental landscapes and be prepared to save those around us at any moment.

Consider the Library of Alexandria, a legendary bastion of ancient wisdom, shrouded in mystery and intrigue, representing a treasure trove of forgotten insights. The Library of Alexandria stood as a beacon of intellect and intrigue, a labyrinth of scrolls and texts that held the secrets and wisdom of ancient civilizations, waiting to be uncovered. The expansive assortment featured an array of subjects, delving into the realms of science, mathematics, philosophy, literature, and beyond. Yet, the obliteration of the library resulted in the disappearance of priceless wisdom and profound revelations. The tale of the Library of Alexandria unfolds as a haunting reminder of the critical need to protect and cherish knowledge, echoing through time to resonate with those who seek to influence the future.[177]

The concept of the Library of Alexandria resonates deeply with the notion of The Long-Lost Library. Much like the paragraph unveils the Thought Vaults as a hidden trove of untapped insights, the Library of Alexandria stood as a beacon of enlightenment, safeguarding the collective wisdom of ancient societies. The obliteration of the library and the ensuing disappearance of priceless wisdom act as a haunting echo of the necessity to protect and cherish our intellectual gems. Immense influence, reminiscent of the Library of Alexandria, carries with it a weighty obligation, highlighting the critical importance of safeguarding our inner worlds and being ready to rescue those in our orbit. The tale of the Library of Alexandria unveils the chilling stakes of protecting knowledge, revealing a haunting reminder of the depths of intellectual curiosity and the brilliance that can emerge from collective minds.

In Conclusion

The Thought Vaults, an enigmatic sanctuary of the mind's most closely held secrets, invite us to plunge into their murky recesses and discover the concealed treasures that lurk just out of sight. The Law of Thoughts Rescue serves as a formidable instrument, allowing us to shield our inner sanctuaries while illuminating the shadowy paths others tread in their intricate mental odysseys. Through the labyrinthine corridors of structured thought and the art of profound dialogue, we can protect the shadowy secrets of the Thought Vaults, allowing them to thrum with vitality and stay perpetually accessible.

As we navigate the shadowy corridors of the mind, we must stay perpetually alert. The Corruptors, those sinister forces, linger in the darkness, ready to poison and annihilate the cherished ideas that reside within the mind. The fate of our shared knowledge hangs precariously in our hands. Shall we face the looming shadows and emerge as the Guardians of the Mind's Sanctuary, or shall we succumb to the malevolent powers that aim to consume our very being?

The path is shrouded in danger, yet the fruits of understanding are limitless. The Thought Vaults beckon, their enigmatic allure pulsating with untapped possibilities. Will you venture into the abyss and uncover the truths concealed within, or will you yield to the darkness that threatens to engulf your very essence? The decision lies in your hands, wanderer of reality. Confront the shadows that loom ahead, for the destiny of our shared knowledge hinges on your resolve and tenacity.

3. Unraveling the Secrets of the Psyche: Exposing the Hidden Vault of Thoughts

(The Law of Thoughts Revelation)

Venture boldly into the intricate labyrinth of Cognitexis—a realm where the essence of thought reigns supreme, transcending mere physicality. Within this enigmatic threshold, cloaked in intrigue and vibrating with an invisible force, resides the Revelation of Thought's Dominion. This is not merely an old textbook; it is a clandestine repository whispering secrets of wisdom teetering on the brink of insanity. Move carefully, for a single misstep in this mysterious realm could lead you straight into the depths of the darkness you have conjured.

Balance on the Precipice

Envision Cognitexis is not merely as a chamber of thought but as an expansive, resonant library, its towering shelves burdened with the weight of forgotten knowledge. These shelves demand a certain courage, a willingness to confront the unknown. The Law of Thoughts Revelation suggests a perilous journey to uncover them—a delicate tightrope walk between Focused Awareness and the alignment of belief. Channel your intellect with precision, steering clear of mundane tasks that dull your edge. No, here, the focus must be a singular, relentless, consuming desire bordering on a frenzied, almost maniacal passion. This intention resonates like a tuning fork, striking a note that draws you closer to the edge of your limits. Combine this with an unwavering conviction, a belief so intense it could consume you whole. In this delicate balance, the threshold to the Revelation of Thoughts may slowly swing ajar, revealing both awe and lurking danger.

The concept of "flow" in psychology, as articulated by Mihaly Csikszentmihalyi, captures the essence of teetering on the edge within the enigmatic world of Cognitexis. Csikszentmihalyi, a notable figure in the realm of psychology, revealed a captivating concept known as "flow," an engrossing state characterized by intense focus, authentic enjoyment, and a remarkable escape from self-consciousness. As people immerse themselves in an activity, they find themselves in a heightened state of awareness, where every detail sharpens and reality shifts, revealing layers previously unseen. This intense engagement often weaves together the pinnacle of success and the abyss of creativity.[178]

To achieve a state of seamless engagement, one must skillfully maneuver through the intricate balance of challenge and ability. The pursuit should weave an intricate web that intrigues the intellect, while avoiding the descent into a daunting abyss that breeds hopelessness. By uncovering this fragile equilibrium, one can seamlessly enter a world of intense focus and limitless creativity. This deep concentration and unwavering conviction, teetering on the edge of obsession, empowers individuals to traverse the intricate labyrinth of their minds and reveal concealed truths. Yet, attaining that seamless state demands a precarious equilibrium between challenge and skill, echoing the treacherous path outlined in the Law of Thoughts Revelation.

The notion of flow, as presented by Mihaly Csikszentmihalyi, seamlessly intertwines with the theme of Delving into the Depths of the Mind: Revealing the Concealed Chambers of Thought. As the narrative unfolds within the treacherous maze of Cognitexis, the state of flow emerges as an intense experience, sharpening awareness and elevating capabilities to an extraordinary level. This psychological landscape allows individuals to traverse the intricate corridors of their minds, reminiscent of the unveiling of cognitive supremacy in Cognitexis. Reaching a state of flow demands an all-encompassing passion and a steadfast belief, reflecting the deep concentration and harmony of conviction illustrated in the Balance on the Precipice. By delving into the depths of flow, one can reveal concealed truths and traverse the fine line between fascination and the ever-present threat that resides within the mind's shadows.

A Peek into the Abyss

The Law implies that this chilling equilibrium within Cognitexis paves the way for the emergence of completely novel CgX system components. Envision the clandestine library, its shelves contorting and writhing, as the very fabric of reality strains and distorts around it. Secrets long hidden, pulsating with an eerie glow, start to unveil themselves right in front of you. This is Thoughts Revelation, a journey that uncovers truths and possibilities that were not just lying in wait but deliberately hidden within Cognitexis. Proceed with caution, seeker, for the truths you uncover may demand a heavy toll. The very essence of one's mind could be the toll required to enter this clandestine repository.

- **Example from Literature:** In a gripping narrative, H.P. Lovecraft's "The Shadow over Innsmouth" masterfully explores the unsettling journey of uncovering concealed realities and the heavy price that comes with such revelations. Robert Olmstead, the central figure, delves into the chilling mysteries lurking within the town of Innsmouth and its eerie residents. As he plunges into the shadows, he uncovers secrets that have been meticulously concealed, protected by the sinister history of the town. The shocking truths unfold, driving Olmstead's mind to the edge as he grapples with the eerie findings that haunt him. This tale delves into the treacherous path of Thoughts Revelation, where the discovery of concealed realities within Cognitexis can result in deep and disquieting repercussions.[179]

The illustration found in H.P. Lovecraft's "The Shadow over Innsmouth" resonates deeply with the concept of A Peek into the Abyss. As the narrative unfolds, the shadowy library reveals its secrets, mirroring the protagonist's quest to expose the sinister truths lurking within the town of Innsmouth. The journey to reveal these truths is perilous and demands a steep price, reflecting the mental strain that accompanies delving into the concealed realms of Cognitexis. The haunting and disquieting discoveries in Lovecraft's tale resonate with the unsettling balance within Cognitexis, where the introduction of new CgX system elements and the unveiling of concealed realities can stretch the limits of existence itself. By exploring this connection, we uncover the deep and possibly dangerous essence of Thoughts Revelation.

The Hidden Influence: An Alluring Call

The Law recognizes the mysterious force that emerges from the unveiling of thoughts. It delves into an enigmatic presence, a sinister murmur that ignites both brilliance and insanity. Envision the concealed library, where not only ancient wisdom lies in wait, but an alluring, ominous force pulses through its shadows. The Law hints at a powerful force lurking beneath the surface, an immense, invisible expanse that offers boundless possibilities yet demands the ultimate sacrifice of your very essence. One misstep, one flirtation with the enigmatic truths, and you may find yourself engulfed by an invisible tide.

The intricate workings of quantum mechanics unveil a captivating truth: the simple act of observation can dramatically shift the outcomes of an experiment. This intriguing phenomenon suggests that our consciousness might shape the very essence of reality itself. It implies that the act of watching holds significant power in molding reality, echoing the principles of perception. Whispers of a hidden power lie just out of sight, promising endless opportunities while requiring the deepest part of your essence as the price for entry.[180, 181]

This idea suggests that our deepest thoughts can shape the reality we inhabit, a theme that has been delved into across various philosophical and spiritual landscapes. By steering our thoughts toward elevated ideas and deliberate intentions, we hold the ability to mold our realities and the journeys we embark upon. Yet, one must navigate with caution, weaving this belief into a firm grasp of reality, avoiding the tempting pull of fanciful notions. The unseen power of our minds, reminiscent of the enigmatic energy lurking in the shadowy corners of a secret library, holds great promise yet poses the danger of being swept away by an unseen current.

This concept explores the enigmatic edges of consciousness and the very essence of existence. It stirs unsettling thoughts about the nature of reality and how our perceptions shape the world around us. Diving deep into the complex maze of our minds might just give us the power to redefine our beliefs, perceptions, and ultimately, the essence of our lives. As we navigate the intricate maze of existence, we are drawn to explore the hidden dynamics of our psyche and the remarkable power we hold to shape our destiny.

The notion of the observer effect in quantum mechanics resonates intriguingly with the theme of The Hidden Influence: An Alluring Call. As the paragraph unveils a mysterious figure and a haunting whisper that sparks both genius and madness, it hints at the unsettling notion that our perceptions and consciousness can shape the essence of existence itself. This intriguing phenomenon reveals both the vast possibilities and the lurking dangers of delving into the shadowy corners of our minds. By delving into and mastering this unseen power, we can manipulate our views, beliefs, and the reality that envelops us, akin to revealing the deep and possibly dangerous secrets lurking within a shadowy archive. This comparison reveals the captivating and enigmatic essence of the hidden power that arises when thoughts are laid bare.

- **Example from Literature:** H.P. Lovecraft's narratives delve into the eerie shadows of reality, exposing the haunting consequences of facing the incomprehensible. His characters often find themselves face-to-face with mysterious figures and hidden realities that drive them to the brink of madness. In "The Call of Cthulhu," the main character, Francis Wayland Thurston, plunges into the enigmatic depths surrounding the ancient and formidable being known as Cthulhu. As he delves deeper into the enigmatic cult surrounding Cthulhu, he becomes entangled in a web of chilling revelations and unfathomable dread. The shocking truths emerge, but not without a steep price, as Thurston's grip on reality teeters under the dark and insidious sway of Cthulhu.[182]

The illustration of H.P. Lovecraft's "The Call of Cthulhu" resonates deeply with the concept of an enigmatic allure that beckons from the shadows. As the paragraph unfolds, it reveals a mysterious figure and a haunting whisper that sparks both genius and madness, reminiscent of Lovecraft's tale where the main character confronts the timeless and formidable being, Cthulhu. Unraveling these sinister truths is perilous and demands a steep price, reflecting the mental strain that accompanies delving into the shadowy realms of Cognitexis. The chilling and disquieting truths unveiled in Lovecraft's narrative resonate with the captivating yet foreboding energy depicted in the paragraph, where the surfacing of concealed realities requires the profound relinquishment of one's core being. By grasping this connection, we uncover the deep and possibly dangerous essence of the mysterious power that arises from revealing our innermost thoughts.

An Unstoppable Drive, a Plunge into Fixation

In spite of the risks, the Law unveils the chilling seduction of its might. It implies that in specific situations, this force transforms into an overwhelming influence. Envision a clandestine library, where the dust of ages conceals not merely lost wisdom but the ultimate gateway to unraveling the enigmas of existence itself. The Law implies that by unraveling the enigma of Thoughts Revelation, you harness a formidable force, empowering you to conquer any challenge and realize any ambition. Yet, this force demands unwavering loyalty. As you plunge into the shadows of the hidden archive, its grip tightens, pulling you further into its enigmatic depths. The boundary separating the pursuit of solutions from the descent into a consuming fixation is alarmingly fragile.

The narrative of Nikola Tesla illustrates an unyielding obsession and a deep dive into singularity. Tesla, a genius with a mind teetering on the edge of brilliance, was consumed by an unquenchable thirst for knowledge and an unrelenting dedication to his craft. His unyielding quest for the unknown sparked revelations that would forever alter the landscape of electricity and electromagnetism. Yet, Tesla's obsession with his visions and creations exacted a heavy toll on his personal life. He spiraled deeper into solitude, his obsession with his craft overshadowing everything else, leaving his well-being and connections in the shadows. Tesla's narrative embodies an intense obsession, showcasing how an unyielding ambition can propel one to remarkable heights while simultaneously teetering on the edge of a dangerous fixation.[183]

The narrative of Nikola Tesla resonates deeply with the concept of an unyielding obsession, a deep dive into an all-consuming fixation. As the paragraph unfolds, it reveals the eerie allure of authority, while Tesla's relentless quest for knowledge and steadfast dedication to his craft embody the powerful grip of an unyielding ambition. His unyielding quest for innovation unveiled astonishing revelations, akin to deciphering the mysteries that empower one to triumph over any obstacle. Yet, Tesla's obsession with his concepts exacted a heavy toll on him, illustrating the delicate line between the quest for answers and the spiral into an all-consuming obsession. Tesla's narrative unfolds as a gripping exploration of boundless ambition intertwined with peril, emphasizing the fragile equilibrium necessary to maneuver through such an overwhelming force.

- **Example from Literature:** Mary Shelley's Frankenstein delves into the dark depths of unchecked ambition, exposing the chilling realities that emerge when the pursuit of knowledge is stripped of ethical boundaries. Victor Frankenstein, driven by an unquenchable desire to defy the boundaries of life itself, conjures a grotesque being that ultimately leads to his own demise. His unyielding pursuit of knowledge shrouds the moral implications of his decisions and the profound consequences they could unleash on humanity.

The story of Frankenstein reverberates with the haunting reminder of the delicate balance and control we must maintain in our ambitions. While the pursuit of achievement can spark a profound evolution, it is essential to maintain a wider perspective and avoid falling into the trap of an all-consuming obsession. By recognizing the limits of our comprehension and the hidden dangers of unchecked power, we can steer clear of catastrophic errors. The tale of Frankenstein reflects an intense obsession, a descent into an all-consuming fixation, where the quest for knowledge and dominance spirals into a chaotic blend of genius and insanity.[184]

The character of Victor Frankenstein in Mary Shelley's Frankenstein embodies an intense obsession, a relentless pursuit that spirals into an all-consuming fixation. As the paragraph unveils the eerie allure of authority, Victor's relentless desire to confront the essence of reality reveals the powerful grip of an unyielding ambition. His unyielding pursuit of understanding gives rise to a terrifying being, akin to the way unlocking the secrets of the mind allows one to overcome any obstacle. Yet, Victor's obsession with his mission exacts a heavy toll, illustrating the delicate line between seeking answers and spiraling into an all-consuming obsession. The tale of Frankenstein unfolds as a gripping exploration of the boundless ambition and lurking dangers that accompany an insatiable pursuit, emphasizing the fragile equilibrium needed to master such a daunting power.

In Conclusion

The Law of Thoughts Revelation unveils a chilling perspective on the latent powers concealed in the depths of the human psyche. By probing into this principle, we can unearth the shadowy corners of our minds, exposing hidden truths and harnessing a formidable force that empowers us to transcend barriers and realize our most profound desires. We must remain vigilant against the lurking perils that threaten to entrap us, pushing us into the depths of obsession, madness, and the devastating erosion of our essence.

In the complex interplay of perception and reality, echoing the observer effect in quantum physics and the unsettling tales of literature, we are compelled to traverse our thoughts with a fusion of awareness and incisive examination. In traversing the murky corridors of our inner selves and facing the chaos that resides there, we possess the power to transform our consciousness into an impenetrable bastion of strength, where enlightenment and deep insights can arise from the abyss of our challenges.

In the end, the Law of Thoughts Revelation looms as a chilling testament to our capacity for both mental and personal transformation, cloaked in the dark recesses of our own minds. It echoes with the caution that through intense focus and unwavering belief, we can navigate the intricate maze of our psyche, transforming our minds into a refuge for deep insight. Yet, we must tread carefully, for within the intricate maze of Cognitexis, the journey toward understanding is fraught with insanity.

As you venture into this treacherous path, seeker of enlightenment, bear in mind that the concealed depths of the mind harbor both unimaginable strength and ominous threats. Welcome the excitement of exploration, yet proceed with caution, as the depths of the psyche are dark and perilous. Will you have the courage to uncover the hidden truths that dwell in the shadows, or will you yield to the mysterious powers that seek to engulf your very soul? The decision lies in your hands, and the consequences loom ominously. Step into the shadows with resolve, for the truths you uncover could irrevocably reshape the fabric of your reality.

4. The Axioms of Thought: Unraveling the Enigma of Cognitexis

(The Law of Thoughts Axioms)

Delve into the intricate depths of Cognitexis, a domain where the essence of existence transcends mere flesh and bone, existing solely within the realm of thought. Here, enveloped in enigma and laden with lurking threats, exists a concealed power— the Laws of Thought Axioms. These axioms are not just principles; they are secrets, murmurs of a force that surpasses the boundaries of human understanding. Move with caution, for in this mysterious domain, each fleeting thought intertwines mastery with the edge of insanity.

The Unveiled Mechanism

It is Cognitexis, perceived not merely as a realm of contemplation but as a clandestine mechanism, its cogs turning with an enigmatic force. The Laws of Thought Axioms suggest that by manipulating these mechanisms in an unconventional manner, we may tap into a force that flirts with the forbidden. This hints at a possibility that transcends ordinary mental processes, enticing with the allure of the taboo and the peril of the uncharted.

Consider a scenario from Mathematics: The notion of Gödel's incompleteness theorems illustrates the intriguing manipulation of thought processes in a way that defies conventional understanding. Kurt Gödel's theorems expose a chilling truth: in any intricate axiomatic system, there exist statements that elude proof or disproof, trapped within the very confines of their own rules. This astonishing revelation disrupts the conventional grasp of mathematical frameworks, unveiling the deep-seated constraints of formal reasoning. Gödel's work hints at truths that elude human understanding, echoing the enigmatic allure of Cognitexis, which dances tantalizingly close to the forbidden and the unknown.[185]

The notion of Gödel's incompleteness theorems intertwines seamlessly with the essence of The Axioms of Thought: Unraveling the Enigma of Cognitexis. As the paragraph unveils a hidden force within Cognitexis that transcends human comprehension, Gödel's theorems expose the constraints of formal logic and the presence of truths that remain unprovable within any established framework. This revelation hints at the possibility that by bending these fundamental principles in unexpected ways, we can access a force that goes beyond typical cognitive functions, reminiscent of the concealed strength found within Cognitexis. Gödel's work captivates with an irresistible charm, drawing one into the shadows of the unknown, resonating with the mysterious and possibly treacherous essence of the Laws of Thought Axioms.

- **Example from Quantum Mechanics:** The world of quantum mechanics unfolds like a suspenseful narrative, exploring the complex interplay of matter and energy at the most fundamental levels, painting a mesmerizing and enigmatic picture of reality itself. One of the most captivating concepts in quantum mechanics is the idea of entanglement, where two particles become inextricably linked, defying the limits of distance. This event suggests a deep and intricate network of interactions in the universe, where elements exert instant influence on each other, seemingly defying the foundational laws of classical physics.[186]

The concept of quantum entanglement reveals the intricate connections that weave our thoughts and ideas into a complex web, hinting at deeper truths lurking beneath the surface. Similar to the mysterious connection shared by intertwined entities, our thoughts and ideas might be intricately stitched into an expansive, universal fabric of consciousness. This suggests that the complexities of our thoughts and actions might extend beyond ourselves, influencing not just our personal narratives but also the larger web of reality that envelops us. This enigmatic and contradictory event hints at deep, hidden forces at play, echoing the mysterious currents that flow through Cognitexis.

The notion of quantum entanglement intertwines seamlessly with the essence of The Unveiled Mechanism. As the paragraph unveils Cognitexis as a secretive apparatus, its gears moving under an elusive influence, quantum entanglement exposes the concealed links between particles that challenge conventional comprehension. By bending these mechanisms in unexpected ways, we engage with a force that dances on the edge of the taboo, reminiscent of the concealed strength found within Cognitexis. The deep connections between intertwined particles mirror the complex relationships within our minds, hinting that the movements of our thoughts and actions can send shockwaves through the wider fabric of reality. This comparison underscores the seductive nature of the forbidden and the risks of the unknown, reflecting the mysterious and possibly treacherous essence of the Laws of Thought Axioms.[187]

Collaboration or Madness?

The fundamental idea behind the Laws of Thought Axioms is an alluring proposition—the convergence of disparate thoughts, forging a powerful entity that transcends the individual elements. This newfound force, capable of transcending the boundaries of reality, carries with it a chilling proposition: collaboration or madness? Is it possible to master these conflicting concepts without being overwhelmed by the chaos of Cognitexis engine? The edge of revolutionary discovery teeters dangerously near the brink of utter psychological collapse.

- **Example from Literature:** In Mary Shelley's Frankenstein, Victor Frankenstein's obsessive quest for knowledge reveals the fragile line between partnership and insanity. As he navigates the shadows of existence, Victor intertwines various scientific theories to forge an extraordinary and uncharted entity—a being that defies the boundaries of life and death. Yet, this merging of insights swiftly descends into chaos, as Victor finds himself engulfed by his own invention and the repercussions that follow. The entity, born from a fusion of diverse scientific pursuits, ultimately transforms into a haunting emblem of insanity and the perilous consequences of unbridled ambition.[188]

Victor's journey highlights the delicate balance between groundbreaking revelation and mental unraveling. His struggle to navigate the tumultuous boundaries between existence and oblivion, while grappling with the turmoil of his own making, highlights the perilous allure of delving into the unknown. The tale of Frankenstein unveils a haunting notion: when the limits of reality are stretched beyond comprehension, the act of collaboration can spiral into a dark abyss of insanity.

The character of Victor Frankenstein in Mary Shelley's Frankenstein embodies the fine line between collaboration and madness, drawing readers into a chilling exploration of ambition and obsession. As the narrative unfolds, the intertwining of fragmented ideas culminates in a formidable force, mirroring Victor's ambitious endeavor to meld diverse scientific principles, leading to an unprecedented revelation. Yet, this emerging power swiftly transforms into a harbinger of chaos as Victor spirals into the depths of his own choices. The tale of Frankenstein unveils the fragile interplay between partnership and mental unraveling, echoing the unsettling notion that transcending the limits of reality can result in groundbreaking revelations and complete insanity.

- **Example from Literature:** H.P. Lovecraft's narratives plunge into the unsettling depths of existence, revealing the chilling repercussions of confronting the unfathomable. In "The Call of Cthulhu," an unnamed narrator spirals into an obsession with a shadowy cult and an ancient, unfathomable being known as Cthulhu, unraveling the very fabric of reality itself. As the storyteller ventures further into the depths of hidden truths, he undergoes a slow spiral into insanity, ultimately yielding to the immense force of the unfathomable dread that lurks beyond comprehension.

The narratives crafted by Lovecraft unfold as a profound warning regarding the perils of unbridled inquisitiveness and the necessity of establishing boundaries. Though the pursuit of knowledge is vital for our evolution, it is imperative to uphold equilibrium and steer clear of the depths of fixation. By acknowledging the boundaries of our comprehension and the

455

lurking threats that come with probing the abyss, we can safeguard our psychological and emotional well-being.[189]

The Five Foundations of the Abyss

The Laws of Thought Axioms reveal five pivotal principles, yet these are not mere signposts along a familiar route. Each foothold on the crumbling cliff face teeters on the edge of reason, where every step becomes a perilous wager with the very fabric of sanity.

1) **Clarity of Intent:** The initial principle requires an unwavering precision of purpose, a singular and consuming focus. Yet, in the shadowy depths of Cognitexis, this intense focus can twist into a perilous fixation, where the boundaries between ambition and illusion start to dissolve. What started as a pursuit of understanding can swiftly transform into a dangerous obsession.

   Mihaly Csikszentmihalyi, a notable figure in psychology, introduced the concept of "flow," a fascinating state of peak experience characterized by intense focus, authentic pleasure, and an enthralling loss of self-consciousness. As individuals immerse themselves fully in a pursuit, they unveil astonishing layers of capability and imagination. This illustrates the essence of a singular and intense focus, compelling individuals to reach remarkable outcomes.[190]

   However, it is essential to recognize that the state of flow can embody a complex duality. When left unchecked, an intense focus can descend into fatigue, discomfort, and a myriad of harmful consequences. The razor-sharp concentration needed to reach that elusive state can morph into a dangerous preoccupation, blurring the lines between drive and fixation. What started as a quest for greatness can quickly spiral into a perilous fixation, revealing the dark undercurrents of Cognitexis.

To unravel the intricacies of life, one must delve into the depths of self-reflection and master the skill of living in the moment. By occasionally stepping back from our obligations and diving into activities that promote calm and rejuvenation, we can prevent the spiral into fatigue and protect our mental and emotional well-being. The delicate interplay between sharp concentration and serene calmness is essential for preserving a clear purpose, ensuring one doesn't slip into the depths of fixation.

The notion of "flow," as articulated by Mihaly Csikszentmihalyi, resonates deeply with the idea of Clarity of Intent. As the paragraph unveils the gripping intensity demanded within the enigmatic realms of Cognitexis, the state of flow emerges as a captivating experience of deep engagement, unlocking unparalleled performance and creativity. Yet, the duality of flow reflects how deep concentration can morph into a dangerous obsession, reminiscent of the path through Cognitexis, where every move turns into a risky gamble with the essence of one's sanity. By navigating the delicate interplay between concentration and ease, we can preserve a sharp sense of purpose and steer clear of the perils of fixation, allowing our quest for greatness to illuminate our path rather than engulf us in darkness.

- **Example from Literature:** In Herman Melville's Moby-Dick, Captain Ahab's relentless chase of the elusive white whale reveals a haunting clarity of purpose that grips the reader's mind. Ahab's relentless obsession propels him into a dark and twisted pursuit of the elusive Moby Dick, his every thought consumed by the singular goal of the hunt. At first, his motives are driven by a thirst for vengeance and clarity, but as the story progresses, this fervent obsession spirals into a dangerous entanglement. The line separating aspiration from delusion begins to blur as Ahab's quest morphs into a perilous fixation, threatening not just his own fate but that of his entire crew.[191]

Ahab's unyielding chase of the elusive white whale reveals the precarious balance between a clear purpose and a consuming fixation. His obsession with the elusive creature dominates his mind and behavior, driving him to make reckless choices that inevitably spiral into his undoing. The tale of Moby-Dick stands as a haunting testament to the dangers of relentless pursuit that spirals into fixation, illuminating the fragile line one must tread while delving into the murky realms of Cognitexis.

The character of Captain Ahab in Herman Melville's Moby-Dick embodies the essence of Clarity of Intent in a hauntingly compelling manner. As the paragraph illustrates the gripping concentration demanded within the enigmatic realms of Cognitexis, Ahab's relentless chase of the elusive white whale reveals how such focus can morph into a dangerous obsession. The story reveals how a quest for insight can quickly spiral into a treacherous fixation, reflecting the path through Cognitexis where every move turns into a risky gamble with the essence of one's mind. Delving into Ahab's narrative reveals the delicate line between aspiration and fixation, highlighting the necessity of keeping our intentions clear, lest they spiral into an all-consuming darkness.

2) **Control or Captivity of the Heart?** The tempest of raw feelings threatens to overwhelm the very machinery designed to maintain control. The idea demands a tight grip—an essential core of existence ensnared in an unyielding embrace. In the enigmatic realm of feelings, the very act of holding back can lead to a chilling detachment, a ruthless precision that teeters on the edge of emotional subjugation. To conquer the

machine, we might find ourselves facing the unsettling prospect of relinquishing our very essence.

- **Example from Literature:** In Aldous Huxley's Brave New World, the society portrayed reveals a chilling exploration of the manipulation and confinement of human emotion. In this chilling reality, the very essence of feelings and personal identity is stifled, all in the name of preserving order and dominance. The administration of a substance known as "soma" guarantees that individuals exist in a facade of bliss, stripped of any genuine emotional resonance. The intricate systems put in place to exert influence have fostered a haunting disconnection, where the suppression of feelings results in a coldly calculated operation of the social order. The individuals in the story, like Bernard Marx and John the Savage, grapple with their emotional confinement, emphasizing the conflict between domination and the erosion of their true selves.[192]

Bernard Marx and John, the Savage's journeys reveal the chilling consequences of stifling emotions and the precarious balance between dominance and entrapment. The relentless grip of conformity stifles true self-expression and authentic emotional connections, leaving a chilling void in its wake. The story unfolds as a chilling exploration of what we risk when we surrender our true selves in the quest for power, revealing the fragile equilibrium needed to traverse the mysterious landscape of emotions.

The illustration of Aldous Huxley's Brave New World resonates deeply with the concept of Manipulation or Enslavement of Emotion. As the narrative unfolds, it captures the chaotic surge of unfiltered emotions poised to dismantle the carefully constructed facade of order, mirroring the way the world in Brave New World stifles genuine feelings to uphold its precarious equilibrium. This repression fosters a cold disconnection and emotional domination, reflecting the notion that restraining feelings can cultivate a merciless clarity. The journeys of Bernard Marx and John the Savage reveal a gripping struggle between the desire for dominance and the haunting fear of losing one's true self. Delving into the story of Brave New World reveals the intricate dance between emotional expression and the desire for control, highlighting the precarious line we tread in our quest for stability, where the essence of our humanity hangs in the balance.

- **Example from Literature:** Mary Shelley's Frankenstein serves as a haunting narrative that explores the perils of unbridled ambition and the relentless quest for knowledge, all while neglecting the moral implications that accompany such pursuits. Victor Frankenstein, consumed by an insatiable quest to surpass the boundaries of human existence, conjures a grotesque entity that inevitably brings about his own downfall. His relentless pursuit of dominion over existence leads to a profound detachment from empathy, compassion, and, in the end, his very essence as a human being.

The tale of Frankenstein underscores the critical nature of emotional awareness and the necessity of harmonizing cerebral endeavors with the essence of human relationships. In his relentless pursuit of knowledge, he disregards the very essence of his humanity, transforming into a sorrowful entity, tormented by the consequences of his actions and overwhelmed by an unshakeable remorse.[193]

3) **Directed Attentiveness or Obsessive Fixation?** Directed Attentiveness or Obsessive Fixation? Like a laser honing in on

its target, our attention demands relentless precision—a singular focus that can illuminate or consume. This principle drives us to direct our mental energies toward the issue at hand, fueling Cognitexis engine with an unyielding intensity of concentration. However, in this mysterious domain, such concentration can easily morph into relentless fixation. The outside world fades into the background, overshadowed by the persistent thrum of the engine—a captivating, yet potentially unsettling rhythm that blurs the line between profound insight and obsessive compulsion.

The concept of directed attentiveness describing focused engagement, as explored by Mihaly Csikszentmihalyi in his work on "flow," illustrates a condition where a person is entirely immersed and involved in an activity, reaching peak performance and fulfillment. This relentless focus enables individuals to shut out the chaos surrounding them, plunging into the task at hand, resulting in a profoundly satisfying and productive journey. In contrast, Jean-Paul Sartre's existential philosophy delves into the more sinister aspects of this phenomenon. In Sartre's perspective, an all-consuming obsession can emerge when intense concentration eclipses reality, pulling the person into a deep and unsettling internal vortex. This unyielding focus can spiral into a haunting sense of despair and a disconnection from the world, revealing the precarious boundary that separates brilliance from insanity.[194]

In the shadowy layers of Cognitexis, focused awareness weaves a vital thread. Echoing Csikszentmihalyi's idea of "flow," it drives us to hone our mental focus on the matter at hand with unwavering intensity, powering Cognitexis engine. This heightened focus is essential to unravel the puzzles and hidden dangers that lie within this enigmatic realm. Yet, as Sartre's existential philosophy implies, this intense focus can morph into an all-consuming obsession, causing the external world to fade into obscurity. The relentless pulse of Cognitexis engine enchants while it disturbs, weaving a cadence that merges control with the brink of madness. In this intricate web of focused thought, the principle of directed attentiveness unveils a chilling reality where every passing notion can either shed light on hidden truths or plunge one into a consuming darkness.

- **Example from Science:** Hyperfocus, often seen in those with ADHD, showcases an intense, almost obsessive concentration on a particular task or interest, drawing one into a world where distractions fade away, and the mind fixates on a singular point of intrigue. This captivating occurrence ensnares individuals, leading them into profound involvement that sparks bursts of heightened productivity and creativity. Yet, this condition can easily descend into an all-consuming obsession, where the mind becomes trapped, unable to shift its gaze, resulting in delays and a withdrawal from social connections.

  People with ADHD frequently navigate the intricate maze of hyperfocus, wrestling with the daunting task of juggling various obligations. They might find themselves ensnared in an all-consuming obsession, losing sight of vital elements of existence—like relationships, health, and the nurturing of their own spirit. Delving into the complex depths of hyperfocus is essential for individuals grappling with ADHD, as it empowers them to master their unique experiences with greater precision. Through the mastery of time management, the art of stress reduction, and the cultivation of social connections, individuals can unlock the power of hyperfocus while navigating its more sinister consequences.[195]

  In the enigmatic realm of Cognitexis, the art of directed attentiveness emerges as a crucial element reminiscent of the intense focus often experienced in ADHD. This principle urges us to direct our mental energies with unwavering intensity, akin to the way some individuals become completely absorbed in their pursuits. The relentless focus of determination drives Cognitexis engine, which is essential for unraveling its mysteries and confronting its dangers.

Yet, much like a captivating narrative, this deep immersion can spiral into an all-consuming obsession, eclipsing everything beyond its grasp. Those immersed in the shadows of Cognitexis may become so entranced by their singular pursuit that they neglect the crucial elements of reality. The relentless hum of Cognitexis engine draws you in, creating an alluring yet disquieting atmosphere. This reveals how intense focus can dangerously intertwine brilliance with insanity. The intricate interplay of focused awareness in Cognitexis reflects the fragile equilibrium required to navigate hyperfocus in ADHD, where every thought can either illuminate or completely consume.

4) **Autosuggestion or Self-Deception?** The whispers of our inner voice wield extraordinary influence. This principle implies that we set the stage for remarkable achievements by persistently nourishing Cognitexis with uplifting affirmations and steadfast confidence in our potential for success. Yet, within the shadowy depths, the boundary between steadfast conviction and haunting self-deception grows alarmingly fragile. Do our affirmations drive the momentum or simply conceal the widening fissures in our psyche?

Autosuggestion, a concept explored by Émile Coué, revolves around the intriguing practice of repeatedly voicing positive affirmations to shape the subconscious mind and ignite personal transformation subtly. This method can unlock remarkable outcomes by fostering an intense belief in one's capabilities and the promise of triumph. Yet, Carl Rogers' perspective on humanistic psychology suggests that these affirmations may spiral into self-deception, particularly when they serve as a shield against facing more profound, uncomfortable truths. Freud's psychoanalytic theory delves deeper into this concept, proposing that the conscious mind often remains oblivious to the hidden conflicts that influence actions, creating a tenuous divide between authentic self-belief, misleading assertiveness, and deceptive self-assurance.[196]

In the enigmatic corridors of Cognitexis, the concept of Autosuggestion or Self-Deception lurks, waiting to unravel its secrets. In a world where the mind's whispers can shape reality, individuals can cultivate their inner strength through powerful affirmations and unwavering belief, paving the way for extraordinary outcomes. These uplifting declarations ignite Cognitexis engine, propelling energy and cultivating an aura of control. Yet, as Carl Rogers and Sigmund Freud imply, there exists a delicate line where unwavering belief can twist into unsettling self-deception. This concept reveals how affirmations, despite their strength, can mask deeper cracks in the mind, creating a delicate tension between true advancement and the allure of comforting illusions. In the mysterious world of Cognitexis, the subtle murmurs of our inner thoughts hold a powerful sway, intertwining the forces of ambition with the shadows of our hidden doubts.

- **Example from the Practice of Positive Psychology:** Embracing an optimistic perspective means steering one's thoughts toward empowering convictions, which can significantly influence one's mental and emotional well-being. Methods like affirmations and visualization possess an undeniable potency, capable of enhancing self-esteem, easing anxiety, and transforming emotional landscapes. Yet, traversing the delicate boundary between authentic optimism and the tempting grip of deception is essential. Though the allure of positivity is enticing, it is crucial to face the darker corners of our feelings and acknowledge the entire range of our mental terrain. The intricate web of self-deception can warp how one views reality, ultimately obstructing the path to personal growth and transformation.[197]

In the enigmatic corridors of Cognitexis, the concept of Autosuggestion or Self-Deception exerts a powerful grip. In a world where the mind's whispers can shape reality, individuals can feed Cognitexis with powerful affirmations and unwavering confidence, creating an atmosphere ripe for extraordinary accomplishments. The uplifting declarations ignite Cognitexis engine, cultivating an atmosphere of control and advancement. Yet, as the illustration of positive psychology suggests, there exists a delicate line where unwavering belief can morph into unsettling self-deception. This concept reveals how affirmations, despite their strength, can obscure deeper cracks in the mind, creating a fragile equilibrium between true advancement and the allure of self-delusion. In the shadowy landscape of Cognitexis, the murmurs of our inner thoughts hold a captivating power, intertwining the forces of ambition with the hidden fears that lie beneath the surface.

5) **The Captivated Will or the Surrendered Spirit?** Ultimately, our will should be dynamically involved in alignment with the fundamental principles of thought. Challenging the boundaries of our perceptions requires deliberate choices; it is an active engagement with the unknown. By harnessing the full force of our determination, we dedicate ourselves to Cognitexis engine, allowing it to reach goals that once appeared beyond our grasp. Yet, this display of resolve may morph into a perilous surrender within the enigmatic realm. The engine retaliates with increasing ferocity, mirroring our relentless drive, as it

exacts a toll—a fragment of our essence—to quench its insatiable thirst for dominance.

The exploration of willpower delves into the intricate layers of human existence, revealing the psychological battles that shape our choices and identities. In Thus Spoke Zarathustra, Friedrich Nietzsche delves into the concept of a relentless drive that propels individuals to shape their own destinies, pushing the limits of what is perceived and understood. Nietzsche highlights the importance of confronting the unknown, suggesting that intentional decisions and unwavering resolve can unlock extraordinary outcomes.

Conversely, Carl Jung's investigation into the hidden layers of the psyche in Man and His Symbols uncovers the perilous consequences of yielding to profound impulses and universal patterns. Jung cautions that while tapping into the depths of determination can propel one toward self-discovery, it may also lead to a dangerous capitulation when the subconscious takes control.

Viktor Frankl's Man's Search for Meaning delves into the intricate dance of resilience. It showcases how individuals, driven by an unyielding spirit, can navigate through profound adversities and emerge transformed, revealing layers of personal evolution. Nevertheless, Frankl emphasizes that an insatiable ambition can spiral into harmful outcomes when one's essence is overtaken by the pursuit of power, resulting in a disconnection from fundamental human qualities.[198]

In the shadowy landscape of Cognitexis, the concept of The Captivated Will or the Surrendered Spirit holds significant weight. Echoing the essence of Nietzsche's philosophy, our drive must be fluid and responsive, intertwining with core ideas and daring to confront the mysteries that lie ahead. With an unwavering resolve, we immerse ourselves in Cognitexis engine, pursuing ambitions that once felt beyond our grasp.

Yet, as Carl Jung's analysis implies, this show of determination could transform into a treacherous capitulation within the mysterious landscape. Cognitexis engine, echoing our unyielding ambition, can exact a price on our very being, embodying the warning of unseen influences lurking in our psyche's shadows. Viktor Frankl's insights reveal the precarious tightrope we walk—our resolve can propel us to extraordinary heights or plunge us into a state of defeat, devoured by an unquenchable thirst for control. In Cognitexis, the intricate dance of willpower weaves a tapestry where vibrant involvement teeters on the brink of dangerous capitulation.

- **Example from Literature:** George Orwell's chilling 1984 narrative explores the disturbing consequences of total control and the slow erosion of individual freedom. In this oppressive world, the governing force utilizes a chilling mix of surveillance, insidious propaganda, psychological manipulation, and ruthless intimidation to control the minds and behaviors of its citizens. Winston Smith, the protagonist of this gripping tale, confronts the stifling power surrounding him, wielding his determination as a weapon against the dark forces at play. Yet, despite his determination, Winston's essence is ultimately crushed by the subtle manipulations and relentless suffering that surround him. This shift from resolute determination to a yielding essence reveals the treacherous journey one navigates when facing insurmountable forces.[199]

In the shadowy landscape of Cognitexis, the concept of The Captivated Will or the Surrendered Spirit holds immense significance. Like Winston Smith's journey in a dystopian world, people must actively wield their resolve, tapping into their inner strength to connect with core ideas and push the limits of their understanding. With a relentless focus on Cognitexis engine and calculated decisions, they pursue ambitions that once felt impossibly distant.

Yet, as Orwell's tale unfolds, this show of determination can twist into a dangerous capitulation lurking in the murky abyss. The Cognitexis engine, reflecting the unyielding ambition of its user, strikes back with escalating intensity, reminiscent of a shadowy authority lurking in the background. This unyielding chase takes a heavy toll on one's very being, revealing how the quest for control can slowly erode personal freedom and the ability to choose one's own path. In this intricate dance of the captivated will against the surrendered spirit within Cognitexis, we see a reflection of Winston's turmoil, emphasizing the fragile line between active involvement and the risks of yielding too much.

In Conclusion

As the final echoes of the Axioms of Thought endure in the shadowy corridors of Cognitexis, a more profound enigma starts to reveal itself. These principles transcend simple guidelines; they serve as the keys to navigating the intricate maze of the mind, where each twist unveils a concealed corridor, and every shadow harbors a mystery yearning to be deciphered.

Venture further, and you will stand at the precipice of an abyss, where focused intent becomes a double-edged weapon, and the control of one's emotions hangs precariously close to the brink of obsession. The odyssey through Cognitexis calls for more than simple comprehension—it necessitates an unyielding quest for truth, traversing the fragile line between enlightenment and insanity.

In this shadowy domain, your thoughts are invaluable treasures zealously protected within the enigmatic Archives of Wisdom. Every shard of your intellectual inheritance demands safeguarding from the creeping void, for in the struggle between illumination and obscurity, the price of surrendering to the abyss is nothing less than devastating.

The Axioms of Thought invite you to delve into the shadowy recesses of your mind, challenging you to face the chaos that resides within, ultimately leading to a rebirth of strength and a deeper comprehension of existence. As you plunge into the shadowy depths of Cognitexis, bear in mind that each truth uncovered demands a toll, and the final sacrifice could be nothing less than the core of your own sanity. Proceed onward with caution, as the real odyssey has only just commenced, and the darkness remains ever vigilant.[xiii]

[xiii] In fact, the Axiom of Thoughts presents a Darker Realm. Here is the Dark Realm of the Power of the Axioms of Thoughts:

The Axioms of Thought: Unlocking the Forbidden Doors of the Mind

Venture deep into the forbidden chambers of Cognitexis, a labyrinthine realm where the very fabric of thought writhes and twists. Here, veiled in shadows and pulsating with unseen energy, lie the Axioms of Thought, a set of principles both potent and perilous. These axioms, whispered through the ages by those who dared explore the furthest reaches of the mind, hold the key to unlocking a power that transcends the mundane–but at a terrible cost.

Imagine Cognitexis not as a well-lit chamber, but as a cavernous, echoing space, its walls shimmering with bioluminescent fungi that cast an eerie glow. The air hangs heavy with an electric tension, a constant reminder of the raw, untamed potential that lies dormant within. The Axioms of Thought are not blueprints for a safe and controlled engine; they are cryptic instructions for a forbidden experiment, a way to tap into a power that could just as easily consume you as elevate you.

The Synergy of Forbidden Might:

The core principle of the Axioms of Thought is both alluring and unsettling. They suggest that by combining diverse thoughts in a specific way, we can breach the boundaries of the known, forge a path into the forbidden. This emergent power, a grotesque chimera of disparate ideas, promises to grant us abilities bordering on the godlike–but the cost of such power is etched in the very fabric of Cognitexis. Imagine feeding a concoction of seemingly unrelated thoughts–the steely resolve of a serial killer, the meticulous planning of a power-hungry dictator, the unhinged creativity of a mad scientist–into this churning vortex. The Axioms of Thought warn that this forbidden engine may take these disparate ideas and forge them into a monstrous force, capable of achieving the seemingly miraculous, but at the potential risk of twisting your very essence in the process.

The Five Forbidden Seals:
The Axioms of Thought outline five key principles, each a forbidden seal guarding the gateway to this perilous power. Breaking these seals unleashes a torrent of raw psychic energy, a maelstrom that threatens to consume both the user and their surroundings.

1) **Unwavering Obsession:** The first principle demands a level of focus bordering on obsession. Cognitexis, once activated by the Axioms, becomes a jealous master, demanding your complete and unwavering devotion. One stray thought, a flicker of doubt, and the engine may malfunction, spewing forth psychic backlash that could warp your perception of reality.

2) **Emotional Maelstrom:** The Axioms warn against the illusion of control. By attempting to harness this forbidden power, you risk becoming a conduit for raw, unchecked emotions. The engine may amplify your darkest desires, twisting your sense of right and wrong, and leaving you a puppet dancing to the strings of your own primal urges.

3) **Fractured Concentration:** Unlike the directed attentiveness of the safeguarded methods, the Axioms demand a fractured form of focus. You must hold a multitude of disparate ideas in your mind's eye simultaneously, feeding them into the engine like fuel into a raging inferno. This mental strain can shatter your concentration, leaving you vulnerable to the psychic backlash that threatens to erupt from the overloaded Cognitexis.

4) **Malignant Self-Affirmation:** The Axioms exploit the power of the subconscious. They instruct you to bombard your mind with affirmations, not of unwavering belief, but of a twisted self-conviction that you are worthy of wielding this forbidden power. This malignant self-affirmation risks warping your sense of self, potentially transforming you into a monster who believes themself to be a god.

5) **Unfettered Will:** The final principle demands the complete surrender of your will. The Axioms are not for the faint of heart; they require a reckless abandon, a willingness to throw open the gates of your mind and allow the raw, untamed power to course through you. This unfettered will can leave you a hollowed-out shell, a husk consumed by the very power you sought to control.

The Axioms of Thought dangle the promise of godlike power before your very eyes, but tread carefully, for the path they illuminate leads not to enlightenment but to a terrifying precipice. Will you dare to unlock the forbidden doors of the mind, or will you turn back before the shadows consume you?

PERCEPTION AND REALITY

ᏁᏔᏁᏔᏁᏔ

PERCEPTION AND REALITY

F inally, we arrive at the threshold where perception and reality intertwine. This group explores the enigmatic nature of our awareness, delving into the subtle interplay between the seen and the unseen. Veils of Perception challenge us to navigate the maze of our thoughts, where reality is often obscured by the shadows of our own making. Echoes of the Spirit guide us into the uncharted depths of the human psyche, where the lines between truth and illusion blur. It is a journey of exploration and revelation as we seek to unravel the mysteries of our own consciousness.

1. Veils of Perception: Thoughts' Maze Obscuring Reality

(The Law of Thoughts' Reality Masking Effect)

Delve into the intricate maze of your consciousness. Here, cloaked in mysterious murmurs and resonating with uncharted potential, exists a concealed tenet—the Law of Thoughts' Reality Masking Effect. Proceed with caution, seeker, for in this domain; one wrong move may plunge you into a world of twisted truths where the boundaries of reason and belief intertwine. The Law unveils the potency of concentrated thought, yet tread carefully—its essence is cloaked in an enigma. Will you harness it to traverse the perilous terrain of your psyche, or will you fall prey to the deceptions it conjures?

The Strength of Concentrated Intent - An Entrance to the Unseen

The Law suggests that deep contemplation, an unwavering mental concentration, can unveil a concealed realm within your mind. This chamber contains the depths of the subconscious, an expansive, fluid web that intertwines with the principles governing existence. As you channel your will with piercing precision towards a desire, your subconscious begins its intricate dance, quietly orchestrating the circumstances around you to bring that desire to fruition. Yet, this force wields a perilous duality.

The notion of focused attention is a subject of profound exploration within the realm of neuroscience, revealing that deep contemplation and steadfast focus can dramatically influence the workings of the brain and significantly affect brain activity. Investigations led by Richard J. Davidson and his team at the University of Wisconsin-Madison reveal that concentrated meditation techniques can induce tangible alterations in the brain's architecture and operation. For example, research on Tibetan monks engaged in concentrated meditation revealed heightened activity in the prefrontal cortex, the area of the brain linked to executive functions and the pursuit of objectives. This intense concentration enables individuals to delve into profound layers of their own minds, unlocking hidden realms of awareness that sharpen their pursuit of particular ambitions and yearnings. Yet, this ability to concentrate intensely harbors a lurking danger, as it can spiral into an all-consuming attachment, paving the way for obsessive tendencies or profound mental exhaustion.[200]

The essence of The Strength of Concentrated Intent - An Entrance to the Unseen in Cognitexis resonates profoundly with the intricate workings of focused attention as explored in the realm of neuroscience. In the shadows of thought, where the mind's labyrinth twists and turns, lies a hidden domain waiting to be uncovered. Just as the stillness of meditation can peel back the layers of awareness, so too does relentless introspection illuminate the obscured corners of our psyche. The investigations into the practices of Tibetan monks reveal a profound truth: When one directs their will with unwavering intent toward a desire, it ignites a surge of activity in the brain's regions tied to ambition, deftly manipulating the very fabric of reality to manifest that longing into existence.

Yet, the dichotomy of this power reveals itself in both the empirical discoveries and the unfolding tale of Cognitexis. In the shadows of concentrated thought lies a duality; the promise of deep understanding and remarkable accomplishments intertwines with the peril of fixation, echoing the haunting specter of obsession and the weariness of the mind. This duality unveils the treacherous equilibrium inherent in the law, where the intensity that fuels ambition may just as easily spiral into self-delusion or catastrophic outcomes.

Thus, The Strength of Concentrated Intent - An Entrance to the Unseen stands as a haunting reminder of the fragile equilibrium necessary when wielding the formidable force of our thoughts. It compels us to traverse the labyrinth of the subconscious with vigilance, acknowledging the duality of extraordinary triumphs and treacherous downfalls that lie in wait.

- **Example from Psychology: Leon Festinger's theory of cognitive dissonance explores the haunting discord that arises when our convictions collide with our deeds.** In the depths of our minds, we wrestle with a tempest of thoughts, employing elaborate strategies to justify our beliefs or decisions. This struggle often leads us down a path of skewed realities and a constricted vision of truth. This intricate psychological journey delves into the shadowy corners of our minds, where the subconscious grapples with and seeks to harmonize the conflicting truths that lie within.

Contemplate a person who partakes in smoking, acutely conscious of the impending health perils that shadow their choice. They may traverse the shadows of their inner chaos, downplaying the detrimental consequences or magnifying the allure of their addiction. This struggle within serves to maintain their self-image, protecting them from the discomfort of facing the contradictions in their own actions. In the shadows of introspection, the smoker's mind weaves a tapestry of justifications, a hidden labyrinth where subconscious machinations entwine with the visible threads of their beliefs and deeds.[201]

The essence of The Strength of Concentrated Intent - An Entrance to the Unseen in Cognitexis resonates deeply with the unsettling nature of cognitive dissonance. As this law implies, profound introspection and steadfast mental focus can reveal a hidden dimension within the psyche. In a shadowy dance of the mind, cognitive dissonance unveils the intricate machinations of the subconscious, where individuals grapple with the discord between their beliefs and actions, weaving a tapestry of rationalization that obscures the truth. This complex mental labyrinth can warp perceptions and narrow focus, reminiscent of the insidious nature of the Law of Thoughts' Reality Masking Effect.

Within the realm of Cognitexis, directing one's will with sharp clarity towards an obsession, like justifying a destructive habit, sparks a haunting interplay within the depths of the subconscious. This intricate ballet subtly manipulates events and perceptions to conform to a chosen conviction, even at the cost of twisting the very fabric of reality. The interplay of this force reveals itself starkly, capable of fostering self-deception and concealing reality, reflecting the treacherous equilibrium outlined in the law.

Thus, The Strength of Concentrated Intent - An Entrance to the Unseen stands as a haunting reminder of the fragile equilibrium needed when traversing the shadowy recesses of our minds. It compels us to wield the force of our thoughts with care, acknowledging the capacity for both deep revelations and treacherous traps as we delve into the shadowy depths of our consciousness.

The Law warns that the deep intensity of this experience could distort one's perceptions. The deep obsession and unusual realization of your desires can warp one's perception, shrouding the essential truths that lie hidden in the recesses of reality. The intricate workings of the universe may compel you to sense them as whispers from unseen forces—a mysterious power answering your desperate pleas for salvation. This misinterpretation can unravel into unforeseen consequences, leading you into a world of deception and potentially disastrous outcomes.

The Deceptive Influence of Anticipation

The Law reveals yet another concealed trap—the deceptive influence of anticipation. At times, the very expectation of an occurrence can warp the essence of reality. One might find themselves encountering a sought-after result ahead of its expected time, fostering a belief in the extraordinary. This distortion emerges from the depths of your subconscious, shaped by your expectations, quietly steering events to conform to your innermost desires. This conjures a deceptive sense of control, a cunning snare that can render you vulnerable to the unforgiving truths that lie ahead.

The Pygmalion Effect illustrates how high expectations, fueled by anticipation, can dramatically elevate performance, transforming potential into reality. This phenomenon highlights the power of expectation in shaping actions and perceptions. Investigations conducted by Robert Rosenthal and Lenore Jacobson revealed a compelling connection between educators' beliefs about their students and the actual outcomes those students achieve. In a striking experiment, students were randomly designated as "intellectual bloomers," leading teachers to believe in their extraordinary potential. The remarkable transformation in these students did not stem from natural talent but rather from the teachers' elevated expectations and the subtle shifts in their interactions.[202]

This underscores how anticipation can create a deceptive influence, obscuring reality by shaping behaviors and outcomes to align with expected results. The Pygmalion Effect serves as a powerful reminder of how our perceptions and beliefs can act as veils, distorting the true nature of reality through the maze of our thoughts.

Rosenthal, R., & Jacobson, L. (1968). Pygmalion in the Classroom: The Intriguing Dynamics of Teacher Expectations and Their Impact on Students' Intellectual Growth. Holt, Rinehart & Winston.

Note that the Pygmalion Effect emerges as an important illustration within the framework of the Deceptive Influence of Anticipation in Cognitexis. The notion that anticipation can distort reality hints at a deeper truth, where the extraordinary emerges from the recesses of expectation, twisting perceptions in unexpected ways. In the research conducted by Rosenthal and Jacobson, the anticipation surrounding students' potential success molded the actual results of their academic achievements, revealing expectations' powerful role in shaping perceived realities.

Much like the way a teacher's belief in a student's potential can manifest in their success, the subtle manipulation of expectation in Cognitexis reveals how our perceptions can twist the fabric of reality itself. This unsettling twist arises from the shadows of the mind, where hidden aspirations quietly manipulate reality to align with our deepest cravings. It fosters an illusion of mastery, reminiscent of the faith in the remarkable capabilities of students. However, this illusion of mastery is a deceptive trap, leaving people exposed to the harsh realities that await, just as the heightened hopes may ultimately prepare students for daunting trials ahead.

Consequently, the Illusory Grip of Anticipation reveals the intricate dynamics between what we expect and what truly is, underscoring the importance of vigilance and discernment as we traverse the labyrinth of our minds and perceptions.

- **Example from Science - The Placebo Effect:** Consider the intriguing notion that perception molds existence: the placebo effect stands as a striking testament to how our anticipations can dramatically transform our physical experiences and psychological conditions. Research indicates that those who firmly believe they are receiving a helpful treatment often experience real improvements in their symptoms, even when the intervention is nothing more than a placebo (Benedetti, 2009). This event uncovers the complex interplay between what we anticipate and what we believe, crafting a narrative that skews our understanding of our influence on our happiness. Yet, the seductive charm of the placebo effect can entangle individuals in a labyrinth of dangers, trapping them in an illusion of safety. They might hold onto futile solutions, deliberately ignoring the essential medical attention they genuinely require (Hróbjartsson & Gøtzsche, 2001).[203]

Within the intricate web of Cognitexis, the deceptive allure of anticipation reveals itself vividly through the striking example of the placebo effect. The notion that mere anticipation can twist the fabric of reality, crafting outcomes that defy the ordinary, is both unsettling and captivating. In the realm of the mind, the power of belief weaves a complex narrative where individuals, convinced of a treatment's potential, experience real transformations in their physical and mental well-being, even when the remedy holds no actual potency.

This occurrence reflects the subtle manipulation of expectation, where the undercurrents of the mind silently guide circumstances to align with one's deepest yearnings. As individuals navigate their journeys, the power of belief can lead to genuine transformations, revealing how anticipation can mold the fabric of reality, inviting the extraordinary into the mundane. Nevertheless, this distortion weaves a web of illusion, crafting a false narrative of control that lures individuals into a comforting embrace, much like a mirage that masks the critical truths they might otherwise confront.

In this labyrinth of thought and perception, the subtle manipulation of anticipation reveals the complex dance between what we expect and what truly is. It serves as a stark reminder to tread carefully, remaining vigilant in our awareness of the shadows lurking in our minds. It acts as a chilling reminder of how easily our expectations can warp our grasp of power and the truth lurking beneath the surface.

- **Example from Literature:** Marcel Proust's monumental work, In Search of Lost Time, delves deep into the shadows of memory and the fleeting nature of time, unraveling the complex threads that shape our very existence. Proust explores the complex nature of our memories, revealing how they can distort and elevate past experiences, weaving a captivating tale of what we once believed to be true. This intriguing phenomenon highlights how the interplay of expectation and recollection shapes our understanding of what is real. As we delve into the shadows, our thoughts craft complex narratives filled with vivid imagery and deep emotion, heightening our aspirations and anxieties in ways that can be both thrilling and disquieting. Yet, the truth behind our interactions frequently disappoints the grand illusions we weave in our thoughts. As we navigate the intricate web of our recollections, they become intricately intertwined with our current emotions and perspectives, leading to distortions and embellishments that obscure the boundaries of what is real.[204]

Here, within the intricate web of Cognitexis, the subtle manipulation of expectation finds a striking parallel in Marcel Proust's profound journey in In Search of Lost Time. The notion that anticipation can distort reality hints at a deeper, unsettling truth, where the extraordinary emerges from the shadows of our expectations. In Proust's tale, the interplay of memory and expectation twists the fabric of reality, crafting a polished reflection of bygone moments shaped by present feelings and yearnings.

This phenomenon reflects the cunning manipulation of expectation, where the mere anticipation of an event can distort reality, nurturing a conviction in the remarkable. Proust's work uncovers the intricate workings of our minds, where the anticipation of what lies ahead can magnify our hopes and fears, distorting our grasp on reality in a thrilling and disconcerting way. This tension rises from the mind's shadows, subtly guiding our recollections and hopes to align with our deepest cravings.

Consequently, the Illusory Grip of Anticipation reveals the complex relationship between what we expect and what truly exists, emphasizing the importance of vigilance and discernment as we traverse the labyrinth of our minds and interpretations. It acts as a cautionary tale about the dangers of letting expectation warp our grasp of power and truth, echoing the intricate dance of recollection and temporality found in Proust's work.

The fundamental concept reveals that what is often regarded as otherworldly phenomena associated with prayer, fortune, or sorcery is, in reality, a manifestation of intense concentration. Your focused awareness stirs the shadows of your subconscious, which relentlessly weaves through the fabric of natural laws, crafting a reality that mirrors your deepest desires. Yet, the enveloping atmosphere of the experience can shroud the true origin, weaving a deceptive tapestry of supernatural intervention or mysterious forces at play.

Unveiling the Rational Behind the Mystical

The Law unveils the truth that beneath the surface of the most baffling occurrences lies a rational explanation waiting to be uncovered. Yet, the journey toward understanding is riddled with peril. The intricate maze of cause and effect may stretch endlessly, but its existence is undeniable, lurking in the shadows of our comprehension. One must endeavor to dissect these encounters with an objective lens, cutting through the illusions of perception to uncover the underlying truths. This journey demands relentless awareness, as yielding to the seductive pull of the otherworldly may divert one from their true course.

The discovery of germ theory serves as a striking example of peeling back the layers of the enigmatic to reveal the logic beneath. In the shadows of history, ailments were frequently attributed to supernatural forces, foul miasmas, or the chaotic dance of bodily humors.[xiv] However, the groundbreaking work of scientists such as Louis Pasteur and Robert Koch uncovered a chilling truth: unseen microorganisms, lurking in the shadows, are the culprits behind numerous diseases.

[xiv] The term "humors" refers to the ancient Greek theory of bodily fluids believed to govern human health and temperament: blood, phlegm, black bile, and yellow bile. This concept, known as "humoral theory," was widely accepted in medieval and Renaissance medicine.

Pasteur's experiments shattered the long-held belief in spontaneous generation, revealing that microorganisms were the hidden agents behind food spoilage and infections. Koch's postulates provided a meticulous framework that intricately linked specific pathogens to distinct diseases, laying the foundation for contemporary microbiology. These discoveries unveiled the rational explanations behind previously mystical beliefs, transforming our understanding of disease and the unseen world.[205]

Within the intricate layers of Cognitexis, the revelation of germ theory emerges as a captivating enigma, inviting deeper exploration into the unseen forces at play. This principle suggests that hidden beneath the most perplexing events is a logical truth waiting to be revealed. The evolution of germ theory shifted our perception of diseases, unraveling the once-enigmatic and supernatural explanations, revealing instead a chilling reality grounded in the existence of microorganisms.

The pursuit of truth in the shadowy world of diseases unfolded like a complex web fraught with obstacles that demanded unyielding vigilance. Visionaries such as Pasteur and Koch navigated the murky waters of perception, dismantling entrenched beliefs and unveiling compelling evidence for their groundbreaking discoveries. Their work delves into the depths of understanding, peeling back layers of complexity to expose the hidden truths of the natural world, transforming enigmatic occurrences into clear, rational insights.

Yet, the path ahead was fraught with danger. Early pushback from the medical establishment and the dominant ideologies of the era created formidable challenges. Still, the unwavering determination of these researchers in their quest for the truth highlights the critical need for unbiased exploration and constant vigilance. Succumbing to the alluring grip of widely accepted fallacies might have led them astray from their genuine path.

In this revelation, the essence of uncovering the logic behind the enigmatic emerges. It showcases how a deep dive into scientific exploration can shed light on the hidden truths of the most baffling occurrences, reshaping our perception of what is real.

• **Example from Science:** The investigation of paranormal phenomena, like ghost encounters, frequently uncovers logical reasons grounded in mental and situational influences. For example, research conducted by Houran and Lange (1996) revealed that numerous ghostly experiences might be linked to environmental factors such as low-frequency sound waves or fluctuations in electromagnetic fields, which can distort human perception. Moreover, the intricacies of the mind, including anticipation and influence, significantly shape these experiences (Wiseman et al., 2003). These revelations underscore the significance of a methodical investigation into the enigmas surrounding what appears to be otherworldly occurrences.[206]

The exploration of otherworldly occurrences presents a captivating illustration of the enigmatic forces at play in Cognitexis. There is an unsettling truth lurking just out of sight, waiting for someone to peel back the layers of confusion and reveal the logic hidden within the chaos. Research into ghost sightings uncovers those numerous encounters, previously deemed otherworldly, can actually be explained by environmental elements like low-frequency sound waves and fluctuations in electromagnetic fields, alongside psychological factors such as anticipation and influence.

The journey to unravel the enigma of paranormal phenomena mirrors a complex web of connections, demanding an objective analysis and a methodical approach to reveal the hidden truths lurking beneath the surface. Researchers such as Houran, Lange, and Wiseman meticulously examined these encounters, peeling back layers of perception to reveal the hidden realities at play. Their discoveries reveal the unsettling truth behind what once seemed inexplicable, reshaping our perception of these enigmatic events.

Yet, the path to enlightenment is fraught with danger. Just as the rules dictate, succumbing to the alluring allure of the unknown can lead one astray from the genuine path of revealing logical truths. Exploring mysterious occurrences highlights the necessity of unwavering vigilance and unbiased investigation, as it uncovers the intricate dynamics between mental states and external influences that mold our understanding of what is real.

The exploration of ghost sightings and other eerie phenomena reveals the essence of uncovering the logic behind the supernatural. It showcases how a deep dive into the unknown can shed light on the hidden truths of the most baffling events, reshaping our perception of reality.

- **Example from Science - Pareidolia:** The phenomenon of pareidolia, where the mind seeks out significance in the chaos of randomness, reveals unsettling ways in which our minds can lead us astray. In fleeting instances when we discern visages in shifting clouds, hear murmurs carried by the wind, or uncover hidden meanings within the tumult of disorder, we engage with the intricate capacity of our minds to create meaning from ambiguity. Research in cognitive neuroscience uncovers that this occurrence stems from the brain's inherent tendency to identify familiar shapes and patterns, a characteristic honed through evolution for the sake of survival. Though pareidolia may inspire wonder and ignite the imagination, it is essential to tread carefully, aware of the shadows that lurk at its edges. Exploring the complex mechanisms of the mind that lead to pareidolia allows us to navigate away from unfounded claims and the dangers of distorted perceptions.[207]

Within the exploration of the rationale behind the enigmatic in Cognitexis, the occurrence of pareidolia serves as a striking illustration. Beneath the shadows of the most perplexing events, a hidden rationale patiently awaits. Pareidolia unveils the intricate workings of our minds, guiding us to discern significance in chaos and exposing a logical foundation for encounters that could easily be dismissed as otherworldly or enigmatic.

Much like the labyrinthine interplay of actions and consequences found in the law, grasping the phenomenon of pareidolia demands a detached perspective to unravel these illusions and reveal the deeper realities lurking beneath. Cognitive neuroscience studies, including those by Voss and colleagues, reveal that pareidolia emerges from the brain's intrinsic inclination to identify familiar shapes and patterns, providing a logical rationale for these enigmatic experiences that often blur the line between reality and illusion.

Yet, the path to enlightenment is fraught with danger, as the shadows of the law forewarn. Succumbing to the alluring grasp of pareidolia may result in unfounded claims and distorted understandings, steering one away from the genuine path of logical exploration. Exploring pareidolia unveils the necessity of unwavering vigilance and impartial scrutiny, exposing the intricate dance between what we perceive and the underlying truths of existence.[208]

In this way, the phenomenon of pareidolia reveals the intricate dance between reason and the enigmatic, showcasing how the pursuit of knowledge can pierce through the shadows of the unknown, reshaping our perception of existence itself.

In Conclusion

As we step into the realm where perception and reality converge, the enigmas of Cognitexis allure us with a fascination that is as captivating as it is dangerous. The Law of Thoughts' Reality Masking Effect calls for an unwavering resilience of the spirit, compelling you to face the formidable power that resides within your own consciousness. In the dim recesses of the mind, hidden truths beckon, urging a journey through the intricate labyrinth of consciousness, where the veils of deception must be pierced to reveal the stark essence of existence.

Veils of Perception surround you, challenging every step as you navigate the intricate labyrinth of your mind. Within these murky recesses, the essence of reality frequently becomes clouded by the intricate designs of your creation, as the boundary between what is real and what is imagined intertwines in a mysterious waltz. Echoes of the spirit guide you into the depths of the human psyche, a domain where exploration unveils the delicate balance between what is perceived and what truly exists.

The complex tapestry of existence reveals itself, necessitating a meticulous perception alignment. As you delve into the intricate web of the mind, the shadows of thought and emotion intertwine, revealing the enigmatic forces that mold your very essence. The decision lies before you: Will you be ensnared by the tempting whispers of the shadows, revealing the treacherous truths they conceal, or will you seize control of your own consciousness, traversing its depths with sharp insight and vigilance?

Proceed ahead with serious caution and utmost vigilance, as the boundary separating truth from deception is perilously fragile. Every move you make has the potential to either shed light on the intricacies of existence or drag you into a realm shaped by your most haunting anxieties. The Axioms of Thought within Cognitexis serve as a dual-edged sword, illuminating the path to intellectual and personal transformation while casting a shadow over the fragile equilibrium necessary to navigate the labyrinthine depths of your own mind.

2. Echoes of the Spirit: A Journey into the Uncharted Depths of the Human Psyche

(The Law of Subconscious Emotional Activator and the Might of Invocations)

Venture forth, fearless seeker, into the intricate shadows of Cognitexis. In this realm, where shadows twist and murmurs resonate through the boundless abyss, a concealed truth awaits— the Law of Subconscious Emotional Activator (SEA). Proceed with caution, as this Law explores the shadowy depths of invocation, a practice that unleashes powerful, yet possibly dangerous, energies lurking within the human mind. In this realm, prayer transcends mere requests to a caring god; it becomes an audacious exploration, a ritual that dances on the edge of existence itself.

The SEA Within: An Entrance to the Hidden

The Law suggests that deep within our minds lies a dormant force, much like a submarine volcano, surrounded by a tumultuous sea of raw emotional energy poised for activation. This is the formidable power of the Subconscious Emotional Activator or SEA. One misstep and the volcano could unleash its fury, leading to catastrophic consequences. The Law presents a singular path to stir the dormant volcano—not through brute strength, but via a carefully chosen catalyst, a meticulously crafted and intricately designed emotional state. Proceed with caution, for the wrong mix of emotions may trigger an unpredictable explosion, distorting your perception of reality in ways you never anticipated.

Exploring emotional triggers reveals how specific emotions can unleash profound reactions buried deep within the human psyche. In his compelling exploration, Antonio Damasio delves into the intricate connections between our emotions and the very fabric of our consciousness, revealing how they shape our choices in profound ways. Emotional triggers can unleash intense responses,

486

often rooted in hidden memories or past experiences. For example, a particular scent or melody can unleash a powerful emotional reaction, awakening memories or sensations that have been buried deep within. These triggers can evoke a spectrum of reactions, occasionally unveiling deep revelations or, on the flip side, plunging one into a whirlwind of emotional chaos.[209]

In the pursuit of the uncharted depths of the human psyche within Cognitexis, the phenomenon of emotional triggers emerges as a stirring depiction. The Law of Subconscious Emotional Activator (SEA) posits that within the recesses of our psyche exists a slumbering power reminiscent of an underwater volcano encased in untamed emotional energy waiting to be unleashed. Emotional triggers, as examined by Damasio, reveal how certain feelings can unleash profound reactions buried deep within our subconscious, creating a web of intrigue and tension.

Similar to the hidden forces of a submarine volcano, emotional triggers can release intense and unpredictable energies within the depths of the human psyche. These meticulously constructed triggers can stir deep emotional reactions, exposing the complex mechanisms of our inner minds. Yet, the warning looms that a single miscalculation in navigating these feelings can spiral into disastrous outcomes, reflecting how a flawed combination of emotional cues can plunge one into chaos or warp one's grasp on reality.

Consequently, the intriguing nature of emotional triggers reveals the essence of the Law of Subconscious Emotional Activator (SEA), showcasing how meticulously selected emotional states can awaken the hidden depths of our minds. It highlights the necessity of treading carefully, as the intensity of these emotional triggers can dramatically influence our views and experiences in deep and often unforeseen manners.

- **Example for Science:** Reflect on the hidden depths of repressed emotions and the intense fallout they can provoke, revealing a more profound insight into the complexities of humanity. Diving into the shadows of the mind uncovers that suppressed feelings, once they surface, can dramatically impact one's mental state and physical health. Research conducted by Gross and Levenson (1997) revealed that the act of suppressing emotions can trigger a surge in physiological responses and amplify stress responses, which may culminate in sudden and erratic outbursts. Moreover, John and Gross (2004) suggest that the ongoing suppression of emotions can result in deep-seated feelings of unease, despair, and a range of psychological afflictions. These revelations highlight the critical importance of skillfully managing and expressing our emotions to prevent catastrophic outcomes.[210]

Within the confines of The SEA Within. An entryway into the concealed depths of Cognitexis reveals the haunting nature of repressed emotions, offering a chilling glimpse into the human psyche. The principle of the Subconscious Emotional Activator unveils a hidden power within our psyche, reminiscent of an underwater volcano, brimming with untamed emotional energy ready to erupt at any moment. As examined by Gross and Levenson, Hidden feelings resonate with this idea by revealing how suppressed emotions can build up and ultimately explode with intense repercussions.

Similar to the hidden depths of a submarine volcano, suppressed feelings can erupt in dramatic and unforeseen ways when they finally break free. The intense emotional outbursts expose the profound influence of the Subconscious Emotional Activator (SEA) and highlight the critical importance of skillfully managing our emotional landscapes. The regulations highlight the significance of a precisely selected trigger, an artfully constructed and intricately woven emotional condition to awaken this latent energy within our minds.

Yet, the contrasting nature of this power is unmistakable in both the research outcomes and the unfolding story of Cognitexis. Grasping and expressing our emotions can unveil deep truths and enhance our mental state, yet failing to navigate these feelings may lead to disastrous outcomes, warping our view of the world around us. This reflects the danger of unaddressed feelings spiraling into deeper issues if not handled wisely.

Consequently, the intricacies of suppressed feelings reveal the essence of The SEA Within: An Entrance to the Hidden, showcasing how deliberately selected emotional states can awaken the latent energies lurking in our minds. It highlights the necessity of moving carefully, aware of the potential for deep revelations and dangerous traps as we explore the complex layers of our feelings.

Invocation: A Portal to the Unknown

The Law reveals that prayer transcends mere petition; it is a meticulously crafted mental state, functioning as a hyper-gate to deeper realms of understanding. Envision it this way: prayer resembles a mystical incantation where emotions act as volatile catalysts, and the will serves as the transformative vessel. In this moment, you might establish a fleeting connection with a colossal, hyper-intelligent entity that saturates the cosmos. Yet, this force is far from a kind-hearted presence; it embodies an ancient intellect beyond human comprehension. To it, the activation of a hyper-gate is akin to gazing into the void—immense potential awaits, yet dangers loom just as large, shrouded in fear.

Delve into the captivating idea that the exploration of altered states of consciousness, whether through meditation or profound prayer, is a realm filled with compelling narratives and investigations. Studies employing advanced neuroimaging techniques have uncovered that these methods can trigger significant changes in brain function, particularly in areas associated with self-perception and emotional regulation (Newberg et al., 2001). These altered experiences might stir a profound connection with something beyond the ordinary, leading to a deeper understanding of life reminiscent of an enigmatic portal. Yet, this journey can morph into a maze of feelings, where insight dances with uncertainty, leading to profound discoveries amid significant psychological challenges.[211]

The exploration of altered states of consciousness unfolds a captivating narrative within the realm of Invocation: A Portal to the Unknown in Cognitexis. The Law unveils that prayer goes beyond simple requests, operating as a carefully constructed mindset—a gateway to profound depths of insight. In a striking revelation, the work of Newberg and his team uncovered how meditation and deep prayer can shift brain activity, leading to experiences that feel eerily akin to an encounter with a higher power.

Similar to the hyper-gate outlined in the law, these transformed states of awareness serve as gateways to profound dimensions of insight. Emotions act as unpredictable triggers, while the will transforms into a powerful conduit, forging a link with a vast, timeless intelligence that eludes human understanding. This journey can unveil deep revelations and an intensified awareness of being, but it also unfolds a maze of feelings where lucidity and uncertainty collide.

The complexity of this journey is striking, revealing layers of profound insights and heightened understanding. Yet, it also presents daunting psychological challenges and the peril of becoming ensnared in an intricate web of emotions. The transformed states of awareness reveal the essence of Summoning: A Gateway to the Unseen, showcasing how intricately designed mental conditions can unveil profound layers of insight akin to the initiation of a dimensional threshold.

Therefore, delving into altered states of consciousness reveals the necessity of navigating these experiences with a blend of intrigue and vigilance. It uncovers the profound influence of the mind when channeled through meditation and prayer, resonating with the notion of prayer as a daring journey that flirts with the very boundaries of reality.

- **Example from Literature:** H.P. Lovecraft's stories delve into the unsettling consequences of probing into the abyss and the dangers of awakening ancient, incomprehensible entities. In narratives like "The Call of Cthulhu," characters become entranced by an unquenchable desire for concealed realities, exploring esoteric rituals that unleash dark forces well beyond their comprehension. Their relentless pursuit of knowledge draws them into a shadowy realm, compelling them to confront the haunting realities of an unfathomable existence.

  Lovecraft's creations serve as a chilling reminder of the limits of human understanding and the importance of respecting the boundaries of what can be grasped. As we delve into the intricacies of life, we might unknowingly stir forces that elude our control, resulting in consequences that could unravel into turmoil. His stories often explore the captivating nature of concealed realities and the dangerous fallout that arises from invoking mysterious, otherworldly powers through arcane rituals and incantations. The whispers from the abyss echo our profound desire to understand the universe and our place within it, even if that journey spirals us toward our own undoing.[212]

  Within the realm of Invocation: A Portal to the Unknown in Cognitexis, the enigmatic journey crafted by H.P. Lovecraft into the depths of the unknown serves as a consuming illustration. The law unveils that prayer goes beyond simple requests, acting as a carefully constructed mindset—a gateway to profound depths of insight. In a similar vein, Lovecraft's tales reveal the unsettling consequences of exploring forbidden knowledge and awakening primordial entities, unleashing formidable and perilous powers that elude human understanding.

Similar to the enigmatic gateways outlined in the law, the rituals found in Lovecraft's narratives function as conduits to profound dimensions of reality, where feelings ignite unpredictable impacts, emotions serve as volatile catalysts, and the will becomes the transformative vessel. These narratives uncover the depths of human curiosity and the pursuit of concealed realities, leading to chilling encounters with ancient, hyper-intelligent beings that permeate the universe. Yet, this path is laden with danger, as these forces are anything but kind; they represent a timeless intellect that can swiftly eclipse human comprehension.[213]

Lovecraft's narratives reveal the intricate dance of allure and peril: the promise of deep understanding intertwined with the ominous fallout of awakening powers we cannot control. This resonates with the law's depiction of prayer as an audacious journey that teeters on the brink of reality. The stories reveal a chilling reminder of the importance of humility and the limits of our understanding, as engagement with such formidable forces can spiral into chaos and devastation if not handled with extreme care.

In Lovecraft's world, the act of summoning ancient entities reveals a chilling truth: it serves as a gateway to the unfathomable. This exploration of carefully constructed mental landscapes unveils profound insights, yet it also warns of the lurking perils that accompany such endeavors. It acts as a cautionary note to navigate these enigmas with respect and caution, acknowledging the delicate boundary between profound revelation and dangerous fallout.

Belief: A Blade with Two Sides

The Law underscores the critical role of belief. In this scenario, faith transcends mere virtue; it morphs into a mental discipline that teeters on the edge of obsession. Envision a tempest brewing in the depths of your consciousness, a chaotic swirl of uncertainties and fears that threaten to shatter the sanctity of your prayer ritual. Belief serves as a psychological barrier, containing the tempest within. Yet, a dam raised beyond its limits or crafted with flaws may transform into a harbinger of catastrophe.

The unsettling concept of cognitive dissonance, first unveiled by Leon Festinger, reveals the intricate and often conflicting layers of belief. When people find themselves caught in a web of conflicting beliefs and actions, it creates a tension that gnaws at their psyche, leaving them in a state of unease. People frequently resort to intricate mental strategies to validate or explain their behaviors to ease this unease, occasionally teetering on the edge of fixation. Consider an individual who prioritizes well-being yet persists in smoking; they might justify their actions by minimizing the dangers or amplifying the advantages. This mental barrier serves to manage the inner turmoil, yet it can spiral into irrational or damaging actions if the underlying beliefs are misguided or pushed to their limits.[214]

Within the context of Belief: A Blade with Two Sides in Cognitexis, the unsettling nature of cognitive dissonance emerges as a striking illustration. The law highlights the profound impact of belief, hinting that faith evolves beyond simple morality into a psychological struggle that flirts with fixation. The clash of conflicting beliefs reveals how the mind can become a fortress, holding back the storm of doubts and anxieties lurking in the shadows of awareness.

In a world where shadows of doubt loom large, the clash between what we believe and how we act creates a tension that can unravel our mental equilibrium. Faith acts as a barrier, restraining the chaos within, reminiscent of a fortress standing firm against a raging storm. Yet, much like a cracked facade that hints at impending doom, a belief system rooted in justifications can spiral into irrational or destructive actions.

The tension between faith and reason unfolds dramatically in the revelations of Cognitexis. Though conviction can offer a sense of mental balance and aid in navigating personal turmoil, it may spiral into chaos if the foundational beliefs are misguided or pushed beyond reasonable limits. This reflects the unsettling possibility that conflicting thoughts can lead to illogical justifications and detrimental actions, emphasizing the fragile equilibrium necessary for emotional health.

Consequently, the intriguing nature of cognitive dissonance reveals the duality of belief, showcasing how it can serve as both a shield and a threat to our mental well-being. It highlights the necessity of scrutinizing and upholding our belief systems, acknowledging the dual potential for uplifting and detrimental consequences as we traverse the intricate layers of our minds.

- **Example from Psychology:** The placebo effect stands as an overpowering testament to the power of belief, revealing how profoundly our perceptions can influence our bodies and minds. When individuals firmly believe that a solution will produce outcomes, their bodies often respond in accordance with that conviction, irrespective of the solution's true effectiveness. The intriguing nature of the placebo effect reveals a range of outcomes, showcasing reduced pain, lowered anxiety, and a heightened sense of well-being. Research reveals that conviction in treatment can evoke genuine physiological reactions, underscoring the profound sway of the mind over the body (Benedetti, 2009).

  However, it is crucial to recognize that an excessive reliance on belief without tangible evidence can result in harmful outcomes. For example, delaying or avoiding necessary medical treatments based on unfounded beliefs can result in severe consequences. In this intricate dance, one must skillfully maneuver through the tension between unwavering belief and the relentless quest for reality, driven by sharp analysis and concrete evidence.[215]

Within the intricate web of Belief: A Blade with Two Sides in Cognitexis, the placebo effect emerges as a striking illustration of the mind's profound influence over reality. The law reveals the profound significance of belief, hinting that faith evolves beyond simple virtue into a mental exercise that hovers perilously close to obsession. The placebo effect reveals the profound influence of entrenched beliefs on both physical and mental health, serving as a psychological shield that confines the shadows of doubt and fear within the depths of the mind.

Similar to the storm raging within the mind's shadows as outlined in the law, the placebo effect hinges on a conviction that can harness and steer the body's reaction to healing. Faith acts as a conduit, harmonizing the body's responses with the expected result, akin to a barrier restraining chaotic currents. Yet, much like a cracked dam that signals impending doom, an unwavering faith in unproven beliefs can spiral into perilous outcomes, including the postponement of essential medical interventions.

The contrasting nature of conviction unfolds within the scientific discoveries and the unfolding story of Cognitexis. Though conviction can spark uplifting physiological reactions and enhance overall wellness, it may spiral into perilous consequences if not balanced with concrete evidence and critical thought. This reflects the intriguing possibility that the mind's influence can lead to either remarkable benefits or severe consequences, emphasizing the fragile equilibrium necessary to sustain mental and physical well-being.

Consequently, the placebo effect unveils the dual nature of belief: a sharp edge that can either shield us or lead us into peril. It reveals the intricate dance between faith and vulnerability in our lives. It highlights the necessity of scrutinizing and upholding our belief systems, acknowledging the dual potential for uplifting and detrimental effects as we traverse the intricate maze of our minds.[216]

The Subtle Menace: Anxiety and Uncertainty as Psychological Intruders

The Law cautions against the perils that fear and doubt can unleash. These are not just fleeting feelings; they are cunning mental invaders that can seep into the sacred act of prayer, distorting your true intentions and possibly drawing the gaze of dark entities lurking beyond the hyper-gate. A mere whisper of fear or uncertainty can taint the bond, spiraling into unexpected outcomes. Stay alert, seeker, for the murmurs of dread may guide you into shadowy realms.

The grip of anxiety is a familiar specter, one that intricately weaves itself into the fabric of thought and choice, casting shadows over clarity and reason. Research conducted by Eysenck, Derakshan, Santos, and Calvo (2007) uncovers the unsettling truth that anxiety can devour cognitive resources, resulting in diminished working memory capacity and compromised task performance. This occurrence becomes strikingly apparent in moments of intense pressure, where individuals may find themselves succumbing to "choking," a deterioration in their abilities brought on by the suffocating grip of anxiety and the insidious whispers of self-doubt.[217]

Within the realm of The Subtle Menace: Anxiety and Uncertainty as Psychological Intruders within Cognitexis, the influence of anxiety on cognitive performance emerges as a haunting illustration. The law warns of the treacherous consequences that fear and doubt can unleash, portraying them as insidious mental intruders that warp genuine intentions and may summon dark, malevolent forces.

Similar to the insidious cognitive disruptions outlined in Eysenck's research, anxiety emerges as a lurking threat, infiltrating the mind and devouring mental resources, ultimately undermining one's ability to perform. This resonates with the portrayal of dread and ambiguity as insidious forces that can corrupt the purity of devotion or any concentrated thought process. The examination reveals how a subtle murmur of unease can unravel the threads of thought, resulting in unforeseen and frequently harmful consequences.

The interplay of anxiety reveals itself through empirical research and the unfolding story of Cognitexis. Though anxiety sharpens perception and readies the mind for lurking dangers, it can just as easily engulf the psyche, resulting in distorted judgment and diminished mental acuity. This reflects the capacity for unease and uncertainty to lead one into murky depths, warping both perceptions and motives.

Consequently, the experience of anxiety unveils the essence of The Subtle Menace: Anxiety and Uncertainty as Psychological Intruders, illustrating the dual nature of these emotions as both guardians and threats to our mental equilibrium. It highlights the critical need to navigate the shadows of anxiety and uncertainty, acknowledging their dual role in awakening us to peril while simultaneously warping our perception of reality.

- **Example from Psychology – Cognitive Behavioral Therapy (CBT):** The insidious grip of anxiety and uncertainty permeates every aspect of our lives, creating an atmosphere thick with tension that deeply influences our thoughts and feelings. Cognitive-behavioral therapy (CBT) acts as a compelling instrument for those eager to explore the intricate layers of their psyche, empowering them to face and deconstruct the insidious negative thought patterns that frequently spiral into anxiety and distress. Delving into the complex labyrinth of the mind reveals hidden routes to conquering anxiety, creating methods that not only ease the turmoil but also shed light on the darker corners of our inner selves.

At the core of CBT is a deep exploration of the complex connections that intertwine our thoughts, feelings, and behaviors. Shifting our perspective can lead to a profound change in how we feel and behave. By facing disturbing thoughts and replacing them with more stable and positive viewpoints, one can lessen the hold of anxiety and enhance their emotional well-being (Beck, 2011).[218]

Within the narrative of The Subtle Menace: Anxiety and Uncertainty as Psychological Intruders within Cognitexis, the tenets of cognitive-behavioral therapy (CBT) emerge as a captivating illustration. The law warns of the dangers that anxiety and uncertainty can unleash, portraying them as sly psychological intruders that warp genuine motives and may invite sinister influences.

Anxiety and uncertainty weave through our minds like unseen intruders, casting dark shadows over our thoughts and emotions, leaving us questioning what lies beneath the surface. CBT acts as a tool to face these unwelcome thoughts, offering tactics to break down harmful mental patterns and transform our psychological terrain. This resonates with the law's focus on remaining vigilant and controlling the sway of fear and uncertainty to keep us from being drawn into murky depths.[219]

The interplay of tension and unpredictability is palpable in both the therapeutic method and the storyline of Cognitexis. Though these feelings can sharpen perception and indicate looming dangers, they can also engulf the psyche if not handled with care. CBT provides a methodical way to reshape our thinking, akin to the alertness needed to confront the unseen forces lurking in Cognitexis.

Consequently, the tenets of cognitive-behavioral therapy reveal the insidious nature of anxiety and uncertainty as unwelcome intruders, illustrating how facing and navigating these feelings can safeguard our mental well-being from the distortions wrought by fear and uncertainty. It highlights the necessity of staying alert and maintaining mental strength as we traverse the intricate layers of our minds.

Honing Your Cognitive Edge: The Dangers of Concentration

The Law underscores the critical significance of psychological liberation. Yet, the pursuit of this freedom can lead one down a perilous path. Envision your mind as a war zone rife with chaotic distractions and lurking anxieties. The Law advocates for eliminating distractions and channeling your mental prowess into a precise and formidable force. Nevertheless, this profound concentration can wield a perilous duality. While it enables you to engage the SEA, it can simultaneously obscure the lurking threats outside your awareness's periphery.

The concept of a flow state, articulated by psychologist Mihaly Csikszentmihalyi, reveals a captivating level of focus that can elevate performance and create an intense engagement in an activity. In a captivating moment, individuals find themselves immersed in an experience where their abilities seamlessly align with the obstacles before them, creating an intoxicating blend of focus and thrill. Neuroimaging studies reveal a striking surge in activity within the prefrontal cortex during flow, a region linked to intense focus and cognitive mastery (Dietrich, 2004). Yet, this deep immersion carries a perilous edge; it can lead individuals to become so engrossed in their pursuits that they remain blind to lurking dangers or shifts in their surroundings.[220]

Within the framework of Sharpening Your Mental Acumen: The Risks of Focus in Cognitexis, the idea of the flow state emerges as a captivating illustration. The law emphasizes the essential importance of mental freedom, urging the removal of distractions to focus one's cognitive power on a sharp and powerful weapon. The flow state captures an intense focus, where individuals reach their highest potential by completely losing themselves in an experience.

Like the intense concentration in a heightened mental state, the law emphasizes the importance of removing distractions to tap into one's intellectual potential fully. Yet, the flow state reveals the intricate balance of intense focus. While it allows individuals to fully immerse themselves in their pursuits, it can also veil the hidden dangers that hover beyond their perception. This reflects the cautionary tale that deep focus, though advantageous for tapping into the hidden depths of the mind, can also render one oblivious to lurking threats in one's surroundings.

The intricate layers of focus reveal themselves through both the empirical evidence and the unfolding story of Cognitexis. Although achieving a flow state can elevate performance and provide a sense of freedom, it can also create a tunnel vision that exposes one to lurking dangers from the outside world. The delicate interplay between concentrated focus and acute awareness is essential, as sustaining a mental advantage requires not just the removal of distractions but also the identification of lurking threats.

Consequently, the concept of the flow state reveals the intricate balance of sharpening one's mental acuity: The Perils of Focus, illustrating how intense concentration can elevate yet simultaneously jeopardize one's cognitive experience. It highlights the necessity of striking a delicate equilibrium between intense concentration and awareness of one's surroundings, skillfully maneuvering through the intricate labyrinth of thoughts with both accuracy and care.

- **Example from Literature:** Oscar Wilde's The Picture of Dorian Gray reveals a chilling tale, delving into the dangerous abyss of unchecked desire and the captivating charm of superficial allure. Dorian Gray's obsessive fixation on his appearance and the pursuit of everlasting youth draws him deeper into a dark abyss of moral decline and self-destruction. His relentless preoccupation with his external image masks the deeper importance of integrity, compassion, and the path of personal transformation.

  This tale underscores the importance of nurturing a balanced perspective and avoiding an unhealthy obsession with any one aspect of life. By delving into varied interests and cultivating deep relationships, we can evade the snares of obsession and welcome a more fulfilling life.[221]

  Within the context of honing your cognitive acuity, the perils of focus in Cognitexis unveil themselves dramatically, much like the haunting narrative of Oscar Wilde's The Picture of Dorian Gray. The law highlights the essential importance of mental freedom, pushing for removing distractions to harness cognitive power into a sharp and powerful weapon. The tale of Dorian Gray captures a haunting narrative, revealing how his relentless fixation on preserving his youth and allure spirals into a dark descent, ultimately sealing his fate.

  Like the gripping obsession outlined in the law, Dorian Gray's relentless preoccupation with his looks allows him to fulfill his shallow ambitions. Yet, this intense focus simultaneously shrouds the dangers threatening his ethical compass and personal evolution. His relentless drive clouds his perception of true character and compassion, reminiscent of a cautionary tale where unwavering focus can conceal hidden dangers just beyond the edge of one's vision.[222]

The intricate layers of focus reveal themselves in Wilde's storytelling and the underlying principles of Cognitexis. Dorian Gray's obsession with his appearance brings him the satisfaction he craves, yet it also spirals into a dark descent of moral corruption and self-destruction. This reflects the possibility that deep focus can bring about both rewards and risks, highlighting the importance of maintaining equilibrium.

In this narrative, the tale of Dorian Gray reveals the perilous nature of an intense fixation: the risks of narrowing one's perspective. It illustrates how an all-consuming obsession can cloud essential truths and spiral into ruinous consequences. It highlights the necessity of preserving a balanced viewpoint while nurturing various interests and relationships, allowing one to maneuver through life's intricate challenges with sharp awareness and careful deliberation.

Determination: Igniting the Unspoken Flame

The principles of the Law reveal the profound significance of unwavering determination. The prayer ritual resembles a flame that demands continuous attention and care. Without relentless determination, this flame will flicker and fade into darkness. Maintaining unwavering focus and a deep emotional intensity over time enables a complete immersion into the depths of the SEA. Yet tread carefully, wanderer, for what begins as a determination can spiral into fixation, and the flame that fuels your ambition may just as easily engulf you.

Consider the concept of grit, described by psychologist Angela Duckworth, revealing the intense influence of relentless commitment and passion in chasing long-lasting dreams. Grit represents an unwavering determination to chase one's ambitions, a fierce commitment that endures through challenges and setbacks.

Research reveals that those with deep resilience tend to maneuver through intricate journeys toward success, whether in the realm of education or the corporate landscape. Yet, one must navigate the fragile line that divides steadfast determination from all-consuming obsession. Heightened focus can plunge into fatigue and mental turmoil, highlighting the essential importance of balance and personal well-being.[223]

Within the framework of Determination: Igniting the Unspoken Flame within Cognitexis, the notion of grit emerges as a captivating illustration. The law unveils the deep implications of relentless resolve, comparing it to a flickering flame that requires constant vigilance and nurturing. Grit embodies an unyielding resolve, where individuals with profound tenacity chase their ambitions with fervor, undeterred by the formidable barriers and trials that lie in their path.

Just as a flickering flame demands unwavering vigilance, those with tenacity exhibit an unyielding concentration and profound emotional depth in their pursuits. Yet, the law also cautions against the perils of obsession, and Duckworth's findings illuminate this complex interplay. While determination can pave the way for extraordinary accomplishments and self-discovery, it can also spiral into fatigue and mental turmoil if not tempered with nurturing and harmony.

The intricate balance of resolve reveals itself in both research outcomes and the core tenet of Cognitexis. Though relentless concentration and deep emotional engagement can pave the way to achievement, they may also descend into obsession and looming danger if not handled cautiously. This reflects the delicate equilibrium outlined in the regulations, highlighting the necessity of a thoughtful and intentional strategy toward one's aspirations.

Thus, the concept of grit unveils the essence of Determination: igniting the Unspoken Flame. It reveals how relentless resolve can illuminate and jeopardize our path. It highlights the necessity of tending to this spark with unwavering focus and caution while being aware of the dangers of obsession.

- **Example from Literature:** In the depths of despair, Victor Hugo's Les Misérables unveils a gripping tale of relentless resolve embodied in the complex figure of Jean Valjean. Valjean's metamorphosis from a callous outlaw to a caring and altruistic figure is fueled by an unyielding resolve to atone for his past and safeguard those dear to him. This relentless drive and deep emotional resonance propel his quest, enabling him to navigate countless challenges and fully dedicate himself to his pursuit of atonement.

Yet, Valjean's resolve casts a shadow that reveals the complexity of this fire. His relentless pursuit of safeguarding Cosette and adhering to his principles often obscures the larger consequences of his choices, plunging him into deep internal struggles and dangerous predicaments. This reflects the essence of resolve, where the same fire that ignites aspiration can also threaten to consume, drawing the individual deeper into an obsession that may overshadow the very drive that pushes them ahead.[224]

Within the narrative of Determination: Igniting the Unspoken Flame within Cognitexis, the figure of Jean Valjean in Les Misérables emerges as a captivating illustration. The law unveils the deep implications of relentless resolve, comparing it to a flickering flame that requires constant vigilance and nurturing. Valjean's journey is a gripping tale of obsession, where his unyielding quest for redemption and a fierce desire to shield his loved ones propel him into a web of choices and consequences.

Like a captivating ritual, Valjean's relentless determination and profound emotional depth allow him to accomplish extraordinary tasks and fully engage in his quest. Yet, the law serves as a cautionary tale about the perils of obsession, and Valjean's narrative underscores this complex tension. His relentless drive often spirals into dangerous territory, showcasing how the passion that ignites success can also consume the person if left unchecked.

The intricate layers of resolve unfold in Hugo's story, mirroring the underlying tenets of Cognitexis. Through relentless concentration and deep emotional engagement can pave the way for remarkable accomplishments and self-discovery, they may also spiral into obsession and looming danger. This reflects the delicate equilibrium outlined in the regulations, highlighting the necessity of a thoughtful and deliberate strategy toward one's aspirations.

In this narrative, Jean Valjean's journey reveals the essence of relentless resolve: a spark that can illuminate the darkest paths, showcasing how steadfast ambition can both uplift and threaten our very existence. It highlights the necessity of tending to this spark with unwavering focus and caution while being aware of the dangers of obsession.

Beyond the Shadows: A Peek into the Uncharted

The Law acknowledges the enigmatic nature of prayer, suggesting its capacity to transcend the natural world's limitations. Yet, the mechanism behind this remains shrouded in mystery. The Law frequently hints at a connection through prayer to power beneath mere physicality—a malevolent force, a swirling tempest of existence that distorts reality into both terrifying and magnificent forms.

Delve into the captivating revelations from neuroscience about the transformative effects of mindfulness meditation and how it reshapes the brain's neuroplasticity. Engaging in mindfulness practices, often characterized by intense concentration through prayer or meditation, reveals a profound ability to break free from the confines of reality, leading to remarkable transformations in brain structure and function. Findings from Sara Lazar and her team at Harvard Medical School unveiled that those who meditate over extended periods show a notable increase in cortical thickness within brain areas linked to attention, sensory processing, and emotional regulation (Lazar et al., 2005). These discoveries suggest a deep link between concentrated mental activities such as prayer and the fundamental neurobiological mechanisms that influence our perception of reality.

Yet, this bond carries an air of mystery that is impossible to ignore. The intricate ways in which mindfulness and prayer shape neuroplasticity linger in the shadows, echoing the sinister presence outlined in the Law. This powerful force, a chaotic whirlwind of life, can twist reality into both haunting and awe-inspiring shapes, mirroring the deep and occasionally disconcerting impacts of these actions on the mind and our perception of the world.[225]

Beyond the Shadows: A Peek into the Uncharted in Cognitexis presents a captivating narrative based on neuroscience revelations about mindfulness meditation. The Law hints at the mysterious essence of prayer, suggesting it possesses the power to rise above the confines of reality. Mindfulness practices, often steeped in intense, concentrated prayer, reveal a profound transformation that alters the brain in ways that transcend the physical realm.

The intricate ties suggested by the Law unveil a deeper narrative, where mindfulness and prayer practices intertwine with the hidden neurobiological mechanisms that sculpt our perception of reality. The heightened cortical thickness seen in those who meditate over long periods hints at deep, transformative shifts in brain structure and function, resonating with the notion of an unseen power lurking just beneath the surface of our tangible reality.

Yet, the exact processes through which these transformations unfold remain shrouded in an enigma reminiscent of a sinister influence lurking in the shadows. This chaotic whirlwind of life can twist reality into forms that are both haunting and awe-inspiring, revealing the intense and occasionally disquieting impact of profound mental exercises on our minds and how we perceive the world.

Consequently, the allure of mindfulness meditation and its effects on neuroplasticity unveil the essence of Beyond the Shadows: A Peek into the Uncharted. It illustrates how prayer and concentrated mental exercises can elevate us beyond the ordinary and link us to profound, mysterious energies. The book highlights the deep importance of these practices while also hinting at the enigmatic and potentially perilous elements that lurk beneath the surface.

The Enigmatic Force of Prayer: Navigating the Dualities of Influence

The Law emphasizes the compelling and ever-evolving essence of prayer. View the SEA as a formidable yet intriguingly erratic instrument. Prayer can serve a multitude of purposes, yet when misused, the outcomes can cast a shadow over their intended light. Grasping the intricacies of the SEA and harnessing the force of emotional activation can empower you to shape your reality in profound and transformative ways. Keep in mind, Seeker, that this wields a dual nature of influence. Employ it with extreme vigilance, as one wrong move could lead to catastrophic outcomes.

The observer effect in quantum physics reveals the captivating and constantly shifting nature of phenomena shaped by the act of observing. This concept suggests that simply watching a quantum system can change its very nature. Take, for example, the renowned double-slit experiment, where particles like electrons reveal a striking transformation in behavior when under scrutiny, oscillating between their particle and wave identities. The observer's role in shaping the outcome reveals the deep-seated effects of engagement on reality, reminiscent of the power of intention and emotional resonance within the SEA.[226]

Within the realm of The Enigmatic Force of Prayer: Navigating the Dualities of Influence in Cognitexis, the observer effect in quantum physics unfolds as a captivating illustration. The law highlights prayer's intriguing and unpredictable nature, comparing the Subconscious Emotional Activator (SEA) to a powerful yet capricious tool. The act of observing reveals a chilling truth: Reality can shift dramatically under scrutiny, echoing the mysterious ways in which fervent wishes and emotional surges can twist outcomes into the unexpected.

Much like the erratic nature of particles in a complex experiment, the SEA's influence can change dramatically depending on the focus and feelings it evokes. This reveals the complex interplay of power, where the ability to mold perceptions is intertwined with the lurking threat of unforeseen repercussions. The observer effect underscores the importance of meticulous maneuvering and acute awareness of the underlying dynamics, stressing the vital need for balance and insight.

The interplay of power is strikingly clear in both the research outcomes and the unfolding story of Cognitexis. The observer effect reveals the intense interaction dynamics, serving as a cautionary tale about the intricate and often unforeseen consequences that arise from these connections. This reflects the law's warning that exploiting the SEA can obscure its true purpose, resulting in dire consequences.

Consequently, the observer effect unveils the essence of The Enigmatic Force of Prayer: Navigating the Dualities of Influence, revealing how our interactions and concentrated attention can intricately mold reality in deeply impactful and transformative manners. It highlights the necessity of wielding this power with acute awareness, acknowledging the duality of effects as we traverse the intricate layers of our minds.

- **Example for Example from Medicine:** The Power of Placebo: The placebo effect serves as a captivating example of how belief and mental focus can wield a powerful sway over our perceptions and experiences. When individuals are convinced that they are undergoing a powerful remedy, their bodies can manifest genuine physiological transformations, regardless of whether the treatment holds any actual healing qualities. This phenomenon reveals the intricate ways in which conviction can mold existence, impacting well-being in strikingly significant manners. Research reveals that the power of belief can dramatically alter experiences of pain, depression, and anxiety, with the mind's expectations playing a pivotal role in the outcomes (Benedetti, 2009).[227]

Within the realm of The Enigmatic Force of Prayer: Navigating the Dualities of Influence in Cognitexis, the placebo effect emerges as a fascinating illustration. The law underscores prayer's intriguing and unpredictable nature, comparing the Subconscious Emotional Activator (SEA) to a powerful yet capricious tool. The placebo effect reveals the intricate dance between belief and mental focus, illustrating how perception can twist reality, echoing the profound impact of unseen forces on transformative outcomes.

Similar to the captivating dynamics explored in the law, the placebo effect uncovers the astonishing power of conviction, demonstrating how firmly rooted beliefs can trigger tangible physiological transformations. This reflects the notion that grasping and utilizing the SEA can enable individuals to manipulate their surroundings in deeply impactful ways. Yet, it highlights the complex interplay of this influence, where the manipulation of belief can spiral into unforeseen and dangerous consequences, reflecting the urgent call for heightened awareness stressed in the law.

The placebo effect reveals a captivating principle: a force that must be cautiously navigated. It shows how belief and mental focus can intricately shape our reality, underscoring the necessity of careful navigation to prevent dire outcomes.

The Echoes of the Mind: A Plea for Awareness

The Law unveils a chilling truth: the real force resides not in the mere utterance of words, but in the psychological landscape you forge in the depths of your prayer. Concentration, an intense determination that flirts with fixation, and a meticulously managed emotional landscape are the essential elements to unleash the SEA's true power. Yet, the Law demands an unwavering watchfulness. The hyper-intelligence you might engage with is not a mere genie-fulfilling desire; it is a power as foreign and erratic as a tempest in the cosmos. Wield this power with profound reverence and a keen awareness of the lurking shadows, for the repercussions of a failed ritual or a misdirected feeling are shrouded in enigma, murmured only in the most sinister recesses of Cognitexis.

The concept of visualization reveals the intense influence of focused intention and the depths of the mind's eye. Athletes frequently engage in vivid mental imagery, conjuring scenarios of triumph in their sports to elevate their confidence and refine their results. Dr. Aymeric Guillot's research unveils a captivating insight into the mind's power, revealing that mental practice through visualization can trigger neural pathways akin to those activated during actual physical practice, ultimately amplifying performance and skill acquisition (Guillot & Collet, 2008).[228]

Within the realm of The Echoes of the Mind: A Plea for Awareness within Cognitexis, the idea of visualization emerges as a captivating illustration. The law reveals a haunting reality: true power lies not in the simple expression of words, but in the intricate mental terrain shaped within the shadows of one's supplication. Visualization captures this essence, where the strength of mental imagery and concentrated intention can profoundly influence tangible results.

Similar to the intricate dynamics of the mind, visualization demands unwavering focus, relentless drive, and a carefully curated emotional environment. Athletes who delve into visualization need to harness an intense concentration and profound emotional connection to truly elevate their performance. Yet, the law requires relentless vigilance, understanding that the heightened awareness cultivated through these intense practices is as unpredictable and alien as a storm raging in the universe.

The intricate layers of visualization reveal themselves through both the psychological insights and the core tenets of Cognitexis. Though envisioning success can elevate abilities and mastery, it also harbors the danger of becoming overly fixated, with possible adverse effects if not approached with caution. This reflects the ominous caution that the consequences of a botched ceremony or a misplaced emotion are cloaked in mystery, demanding deep respect and sharp insight.

Consequently, the idea of visualization reveals the essence of The Echoes of the Mind: A Plea for Awareness. It showcases how mental imagery and concentrated intention can unleash significant power while emphasizing the necessity of vigilance and meticulous oversight of one's psychological terrain.

- **Example from Science:** The complexities of obsessive-compulsive disorder (OCD) unveil a captivating link to the profound realms of relentless concentration and steadfast obsession. The mind becomes a battleground, plagued by intrusive thoughts that refuse to fade, driving individuals to perform compulsive rituals in a frantic bid to silence the chaos that envelops them. This scenario highlights the intense effects of focused thinking, showcasing how a misstep can lead to a descent into psychological chaos and a distorted perception of reality. Studies reveal that increased engagement in specific regions of the brain, especially the orbitofrontal cortex and the striatum, plays a crucial role in these phenomena (Stein et al., 2020). Thus, the imperative to carefully traverse the complexities of the mind, as cautioned by the Law, profoundly echoes the clinical understanding of OCD.[229]

Within the narrative of The Echoes of the Mind: A Plea for Awareness within Cognitexis, the complexities of obsessive-compulsive disorder (OCD) unfold in a captivating manner. The law reveals a haunting reality: the true power lies not in the simple act of speaking but in the intricate mental terrain shaped within the shadows of one's devotion. The essence of this condition lies in its unyielding grip, where intrusive thoughts and compulsive behaviors emerge from a deep-seated obsession that refuses to let go.

Similar to the intricate dynamics of the mind explored in various narratives, OCD embodies a focus and resolve that teeter on the edge of obsession. People grappling with OCD find their minds racing in specific areas, revealing how intense, misguided focus can spiral into profound inner conflict and a distorted perception of reality. This resonates with the notion that heightened intellect, cultivated through intense mental exercises, can be as unpredictable and chaotic as a storm raging in the universe.

The intricate layers of focus reveal themselves not only in the research but also in the unfolding story of Cognitexis. While focus and resolve can enable individuals to tap into the Subconscious Emotional Activator (SEA), they can also spiral into obsession and deep psychological ramifications if not handled with caution. This reflects the ominous reminder that the consequences of a botched ritual or a misplaced emotion are cloaked in mystery, demanding deep respect and sharp insight.

Consequently, the intricacies of obsessive-compulsive disorder reveal the essence of The Echoes of the Mind: A Plea for Awareness, showcasing how intense focus and relentless preoccupation can simultaneously elevate and threaten our mental health. It highlights the necessity of carefully tending to one's inner landscape, maintaining a sharp awareness to maneuver through the intricate labyrinth of the mind with caution.

The Cost of Authority: A Journey into Insanity

The Law cautions against the potential unraveling of the mind that may ensue. The relentless intensity, the intricate dance of emotions woven through prayer, can be utterly draining for the human psyche. Those intrepid seekers who delve too far, driven by an insatiable urge to control the depths of the SEA, find themselves spiraling into madness, ensnared by paranoia and delusion. Echoes from the depths can resonate with a deafening clarity; the psyche twists, reshaping reality into a distorted lens, compelling one to tread the perilous path of self-destruction. Heed the murmurs, seeker; they may not belong to you.

Within the complex tapestry of human experience, the delicate interplay of belief and perception unfolds, drawing us into the unsettling depths of psychosis, especially as it intertwines with the revered stories of diverse faiths. This journey compels us to delve into the mind's shadows and question the very fabric of existence. Research indicates that intense spiritual experiences can sometimes lead to episodes of altered perception, characterized by striking delusions and vivid hallucinations (Pierre, 2001). A captivating exploration emerges when delving into the lives of those who, consumed by fervent devotion, begin to exhibit unsettling signs of paranoia and delusion, ultimately requiring psychiatric intervention

(Pietkiewicz et al., 2018). This suggests that deep emotional and mental engagement in spiritual practices can, at times, result in a significant psychological weight.[230]

Within the narrative of The Cost of Authority: A Journey into Insanity within Cognitexis, the convergence of the ethereal and the disturbed creates a gripping exploration. The law warns of the mind's precarious descent, caught in the relentless grip of intensity and the complex interplay of emotions entwined within prayer. The intense spiritual experiences that can occasionally lead to psychosis, as illustrated in the research by Pierre and Pietkiewicz, highlight this concept, showcasing how deep emotional and intellectual engagement can result in a significant psychological weight.

Similar to the cautionary tales shared among the devoted, those consumed by fervent beliefs may find themselves ensnared in a web of paranoia and delusion, ultimately necessitating psychological assistance. This reflects the notion that the unyielding pressure and complex emotional interplay of spiritual pursuits can exhaust the mind, resulting in a warped perception of reality. The haunting reverberations from the abyss pierce through the silence, warping perception, and bending reality into a surreal tapestry reminiscent of the journeys faced by those grappling with the aftermath of profound, unsettling experiences.

The interplay between spiritual authority and manipulation is strikingly clear in the scientific discoveries and the core tenet of Cognitexis. While deep spiritual journeys can unveil extraordinary insights and connections, they may also spiral into mental chaos and a distorted perception of reality if not cautiously navigated. This reflects the ominous reminder that the consequences of a botched ritual or a misplaced emotion can spiral into devastating results.

The intersection of spirituality and psychosis reveals a chilling narrative about the price of authority, illustrating how deep emotional and intellectual engagement in spiritual practices can ignite inspiration while simultaneously threatening our mental stability. It highlights the necessity of adopting a cautious and deliberate stance towards spiritual practices, acknowledging the possibility of deep revelations alongside dangerous outcomes.

- **Example from Literature:** Joseph Conrad's Heart of Darkness delves into the chilling unraveling of the character Kurtz as he spirals deeper into the abyss of his own psyche. Consumed by an unquenchable thirst for dominance and influence in the heart of the African Congo, Kurtz's fervent intensity and unchecked ambition plunge him into the shadowy depths of his mind. His relentless pursuit of control over the territory and its inhabitants' spirals into a dark descent, where paranoia and delusion take hold, leading to a total breakdown of his mental state. Kurtz's last utterance, "The dread!" The dread!" captures the chilling awareness of his impending downfall.[231]

Within the intricate layers of The Cost of Authority: A Journey into Insanity within Cognitexis, one can find a haunting reflection in Joseph Conrad's Heart of Darkness. The law warns of the perilous descent into chaos that can arise from unyielding pressure and the complex interplay of feelings. Kurtz's spiraling journey into insanity, driven by an insatiable hunger for dominance and authority, vividly illustrates this concept, as his mental realm becomes completely depleted and warped.

In a chilling descent, Kurtz plunges into the abyss of his ambition, compelled by an unquenchable desire for dominance. This unyielding tension breeds suspicion and madness, reflecting the notion that whispers from the abyss can reverberate with startling precision, distorting the mind and altering the fabric of existence. Kurtz's descent into chaos highlights the dangerous trajectory of self-destruction that can emerge from the relentless pursuit of mastering the hidden realms of the Subconscious Emotional Activator (SEA).

The interplay of power and manipulation is strikingly clear in both Conrad's tale and the underlying concept of Cognitexis. The pursuit of dominance can propel people to remarkable heights, yet it may also plunge them into deep psychological chaos and a distorted perception of reality if left unchecked. This reflects the ominous caution that the consequences of a botched ceremony or a misplaced emotion can spiral into devastating results.

In Heart of Darkness, Kurtz's tale unveils the dark undercurrents of power and obsession, revealing how an unyielding drive for dominance can erode sanity and spiral into chaos. It highlights the necessity of navigating one's aspirations with caution and awareness, acknowledging the possibility of remarkable successes and dangerous outcomes.

The Hidden Truth: A Cautionary Tale

The law implies that understanding the SEA and its link to hyper-intelligence has remained a well-kept secret, shrouded in mystery throughout the ages. Ancient manuscripts whisper of clandestine rites and the tragic fates of societies that ventured too close to these enigmatic powers. The Law stands as a stark reminder, a chilling testament to the perils of probing too far into the enigmas of the human psyche and the shadowy forces that may lie in wait.

A Cautionary Tale: The Perils of Artificial Intelligence. In the landscape of scientific exploration, the emergence and utilization of artificial intelligence (AI) stands as a striking illustration. Advanced AI systems, especially those utilizing deep learning and neural networks, promise to reveal extraordinary capabilities, allowing machines to tackle intricate challenges, make informed choices, and adapt through data in manners once thought exclusive to human thought processes. Yet, this formidable technology harbors profound dangers lurking beneath its surface. AI's unintended twists and dark turns can spiral into disastrous scenarios, revealing hidden biases, eroding privacy, and even paving the way for autonomous weapons. [232]

Within the narrative of The Hidden Truth: A Cautionary Tale within Cognitexis, the evolution of AI unfolds as a gripping illustration. The law suggests that the grasp of the Subconscious Emotional Activator (SEA) and its connection to heightened intelligence has been a closely guarded secret, enveloped in intrigue across time. The swift evolution of AI technology and the lurking threats tied to it echo the mysterious forces and doomed destinies found in age-old texts.

Similar to the hidden rituals and grim destinies of those who dared to approach these mysterious forces, AI's exploitation or unforeseen repercussions can result in devastating consequences. The law serves as a chilling reminder of the dangers that lurk when one dares to delve too deeply into the mysteries of the human mind and the dark influences that may be lurking just out of sight. The evolution of AI, teeming with both extraordinary possibilities and daunting dangers, highlights the necessity of navigating these formidable technologies with a blend of caution and deep respect.

Thus, the example of AI unveils the principle of The Hidden Truth: A Cautionary Tale, revealing how the quest for hyper-intelligence can simultaneously ignite inspiration and pose a grave threat to our existence. It highlights the necessity of a cautious and deliberate stance towards technological progress, acknowledging the possibility of remarkable breakthroughs alongside ominous repercussions.

- **Example from History:** The tale of the Library of Alexandria unfolds with a haunting resonance. This intriguing hub of intellect was rumored to conceal vast archives of wisdom, featuring ancient scrolls and enigmatic writings on a multitude of topics, some of which allegedly held profound insights and arcane mysteries. The conflagration of the library, whether a mere mishap or a deliberate act, represents the devastating erasure of invaluable wisdom and acts as a chilling reminder of the perils that lie in probing too far into the enigmas of human consciousness and the uncharted realms.[233]

The destruction of the Library of Alexandria serves as a haunting illustration within the narrative of The Hidden Truth: A Cautionary Tale within Cognitexis. The law suggests that the grasp of the Subconscious Emotional Activator (SEA) and its connection to extraordinary intelligence has been a hidden enigma, cloaked in intrigue across time. The disappearance of the Library of Alexandria, with its vast troves of ancient manuscripts and clandestine texts, reflects a concealed reality, hinting that some truths are too deep and perilous to be entirely understood.

Similar to the hidden narratives that hint at secret rituals and the fateful downfalls of those who dared to explore the depths of mysterious influences, the obliteration of the Library of Alexandria stands as a chilling testament to the dangers of delving too deeply into the complexities of the human mind and the dark forces that may lurk just beyond our understanding. The destruction of the library represents a haunting void of deep understanding and the chilling repercussions of pursuing truths that might be too dark to grasp.

The tension between the pursuit of knowledge and its consequences is strikingly clear in both the historical case and the underlying principle of Cognitexis. The quest for knowledge can unveil astonishing revelations and progress, yet it harbors the potential for devastating consequences if navigated without care and respect. This reflects the cautionary tale that the comprehension of the SEA and its connection to heightened intellect demands a deep sense of reverence and vigilance.

Consequently, the destruction of the Library of Alexandria serves as a stark reminder of the principle of The Hidden Truth: A Cautionary Tale. It illustrates how the quest for concealed wisdom and exploration of uncharted territories can ignite inspiration while simultaneously posing grave risks. It highlights the necessity of adopting a cautious and thoughtful stance when delving into the mysteries of the human mind and the lurking influences that may be concealed beneath the surface.

In Conclusion

The Law of Subconscious Emotional Activator unveils a haunting notion that resides in the recesses of the mind, a murmur in the void that draws you into an exploration of the unexplored corners of your own consciousness. The allure of choices reveals a portal to infinite potential, where the control of existence hangs precariously above a chasm of uncertainty. Yet, heed the foreboding warning that looms over this threshold: the constant peril of self-ruin and the awakening of powers that may spiral into realms far beyond the reach of conventional understanding.

Through the prism of the human psyche, the written word, empirical inquiry, and the annals of time, we have caught a glimpse of the complex and frequently treacherous consequences of summoning the SEA. The power to shape reality is both magnificent and profoundly disturbing, requiring profound mindfulness and unwavering vigilance. The whispers of the soul, the odyssey through Cognitexis, is a path reserved for the brave.

Are you, intrepid seeker, poised at the edge of obscured realities, prepared to dive into the intricate maze of your own consciousness? Your choice is yours to make, yet proceed with caution: the journey to power is fraught with peril, and the truths whispered by the depths may be cloaked in uncertainty. To traverse this perilous landscape demands a keen mind, unwavering determination, and a deep respect for the hidden forces that shape our destinies.

As you move ahead, tread carefully, for the whispers of the spirit hold both the promise of enlightenment and the lurking threat of madness. Every move you make in this intricate journey may either shed light on deep truths or drag you into the murky depths of your most haunting anxieties. The exploration of the shadowy recesses of the mind unfolds as a captivating plunge, where the distinction between what is real and what is imagined intertwines in a mysterious ballet.

Will you have the courage to delve into the mysteries concealed in the soul's whispers? The path lies ahead, cloaked in enigma and teeming with peril, yet the insights gained may transcend the boundaries of comprehension. The decision rests with you, wanderer—step into the domain of Cognitexis and unveil the truths hidden in the darkness.

3. The Shadowy Dance: Repulsive Thoughts and the Mind's Defenses

(The Law of Repulsive Thought Processes)

Within the intricate maze of Cognitexis lies a hidden dread—the Law of Repulsive Thought Processes. The law unveils a gripping and unsettling truth: even the most innocuous thoughts can harbor the potential for conflict. Envision Cognitexis as an expansive chamber where the atmosphere is thick with swirling currents of ideas and reflections. In the realm of the mind, the Law of Repulsive Thought Processes reveals a chilling truth: While these waves may seem innocuous on their own, they can morph into lethal poison when they collide with discordant frequencies. The consequences of such clashes are nothing short of catastrophic.

The Disturbing Confrontation

Just as conflicting energies push away from each other, thoughts that resonate at opposing frequencies generate a violent confrontation—a destructive force that undermines the entire mental framework. Imagine two powerful currents of thought— one steeped in trepidation, the other brimming with conviction— colliding with an intensity that shakes the very foundations of the mind. The resulting dissonance can be paralyzing, plunging the mind into a labyrinth of confusion and uncertainty.

Reflect on how conflicting thoughts shape choices. Leon Festinger introduced the unsettling nature of cognitive dissonance, which reveals the dark undercurrents of turmoil created by clashing thoughts. When a person finds themselves caught in a web of conflicting beliefs and actions, tension gnaws at their mind, stirring a deep sense of unease. This unease emerges from the battle of opposing thoughts swirling in the mind, creating a chaotic energy that erodes mental clarity and the ability to make sound choices.

In moments when an individual faces a choice between two equally enticing yet conflicting paths, the ensuing mental turmoil can spiral into profound stress and paralyzing uncertainty. Research utilizing neuroimaging techniques has revealed that this internal struggle triggers brain regions linked to managing emotions and resolving conflicts, including the anterior cingulate cortex and the prefrontal cortex (Van Veen et al., 2009). The ensuing psychological chaos can be immobilizing, plunging one into a labyrinth of doubt and ambiguity.[234]

Within the unsettling dynamics of The Disturbing Confrontation in Cognitexis, the influence of conflicting beliefs on choices creates a gripping narrative. The principle indicates that clashing thoughts, vibrating at discordant frequencies, ignite a tumultuous clash, unleashing a chaotic energy that threatens to dismantle the very structure of the mind. The tension of opposing thoughts creates a haunting unease, unraveling the mind and plunging it into a state of turmoil.

The mind becomes a battleground, where two formidable forces clash—one laced with fear, the other pulsating with unwavering belief. This tumultuous encounter reverberates through the psyche, unsettling everything in its path. The ensuing discord can be immobilizing, thrusting the person into a maze of bewilderment and doubt, echoing the dire outcomes cautioned by the Law of Repulsive Thought Processes.

The interplay of conflicting ideas is strikingly clear in the neuroscientific discoveries and the unfolding story of Cognitexis. Though solitary musings might appear harmless, their clash with jarring elements can spiral into profound mental distress. This reflects the notion that disturbing mental patterns can transform into a dangerous toxin, highlighting the need for a vigilant and thoughtful strategy in navigating the clash of ideas within one's psyche.

Consequently, cognitive dissonance's unsettling nature reveals the clash of opposing thoughts, showcasing how this turmoil can destabilize the mind and evoke deep psychological unease. It highlights the critical need to identify and address these inner struggles to preserve one's mental health and maneuver through the intricate labyrinth of thoughts.

The Intricacies of Mind

The Law parallels the unsettling dynamics of thoughts with the seemingly innocuous mingling of chemicals that can unexpectedly yield a lethal poison. This implies that the core of our thinking, much like the fabric of reality, is governed by essential principles of connection. The intricate interplay of brain chemistry may hold the key, where specific thought-wave combinations unleash chaotic responses within the neural pathways.

Examining the theory related to the influence of chemical messengers on psychological well-being shows that the complex dance of neurotransmitters within the mind reveals how subtle chemical exchanges can lead to profound consequences for one's mental well-being. Neurotransmitters act as unseen messengers, weaving intricate connections between nerve cells and subtly influencing our emotions, thoughts, and actions in ways we often overlook. Disruptions in the delicate balance of neurotransmitters can unravel the mind, giving rise to a spectrum of mental health challenges, including the shadows of depression, the grip of anxiety, and the complexities of schizophrenia.

Consider this: Serotonin acts as a crucial messenger in the brain, influencing our emotions, cravings, and rest patterns. Decreased serotonin levels frequently correlate with feelings of despair and heightened anxiety, creating a shadowy backdrop for the mind's turmoil. In a world where the mind's intricate pathways intertwine with our deepest desires, the role of dopamine emerges as a pivotal player. Its delicate balance holds the key to understanding the shadows of conditions such as schizophrenia and addiction, revealing the fine line between reward and chaos. The intricate interplay of these substances is crucial for preserving psychological stability, and any disturbances can lead to significant shifts in a person's mental landscape.[235]

Within the labyrinth of Cognitexis, the influence of neurotransmitters on mental health unveils a captivating narrative. The intricate interplay of thoughts mirrors the disquieting fusion of elements, where what appears harmless can suddenly transform into something dangerously toxic. This suggests that the essence of our thoughts, akin to the intricate weave of existence, is dictated by fundamental laws of interrelation.

The delicate dance of neurotransmitters in the brain reflects the tangled web of thought waves swirling within the mind. Just as particular blends of neurotransmitters can trigger tumultuous reactions within the brain's intricate networks, certain thought patterns can spiral into unforeseen and possibly dangerous psychological states. The intricate interplay of neurotransmitters is crucial for preserving mental equilibrium, just as the meticulous control of thought waves is vital to averting psychological turmoil.

Thus, the example of neurotransmitters unveils the complexities of the mind, illustrating how the delicate dance of brain chemistry can dramatically influence mental well-being. It highlights the necessity of unraveling and controlling these complex ties to preserve psychological health and maneuver through the labyrinth of the mind.

The Universality of Repulsion

This law reveals that the phenomenon of repulsion transcends mere clashes between disparate personalities; it is a pervasive force that operates within the confines of a single mind itself. Observe the intense battle raging within, where fear and faith clash violently, each vying for supremacy in the mind. These opposing forces are locked in a relentless struggle, refusing to share the same mental realm; one must inevitably rise to power, leaving the other in a state of temporary defeat.

A reflection from the realm of psychology: The Struggle Between Anxiety and Self-Assurance. The harrowing struggle between anxiety and self-confidence serves as a haunting reflection of the pervasive repulsion that resides within the human psyche. Anxiety emerges as a formidable, dread-laden specter, capable of eroding one's confidence and distorting the very essence of self-worth. On the other hand, self-confidence emerges as a formidable, belief-driven energy, enabling one to confront adversities and chase aspirations with unwavering resolve. The clash of these opposing forces unfolds in a ceaseless battle within the mind, each one striving for dominance.

Studies reveal that elevated anxiety can profoundly undermine self-assurance, plunging individuals into a paralyzing abyss of doubt and uncertainty. On the other hand, when self-assurance is fortified, it can serve to alleviate anxiety, enabling individuals to confront their fears with greater efficacy. This tumultuous struggle unveils the relentless tension within a solitary psyche, where dread and belief engage in a fierce battle, each refusing to yield to the other in a fragile coexistence.[236]

Within the realm of The Universality of Repulsion in Cognitexis, the struggle between anxiety and self-assurance emerges as a haunting illustration. The law unveils a chilling truth: The phenomenon of repulsion extends beyond the mere conflicts of opposing souls; it is a haunting force that dwells within the very recesses of one's own psyche. The fierce struggle between anxiety and self-confidence embodies this principle, as these conflicting forces clash for dominance within the psyche.

Anxiety and self-confidence engage in a fierce duel in a shadowy arena of the mind, each determined to dominate the other, neither willing to coexist within the same mental landscape. As anxiety surges, it can engulf self-assurance, plunging the individual into a momentary abyss of despair. In stark contrast, when self-confidence is fortified, it becomes a formidable force against the encroaching shadows of anxiety, empowering the individual to traverse the labyrinth of challenges with a newfound resilience.

The interplay of these opposing forces is starkly revealed in both the psychological revelations and the unfolding tale of Cognitexis. Though anxiety and self-confidence may appear harmless in isolation, their collision can unleash profound psychological chaos. This reflects the notion that abhorrent mentalities can transform into a deadly toxin, demanding a vigilant and contemplative strategy for navigating these inner struggles.

In this way, the interplay of anxiety and self-confidence reveals a deeper truth about the human psyche, illustrating how the collision of conflicting forces can yield unsettling psychological ramifications. It highlights the necessity of acknowledging and grappling with this inner turmoil to preserve one's mental equilibrium and traverse the intricate labyrinth of the psyche.

The Harmful Consequences of Disturbing Confrontations

The Law of Repulsive Thought Processes carries with it a weight of inevitable repercussions. When these conflicts arise within Cognitexis, they can profoundly disrupt the psyche:

a. **Cognitive Dissonance:** This unsettling tension emerges when opposing beliefs or ideas clash within the psyche. The disturbing collision of these thoughts breeds palpable tension, obstructing clarity and the ability to make sound decisions. Picture yourself ensnared in a mental tug-of-war, with relentless thoughts clashing over the merits and dangers of a perilous choice. The clash of thoughts can ensnare you, rendering you motionless, trapped in a web of indecision.

- **Example from Psychology – The Dynamics of Imposter Syndrome:** The unsettling reality of imposter syndrome serves as a gripping illustration of the Law of Repulsive Thought Processes and the detrimental effects of unsettling confrontations. Imposter syndrome grips those who have reached great heights, leaving them haunted by relentless self-doubt and a chilling fear of being unmasked as impostors, even in the face of undeniable achievements. This condition emerges from the intense struggle within, where self-doubt battles against the need for external approval, creating a profound sense of psychological turmoil and unease.

A quintessential scenario features individuals in scholarly or career environments who perpetually grapple with feelings of inadequacy regardless of their achievements and harbor a deep-seated dread of being unmasked as frauds. This inner turmoil can spiral into overwhelming anxiety, relentless stress, and a haunting sense of diminished self-worth. The battle within—between crippling self-doubt and the glaring signs of achievement—fuels a deep-seated turmoil that can erode one's mental fortitude and cloud judgment.[237]

Within the framework of the Law of Repulsive Thought Processes in Cognitexis, the experience of imposter syndrome emerges as a striking illustration. The unsettling clash of conflicting beliefs or ideas within the mind can create a gripping tension that threatens to unravel one's mental equilibrium. The sensation of being an imposter vividly illustrates this concept, as the battle of opposing thoughts within the mind generates an intense atmosphere, hindering clarity and the capacity to make wise choices.

The internal battle reminiscent of a gripping narrative, imposter syndrome manifests as a ceaseless conflict within the mind, where thoughts collide over self-worth and abilities, resulting in profound psychological unease. This reflects the notion that disturbing mental patterns can provoke a clash, resulting in a chilling sense of immobility and uncertainty. The illustration of imposter syndrome reveals how conflicting thoughts can ensnare individuals, leaving them paralyzed and ensnared in a labyrinth of self-doubt and anxiety.

The clash of ideas reveals itself in the intricate psychological insights and the unfolding story of Cognitexis. Though solitary musings might appear harmless, their clash with jarring vibrations can spiral into deep psychological chaos. This highlights the critical need to identify and address these tensions to safeguard mental health and maneuver through the intricate labyrinth of the psyche.

The experience of imposter syndrome reveals the unsettling dynamics of the mind. It showcases how the battle between opposing thoughts can unravel one's sense of self and plunge one into deep internal turmoil. It highlights the necessity of a vigilant and deliberate strategy in navigating one's inner thoughts, acknowledging the possibility of both deep revelations and dangerous outcomes.

b. **Stuck in a Web of Contemplation:** The relentless onslaught of contradictory ideas can trap one in a cycle of overthinking. The mind spirals into a labyrinth of conflicting perspectives, paralyzed by the tension of indecision. Imagine the struggle of crafting a paper, where each sentence is relentlessly scrutinized by an inner voice that thrives on doubt and criticism. The battle can ensnare you in a web of confusion, leaving you paralyzed and stagnant in your journey.

- **Example from Psychology – Analysis Paralysis:** The intricate dance of overthinking reveals a captivating struggle, ensnaring one in a labyrinth of thoughts and decisions. Analysis paralysis creeps in when someone becomes ensnared in a web of overthinking and relentless scrutiny, leaving them trapped in a cycle where decision-making and action become elusive shadows. This state frequently emerges from the unyielding barrage of conflicting thoughts and the strain of uncertainty, resulting in a chilling mental standstill.

A typical instance of being trapped in indecision can be seen in situations where one must navigate the complexities of selecting from various job offers. A person could find themselves ensnared in a web of choices, meticulously analyzing each facet and possible consequence, caught in a relentless cycle of doubt and intrigue. This relentless spiral of thought ensnares them, leaving them ensconced in a web of doubt, immobilizing their capacity to choose a path and advance.[238]

Within the intricate maze of Stuck in a Web of Contemplation in Cognitexis, the gripping experience of analysis paralysis unfolds as a captivating illustration. The relentless barrage of conflicting thoughts can ensnare the mind, spiraling into a labyrinth of overanalysis that ultimately paralyzes decision-making. The concept of analysis paralysis vividly illustrates this principle, where the relentless scrutiny of choices and consequences can trap one in a web of indecision and stagnation.

The battle within the mind mirrors a complex narrative, where thoughts twist and turn through a maze of opposing viewpoints, ensnared by the gripping hold of uncertainty. The scenario of someone obsessively analyzing job offers illustrates how the battle of conflicting thoughts can ensnare a person, rendering them paralyzed and caught in a tangled web of uncertainty. This reflects the notion that disturbing mental patterns can provoke a fierce clash, resulting in a state of psychological immobility and stagnation.

The clash of inner turmoil is strikingly apparent in both the psychological insights and the unfolding story of Cognitexis. Though solitary musings might appear harmless, their clash with jarring elements can spiral into deep psychological chaos. This highlights the critical need to identify and address these tensions to preserve psychological health and maneuver through the intricate labyrinth of the psyche.

Consequently, the intricacies of analysis paralysis reveal the unsettling nature of being ensnared in a labyrinth of thoughts, showcasing how the collision of opposing ideas can spiral into profound internal turmoil and mental stagnation. It highlights the necessity of a vigilant and introspective strategy in navigating one's inner thoughts, acknowledging the possibility of both deep revelations and dangerous outcomes.

c. **Emotional Turmoil:** Disturbing confrontations can ignite profound emotional reactions. Imagine the intense struggle between dread and exhilaration—a confrontation that can render an individual immobilized or engulfed in chaos. Maybe an exhilarating chance has come your way, yet the shadows of uncertainty murmur unsettling thoughts in your mind. The inner chaos can obscure the thrill of seizing the moment.

- **Example from Psychology – The Yerkes-Dodson Law:** The Yerkes-Dodson Law illustrates how disturbing encounters can trigger intense emotional responses. This intriguing concept suggests that there exists a perfect balance of excitement for achieving peak performance: insufficient excitation may result in a lack of drive. In contrast, excessive excitation can spiral into crippling anxiety, ultimately hindering success. The delicate interplay between excitement and execution unfolds like a suspenseful narrative, revealing that while a touch of stimulation can elevate one's abilities, an overwhelming surge can lead to a dramatic downfall.

  Imagine an individual standing on the brink of a public presentation, the weight of anticipation hanging in the air.

The thrilling chance to reveal their skills can be clouded by a gripping sense of fear and unease about facing an audience. The clash of exhilaration and dread can spiral into a whirlwind of emotions, risking paralysis or a descent into disorderly actions. The Yerkes-Dodson Law reveals a captivating truth: a certain degree of arousal can enhance performance, yet when anxiety spirals out of control, it can sabotage even the most capable individuals.[239]

Amidst the swirling chaos of Emotional Turmoil within Cognitexis, the Yerkes-Dodson Law emerges as a captivating illustration. The rules indicate that unsettling encounters can spark deep emotional responses, creating a tension between fear and excitement. The Yerkes-Dodson Law reveals a captivating dynamic, showcasing how different arousal degrees can dramatically influence performance and emotional equilibrium.

The gripping tension illustrated in the law reveals the delicate equilibrium between stimulation and achievement. When an electrifying opportunity arises, the whispers of doubt can stir unsettling thoughts, weaving a tapestry of inner turmoil that clouds the excitement of embracing the moment. The scenario of an individual preparing for a public presentation highlights the intense clash between exhilaration and dread, creating a psychological storm that could disrupt their performance.

The contrasting layers of emotional reactions are strikingly apparent in both the psychological insights and the unfolding story of Cognitexis. While a certain level of excitement can boost performance and drive, too much intensity can spiral into anxiety and diminish effectiveness. This reflects the notion that unsettling encounters can stir deep emotional unrest, highlighting the need for a thoughtful and deliberate strategy in navigating emotional responses.

Thus, the Yerkes-Dodson Law unveils the intricate dance of Emotional Turmoil, revealing how the delicate balance between arousal and performance can spiral into profound emotional and psychological repercussions. It highlights the crucial need to identify and control emotional reactions to maneuver through the intricate labyrinth of the psyche and grasp opportunities with precision.

The Strength of Focused Awareness

Thankfully, the Principle of Aversion in Thought Patterns does not condemn us to a state of psychological turmoil. It presents a flicker of possibility through the lens of Directed Attention. This notion surfaces as a pivotal tactic in the psychological struggle against abhorrent confrontations. Envision Cognitexis as an expansive arena, resonating with the tumult of myriad thought waves battling for supremacy. Directed Attention acts as the maestro's wand, enabling us to deliberately hone in on a particular thought wave, elevating it to the center of our cognitive performance.

The Craft of Elevation

By deliberately directing our focus toward a specific thought, we can enhance its resonance. Consider the mechanics behind this amplification:

a. **Neural Reinforcement:** Concentrating on a particular thought intensifies the neural connections tied to it. Envision a winding trail cutting through a sea of swaying blades, each whispering secrets of the mind. The deeper you delve into that journey, the sharper and more distinct it reveals itself to be. In a parallel manner, concentrating on a particular thought fortifies the neural connections that underpin it, enabling it to echo with greater intensity within Cognitexis.

- **Example from Science – Hebbian Learning in Neuroscience:** Delve into the concept of Hebbian learning in neuroscience, a fascinating exploration of connections and the complex interplay of ideas and experiences. Hebb's principle often encapsulated in the phrase "cells that fire together, wire together," implies that when neurons synchronize their activity, they create more robust connections. This suggests that prolonged focus on a specific idea or experience strengthens the neural connections linked to it (Hebb, 1949). This enhancement intensifies the power and speed of neural connections, making the concept stand out vividly in the mind's eye.[240]

Within the narrative of The Hidden Truth: A Cautionary Tale in Cognitexis, the concept of Hebbian learning emerges as a fascinating element. The law suggests that the grasp of the Subconscious Emotional Activator (SEA) and its connection to heightened intelligence has been a closely guarded secret, cloaked in an enigma over time. Hebbian learning reveals the complex and frequently concealed mechanisms that shape our mental and emotional landscapes.

Echoing the secretive rituals and fateful tales found in forgotten texts, Hebbian Learning uncovers the deep and often hidden forces that mold our psychological terrain. By fixating on a specific thought or experience, we intensify the neural connections tied to it, elevating its significance within our mental landscape. This reflects the notion that exploring the mysteries of the psyche can unveil astonishing revelations while also inviting dangerous outcomes.

The interplay between concentrated awareness and neural conditioning unfolds intriguingly in the scientific discoveries and the story of Cognitexis. As the intricate web of our thoughts evolves, the sharpening of neural connections can illuminate our minds, revealing both brilliance and peril. It serves as a chilling reminder of how easily one thought can overshadow the rest, lurking in the shadows of our consciousness. This reflects the cautionary tale that comprehending the SEA and its connection to heightened intellect requires deep reverence and acute awareness.

Thus, the concept of Hebbian learning unveils the principle of The Hidden Truth: A Cautionary Tale. It illustrates how a concentrated focus on particular thoughts can trigger profound cognitive enhancement while simultaneously warning of the lurking dangers that accompany such intense mental immersion. It highlights the necessity of adopting a cautious and thoughtful stance when delving into the mysteries of the human mind and the lurking influences that may be concealed beneath the surface.

b. **Attentional Spotlight:** Our focus operates as a piercing beam, casting light on a singular thought wave while shrouding the others in shadow. By honing our focus, we can silence the cacophony of discord and concentrate on the idea we wish to dominate. This enables it to claim a more significant portion of our mental landscape, thereby wielding a more profound impact on our entire cognitive framework.

- **Example from Psychology – The Concept of Selective Attention:** The idea of selective attention in psychology unveils a fascinating glimpse into the workings of our mental focus. Selective attention is the intriguing process where the mind zeroes in on a particular piece of information, deliberately tuning out the surrounding noise and distractions. This mental prowess enables individuals to hone in on crucial details while dismissing distractions, illuminating a singular stream of thought and cloaking others in obscurity.

A timeless illustration of focused perception is the phenomenon known as the "cocktail party effect." Amidst the chaos of a bustling room, one can hone in on a solitary conversation, skillfully drowning out the cacophony surrounding them. The capacity to focus on a specific stimulus while surrounded by a whirlwind of distractions reveals the profound influence of selective attention on how we process information.[241]

Within the intricate web of Cognitexis, the notion of selective attention emerges as a captivating focal point, drawing the mind into its depths. The law indicates that our attention functions like a sharp spotlight, illuminating one thought while leaving the rest cloaked in darkness. Selective attention embodies this concept, allowing individuals to hone in on crucial details while dismissing the noise around them.

Like how a focused lens sharpens a single image amidst chaos, selective attention enables the mind to drown out the noise and hone in on a particular thought. The cocktail party effect phenomenon reveals how one can hone in on a singular dialogue, skillfully drowning out the chaos that surrounds them. This reflects the idea that by sharpening our attention, we can allow a specific thought to take control of our minds, influencing our perception in a deeper and more significant way.

The interplay between concentration and diversion is strikingly clear in the psychological insights and the unfolding story of Cognitexis. Amidst the relentless onslaught of stimuli that flood our minds, a powerful mechanism enables us to hone in on specific information, elevating its significance in our mental landscape. This highlights the crucial need to acknowledge and utilize concentrated focus to maneuver through the intricate labyrinth of the psyche and elevate mental capabilities.

In this intricate dance of the mind, the notion of selective attention reveals the power of the Attentional Spotlight, showcasing how a calculated focus on particular thoughts can unlock profound cognitive depth and insight.

c.   **Emotional Anchoring:** By linking a thought wave to a positive emotion, we can amplify its impact. Envision a helium balloon tethered to a thought—the emotional bond elevates it, amplifying its presence in the intricate terrain of the mind. By intertwining a sought-after notion with emotions of assurance, elation, or resolve, we can fortify it to dominate the adverse forces of a jarring confrontation.

Example from Psychology – The Power of Positive Affirmations: The notion of positive affirmations in psychology serves as a fascinating illustration of emotional grounding. Repetitive declarations echo in mind, crafting a landscape where positivity thrives, and the shadows of doubt are kept at bay, shaping behaviors and thoughts into something more desirable. By connecting these affirmations to uplifting feelings, people can enhance their influence, reminiscent of a helium balloon anchored to a fleeting idea. This intense connection amplifies the validation, rendering it more striking and persuasive in the psyche.

Studies reveal that consistently engaging in positive affirmations can elevate self-esteem, diminish stress, and enhance overall well-being. When people connect affirmations with sensations of confidence, joy, or determination, these feelings amplify the power of the affirmations, creating a stronger defense against negative thoughts and self-doubt (Creswell et al., 2013).[242]

Within the intricate web of Emotional Anchoring in Cognitexis, the notion of positive affirmations emerges as a captivating illustration. The principle indicates that by connecting a thought wave to an uplifting feeling, we can amplify its effect. Positive affirmations embody this concept, intertwining affirmations with uplifting emotions to enhance their impact and sway within the psyche.

Similar to a helium balloon anchored to a fleeting idea, positive affirmations gain strength through the emotional connection, amplifying their presence and influence. The illustration of people engaging in positive affirmations reveals how linking these declarations with feelings of confidence, joy, or determination can shield them from the shadows of negativity and self-doubt. This reflects the idea that blending a coveted concept with uplifting feelings can overpower negative influences and forge a stronger psychological foundation.

The interplay between thought and emotion unfolds dramatically in the psychological revelations and the storyline of Cognitexis. Though solitary thoughts might seem feeble at first, intertwining them with uplifting emotions can dramatically sharpen their focus and influence. This highlights the necessity of understanding and utilizing emotional anchoring to maneuver through the intricacies of the psyche and improve mental acuity.

Consequently, positive affirmations reveal the intriguing principle of Emotional Anchoring, showcasing how intentionally connecting thoughts to uplifting emotions can yield profound cognitive and psychological advantages. They highlight the necessity of a meticulous and thoughtful strategy for navigating emotions, acknowledging the possibility of significant mental and emotional enhancements.

Conclusion: The Enigmatic Waltz of Cognitexis

The Shadowy Dance within Cognitexis reveals the profound and often perilous intricacies of disquieting psychological realms. As we navigate this intricate psychological landscape, we face the unsettling truth that even the purest of thoughts may harbor the potential for chaos. The Law of Repulsive Thought Processes unveils the complex skirmishes that rage within the psyche, laying bare the capacity for cognitive dissonance, emotional turmoil, and an oppressive maze of introspection.

In the depths of turmoil, a glimmer of possibility surfaces, guided by the enigmatic force of focused intent. This mysterious force provides a means to traverse the chaos, enabling us to enhance specific streams of consciousness, strengthen mental connections, and anchor them to positive emotions. This deliberate orchestration transforms the tumultuous realm of Cognitexis into a unified tapestry of contemplation.

The journey toward mental dominance is riddled with challenges, demanding relentless commitment and unwavering toil. Through deep reflection and heightened consciousness, the intricate shaping of one's internal realm becomes essential, a skill honed to navigate the stormy seas of clashing thoughts. By refining these abilities, we can steer our awareness into the realms of clarity, imagination, and a deep-seated sense of meaning.

Ultimately, the Shadowy Dance unveils the complex dimensions of our being, mirroring our vulnerability and the deep resilience that arises from the abyss of hopelessness. It stands as an ominous reminder that by meticulously traversing our thoughts and examining the dark corners of our psyche, we can shield our innermost selves from the tumultuous forces that lie hidden beneath the surface. In the shadows of our consciousness, where turmoil often reigns, we can forge our thoughts into an impenetrable bastion of strength and equilibrium.

Venture into the shadows, intrepid seeker. The eerie strains of contemplation guide us toward disquieting truths and a deeper understanding of our very being. The odyssey through Cognitexis is laden with danger and potential, a maze where only the watchful and steadfast may find triumph. Will you embrace the enigmatic rhythm of the Shadowy Dance and unveil the concealed realities lurking in the depths of your consciousness?

ODYSSEY OF THE INTELLECT - CONQUERING THE MINOTAUR OF TRUTH

§❧ §❧ §❧

The formidable labyrinthine passageways of Cognitexis unfolded before you; you embarked on a journey into this vast and enigmatic realm. Armed with the flickering glow of insight from part two, you embark on a solitary quest, a journey through the realms of thought. The path forward was fraught with danger; it twisted and turned like a cosmic maze, where whispers of hidden truths echoed, and darkness danced around every corner. Your mission is to navigate through the depths of the maze, where the fearsome Guardian of Secrets awaits, a mythical beast shrouded in enigma and power.

Peril lurked at every turn along the path. Whispers of deception surrounded you, shadows of your own biases that twisted the truth of reality. Unbridled passion forged a haunting atmosphere that clouds clarity and demands unwavering vigilance. Yet, you pressed on, brandishing the map of Cognitexis—a map you had forged and honed through your own trials.

Amidst these winding corridors, you came to recognize the steadfast edge of reason from the capricious spark of feeling. You navigated the chaotic web of your mind, distinguishing the clear truths from the seductive echoes of unproven yearnings. Every stride was a battle, a duel with your own boundaries, a declaration of your relentless quest for enlightenment.

In the heart of the labyrinth stood the Minotaur of Truth, poised for your arrival. To others, this creature was an enigma, but to you, it was a challenge that tested the core of your faith in your own abilities. These were not mere puzzles but a trial of the spirit, forcing one to face the flaws in reasoning, gaps in understanding, and biases that colored their view of what exists.

The confrontation was intense. You battled with enigmas, clashed with conflicting truths, and maneuvered through the perilous landscape of doubt. Yet, with each trial faced, your mind sharpened, becoming more formidable and astute. You have come to accept uncertainty not as a flaw but as a powerful force driving you toward greater insight.

You unraveled the enigma of the Minotaur with determination and cunning. The formidable adversary disappeared into a shimmering stream of knowledge. Instead of a fabric crafted from isolated views, logical deductions, and a firm understanding of nature, this was a tapestry woven from diverse perspectives, sensible conclusions, and our ever-evolving grasp of the universe.

You emerged changed, unrecognizable to those who knew you, for you were no longer the brave soul who ventured into the depths of the maze. You have been transformed into a remarkable being, a living testament to the extraordinary potential that emerges when one faces one's inner struggles and relentlessly seeks the ultimate truth. You discovered truths, yet more crucially, you forged the tool of exploration—a discerning intellect—that lies at the core of the ADAM-GENE quest.

Once shrouded in shadows and doubt, the labyrinth now radiated a newfound allure. You recognized that the real adventure was not a straightforward quest to a single endpoint but an ongoing odyssey, a familiarization with the constantly shifting Minotaur of Truth.

And so, you turned your gaze back towards the labyrinth, prepared to embark on countless more journeys of the mind, forever a seeker in the vast expanse of human understanding.

FOURTH BOOK:
THE SUPREMACY OF SELECTIVE AWARENESS

ɞɞɞ

Whispers of the Soul – A New Symphony of Being

Congratulations, intrepid explorer! You have successfully navigated the intricate pathways of "The Cognitexis Enigma," emerging with a deeper understanding of your own intellect and the vast potential it holds. Your journey through the labyrinth of thought has equipped you with the tools to master your inner world, and now, you stand on the threshold of a new adventure.

As you prepare to embark on the next chapter, "The Supremacy of Selective Awareness," know that you are armed with the power you have acquired. This book will guide you in harnessing the transformative power of selective awareness, a multifaceted gem that will illuminate your path to peak performance and success.

In this new symphony of being, you will explore the resonance of a determined mind, learning to define and master the art of selective focus. You will delve into the dance of concentration, balancing duration and intensity, and go beyond mere concentration to achieve the piercing focus of disciplined perception. You will uncover the sources of power that can ignite selective awareness and learn to guard against the kryptonite of lost focus.

The transformative power of selective awareness will reveal itself as a multifaceted powerhouse, enabling you to conduct the orchestra within your mind for peak performance. You will learn to see through the veil with focused attention, channel knowledge for peak performance, and sculpt your reality through autosuggestion and focused intention. The power of purpose will conserve your energy and fuel your actions, attracting opportunities and fueling your success.

As you harness selective awareness, you will unlock the gateway to the law of harmonious attraction. You will design your definite purpose, supercharge your awareness with intellectual synergy, and fuel it with unwavering conviction. You will learn the power of organized individual endeavor, self-discipline, and creative vision, sharpening your thinking and clearing your path. Learning from defeat will fuel your unstoppable growth, and the spark within will harness inspiration for peak performance and unbounded potential.

You will explore the multifaceted aspects of education, purpose, and leadership, understanding the role of education in planting the seeds of selective awareness. You will cultivate definiteness of purpose, embark on the thrilling hunt for your life's mission, and cultivate the symphony of leadership.

Life specialization will fuel your selective awareness, guiding you on the path to mastery and the power of united expertise. You will journey to your niche, climb the ladder of specialization, and evolve through selective awareness, weaving the tapestry of benefits for your destiny.

Disciplined devotion will shape your reality with prayer and love, unveiling the hidden power of prayer as a portal to perception and reality. Love's journey of discovery through insight and focus will take you beyond the veil.

Finally, you will learn to shape the collective mind and build a better world, harnessing awareness to conquer economic challenges and forging unity from the ashes. You will unite for prosperity, learn lessons from economic challenges and global cooperation, and heed a call to collective harmony.

Prepare yourself for this new symphony of being. With the power of selective awareness, you are ready to shape your reality, achieve peak performance, and contribute to a better world. The journey continues, and the possibilities are limitless.

REFERENCES

[1] https://www.bible.com/bible/compare/EPH.2.8-9

[2] The Role of the Amygdala in Value-Based Learning https://www.jneurosci.org/content/37/28/6601?form=MG0AV3

[3] What is the role of dopamine in reward: hedonic impact, reward learning, or incentive salience? https://www.sciencedirect.com/science/article/abs/pii/S016501739800 0198

[4] Theories of Selective Attention in Psychology https://www.simplypsychology.org/attention-models.html?form=MG0AV3

[5] The Influences of Emotion on Learning and Memory https://www.frontiersin.org/journals/psychology/articles/10.3389/fpsyg .2017.01454/full?form=MG0AV3

[6] Effects of Directed Attention on Subsequent Processing of Emotions: Increased Attention to Unpleasant Pictures Occurs in the Late Positive Potential https://www.frontiersin.org/journals/psychology/articles/10.3389/fpsyg .2018.01127/full?form=MG0AV3

[7] Physiology and Neurobiology of Stress and Adaptation: Central Role of the Brain https://journals.physiology.org/doi/full/10.1152/physrev.00041.2006

[8] Emotional intelligence: Theory, findings, and implications. https://psycnet.apa.org/record/2004-18872-002

[9] Contributions of the amygdala to emotion processing: from animal models to human behavior https://pubmed.ncbi.nlm.nih.gov/16242399/

[10] References (Adopted from Microsoft Bing AI): Bandura, A. (1997). Self-efficacy: The exercise of control. W.H. Freeman; Schunk, D. H., & DiBenedetto, M. K. (2020). Motivation and social cognitive theory. Contemporary Educational Psychology, 61, 101861.

[11] References (Adopted from Microsoft Copilot AI): Dweck, C. S. (2006). Mindset: The New Psychology of Success. Random House; Dweck, C. S. (2016). Mindsets: The Power of Believing That You Can Improve. In

World-changing Reflections on the Power of Working on Purpose (pp. 117-126). Routledge.

[12] References (adopted from Microsoft Copilot AI): Surowiecki, J. (2005). The Wisdom of Crowds. Anchor Books; Page, S. E. (2007). The Difference: How the Power of Diversity Creates Better Groups, Firms, Schools, and Societies. Princeton University Press.

[13] References (Adopted for Microsoft Copilot AI): Johnson, D. W., & Johnson, F. P. (2009). Joining Together: Group Theory and Group Skills. Pearson; Salas, E., Sims, D. E., & Burke, C. S. (2005). Is there a "big five" in teamwork? Small Group Research, 36(5), 555-599.

[14] References (Adopted from Microsoft Copilot AI): Hackman, J. R. (2002). Leading Teams: Setting the Stage for Great Performances. Harvard Business Review Press; Salas, E., Cooke, N. J., & Rosen, M. A. (2008). On Teams, Teamwork, and Team Performance: Discoveries and Developments. Human Factors: The Journal of the Human Factors and Ergonomics Society, 50(3), 540-547.

[15] References (Adopted from Microsoft Copilot AI): Edmondson, A. (1999). Psychological Safety and Learning Behavior in Work Teams. Administrative Science Quarterly, 44(2), 350-383; Frazier, M. L., Fainshmidt, S., Klinger, R. L., Pezeshkan, A., & Vracheva, V. (2017). Psychological Safety: A Meta-Analytic Review and Extension. Personnel Psychology, 70(1), 113-165.

[16] References (Adopted from Microsoft Copilot AI): Asch, S. E. (1956). Studies of Independence and Conformity: I. A Minority of One Against a Unanimous Majority. Psychological Monographs, 70(9), 1-70; Cialdini, R. B., & Goldstein, N. J. (2004). Social Influence: Compliance and Conformity. Annual Review of Psychology, 55(1), 591-621; Janis, I. L. (1972). Victims of Groupthink: A Psychological Study of Foreign-Policy Decisions and Fiascoes. Houghton Mifflin.

[17] References (Adopted from Microsoft Copilot AI): Rizzolatti, G., & Craighero, L. (2004). The Mirror-Neuron System. Annual Review of Neuroscience, 27(1), 169-192; Iacoboni, M. (2009). Mirroring People: The Science of Empathy and How We Connect with Others. Picador.

[18] References (Adopted from Microsoft Copilot AI): Bandura, A. (1977). Social Learning Theory. Prentice Hall; Bandura, A. (1986). Social Foundations of Thought and Action: A Social Cognitive Theory. Prentice-Hall.

[19] Reference (Adopted from Microsoft Copilot AI): Tajfel, H., & Turner, J. C. (1986). The Social Identity Theory of Intergroup Behavior. In S.

Worchel & W. G. Austin (Eds.), Psychology of Intergroup Relations. Nelson-Hall.

[20] References (Adopted form Microsoft Copilot AI): Festinger, L. (1957). A Theory of Cognitive Dissonance. Stanford University Press; Aronson, E. (1992). The Return of the Repressed: Dissonance Theory Makes a Comeback. Psychological Inquiry, 3(4), 303-311.

[21] References (Adopted from Microsoft Copilot AI): Durkheim, E. (1912). The Elementary Forms of the Religious Life. Free Press; Baumeister, R. F., & Leary, M. R. (1995). The Need to Belong: Desire for Interpersonal Attachments as a Fundamental Human Motivation. Psychological Bulletin, 117(3), 497-529.

[22] References (Adopted from Microsoft Copilot AI): Kosfeld, M., Heinrichs, M., Zak, P. J., Fischbacher, U., & Fehr, E. (2005). Oxytocin increases trust in humans. Nature, 435(7042), 673-676; Bartz, J. A., Zaki, J., Bolger, N., & Ochsner, K. N. (2011). Social effects of oxytocin in humans: context and person matter. Trends in Cognitive Sciences, 15(7), 301-309.

[23] Kanigel, R. (1991). The Man Who Knew Infinity: A Life of the Genius Ramanujan. Scribner.

[24] Reference – adopted form Microsoft Copilot AI: Shonkoff, J. P., & Garner, A. S. (2012). The lifelong effects of early childhood adversity and toxic stress. Pediatrics, 129(1), e232-e246.

[25] Reference – adopted from Microsoft Copilot AI: Salinger, J. D. (1951). The Catcher in the Rye. Little, Brown and Company.

[26] Reference – adopted from Google Gemini AI: The citation of Napoleon Hill's book Think and Grow Rich.

[27] References – adopted from Microsoft Copilot AI:
- Kempermann, G. (2019). Environmental enrichment, new neurons and the neurobiology of individuality. Nature Reviews Neuroscience, 20(4), 235-245.
- Hertzog, C., Kramer, A. F., Wilson, R. S., & Lindenberger, U. (2008). Enrichment Effects on Adult Cognitive Development: Can the Functional Capacity of Older Adults Be Preserved and Enhanced? Psychological Science in the Public Interest, 9(1), 1-65.

[28] References – adopted from Microsoft Copilot AI:
- American Psychological Association. (2022). Resilience. https://www.apa.org/topics/resilience
- Iacoboni, M. (2009). Mirroring People: The Science of Empathy and How We Connect with Others. Picador.

- Kosfeld, M., Heinrichs, M., Zak, P. J., Fischbacher, U., & Fehr, E. (2005). Oxytocin increases trust in humans. Nature, 435(7042), 673-676.

[29] References – adopted form Google Gemini AI:
- Kandel, E. R., Schwartz, J. H., & Jessell, T. M. (2013). Principles of Neural Science (5th ed.). McGraw-Hill Medical.
- Kosslyn, S. M., & Koenig, O. (1992). Wet Mind: The New Cognitive Neuroscience.

[30] Reference – adopted from Google Gemini AI: The Citation of Daniel Kahneman's book Thinking, Fast and Slow.

[31] The direct quote from the novel adopted from Google Gemini AI.

[32] Reference – adopted from Google Gemini AI: Henry Chesbrough original quote *'Open innovation recognizes the fact that innovation is distributed across many organizations and individuals.'*

[33] Reference – adopted form Google Gemini AI: Thinking Fast and Slow.

[34] Reference – adopted from Microsoft Copilot AI: The Network Propaganda book.

[35] Reference – adopted from Google Gemini AI: Where Good Ideas Come from by Steven Johnson.

[36] Referencing Irving Janis was adopted through Google Gemini AI.

[37] Reference – adopted from Google Gemini AI: AIJ.R.R. Tolkien's The Lord of the Rings.

[38] Reference – adopted from Google Gemini AI: Bruce Schneier

[39] Reference – adopted from Google Gemini AI: John Bell.

[40] Reference – adopted from Google Gemini AI: Michael Gazzaniga.

[41] Reference -adopted from Google Gemini AI: Harold Bloom.

[42] Reference – adopted from Google Gemini AI: Leon Festinger.

[43] Reference for Aaron Beck adopted from Google Gemini AI.

[44] Reference for Harold Bloom's analysis of Frankenstein adopted from Google Gemini AI.

[45] Reference – adopted from Microsoft Copilot AI: Reference: Rhodes, R. (1986). The Making of the Atomic Bomb. Simon & Schuster.

---

[46] Reference – adopted from Google Gemini AIAs Heisenberg himself recalled, *'Bohr was not only a great scientist but also a great teacher.'*

[47] The direct quote from the film adopted from Google Gemini AI.

[48] Reference – adopted from Microsoft Copilot AI: Reference: Kleinbaum, N. H. (1989). Dead Poets Society. Bantam Books.

[49] Reference – adopted from Google Gemini AI: Walter Isaacson's biography of Steve Jobs

[50] The direct quote from the novel adopted from the Google Gemini AI.

[51] The direct quote from the novel adopted from Google Gemini AI.

[52] Reference – adopted from Google Gemini AI: Susan Quinn's biography of Marie Curie.

[53] Reference – adopted from Google Gemini AI: Walter Isaacson's biography of Elon Musk.

[54] The direct quote from the novel adopted from Google Gemini AI.

[55] Reference – adopted from Microsoft Copilot AI: Reference: Beck, A. T. (1979). Cognitive therapy of depression. Springer, 6(1), 18-28.

[56] The Citation of Norman Doidge's book The Brain That Changes Itself adopted from Google Gemini AI.

[57] Reference – adopted from Microsoft Copilot AI: Kabat-Zinn, J. (1990). Full catastrophe living: Using the wisdom of your body and mind to face stress, pain, and illness. Springer, 4(2), 191-206.

[58] The direct quote from the novel adopted from Google Gemini AI.

[59] The reference for psychologists Richard Tedeschi and Lawrence Calhoun book's Post-traumatic Growth adopted from Google Gemini AI.

[60] The direct quote from the novel adopted from Google Gemini AI.

[61] Reference – adopted from Google Gemini AI: American Prometheus: The Triumph and Tragedy of J. Robert Oppenheimer" by Kai Bird and Martin J. Sherwin.

[62] Reference – adopted from Google Gemini AI: Isaacson, Walter. Steve Jobs. Simon & Schuster, 2011.

[63] Reference – adopted from Microsoft Copilot AI: Reference: Duckworth, A. L., Peterson, C., Matthews, M. D., & Kelly, D. R. (2007). Grit: Perseverance and passion for long-term goals. Journal of Personality and Social Psychology, 92(6), 1087-1101.

[64] Reference – adopted from Google Gemini AI: Tedeschi and Calhoun's book on post-traumatic growth.

[65] Reference – adopted from Microsoft Copilot AI: Seligman, M. E. (1972). Learned helplessness. Annual Review of Medicine, 23(1), 407-412.

[66] The direct quote from the series adopted from the Google Gemini AI.

[67] Reference – adopted from Microsoft Copilot AI: Clough, P., Earle, K., & Sewell, D. (2002). Mental toughness: The concept and its measurement. Solutions in Sport Psychology, 32(2), 36-41.

[68] Reference – adopted from Google Gemini AI: Wood, W. (2019). Good Habits, Bad Habits: The Science of Making Positive Changes That Stick. Penguin Press.

[69] Reference – adopted from Microsoft Copilot AI: https://en.wikipedia.org/wiki/Bilal_ibn_Rabah?form=MG0AV3

[70] Reference – adopted from Microsoft Copilot AI:

- Churchill's Character: Hardiness, Resilience and Personal Toughness https://winstonchurchill.hillsdale.edu/churchill-character-hardiness/

- The Pivotal Role of Winston Churchill in WWII Strategy and Leadership https://totalmilitaryinsight.com/the-role-of-winston-churchill-in-wwii/

- Winston Churchill Leadership Style: The Pillars of Resilience and Inspiration https://hidayatrizvi.com/winston-churchill-leadership-style/

[71] Reference adopted from Google Gemini AI: Doidge, N. (2007). The Brain That Changes Itself. Penguin Books.

[72] Reference – adopted from Google Gemini AI: Gazzaley, A. (2018). The Distracted Mind: Ancient Brains in a High-Tech World. MIT Press.

[73] Reference adopted from Google Gemini AI: Bowman, E. D., & Levine, L. E. (2001). The impact of self-selected multitasking on college students' learning. Computers in Human Behavior, 17(4), 329-345.

[74] Reference – adopted from Microsoft Copilot AI: Reference: Newell, A. (1990). Unified Theories of Cognition. Harvard University Press.

[75] Sun Tzu. (2010). The Art of War. Penguin Classics.

76 Reference – adopted from Microsoft Copilot AI: Reference: Csikszentmihalyi, M. (1990). Flow: The Psychology of Optimal Experience. Harper & Row.

77 Reference – adopted from Google Gemini AI: Kabat-Zinn, J. (1994). Wherever You Go, There You Are: Mindfulness Meditation in Everyday Life. Hyperion.

78 Reference – adopted from Microsoft Copilot AI: Reference: Leroy, S. (2009). Why is it so hard to do my work? The challenge of attention residue when switching between work tasks. Organizational Behavior and Human Decision Processes, 109(2), 168-181.

79 Reference – adopted from Google Gemini AI: Sweller, J., van Merriënboer, J. J. G., & Paas, F. G. W. C. (1998). Cognitive architecture and instructional design. Educational Psychology Review, 1 10(3), 251-296.

80 Reference – adopted from Microsoft Copilot AI: Reference: Sweller, J. (1988). Cognitive load during problem-solving: Effects on learning. Cognitive Science, 12(2), 257-285.

81 Reference adopted from Google Gemini AI: Hesse, H. (1927). Steppenwolf. Fischer Verlag.

82 Reference – adopted from Microsoft Copilot AI: I hope this example provides a clear illustration! If you need further information or another reference, feel free to ask.

83 Reference – adopted from Google Gemini AI: Beck, A. T. (1976). Cognitive Therapy and the Emotional Disorders. International Universities Press.

84 Reference – adopted from Microsoft Copilot AI: Reference: Gross, J. J. (2002). Emotion regulation: Affective, cognitive, and social consequences. Psychophysiology, 39(3), 281-291.

85 Reference – adopted from Google Gemini AI: Tolkien, J. R. R. (1954). The Lord of the Rings. George Allen & Unwin.

86 Reference – adopted from Microsoft Copilot AI: Segal, Z. V., Williams, J. M. G., & Teasdale, J. D. (2002). Mindfulness-Based Cognitive Therapy for Depression: A New Approach to Preventing Relapse. Guilford Press.

87 Reference – adopted from Microsoft Copilot AI: Ryan, R. M., & Deci, E. L. (2000). Self-determination theory and the facilitation of intrinsic motivation, social development, and well-being. American Psychologist, 55(1), 68-78.

[88] Reference – adopted from Google Gemini AI: Doidge, N. (2007). The Brain That Changes Itself. Penguin Books.

[89] Reference – adopted from Microsoft Copilot AI: Nolen-Hoeksema, S. (2000). The role of rumination in depressive disorders and mixed anxiety/depressive symptoms. Journal of Abnormal Psychology, 109(3), 504-511.

[90] Alighieri, D. (1995). The Divine Comedy. Penguin Classics.

[91] Reference – adopted from Microsoft Copilot AI: Tedeschi, R. G., & Calhoun, L. G. (2004). Posttraumatic growth: Conceptual foundations and empirical evidence. Review of General Psychology, 8(3), 280-294.

[92] Reference – adopted from Google Gemini AI: Long, A. A. (2016). How to Be a Stoic: Using Ancient Philosophy to Live a Modern Life. Hodder & Stoughton.

[93] Reference – adopted from Microsoft Copilot AI: Reference: Heisenberg, W. (1930). The Physical Principles of the Quantum Theory. Dover Publications.

[94] Reference adopted from Google Gemini AI: Kuhn, T. S. (1962). The Structure of Scientific Revolutions. University of Chicago Press.

[95] Reference – adopted from Microsoft Copilot AI: Reference: Hofstadter, D. R. (1979). Gödel, Escher, Bach: An Eternal Golden Braid. Basic Books.

[96] Reference adopted from Google Gemini AI: Dick, P. K. (1968). Do Androids Dream of Electric Sheep? Doubleday.

[97] Reference – adopted from Microsoft Copilot AI: Reference: Frankl, V. E. (1946). Man's Search for Meaning. Beacon Press.

[98] Reference – adopted from Google Gemini AI: Kapleau, P. (1966). The Three Pillars of Zen: Teachings from the Masters of Japan. Doubleday.

[99] Reference – adopted from Google Gemini AI: Feynman, R. P., Leighton, R. B., & Sands, M. (1965). The Feynman Lectures on Physics. Addison-Wesley.

[100] Reference – adopted from Google Gemini AI: Wheeler, J. A. (1990). Information, physics, quantum: The search for links. In Zurek, W. H. (Ed.), Complexity, entropy, and the physics of information. Addison-Wesley.

[101] Reference – adopted from Microsoft Copilot AI: Reference: Plato. (380 BCE). The Republic. (Book VII, The Allegory of the Cave).

[102] Reference – adopted from Google Gemini AI: Isaacson, Walter. Leonardo da Vinci. Simon & Schuster, 2017

[103] Reference – adopted from Google Gemini AI: Bloom, Harold. Blake's Apocalypse: A Study in Poetic Argument. Cornell University Press, 1963.

[104] Reference – adopted from Google Gemini : Hilma af Klint: Paintings for the Future. Tate Publishing, 2018.

[105] Reference – adopted from Google Gemini AI: Naifeh, Steven, and Gregory White Smith. Van Gogh: The Life. Random House Trade Paperback, 2011.

[106] Reference – adopted from Microsoft Copilot AI: Reference: Kahneman, D. (2011). Thinking, Fast and Slow. Farrar, Straus and Giroux.

[107] Reference – adopted from Google Gemini AI: Popper, K. R. (1959). The Logic of Scientific Discovery. Routledge.

[108] Reference – adopted from Microsoft Copilot AI: Reference: Gross, J. J. (2002). Emotion Regulation: Affective, Cognitive, and Social Consequences. Psychophysiology, 39(3), 281-291.

[109] Reference – adopted from Google Gemini AI: Coelho, P. (1988). The Alchemist. HarperCollins.

[110] Reference – adopted from Microsoft Copilot AI: Reference: Toffler, A. (1970). Future Shock. Bantam Books.

[111] Reference – adopted from Google Gemini AI: Postman, N. (1985). Amusing Ourselves to Death: Public Discourse in the Age of Show Business. Viking.

[112] Reference – adopted from Google Gemini AI: Doidge, N. (2007). The Brain That Changes Itself. Penguin Books.

[113] Reference – adopted from Microsoft Copilot AI: Reference: Johansson, F. (2004). The Medici Effect: Breakthrough Insights at the Intersection of Ideas, Concepts, and Cultures. Harvard Business School Press.

[114] Reference – adopted from Google Gemini AI: Watson, J. D. (1968). The Double Helix. Atheneum.

[115] Reference – adopted from Microsoft Copilot AI: Reference: Collins, J. C., & Porras, J. I. (1994). Built to Last: Successful Habits of Visionary Companies. HarperBusiness.

[116] Reference – adopted from Google Gemini AI: Tolkien, J. R. R. (1954). The Lord of the Rings. George Allen & Unwin

[117] Reference – adopted from Microsoft Copilot AI: Reference: Shirer, W. L. (1960). The Rise and Fall of the Third Reich: A History of Nazi Germany. Simon & Schuster.

[118] Reference – adopted from Google Gemini AI: Loftus, E. F. (2017). The Witness for the Defense. St. Martin's Press.

[119] Reference – adopted from Microsoft Copilot AI: Reference: Popper, K. (1959). The Logic of Scientific Discovery. Routledge.

[120] Reference – adopted from Google Gemini AI: Feynman, R. P. (1965). The Feynman Lectures on Physics. Addison-Wesley.

[121] Reference – adopted from Microsoft Copilot AI: Reference: Dweck, C. S. (2006). Mindset: The New Psychology of Success. Random House.

[122] Reference – adopted from Google Gemini AI: Carey, N. (2012). The Epigenetics Revolution: How Modern Biology Is Rewriting Our Understanding of Genetics, Disease, and Inheritance. Dutton.

[123] Reference – adopted from Google Gemini AI: Shelley, M. (1818). Frankenstein; or, The Modern Prometheus. Lackington, Hughes, Hardman, Mavor, and Jones.

[124] Reference – adopted from Microsoft Copilot AI: Reference: Chesbrough, H. W. (2003). Open Innovation: The New Imperative for Creating and Profiting from Technology. Harvard Business School Press.

[125] Reference – adopted from Google Gemini AI: Drucker, P. F. (1999). Management Challenges for the 21st Century. HarperCollins.

[126] Reference – adopted from Microsoft Copilot AI: Reference: Janis, I. L. (1972). Victims of Groupthink: A Psychological Study of Foreign-Policy Decisions and Fiascoes. Houghton Mifflin.

[127] Reference – adopted from Google Gemini AI: Loftus, E. F. (2017). The Witness for the Defense. St. Martin's Press.

[128] Reference – adopted from Google Gemini AI: Vosoughi, S., Roy, D., & Aral, S. (2018). The spread of true and false news online. Science, 359(6380), 1146-1151.

[129] Reference – adopted from Microsoft Copilot AI: Reference: Beck, J. S. (2011). Cognitive Behavior Therapy: Basics and Beyond. Guilford Press.

[130] Reference – adopted from Google Gemini AI: Orwell, G. (1949). 1984. Secker & Warburg.

[131] Reference – adopted from Microsoft Copilot AI: Reference: Piaget, J. (1952). The Origins of Intelligence in Children. International

Universities Press. Reference: Vygotsky, L. S. (1978). Mind in Society: The Development of Higher Psychological Processes. Harvard University Press.

[132] Reference – adopted from Google Gemini AI: Doidge, N. (2007). The Brain That Changes Itself. Penguin Books.

[133] Reference – adopted from Google Gemini AI: Coelho, P. (1988). The Alchemist. HarperCollins.

[134] Reference – adopted from Google Gemini AI: Tedeschi, R. G., & Calhoun, L. G. (1996). Post-traumatic growth: Conceptual foundations and empirical evidence. Psychology Press.

[135] Reference – adopted from Microsoft Copilot AI: Reference: Frankl, V. E. (1946). Man's Search for Meaning. Beacon Press.

[136] Reference – adopted from Microsoft Copilot AI: Reference: Csikszentmihalyi, M. (1990). Flow: The Psychology of Optimal Experience. Harper & Row.

[137] Reference – adopted from Google Gemini AI: Frankl, V. E. (1959). Man's Search for Meaning. Beacon Press.

[138] Reference – adopted from Google Gemini AI: Naifeh, M., & Smith, G. K. (1991). Van Gogh: The Life. Random House.

[139] Reference – adopted from Microsoft Copilot AI: Reference: Shelley, M. (1818). Frankenstein; or, The Modern Prometheus. Lackington, Hughes, Harding, Mavor & Jones.

[140] Reference – adopted from Google Gemini AI: Sapolsky, R. M. (2017). Why Zebras Don't Get Ulcers: A Guide to Stress, Stress-Related Diseases, and Coping. St. Martin's Press.

[141] Reference – adopted from Microsoft Copilot AI: Reference: Fischer, L. (1950). The Life of Mahatma Gandhi. Harper & Brothers.

[142] Reference – adopted from Google Gemini AI: Coelho, P. (1988). The Alchemist. HarperCollins.

[143] Reference – adopted from Google Gemini AI: Isaacson, W. (2017). Elon Musk: Tesla, SpaceX, and the Quest for a Fantastic Future. Simon & Schuster.

[144] Reference – adopted from Microsoft Copilot AI: Reference: Pernoud, R., & Clin, M. (1999). Joan of Arc: Her Story. St. Martin's Press.

[145] Reference – adopted from Microsoft Copilot AI: Reference: Doidge, N. (2007). The Brain That Changes Itself: Stories of Personal Triumph from the Frontiers of Brain Science. Viking Press.

[146] Reference – adopted from Google Gemini AI: Kandel, E. R., Schwartz, J. H., & Jessell, T. M. (2013). Principles of Neural Science. McGraw-Hill Education.

[147] Reference – adopted from Microsoft Copilot AI: Reference: Doidge, N. (2007). The Brain That Changes Itself: Stories of Personal Triumph from the Frontiers of Brain Science. Viking Press.

[148] Alighieri, D. (1995). The Divine Comedy. Penguin Classics.

[149] Reference – adopted from Microsoft Copilot AI: Reference: Kahneman, D. (1973). Attention and Effort. Prentice-Hall.

[150] Reference – adopted from Google Gemini AI: Kabat-Zinn, J. (1994). Wherever You Go, There You Are: Mindfulness Meditation in Everyday Life. Hyperion.

[151] Reference – adopted from Microsoft Copilot AI: Reference: Festinger, L. (1957). A Theory of Cognitive Dissonance. Stanford University Press.

[152] Reference – adopted from Microsoft Copilot AI: Reference: Merton, R. K. (1948). The Self-Fulfilling Prophecy. Antioch Review.

[153] Reference – adopted from Microsoft Copilot AI: Reference: Csikszentmihalyi, M. (1990). Flow: The Psychology of Optimal Experience. Harper & Row.

[154] References – adopted from Google Gemini AI: Mack, A., & Rock, I. (1998). Inattentional Blindness. MIT Press; Kahneman, D. (2011). Thinking, Fast and Slow. Farrar, Straus and Giroux; Simons, D. J., & Chabris, C. F. (1999). Gorillas in our midst: Sustained inattentional blindness for dynamic events. Perception, 28(9), 1059-1074.

[155] Reference – adopted from Microsoft Copilot AI: Reference: Nolen-Hoeksema, S. (2000). The Role of Rumination in Depressive Disorders and Mixed Anxiety/Depressive Symptoms. Journal of Abnormal Psychology.

[156] Reference – adopted from Google Gemini AI: Shakespeare, W. (1606). Macbeth. First Folio.

[157] Reference – adopted from Microsoft Copilot AI: Reference: Byrne, R. (2006). The Secret. Atria Books/Beyond Words.

[158] Reference – adopted from Google Gemini AI: Byrne, R. (2006). The Secret. Atria Books.

[159] Reference – adopted from Microsoft Copilot AI: Reference: Doran, G. T. (1981). There's a S.M.A.R.T. way to write management's goals and objectives. Management Review, 70(11), 35-36.

[160] References – adopted from Google Gemini AI:
- Locke, E. A., & Latham, G. P. (1990).
- A Theory of Goal Setting & Task Performance. Prentice Hall; Dweck, C. S. (2006). Mindset: The New Psychology of Success. Random House.

[161] Reference – adopted from Microsoft Copilot AI: Yates, F. A. (1966). The Art of Memory. University of Chicago Press.

[162] Reference – adopted from Google Gemini AI: Smithsonian Institution. (2010). Smithsonian Cultural Rescue Initiative: Haiti. Smithsonian Institution.

[163] Reference – adopted from Microsoft Copilot AI: Hagan, J. F., Shaw, J. S., & Duncan, P. M. (Eds.). (2017). Bright Futures: Guidelines for Health Supervision of Infants, Children, and Adolescents. American Academy of Pediatrics.

[164] Reference – adopted from Google Gemini AI: Bradbury, R. (1953). Fahrenheit 451. Ballantine Books.

[165] Reference – adopted from Google Gemini AI: Kabat-Zinn, J. (1994). Wherever You Go, There You Are: Mindfulness Meditation in Everyday Life. Hyperion.

[166] Reference – adopted from Microsoft Copilot AI: Beck, A. T. (1976). Cognitive Therapy and the Emotional Disorders. International Universities Press.

[167] Reference – adopted from Google Gemini AI: Kahneman, D. (2011). Thinking, Fast and Slow. Farrar, Straus and Giroux.

[168] Reference – adopted from Microsoft Copilot AI: Reynolds, S. (1991). Medieval Reading: Grammar, Rhetoric, and the Classical Text. Cambridge University Press.

[169] Reference – adopted from Google Gemini AI: Eco, U. (1980). The Name of the Rose. Bompiani.

[170] Reference – adopted from Microsoft Copilot AI: Beck, J. S. (2011). Cognitive Behavior Therapy: Basics and Beyond. Guilford Press.

[171] Reference – adopted from Google Gemini AI: Beck, A. T. (1976). Cognitive Therapy and the Emotional Disorders. International Universities Press.

[172] Reference – adopted from Microsoft Copilot AI: Beck, A. T. (1976). Cognitive Therapy and the Emotional Disorders. International Universities Press.

[173] Reference – adopted from Microsoft Copilot AI: Gross, J. J., & John, O. P. (2003). Individual differences in two emotion regulation processes: Implications for affect, relationships, and well-being. Journal of Personality and Social Psychology, 85(2), 348-362.

[174] Reference – adopted from Google Gemini AI: Topping, K. J., & Ehly, S. W. (1998). Peer Tutoring: A Practical Guide. Routledge.

[175] Reference – adopted from Microsoft Copilot AI: Bass, B. M., & Avolio, B. J. (1994). Improving Organizational Effectiveness through Transformational Leadership. Sage Publications.

[176] Reference – adopted from Microsoft Copilot AI: Lévy, P. (1997). Collective Intelligence: Mankind's Emerging World in Cyberspace. Perseus Books.

[177] Reference – adopted from Microsoft Copilot AI: Reference: El-Abbadi, M. (1990). The Life and Fate of the Ancient Library of Alexandria. UNESCO.

[178] Reference – adopted from Microsoft Copilot AI: Csikszentmihalyi, M. (1990). Flow: The Psychology of Optimal Experience. Harper & Row.

[179] Reference – adopted from Microsoft Copilot AI: Lovecraft, H.P. (1936). The Shadow over Innsmouth. The Visionary Publishing Company.

[180] References – adopted from Google Gemini AI:
- Wheeler, J. A. (1990). Information, physics, quantum: The search for links. In Zurek, W. H. (Ed.), Complexity, entropy, and the physics of information. Addison-Wesley.
- Zeilinger, A. (2010). Dance of Photons: From Einstein to Quantum Teleportation. Farrar, Straus and Giroux.

[181] Reference – adopted from Microsoft Copilot AI: Wheeler, J. A., & Zurek, W. H. (1983). Quantum Theory and Measurement. Princeton University Press.

[182] Reference – adopted from Microsoft Copilot AI: Lovecraft, H.P. (1928). The Call of Cthulhu. Weird Tales.

[183] Reference – adopted from Microsoft Copilot AI: Carlson, W. B. (2013). Tesla: Inventor of the Electrical Age. Princeton University Press.

[184] Reference – adopted from Google Gemini AI: Shelley, M. (1818). Frankenstein; or, The Modern Prometheus. Lackington, Hughes, Hardman, Mavor, and Jones.

[185] Reference – adopted from Microsoft Copilot AI: Gödel, K. (1931). Über formal unentscheidbare Sätze der Principia Mathematica und verwandter Systeme I. Monatshefte für Mathematik und Physik, 38, 173-198.

[186] Reference – adopted from Google Gemini AI: Greene, B. (1999). The Elegant Universe: Superstrings, Hidden Dimensions, and the Quest for the Ultimate Theory. W.W. Norton & Company. https://medium.com/@rafagarza/is-the-universe-a-living-organism-477d84c70a9

[187] Reference – adopted from Microsoft Copilot AI: Aspect, A., Dalibard, J., & Roger, G. (1982). Experimental Test of Bell's Inequalities Using Time-Varying Analyzers. Physical Review Letters, 49(25), 1804-1807.

[188] Reference – adopted from Microsoft Copilot AI: Shelley, M. (1818). Frankenstein; or, The Modern Prometheus. Lackington, Hughes, Harding, Mavor & Jones.

[189] Reference – adopted from Google Gemini AI: Lovecraft, H. P. (1928). The Call of Cthulhu and Other Weird Stories.

[190] Reference – adopted from Google Gemini AI: Csikszentmihalyi, M. (1990). Flow: The Psychology of Optimal Experience. Harper Perennial.

[191] Reference – adopted from Microsoft Copilot AI: Melville, H. (1851). Moby-Dick; or, The Whale. Harper & Brothers.

[192] Reference – adopted from Microsoft Copilot AI: Huxley, A. (1932). Brave New World. Chatto & Windus.

[193] Reference – adopted from Google Gemini AI: Shelley, M. (1818). Frankenstein; or, The Modern Prometheus. Lackington, Hughes, Hardman, Mavor, and Jones.

[194] References – adopted from Microsoft Copilot AI:
- William James - The Principles of Psychology (1890).
- Mihaly Csikszentmihalyi - Flow: The Psychology of Optimal Experience (1990).
- Jean-Paul Sartre - Being and Nothingness (1943).

[195] References – adopted from Google Gemini AI:

- Hallowell, E. M., & Ratey, J. J. (1994). Driven to Distraction: Recognizing and Coping with Attention Deficit Disorder. Simon & Schuster
- National Institute of Mental Health (NIMH): The NIMH provides comprehensive information on ADHD, including its symptoms and impact on daily life.
- Attention Deficit Disorder Association (ADDA): The ADDA offers resources and support for individuals with ADHD and their families.

[196] Reference – adopted from Microsoft Copilot AI:
- Émile Coué - Self-Mastery Through Conscious Autosuggestion (1922).
- Carl Rogers - On Becoming a Person (1961).
- Sigmund Freud - The Ego and the Id (1923).

[197] Reference – adopted from Google Gemini AI: Seligman, M. E. P. (2006). Learned Optimism: How to Change Your Mind and Your Life. Random House.

[198] References – adopted from Microsoft Copilot AI:
- Friedrich Nietzsche - Thus Spoke Zarathustra (1883-1891).
- Carl Jung - Man and His Symbols (1964).
- Viktor Frankl - Man's Search for Meaning (1946).

[199] Reference – adopted from Google Gemini AI: Orwell, G. (1949). 1984. Secker & Warburg.

[200] Reference – adopted from Microsoft Copilot AI: Lutz, A., Slagter, H. A., Dunne, J. D., & Davidson, R. J. (2008). "Attention regulation and monitoring in meditation." Trends in Cognitive Sciences, 12(4), 163-169.

[201] Reference – adopted from Google Gemini AI: Festinger, L. (1957). A Theory of Cognitive Dissonance. Stanford University Press.

[202] Reference – adopted from Microsoft Copilot AI: Rosenthal, R., & Jacobson, L. (1968). Pygmalion in the Classroom: Teacher Expectation and Pupils' Intellectual Development. Holt, Rinehart & Winston.

[203] References – adopted from Microsoft Copilot AI and Google Gemini AI:
- Benedetti, F. (2009). Placebo Effects: Understanding the mechanisms in health and disease. Oxford University Press.
- Hróbjartsson, A., & Gøtzsche, P. C. (2001). "Is the placebo powerless? An analysis of clinical trials comparing placebo with no treatment." New England Journal of Medicine, 344(21), 1594-1602.

[204] Reference – adopted from Microsoft Copilot and Google Gemini AI: Proust, M. (1913-1927). In Search of Lost Time.

[205] References – adopted from Microsoft Copilot AI:
- Pasteur, L. (1864). "Germ Theory and Its Applications to Medicine and Surgery."
- Koch, R. (1884). "The Etiology of Tuberculosis."

[206] References – adopted from Microsoft Copilot AI:
- Houran, J., & Lange, R. (1996). "Hauntings and poltergeist-like experiences: A survey of theories and explanations." Journal of the Society for Psychical Research, 61, 114-128.
- Wiseman, R., Watt, C., Stevens, P., Greening, E., & O'Keeffe, C. (2003). "An investigation into the alleged haunting of Hampton Court Palace: Psychological variables and magnetic fields." Journal of Parapsychology, 67, 507-522.

[207] Reference – adopted from Microsoft Copilot AI: Voss, J. L., Federmeier, K. D., & Paller, K. A. (2012). "The neural basis of illusory face and word perception." Neuropsychologia, 50(14), 3294-3305.

[208] Reference – adopted from Google Gemini AI: Kandel, E. R., Schwartz, J. H., & Jessell, T. M. (2013). Principles of Neural Science. McGraw-Hill Education.

[209] Reference – adopted from Microsoft Copilot AI: Damasio, A. (1999). The Feeling of What Happens: Body and Emotion in the Making of Consciousness. Harcourt Brace.

[210] References – adopted from Microsoft Copilot AI:
- Gross, J. J., & Levenson, R. W. (1997). "Hiding feelings: The acute effects of inhibiting negative and positive emotion." Journal of Abnormal Psychology, 106(1), 95-103.
- John, O. P., & Gross, J. J. (2004). "Healthy and unhealthy emotion regulation: Personality processes, individual differences, and life span development." Journal of Personality, 72(6), 1301-1334.

[211] References – adopted from Microsoft Copilot AI:
- Newberg, A. B., d'Aquili, E. G., & Rause, V. (2001). Why God Won't Go Away: Brain Science and the Biology of Belief. Ballantine Books.
- Newberg, A. B., & Waldman, M. R. (2009). How God Changes Your Brain: Breakthrough Findings from a Leading Neuroscientist. Ballantine Books.

[212] Reference – adopted from Google Gemini AI: Lovecraft, H. P. (1928). The Call of Cthulhu and Other Weird Stories.

[213] Reference – adopted from Microsoft Copilot AI: Lovecraft, H. P. (1928). The Call of Cthulhu. Weird Tales.

[214] Reference – adopted from Microsoft Copilot AI: Festinger, L. (1957). A Theory of Cognitive Dissonance. Stanford University Press.

[215] Reference – adopted from Microsoft Copilot AI: Benedetti, F. (2009). Placebo Effects: Understanding the mechanisms in health and disease. Oxford University Press.

[216] Reference – adopted from Google Gemini AI: Moerman, D. E. (2002). Placebo Effects and the New Medicine: Discoveries in Health and Healing. Oxford University Press.

[217] Reference – adopted from Microsoft Copilot AI: Eysenck, M. W., Derakshan, N., Santos, R., & Calvo, M. G. (2007). "Anxiety and cognitive performance: Attentional control theory." Emotion, 7(2), 336-353.

[218] Reference – adopted from Microsoft Copilot AI: Beck, J. S. (2011). Cognitive Behavior Therapy: Basics and Beyond. Guilford Press.

[219] Reference – adopted from Google Gemini AI: Beck, A. T. (1976). Cognitive Therapy and the Emotional Disorders. International Universities Press.

[220] Reference – adopted from Microsoft Copilot AI: Dietrich, A. (2004). "Neurocognitive mechanisms underlying the experience of flow." Consciousness and Cognition, 13(4), 746-761.

[221] Reference – adopted from Microsoft Copilot AI: Wilde, O. (1890). The Picture of Dorian Gray. Lippincott's Monthly Magazine.

[222] Reference – adopted from Google Gemini AI: Wilde, O. (1890). The Picture of Dorian Gray. Ward, Lock, Bowden & Co.

[223] Reference – adopted from Microsoft Copilot AI: Duckworth, A. L., Peterson, C., Matthews, M. D., & Kelly, D. R. (2007). "Grit: Perseverance and passion for long-term goals." Journal of Personality and Social Psychology, 92(6), 1087-1101.

[224] Reference – adopted from Microsoft Copilot AI: Hugo, V. (1862). Les Misérables. A. Lacroix, Verboeckhoven & Cie.

[225] Reference – adopted from Microsoft Copilot AI: Lazar, S. W., Kerr, C. E., Wasserman, R. H., Gray, J. R., Greve, D. N., Treadway, M. T., ... & Fischl, B. (2005). "Meditation experience is associated with increased cortical thickness." Neuroreport, 16(17), 1893-1897.

[226] Reference – adopted from Microsoft Copilot AI: Wheeler, J. A., & Zurek, W. H. (Eds.). (1983). Quantum Theory and Measurement. Princeton University Press.

[227] Reference – adopted from the Microsoft Copilot AI: Benedetti, F. (2009). Placebo Effects: Understanding the mechanisms in health and disease. Oxford University Press.

[228] Reference – adopted from Microsoft Copilot AI: Guillot, A., & Collet, C. (2008). "Construction of the motor imagery integrative model in sport: a review and theoretical investigation of motor imagery use." International Review of Sport and Exercise Psychology, 1(1), 31-44.

[229] Reference -adopted from Microsoft Copilot AI: Stein, D. J., Fineberg, N. A., & Blanco, C. (2020). "Obsessive-compulsive disorder." The Lancet, 396(10256), 1231-1243.

[230] References – adopted from Microsoft Copilot AI:
- Pierre, J. M. (2001). "Faith or delusion? At the crossroads of religion and psychosis." Journal of Psychiatric Practice, 7(3), 163-172.
- Pietkiewicz, I. J., Kościesza, A., Chudy, N., & Wojciechowski, T. (2018). "Spiritual struggles and mental health: Exploring the associations between religious coping and psychological distress in a Polish sample." Journal of Religion and Health, 57(1), 193-205.

[231] Reference – adopted from Microsoft Copilot AI: Conrad, J. (1899). Heart of Darkness. Blackwood's Magazine.

[232] Reference – adopted from Microsoft Copilot AI: Jiang, M., Zhu, Z., & Logares, R. (2022). "The Role of Artificial Intelligence Algorithms in Marine Scientific Research." Frontiers in Marine Science, 9, 920994

[233] Reference – adopted from Microsoft Copilot AI: El-Abbadi, M. (1992). Life and Fate of the Ancient Library of Alexandria. UNESCO.

[234] References – adopted from Microsoft Copilot AI:
- Van Veen, V., Krug, M. K., Schooler, J. W., & Carter, C. S. (2009). "Neural activity predicts attitude change in cognitive dissonance." Nature Neuroscience, 12(11), 1469-1474.
- Festinger, L. (1957). A Theory of Cognitive Dissonance. Stanford University Press.
- Harmon-Jones, E., & Harmon-Jones, C. (2012). Cognitive Dissonance Theory after 50 Years of Development. Zeitschrift für Sozialpsychologie, 41(1), 7-16.

[235] References – adopted from Microsoft Copilot AI:
- National Human Neural Stem Cell Resource. (2023). "Understanding Brain Chemistry: Key Chemicals and Their Functions." Retrieved from nhnscr.org.

- Snyder, S. H. (1976). The role of dopamine in schizophrenia. Schizophrenia Bulletin, 2(4), 56-77.
- Stahl, S. M. (2008). Stahl's Essential Psychopharmacology: Neuroscientific Basis and Practical Applications. Cambridge University Press.

[236] Reference – adopted from Microsoft Copilot AI: Clark, D. A., & Beck, A. T. (2010). Cognitive Therapy of Anxiety Disorders: Science and Practice. Guilford Press.

[237] Reference – adopted from Microsoft Copilot AI: Clance, P. R., & Imes, S. A. (1978). "The imposter phenomenon in high achieving women: Dynamics and therapeutic intervention." Psychotherapy: Theory, Research & Practice, 15(3), 241-247.

[238] References – adopted from Microsoft Copilot AI:
- Schwartz, B. (2004). The Paradox of Choice: Why More Is Less. HarperCollins.
- Iyengar, S. S., & Lepper, M. R. (2000). When choice is demotivating: Can one desire too much of a good thing? Journal of Personality and Social Psychology, 79(6), 995-1006.

[239] Reference – adopted from Microsoft Copilot AI: Yerkes, R. M., & Dodson, J. D. (1908). "The relation of strength of stimulus to rapidity of habit-formation." Journal of Comparative Neurology and Psychology, 18(5), 459-482.

[240] Reference – adopted from Microsoft Copilot AI: Hebb, D. O. (1949). The Organization of Behavior: A Neuropsychological Theory. Wiley.

[241] Reference – adopted from Microsoft Copilot AI: Cherry, E. C. (1953). "Some experiments on the recognition of speech, with one and with two ears." Journal of the Acoustical Society of America, 25(5), 975-979.

[242] Reference – adopted from Microsoft Copilot AI: Creswell, J. D., Lam, S., Stanton, A. L., Taylor, S. E., Bower, J. E., & Sherman, D. K. (2013). "Does self-affirmation, cognitive processing, or discovery of meaning explain cancer-related health benefits of expressive writing?" Personality and Social Psychology Bulletin, 39(3), 275-286.